ETCHING WITH PERMEABLE GROUNDS

Etching with Permeable Grounds

RICHARD STAUFFACHER

Hickory Bud Press
Fayetteville
2012

ISBN: 978-0-9829455-7-5

All photographs by Richard Stauffacher.
etchings.org

Designed by Liz Lester.

To my wife, Martha, with thanks for her constant support

CONTENTS

INTRODUCTION

In 1963, artist Frank Cassara wrote an article published in *Artist's Proof*, Issue No. 5, spring/summer 1963, Vol. 3, No. 1 (a semiannual publication of the Pratt Graphic Art Center) titled "A Unique One-bite White Etching Ground," that has intrigued etchers ever since. The reason White Ground (also called a "soap ground") is intriguing is because whereas previously grounds and stopouts had completely stopped out the acid from etching the plate (or left the metal completely exposed to the acid where they were absent), White Ground only blocked the action of the acid for a limited amount of time, depending on how thick or thin the coating. Thus, White Ground is "permeable" (see Appendix 7). This creates the possibility of modulated tonal areas with soft edges, instead of only flat tonal areas with hard edges.

It's a rough comparison, but the choice between nonpermeable and permeable grounds is analogous to the choice between drawing with pen and ink, and doing ink and water wash renderings with a brush. It is a technique that can result in loose, "painterly" but controllable rendering.

In 1976, Ruth Leaf included a section about the Cassara recipe in her book *Intaglio Printmaking Techniques*, which further popularized it.

I was given a copy of Ruth Leaf's book in the early 1980s and developed an enduring interest in Cassara's White Ground recipe. However, I found it to yield results that were more contrasty than what I was after so I began experimenting with ways to modify it to better suit my particular needs. I have been experimenting ever since with the challenging and fascinating subject of permeable grounds, and I gratefully acknowledge my debt to Ruth Leaf and Frank Cassara.

In this book two specific recipes are presented. One is the best permeable ground recipe I have come up with as of 2011, therefore named "PG-11." It is white in appearance and has other similarities to the Cassara recipe. The other recipe is a nonpermeable stopout: "SO-11." It is brown in color and is more compatible with PG-11 than are the common traditional stopouts like asphaltum, hard ground, and shellac. There are also permeable grounds that are not in this "soap-based" family, but I focus on these two grounds, one permeable and one not, both of which contain soap.

For the sake of clarity, I will avoid using the term "white ground" except when referring to the Cassara recipe which has been familiar to many etchers since the 1970s.

My perspective on working with permeable grounds has been shaped both by my own work and by my experience working for seven years (1986–1993) as master printer for Island International Artists on Guemes Island near Anacortes, Washington in Puget Sound.

I worked with established artists, some of whom had prior knowledge of etching, but most of whom did not. They previously worked in oil, acrylic, watercolor, or other media and were interested in intaglio, so most of my work consisted of teaching them etching techniques that would allow them to carry their style, strengths, and habits over into intaglio as effectively as possible. I relied heavily on permeable grounds, along with all the other standard intaglio techniques.

We also needed a fairly accurate way to plan, discuss, and achieve target tonal values during the development of images on plates, so I devised acid timing charts (see Appendix 2) which can be useful in timing the step biting of target tones in aquatints.

This book is a discussion of permeable grounds as used in intaglio etching, not about the basics of the technique. Since there are already many excellent resources available about intaglio etching, I assume the reader will be familiar with basic techniques including hard ground, soft ground, aquatints, preparation of plates, ferric chloride, scraping and burnishing, operation of presses, inks, wiping and printing issues, etc.

The term "permeable ground" covers a broad range of products. If you combine some kind of soap, some kind of grease or oil, pigment, and water, you will get a permeable ground. The challenge is to get something that works the way you want it to, and this brings into the mix different artists with different styles, tastes, and demands.

Also intaglio etching terminology can be ambiguous. A "ground" is pretty much any material that is applied to the surface of a metal plate to provide a protective coating that will control the way the etchant etches the plate. They are usually used to coat the entire plate, or large areas of it, and are further manipulated (scratched, scraped, have things pressed into them) to create openings in the coating where the acid/ etchant can get through and etch the surface of the plate, creating imagery.

A "stopout" is something painted on to the surface of the plate, usually in small, detailed, or restricted areas, and often on top of a ground to block the etchant (acid) from etching the plate. The terms "ground" and "stopout" can refer to any number of materials. Most grounds can be used as stopouts, and stopouts used as grounds. If any of these are applied through spray cans, transfers, aquatint boxes, photomechanical processes, etc., they tend to be referred to as "resists," though the same or similar materials may be used.

In developing permeable ground recipes I have tried to get something that not only would work the way I wanted it to but could be made from generic ingredients that can be easily found and are likely to remain available. At least one of the ingredients (Ivory Snow) in the Cassara recipe is no longer available, but fortunately the principles on which the recipe is based allow for endless substitutions. There will always be experimentation, adjustments for individual tastes, and the occasional need for substitutions, but I feel that consistency and predictability are also vital.

An artist has to be able to control his/her materials and with permeable grounds that has to include being able to control the degree of permeability of the ground. I'm referring to more than the obvious measure of putting it on thinner or thicker. The permeability of PG-11 is increased by mixing glycerin (available in the health and beauty aid section of most grocery or drug stores) with it. (Surprisingly, this doesn't seem to work with White Ground. See Appendix 5 for the specifics on varying the permeability of PG-11.)

Many of the techniques depicted in this book would work similarly if done using other permeable ground recipes, but they would also have significant differences. They would all work as permeable grounds, but might be more or less permeable, might have consistencies that would make them easier or harder to brush on to a plate, might dry to a harder or softer coating, might have some characteristic pattern or texture (or lack thereof) in the tones they create, might respond differently to heat or drying time, be compatible with different solvents, be more or less stable over time, etc. Any individual permeable ground will contribute its own character to the imagery that is created using it.

The material in this book focuses on using permeable grounds in connection with etching copper with either ferric chloride or Edinburgh Etch (see Appendix 4). Friedhard Kiekeben, developer of Edinburgh Etch, created variations of the recipe specifically for copper, zinc, and other metals. This book will only discuss Edinburgh Etch used with copper, since each metal has its own particular requirements regarding etchants and the utilization of permeable grounds. For instance, I have no doubt that permeable grounds on zinc would etch just fine with the Edinburgh Etch recipe for zinc. Zinc is much more chemically active than copper, and permeable grounds on it tend to be more permeable than when they're on copper, so allowances would have to be made with both the application of the ground and the characteristics of the etchant just as with copper.

Regarding the use of White Ground, Cassara's article only mentions etching zinc with nitric acid, and Leaf talks about etching zinc and possibly steel with nitric, but warns, "Don't, however, use White Ground on copper" (*Intaglio Printmaking Techniques*, p. 11). I would agree with her that anyone using the Cassara recipe should use it on zinc (or steel), and if using it on copper should apply it very thinly and etch it with undiluted (40° Baumé) copper recipe Edinburgh Etch, which very aggressively penetrates permeable grounds.

For the sake of brevity, in places where specificity is not required I will occasionally use the term "acid" to refer to either ferric chloride or Edinburgh Etch though the term is not strictly accurate.

All of the prints made from sample plates illustrating various techniques in Chapters 2–6 are printed using Graphic Chemical No. 514 Bone Black ink and Rives BFK white paper. Pictures of prints made from the plates have been flipped for easier comparison with the plates, or vice versa. Also, pictures of prints have a paper edge to distinguish them from pictures of plates.

The amount of time a plate is placed in the acid will be shown in minutes and seconds. This may be written out (5 minutes and 12 seconds) or it may be abbreviated (5:12). None of the examples in this book involved individual bites in the acid for longer than 60 minutes.

For updates, addenda, and feedback go to www.etchings.org/ PermeableGrounds/PG-11.html.

Acknowledgments

Thanks to Liz Lester for her transfiguration of the manuscript into the book, and to Susan Raymond and Bob Lowe for proofreading and making many important suggestions.

CHAPTER 1

Methods and Suggestions

Making the grounds

When making a batch of permeable ground from a particular recipe, there are some procedures and techniques that are broadly useful. Whether or not to use some of these procedures will depend on how smooth a ground you want to end up with. For instance, the Cassara recipe for White Ground that many people are familiar with only calls for the ingredients to be mixed with a spatula or putty knife until they are blended. This results in a somewhat grainy compound, which is adequate and even preferable for many people's purposes and expectations since it's often used to create loose textures and a bit of granularity can make it more interesting. However, if you're doing finer renderings or trying to apply it with an airbrush, you need something smoother. Following are some things I commonly do to get grounds that are smoother and better blended. Also, since I'm presenting a "do it yourself" approach to permeable grounds generally, I will mention some simple ways to check a batch of ground for performance characteristics or possible problems since some people may want to experiment with different ingredients or altering recipes to suit their taste.

Here are the tools and processes I would recommend for making a batch of PG-11, SO-11, or any similar ground.

STEP 1. *Measure out the ingredients.*

I like to actually place the measured amounts of ingredients out on a glass slab before I start mixing, so I don't end up wondering whether or not I actually put in the right number of tablespoons of soap, etc.

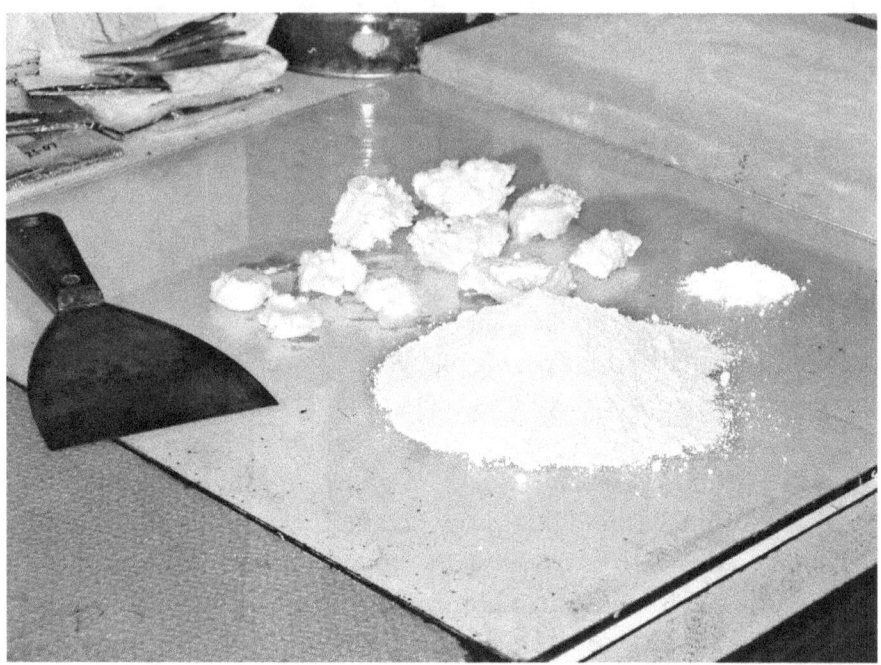

FIGURE 1.1: PG-11 ingredients

STEP 2. *Mix the ingredients.*

I've found that a wide (4-inch) putty knife works well for mixing quantities like this, along with a plastic Bondo spreader to help manage the material.

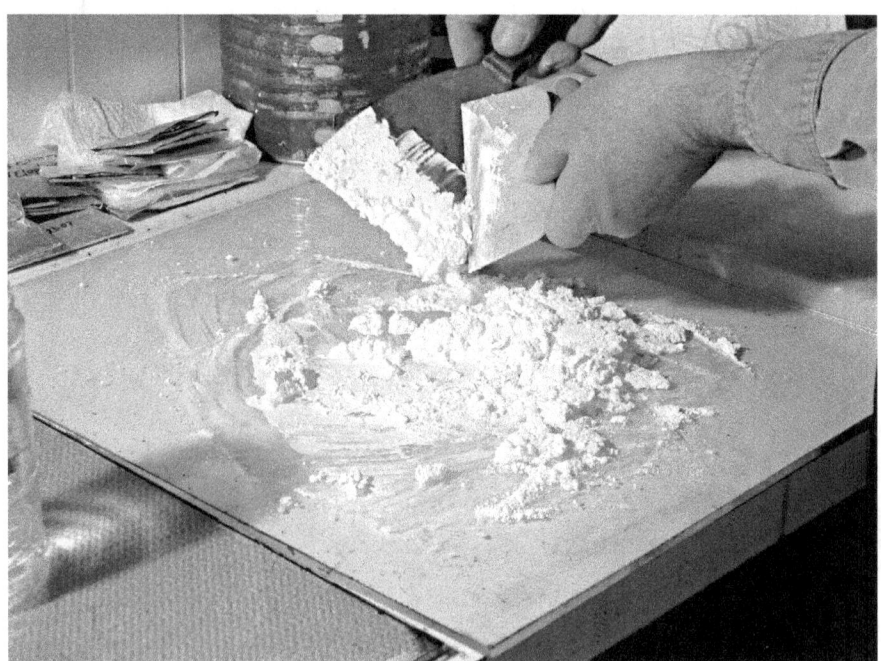

FIGURE 1.2

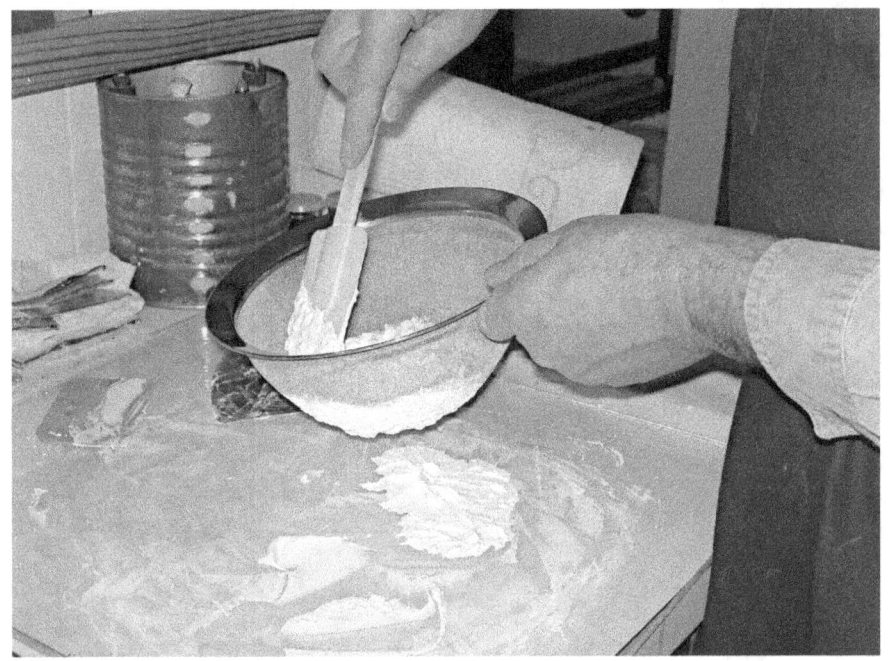

FIGURE 1.3

STEP 3. *Screening*

This is a good way to get rid of lumps and to ensure thorough mixing. Use a rubber scraper or a spoon to force the ground through the strainer. You may need to do it more than once. If the material is too thick, add a small amount of water. Alternatively, you can skip this step and go straight from mixing to mulling if lumps aren't too much of a problem.

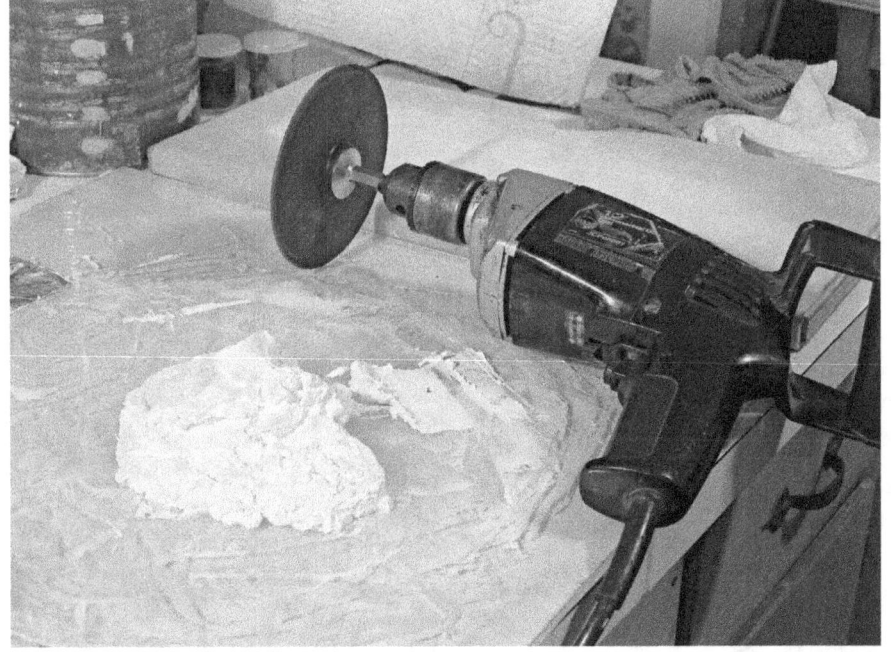

FIGURE 1.4

STEP 4. *Mulling*

A heavy duty drill with a 5-inch backup pad for sanding discs makes a good mulling machine. (Just use the plastic backup pad, not the sanding discs.) The drill has to be a variable speed drill that will operate at very low rpm.

Work in a generally circular pattern with the drill tipped a bit so the plastic pad isn't sitting flat on the glass and try to pull the ground towards the center. If you let the drill start turning too fast you'll sling blobs of ground in unpredictable directions. Of course you could also use a standard glass or steel muller.

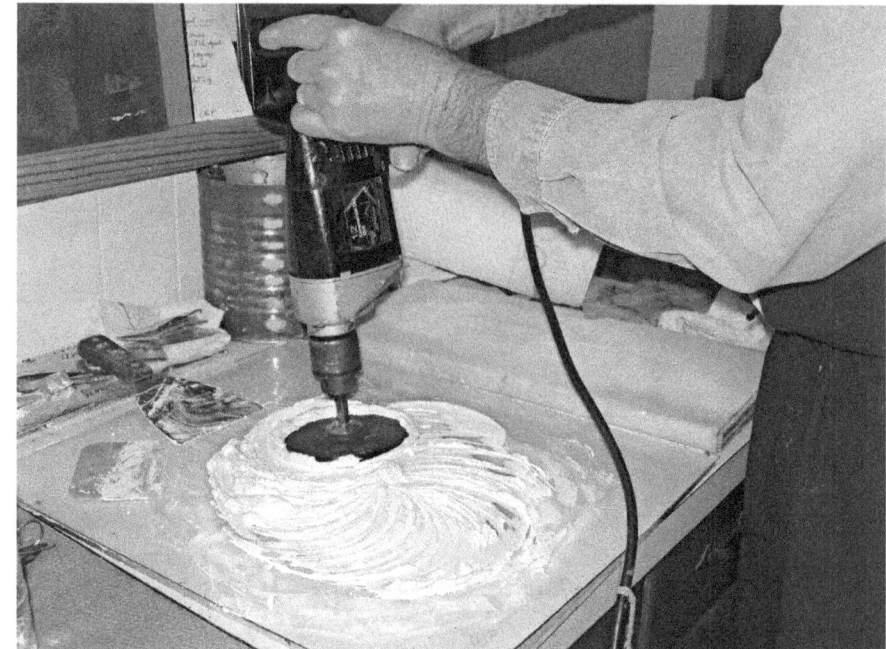

FIGURE 1.5

Mulling will give you a batch of ground with a wonderful, smooth, buttery consistency. Store the ground in a plastic container since the water in it will cause a metal container (or a metal lid) to rust.

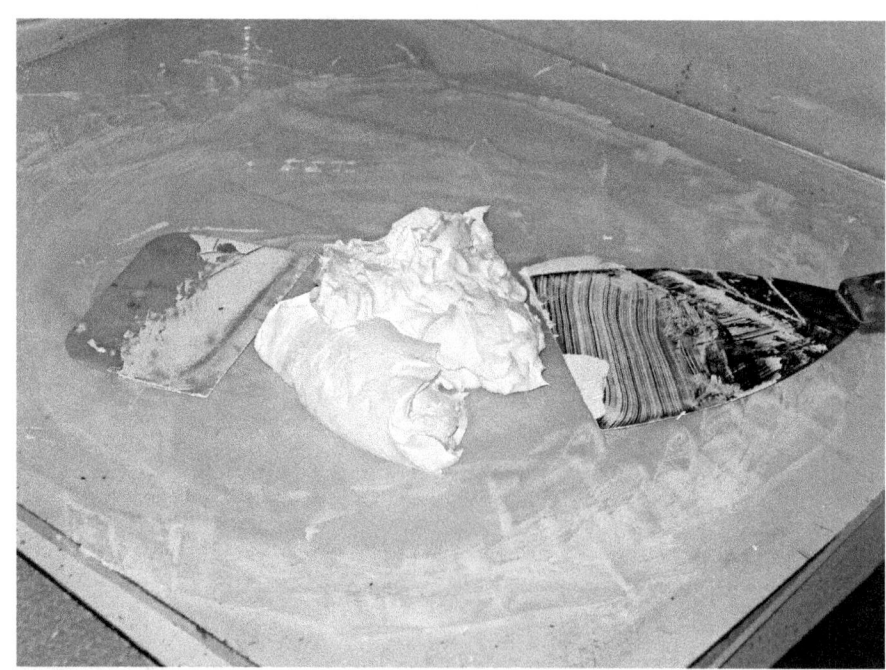

FIGURE 1.6

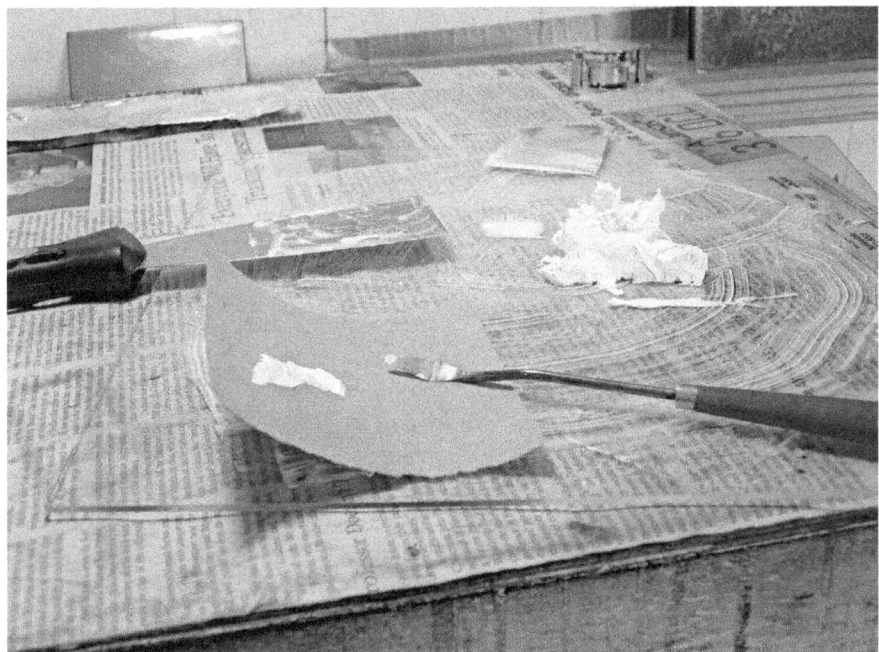

FIGURE 1.7

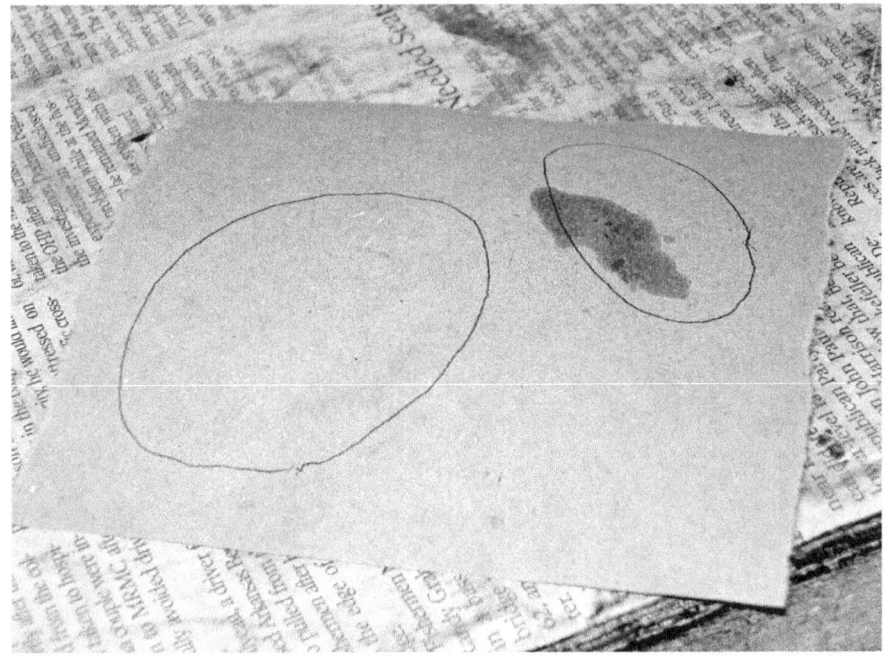

FIGURE 1.8

SIMPLE TESTS:

1. *Excess Oil*

One very simple test you can do is for excess oil. Spread a small blob of ground on a piece of brown Kraft paper. Make one edge thick and the other edge thin and feathered.

After anywhere from ten minutes to overnight, look at the back side of the Kraft paper. The circle on the left in Figure 1.8 is the back side of where some PG-11 was smeared, and on the right where some petroleum jelly was smeared. If you see oil soaking through the paper you may have too much oil in the ground.

Oil can be an issue because if there is too much of it in the mixture it can seep out after the ground has been applied to the plate and cause a "haloing" effect. This is particularly problematic when you are doing step biting of an aquatint and allow the plate to sit for a day or a week between step bites. The oily "halo" may or may not be visible but will act as a stopout which blocks further etching of the darker tones in the aquatint. If you are only doing a single application of ground and etching immediately afterward then this isn't a problem. Oil in a permeable ground needs to be balanced by the soap. If there's too much oil, add more soap.

SIMPLE TESTS:

2. Permeability

Here is a quick way to get a feel for the permeability of a ground. Take a scrap piece of copper and scrub it with steel wool until it is bright.

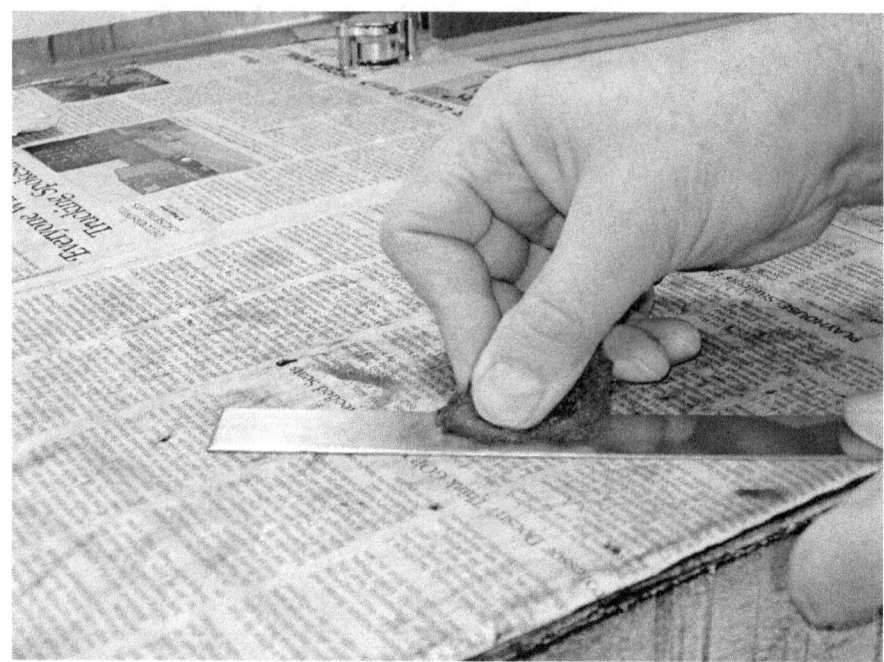

FIGURE 1.9

Dab a small amount of the ground on to the copper with a finger. Make the application thicker at one end and very thin at the other.

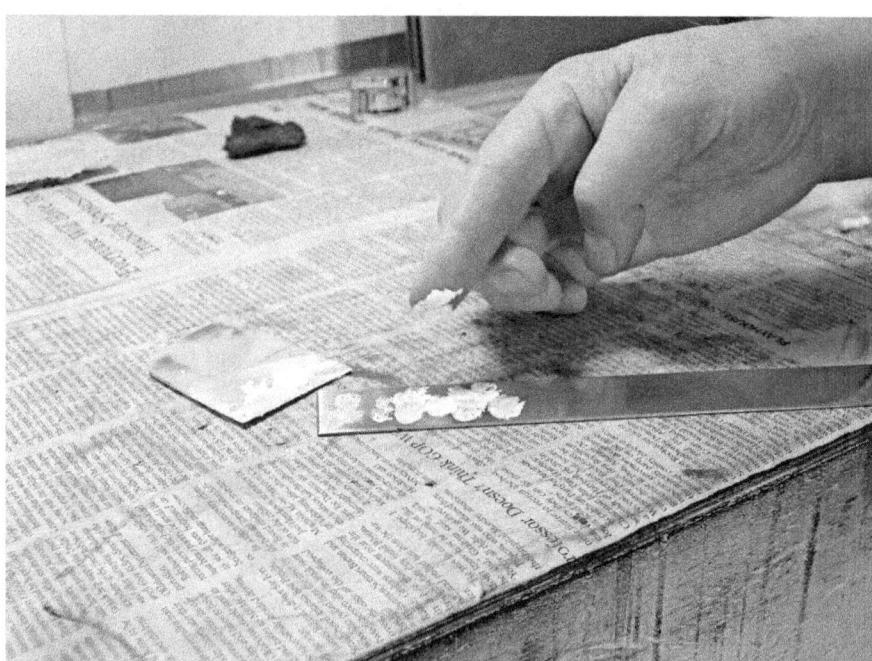

FIGURE 1.10

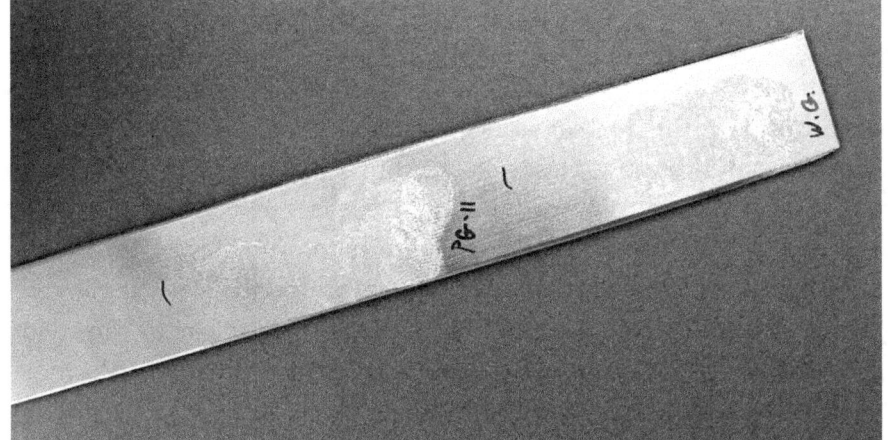

FIGURE 1.11

It should look something like this. Here I was comparing PG-11 and White Ground. I used a Sharpie pen to identify the grounds and to mark the edge of where the thinnest ground came to.

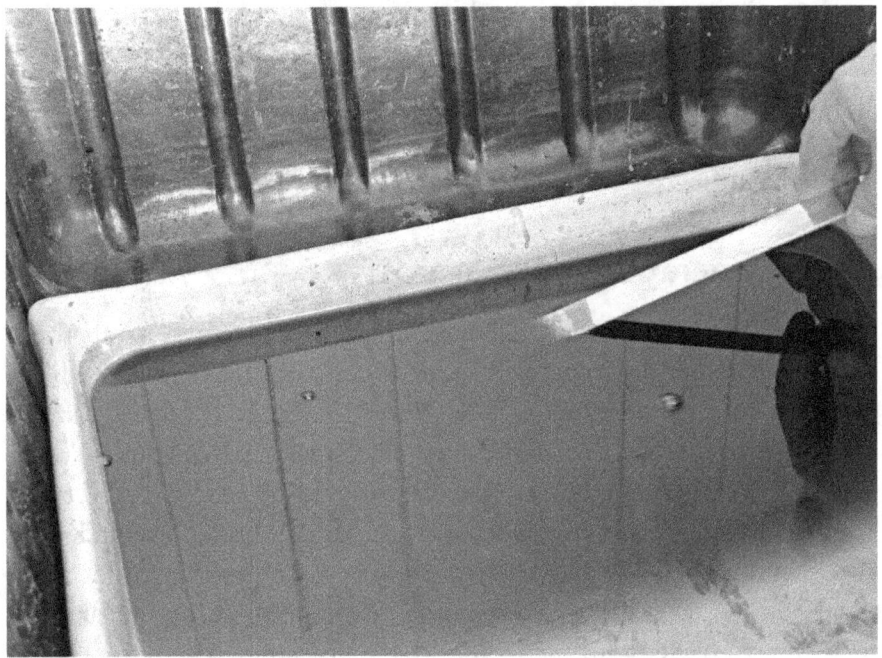

FIGURE 1.12

Place the copper strip in the acid for a minute or two.

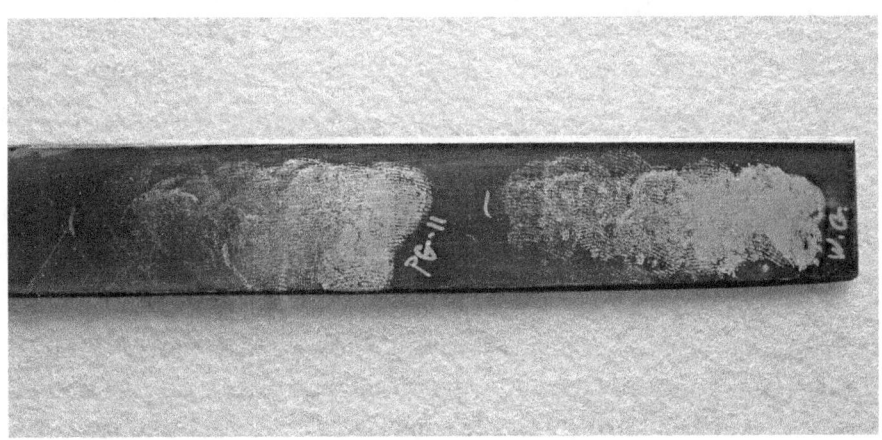

FIGURE 1.13

This is what the strip should look like after being in the ferric chloride for a minute. You have to look closely and some experience helps, but even a brief test like this can yield indications. The grounds have a different look, and near the mark indicating where the thinnest ground came to, there is more permeation with the PG-11 than there was with the White Ground.

There is a list of characteristics I either look for, or seek to avoid when experimenting with different recipes. I suppose by definition, permeability would have to head-up the list. A ground needs to have a degree of permeability that works well for whatever an artist is doing. If it's too permeable, things tend to come out too dark or lacking contrast, and if it's not permeable enough, there are too many hard edges and white areas that were supposed to have something in them. Also by definition, permeability depends on how thick or thin the artist applies the ground, but the ground needs to offer a range that the artist can adapt to in order to work comfortably and learn to get the desired results most of the time. Other things I watch out for are that it doesn't react chemically with copper or zinc, if thinned with water doesn't form reticulated patterns or migrate to the center or to the perimeter while drying on the plate, has good brush-flow characteristics (i.e. acts like paint, not gel), works well for stopping out both shallow and deeply bitten aquatints (doesn't "bleed"), is tolerant of being re-worked if corrections are necessary (doesn't lift underlying layers), makes smooth gradations from lights to darks, doesn't break down too fast where thin (or flake off) and too slowly where thicker, and has a good shelf life.

Plate Preparation and Hazards

Probably the biggest hazard I have encountered when using these grounds is poor adhesion to the plate when airbrushing the modified Medium and Soft versions of PG-11 (see Appendix 5) onto a plate to do soft ground techniques like pencil-line (tracing paper) overlays (see Chapter 5). This seems to have been associated with copper plates that have been cleaned using scouring powder or plates that have had these two grounds applied and then left to sit for a day or more without being dipped in vinegar. There seems to be a residue of something left on the plate from the scouring powder that causes the ground to become unstable and causes it to detach from the plate if left for several hours, or to break down prematurely in the acid. I would suggest cleaning a plate by whatever means is necessary, and finishing with a dip in vinegar, rinsing and drying, and then vigorous scrubbing with a clean dry paper towel.

Another thing that sometimes happens concerns the stopout, SO-11. If it is applied in a thinned consistency to a plate, sometimes as it dries, patches that resist drying form on the thicker spots. This is mostly associated with using SO-11 that has dried and then been reconstituted by wetting it with a brush and applying it to a plate like watercolor from dried cakes, and applying it in a juicy uneven layer. To avoid this, thin with a minimum amount of water to get a brushable consistency and keep it in a small airtight container so it doesn't dry out when not being used. I like to use the small plastic cups with snap on lids that salad dressing or tartar sauce comes in with take-out food, or any small jar with a lid. These patches will eventually dry after 2 or 3 hours, compared to the 15 or 20 minutes the rest of the stopout requires to dry. One way to deal with them is to dunk the plate in vinegar, which will harden the soft patches, and then to reinforce those areas with some thicker SO-11. When stopping out with SO-11 it is generally better to apply two thin, even coats with vinegar immersion between them than to apply one thick coat.

Vinegar (with or without salt) is a very important accessory when using these grounds. I use the clear "white" kind from the grocery store. It is good for cleaning and preparing the surface of the plate for application of the grounds (as mentioned previously) and a 10 or 20 second dip in vinegar converts the grounds from being readily water-soluble to being water-*in*soluble (more effectively than immersion in ferric chloride). It also stabilizes them chemically so that if they are left on a plate for a day, week, or month they won't flake off and float away when put back in the acid as they are prone to do when modified with glycerin. Forming the habit of dipping the plate in a tray of vinegar after (and before) any application of grounds is a good way to avoid having unscripted adventures. It does make them slightly physically tougher and less permeable than when fresh, but they are soft enough in either case that this does not really have a significant effect on the way they perform. After immersion in vinegar these grounds are stable on the plate indefinitely.

Transfer Methods

In etching it is frequently necessary to transfer lines from a drawing or tracing to a plate, either to create etched lines in the plate or for visual reference only. These grounds are too soft to use standard "graphite-transfers," where you run a plate coated with asphaltum hard ground through a press with a tracing that has graphite lines on it laid on top of the plate—the graphite from the lines transfers to the hard ground on the plate.

For this reason I have relied on various kinds of transfer sheets. Many different kinds are commercially available, but I usually make my own. Probably the most useful one is a piece of tissue paper with white titanium dioxide dry pigment rubbed on it. "Titanium white," or titanium dioxide pigment, is a phenomenal pigment for making transfers like this. Other pigments work, but usually do not transfer as well. I like to keep transfer sheets of different colors to use as underlays for doing line transfers and have found that other dry pigments transfer better if they have some titanium white mixed in with them. Some other dry pigments that transfer reasonably well are Indian Red, Chromium Green Oxide, Lampblack, and Milori (Prussian) Blue.

Visual reference lines can be transferred to the surface of an oxidized copper plate using a titanium dioxide white dry pigment transfer sheet. The lines are visible and transfer well, but since they lack any binder they wipe away extremely easily. Lines transferred this way (dry pigment transfer sheet) to an etched copper surface are much more persistent.

For a detailed description of a way to put nonprinting lines on a copper plate using copper oxidizing solution, see Chapter 2, Example 7. Also, see the Hydrogen Peroxide Copper Oxidizer recipe in Appendix 1 for a way to do this using a counterproofed resist.

Transferring lines usually involves registering drawings or tracings to a plate. A reliable way of doing this can be very useful in etching because often etched features on a plate or reference lines can be obscured by grounds and can be difficult or impossible to see. If you have a well-registered tracing you can always re-establish reference lines to guide the placement of additional imagery on a plate.

One way I use for registering overlays to a plate is described in Chapter 6, "Winter Crow."

Application tips

As with paint, successful application of PG-11 depends on sensitivity to and precise control of the consistency of the material, and consistency is usually controlled by adding water or allowing it to dry out a bit. Unlike many creative situations involving paint, it is being applied to a completely non-absorbent surface so it dries more quickly while being worked and there is a shorter window of time when the consistency is right. However, unlike most paints, PG-11 never completely hardens and is indefinitely re-workable.

Leaf and Cassara both discuss in detail various tools and techniques for applying White Ground, all of which also apply to PG-11 or any other permeable ground. Basically, you get it to a workable consistency by thinning it with water and then apply it with a brush, dauber, roller, wad of cloth or paper towel, sponge, or whatever. Aluminum or plastic pie pans, small jars and plates are also useful. For doing controlled imagery (as opposed to loose textural or spontaneous painterly effects), standard sable or bristle brushes are useful. Also useful for blending or distributing PG-11 after it has partially dried are bristle brushes that have had the bristles cut off short. Brights can be used for blending, but rounds, flats, or filberts that have had the bristles cut off a little shorter than most brights are more effective. Gradually trim the bristles shorter

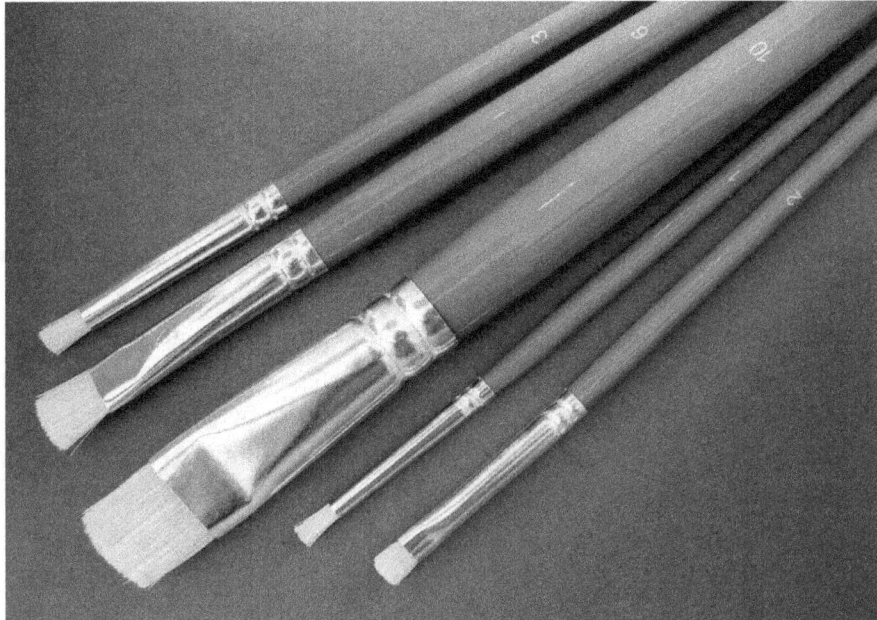

FIGURE 1.14: Bristle brushes with truncated bristles

until it works well. Moisture being a critical issue, it is sometimes useful when manipulating the ground to moisten a brush by touching it to a wet paper towel, or dip it in water and then touch it to a paper towel to remove the excess water. Other useful items are rolled paper blending "stumps" or points, and edges cut from cardboard, plastic, or wood. (See Chapter 2, Example 8 for a detailed description of using cotton or polyester fiber for applying ground.)

Sprayers are also useful both for applying PG-11 and for moistening it with water while it is being worked. Diluted about 1 part PG-11 to 4 parts water and strained, PG-11 will go through an airbrush or a small plastic bottle with a pump sprayer that makes a fine mist such as those used for non-aerosol hairspray. The cheapest ones seem to work best. At a 1:4 dilution, the PG-11 will settle out and thicken on the bottom of a container if left for a period of time, so when using one of these bottles I follow the lead of the spray paint manufacturers and put a lock washer or some other small object in the bottle and swirl it until it rattles freely before spraying. If one of these spray bottles becomes stopped up, you can usually open it up by inserting the end of a fine wire into the pinhole in the nozzle where the spray comes out.

Though spray bottles can be useful, they are not adequate for some of the techniques presented. I would highly recommend the procurement of some kind of an airbrush. For use with the materials being discussed here, the low-end ones are probably preferable to the high-end ones. They are very useful for etching in general, and I would go so far as to say they are mandatory for the soft ground techniques discussed in Chapter 5. For these techniques you have to have a thin, even film of ground on the plate; something which is easy to get with an airbrush but in my experience is impossible otherwise. For doing all the examples illustrated and discussed in this book I used a Paasche VL airbrush with a #5 (coarse) tip and needle, a ¼ oz. side-cup, and air pressure of 10, 20, or 30 psi. Though straining materials for use in an airbrush is always recommended, I used most of the diluted grounds without straining and had very little trouble with them going through the airbrush.

The thickness of the coating of ground has to be coordinated with the planned time in the acid to achieve the desired range of tones, and once the darkest tones desired in a given area have been achieved, if more etching is to be done on the plate, the area has to be stopped out with something like asphaltum or SO-11 to keep it from etching further and getting too dark. A sense of how heavily to apply the ground will develop with experience. Appendix 5 discusses adding glycerin to PG-11 to increase permeability. Adding glycerin not only boosts permeability but makes PG-11 dry to a physically softer consistency so it is easier to spread and blend for soft-edged effects or use as a soft ground. I usually use compressed air or a hair dryer to dry grounds or stopouts freshly applied to a plate.

Aquatint Options

The utilization of aquatint in relation to permeable ground is a pervasive and important subject and as such is touched on in numerous places throughout the book.

Permeable grounds can certainly be used without any aquatint, but my experience has been that aquatint is typically a companion technique to permeable ground. Whether aquatint is involved or not, it is important to understand the available options.

With regard to using aquatint with permeable ground, there are three options: (1) no aquatint, (2) aquatint under the permeable ground, and (3) aquatint on top of the permeable ground. Any of the three can be called for, depending on the situation. Basically, if you want to etch mostly textures rather than tones, use no aquatint. If you want to etch tones, use an aquatint under the permeable ground. If you want to etch tones with heightened value contrasts in the resulting imagery, use an aquatint on top of the permeable ground. (See Chapter 2, Example 3.)

You can use a spray aquatint, or a heated rosin aquatint. I use a variety of resist materials when creating aquatints, including spray enamel, PG-11, and SO-11, and frequently I use box aquatints. I usually prefer the brown powdered rosin from Graphic Chemical & Ink Co. since

I've found this to be more easily visible on the plate (or on permeable ground) and more durable than pulverized (amber) lump-rosin, or PG-11 spattered from an airbrush, which is fragile but quick and convenient. (See Appendix 3 for a detailed examination of White Ground, PG-11, heat and rosin aquatint; and Appendix 6 for more information about using PG-11 and SO-11 as a resist for sprayed aquatints.)

Both Cassara and Leaf only discuss using permeable ground (White Ground) with no aquatint, or with aquatints applied on top of it. With no aquatint, the acid tends to flat bite except where irregularities in the permeable ground create shallow tonal effects. With the aquatint under the permeable ground, the aquatint creates a tone as usual and the ground controls how much acid the aquatint (i.e. the plate) gets exposed to. With the aquatint on top of the permeable ground, exposed areas (where there is little or no ground) which would normally flat bite get reinforced with aquatint and trap more ink, creating darker grays; and areas covered with permeable ground, which would normally produce shallow grays or whites, are now covered with ground that has become less permeable because it has extra resist sprayed or sprinkled on top of it, so produces shallower grays and more whites; hence, greater contrast is created in the overall image.

The aquatint can be applied before any etching happens, or after the plate and the permeable ground have had some exposure to the acid. (See Chapter 2, Example 2B, Figure 2.10.) Since I'm basing this book primarily on my own experience, which has mostly consisted of using permeable ground on top of an aquatint, that is what will be most thoroughly covered in the following illustrations and examples.

Etching issues

The ferric chloride solution I use is made by adding 1 lb. of iron perchloride crystals to 2 pints of water, which is equivalent to 1 pint of 40° Baumé solution diluted with 1 pint of water. This may be referred to as "1:1 ferric chloride." I never use the full strength ferric chloride (40° Baumé, made by dissolving 1 lb. of iron perchloride crystals in 1 pint of water) for etching copper. All the plates for this book were etched in a flat tray, face up with occasional gentle agitation caused by lifting an edge or corner of the tray. I usually don't etch lines or aquatints for more than a total of 20 minutes.

When etching PG-11 on copper using Edinburgh Etch, I use a half strength dilution of it, which is 1 volume of the 40° full strength Kiekeben recipe diluted with an equal volume of water. I will refer to this as "1:1 Edinburgh Etch." The full strength recipe works well for etching White Ground (Cassara recipe) on copper but is, in my opinion, too aggressive for etching PG-11 on copper (see Appendix 4).

The fact that permeable grounds have a built-in time component means that their use automatically requires effective coordination of the time they are left in the acid with the darkness or lightness of the tones one is trying to create. This is true as well, of course, when aquatints are being stopped out by nonpermeable stopouts like asphaltum, shellac, or rosin varnish, but with permeable grounds (stopouts) the situation is much more dynamic and flexible.

You can use a one-step strategy, or a multi-step strategy depending on the range of values and the complexity of the image being etched. A cardinal asset of permeable ground, one emphasized by Frank Cassara, is that it can do in one step what it takes many steps (plus probably a lot of burnishing or scraping) to do with nonpermeable grounds and stopouts. It boils down to a question of how much risk is acceptable. A one-step strategy may appear to be the intuitive choice with permeable grounds, generally speaking, especially if you are working loosely and spontaneously, but if you want to sacrifice some spontaneity to gain some certainty you can subdivide one step into two or more.

Instead of etching all of the range of values from white to black in one immersion in the acid, you can do a series of step bites. To do it in two steps, only apply the permeable ground to areas or elements in the image where you want a 50% tone (middle gray) or lighter. The thinnest ground would be on the areas that will print close to the middle gray and the thicker ground would be on areas targeted for white or lighter grays. On all areas that are to print darker than middle gray, the aquatint would be left open with no permeable ground applied. After the plate has been in the acid long enough to etch the middle gray tone, it is taken out, rinsed, and dried. You have now etched the middle gray tone (open aquatint), plus any lighter tones created wherever the permeable ground was thin enough for the acid to penetrate.

Additional permeable ground, SO-11, or asphaltum is applied to block further etching in the highlights, light grays, or areas where no more etching is desired. Permeable ground is then applied to the areas that get darker values than mid-gray, and the plate is put back in the acid for a second time and etched to the maximum dark value desired. This method guarantees that you will at least have some of the tones that you wanted in the image. (This issue is discussed in greater detail in Appendix 5.) It doesn't have to be a complex, rigid approach. You can paint on some permeable ground, put it in the acid, take it out, rinse, dry, paint on some more, etc., until you have your image. Experimentation and experience are the important things.

Permeable ground that is being used with no aquatint or that has aquatint on top of it is usually given the full etch in one bite, though, of course, you can apply more ground during the process if the existing ground is not too easily disturbed. Cassara mentions a technique of building up thin washes of White Ground to develop an image.

When rinsing a plate coated with PG-11 or any other grease/soap ground with water after taking it out of the acid, there are some things to remember. These grounds have an interesting property. They are water soluble, and in most cases dried ground on a plate will wash off if exposed to water unless (as mentioned above) the ground has been immersed in vinegar for 10 or 20 seconds or has been in the acid for around 30 seconds or more. Exposure to acid "fixes" the surface of the ground so that it is no longer water soluble, and can be rinsed with water without affecting the ground. In any case though, extreme care is called for when rinsing and drying these grounds so as not to disturb them. It is particularly risky when they have been put in the acid before they are thoroughly dry or when they have been in the acid for less than a minute. In this situation, it is a good idea to rinse them by immersion in a tray of cold water and always a good idea to be very careful when running water over them from a tap (I wouldn't ever use a sprayer), or using compressed air to dry them off. It is important to avoid exposing them to warm water which is much more likely to dislodge the ground.

Being able to evaluate how much etching has occurred by inspecting the plate with a magnifying glass and observing other indicators is a critical skill that comes with experience. Be aware of the strength of your etchant. I like to test it by measuring the amount of time it takes to etch through a thin copper wire, but there are any number of ways to "check the acid."

When etching with ferric chloride, you can usually see a black residue coming off of the plate when the acid drains off of it. It's especially visible if the plate is coated with something light colored, like PG-11. If you see lots of the residue, etching is happening quickly. If you don't see any or very little, then etching is probably happening more slowly. See if bare copper on the edge or bevel of the plate seems to be etching quickly or not. If there is deep pitting, then you at least know the acid is working. View the plate in various kinds of light; with the light glaring off of the ground, off of the copper, or at an angle so that shadows are created in etched recesses making them more visible.

Another indicator of etching depth is that when you are drying a rinsed plate with compressed air during the step biting of an aquatint, deeply bitten aquatints take longer to dry than shallow ones.

Permeable grounds that are breaking down in the acid look different from ones that are remaining intact. Look for barely visible pits and fissures or more obvious erosion which indicates that etching has happened. Sometimes small or large patchy holes or pits appear in permeable ground that is in a more advanced state of breakdown.

See the enlarged split images in Appendix 3 which show close-ups of grounds and aquatints before and after etching, and Appendix 4, Figures A4.4–A4.9.

Once etching has been completed, PG-11 can be removed from the plate with mineral spirits or other grease-cutting cleaners. I have a habit of giving plates a final cleaning with a toothbrush and Brasso (metal polish) after etching and removing grounds and before proofing. This removes residual rosin, asphaltum, and ferric chloride, and also oxidation or deposits which may print a tone for a few prints and then disappear.

I usually use PG-11 similarly to the way I would use a nonpermeable stopout, which is a series of step bites followed by scraping, sanding, etc. I will illustrate this in Chapter 2, Examples 5, 6, 8A, and 9. Most of the larger illustrations in Chapter 6 have some additional direct work, as noted.

Other than what is described with the illustrations, no additional work was done on any of the sample plates.

CHAPTER 2

PG-11 Used As a Stopout

This chapter and the following chapters through Chapter 6 will contain mostly illustrations showing different ways PG-11 can be applied along with samples of the different results that can be obtained. The topic for this chapter is probably a misnomer since everywhere in this book where PG-11 is mentioned it is used as a stopout. This chapter's title derives from usage, not from fact. As was mentioned in the introduction, when etchers talk about a "stopout" or "stopping out" they usually mean picking up a brush and directly painting something on to a more or less restricted area of a plate to stop the acid from doing anything more there for the purpose of making a visible difference in the image that is being created. That is what the illustrations in this chapter are about.

The copper plates for these examples are 2.5 inches by 4 inches (6.3 cm. by 10.1 cm.) and plates and prints are shown actual size.

EXAMPLE 1: Airbrush—Single Step

(etchant: 1:1 ferric chloride; 20 minutes)

I wanted to include a very basic example of what happens when PG-11 is applied with an airbrush. The stopout I applied was unaltered PG-11 and it was applied on top of a rosin aquatint. I diluted it with water to get it thin enough to go through the airbrush. I thinned 1 part of PG-11 with 4 parts water, and strained it through a coffee filter cone strainer. I used 30 psi air pressure, and it went through the airbrush with no problem whatsoever. A 1:4 dilution is fairly runny and so I had to spray it on with the plate lying flat instead of propped up. It might have worked better with a 1:3 dilution and the same or somewhat higher air pressure. As can be seen, the tonal gradation in the print has a pronounced granularity compared to the smooth gradation on the stopped out plate. This may or may not be a concern. I've experienced a similar granularity in the same type of situation when using asphaltum applied with an airbrush to get gradations in an aquatint. The granularity happens most when etching a wide tonal range in one step, as in this example. It can be minimized by breaking down the operation into multiple steps, or by reducing the difference between the lightest and darkest tones. It could probably be further minimized by having the airbrush at a 90° angle to the plate instead of a 30° angle as it was in this case, and by using a Medium or Soft version of PG-ll.

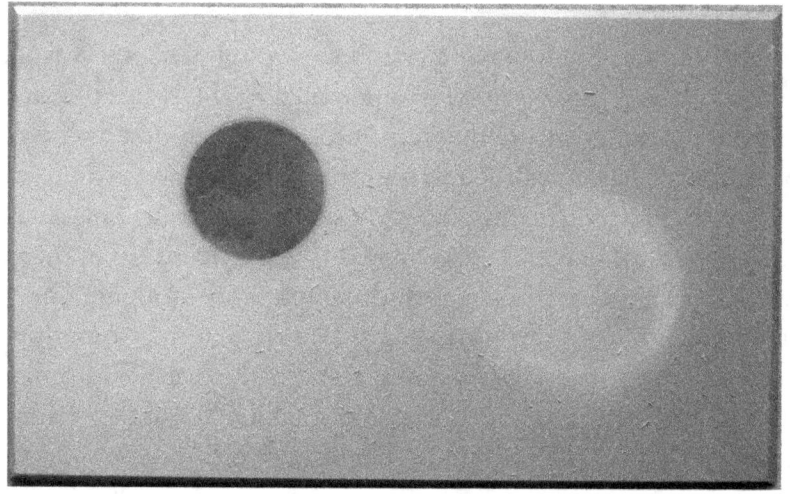

FIGURE 2.1: This is the aquatinted plate with PG-11 sprayed on with an airbrush.

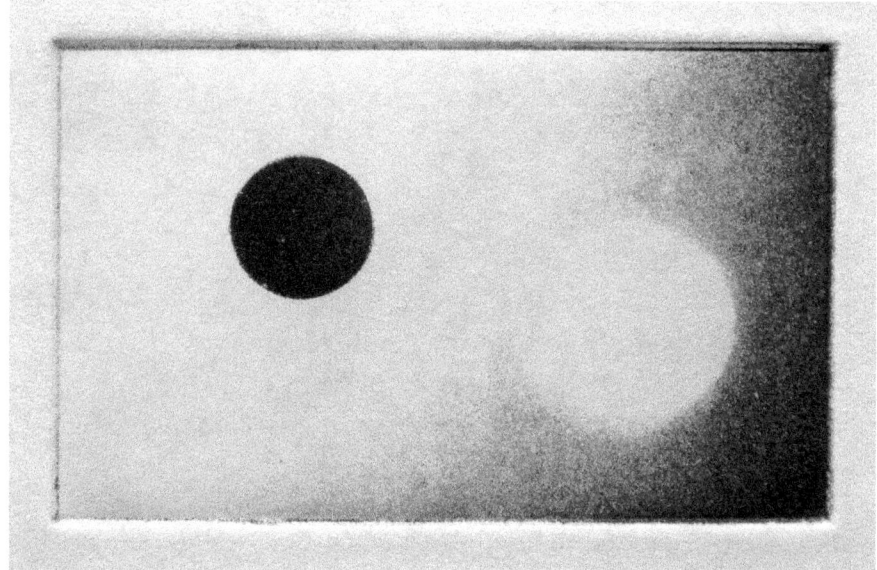

FIGURE 2.2: This is a print from the plate above, after a single 20-minute etch in 1:1 ferric chloride.

Example 2A: Monotype on Oxidized Plate (Abstract)

(etchant: 1:1 ferric chloride; 20 minutes)

Examples 2A and 2B have a similarity to the monotype technique, but only in that the "ink" (in this case, the ground) is manipulated on a blank unetched plate and you tend to get painterly effects with dramatic lights and darks. However the similarity quickly ends when you etch the image into the plate and print an edition. The ground (PG-11) dries quickly compared to ink, but can be re-dampened and manipulated in ways similar to the ways ink is manipulated on the plate when doing a monotype. It is a fun, easy, and spontaneous way to create an image.

■ ■ ■

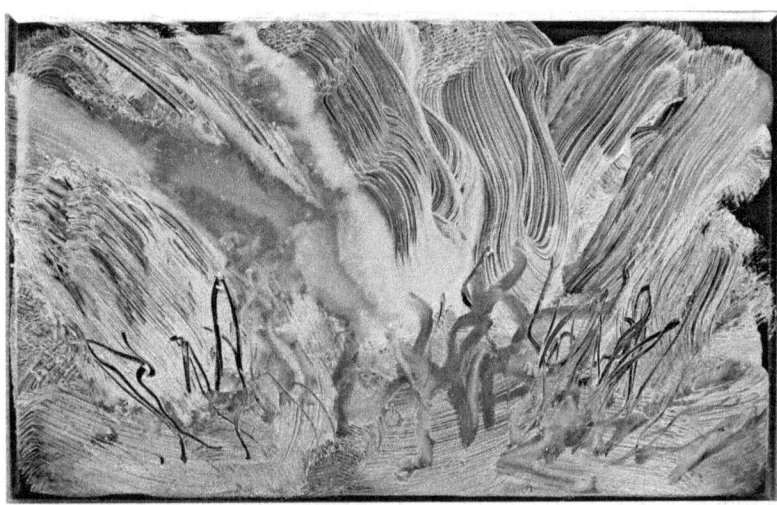

FIGURE 2.3

Figure 2.3 shows the plate, before etching. The procedure was as follows.

1. Clean the copper plate thoroughly with scouring powder and rinse thoroughly.

2. With the plate still wet (holding a film of water) put it in some peroxide and ferric chloride oxidizer (see Appendix 1) until it is visibly oxidized/darkened. Rinse and dry with a clean cotton towel. The oxidation acts as a primer to keep thin washes of PG-11 from beading on the surface of the plate, as well as a dark background which makes it easier to judge the thickness of the ground.

3. Apply the PG-11 to the plate. For this plate I used my fingers, a cotton swab, a bristle brush, and the corner of a plastic spreader. If you encounter beading of the thinned PG-11 washes, use a wet brush to pick up a small amount of soap from a bar of hand soap and mix it into the thinned PG-11 until the beading is brought under control. After the ground has been applied and allowed to dry, immerse it in vinegar for about 20 seconds. Rinse and dry with compressed air. The vinegar may remove most of the oxidation.

4. Create an aquatint by spattering it sparingly with an airbrush loaded with thinned SO-11. (You could also spatter it with PG-11.) I normally use 20 psi for my airbrush, but for this I increased the air pressure to 30 psi to get a finer spatter. Spatter with caution. It's easy to get too much on, in which case the show is probably over and your only option is to clean the plate and start over.

In a situation like this (unlike with rosin aquatints) you can use a "spatter as you go" approach. I usually start out with about 30% coverage with the SO-11 spatter. (On an area of bare copper, about 30% of the surface would be covered with the spattered ground leaving about 70% of the surface between the dots open and exposed to the acid.) After some etching you can better see how much of the copper is covered and can add more spatters as necessary. With brown SO-11 there tends to be more coverage than you think.

Since the spatter density is so critical, you can do the following to promote visibility (in situations where visibility is a problem) as an aid in judging the amount of material you are adding when adding spatters to an existing aquatint. If spraying brown SO-11 on to white PG-11 that already has some spatter on it, pick a spot that is already stopped out and paint a small patch of fresh PG-11 there so that you will have a fresh white surface that will show only new dots of spatter. If there is no such stopped-out spot available, then paint it on to something set next to the edge of the plate. Conversely, if spraying with white PG-11, paint a patch of brown SO-11 to use as an indicator.

5. Etch. This plate was etched for a single 20-minute bite. If you see that the aquatint is starting to break down before you think you have a good black, you can add some more spatter and keep etching.

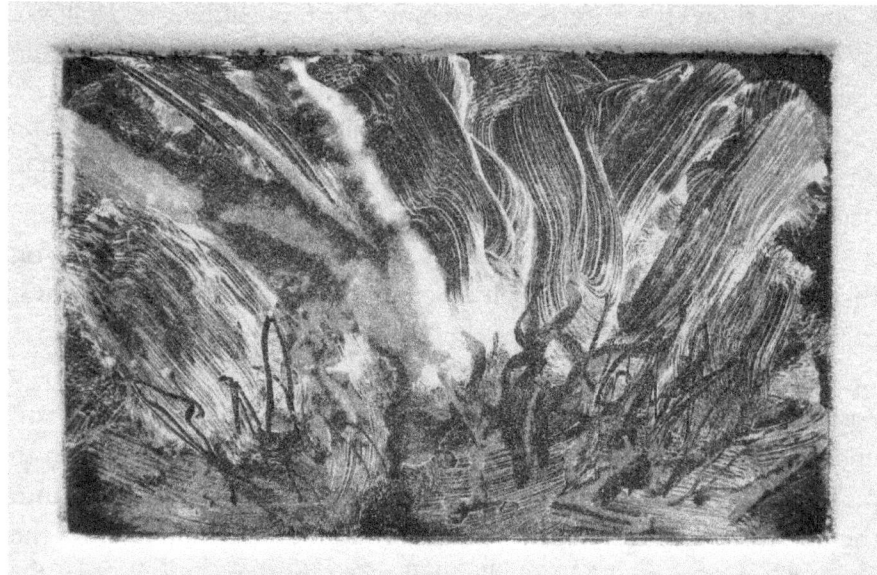

FIGURE 2.4: This is the print resulting from the above steps.

Example 2B: Monotype on Unoxidized Plate (Cliff Dwelling)

(etchant: 1:1 ferric chloride; 20-minute timing chart)

From a photograph of White House Ruins, Canyon de Chelly, Arizona. *Irene Klar, photographer.*

FIGURE 2.5

This is an additional example of the technique described in Example 2A. There was a procedural difference in that the ground was airbrushed on to an unoxidized plate and then manipulated instead of being painted on to an oxidized plate. (Again, not a monotype, but reminiscent of.)

Figure 2.5 shows the copper plate with a thin, even coating of PG-11 airbrushed on to it. This was allowed to dry, and lines from a tracing were transferred to it with a gray dry-pigment transfer sheet. It was not dipped in vinegar, since the next step requires that the ground should remain water soluble.

I wanted hard, crisp lines so I transferred the lines this way with very light pencil pressure and then "needled" them in the ground with a hard mechanical (0.5 mm.) pencil lead (heavy lines), and an etching needle (fine lines). If I had wanted soft lines, I could have dispensed with the transfer sheet, laid the tracing directly on the ground and pressed harder with the pencil. This would have pressed the tracing paper into the ground and created soft ground overlay lines. (See Chapter 5, Example 8.)

Figure 2.6 shows the plate after needling the lines and manipulating the PG-11 with a small dampened brush with stiff bristles. I mostly removed ground by repeatedly dipping the brush in water, wiping it on a paper towel and scrubbing the ground with it until it lifted. During this process lines can be obliterated or left intact as desired. New lines can be added, ground can be re-applied to rework areas, etc.

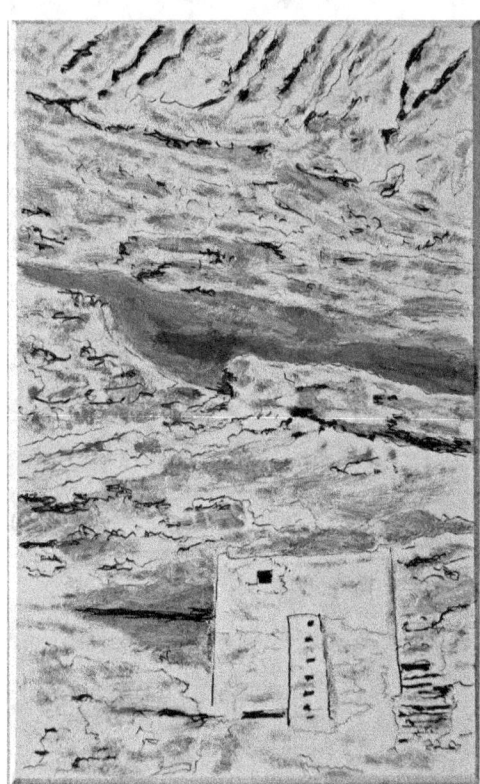

FIGURE 2.6

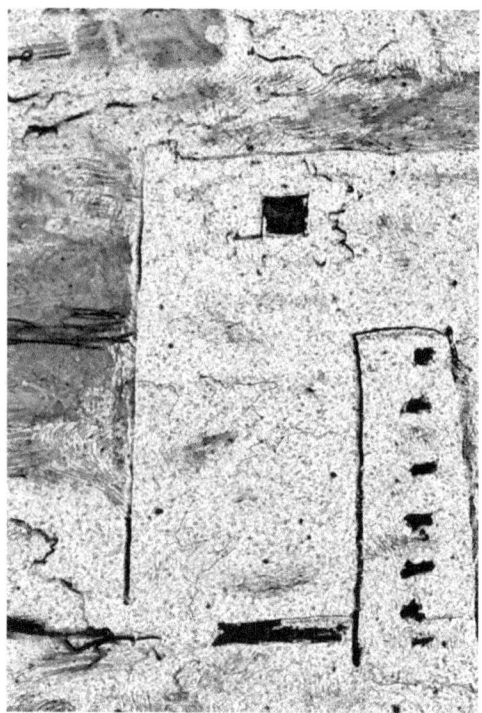

FIGURE 2.7

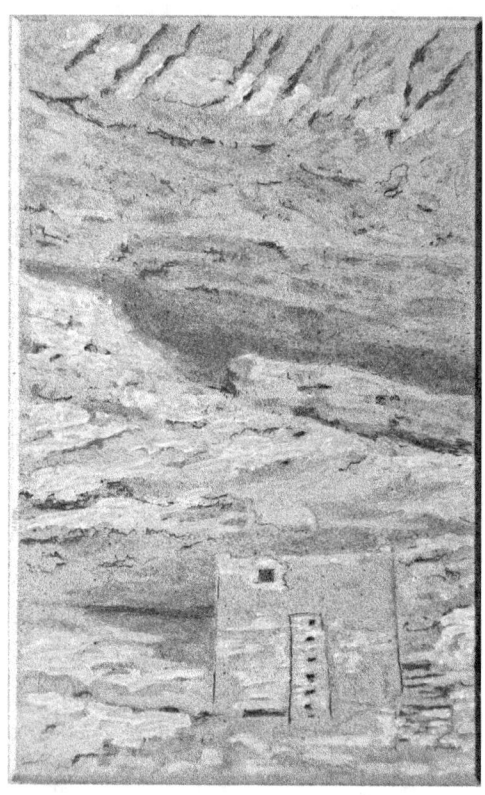

FIGURE 2.8

When I finished manipulating the ground, I applied an aquatint on top of the ground by spattering it with the airbrush loaded with some diluted SO-11. Figure 2.7 is a close-up detail picture showing the SO-11 aquatint spatters on top of the exposed plate and the white PG-11.

The blacks were created with the hard mechanical pencil lead used as a scraper, since the brush tended to leave at least a small amount of ground on the plate.

After spattering the plate with the airbrush and SO-11, I put it in the acid for 8 minutes. I wanted some areas to etch lighter than others, so after 8 minutes I took the plate out of the acid, rinsed and dried it and painted some additional PG-11 on in some areas to stop them out (visible in Figure 2.8 as the whiter brushstrokes) and put it back in the acid for another 12 minutes, for a total etch time of 20 minutes.

Figure 2.9 shows the print that resulted from the above steps. My highlighted areas that I stopped out after 8 minutes pretty much failed to materialize. They could be created by scraping and burnishing.

Figure 2.9 was actually my second attempt at this image. Figure 2.10 is the print that resulted from my first attempt. The only difference in the proceedings was that with this plate I waited until after the first 8-minute etch to spatter it with the airbrush and SO-11. My thinking was that I would etch it for 8 minutes to make sure that all the fine details got etched, then spatter it to create darks in areas that would otherwise flat bite.

The actual result was just the opposite. By putting it in the acid for 8 minutes with no aquatint to reinforce them, the thinnest layers of ground were burned off by the acid, leaving those areas open. Then when I spattered the plate and put it back in the acid for 12 minutes, I etched the same dark aquatint tone on all those open areas. The net result was to push the contrast toward blacks and whites, with fewer grays. This turns it into a moonlit night-time scene.

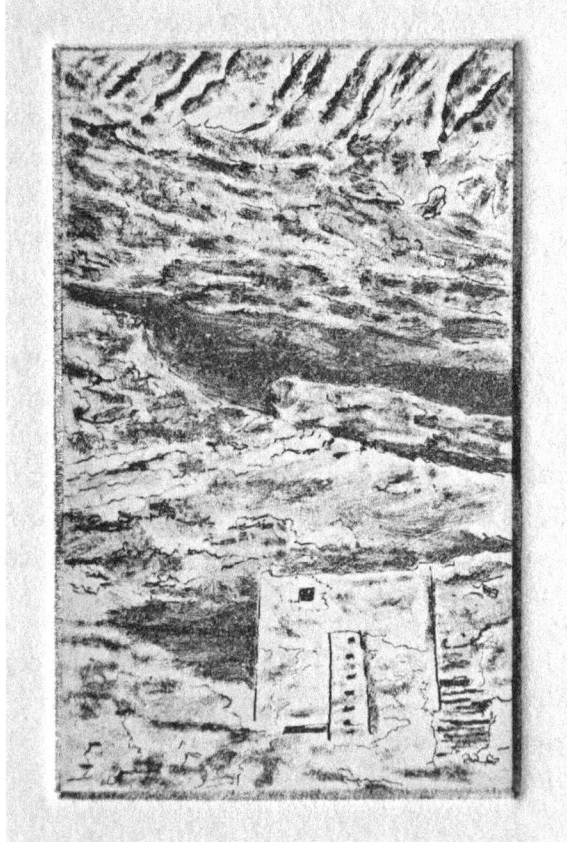

FIGURE 2.9

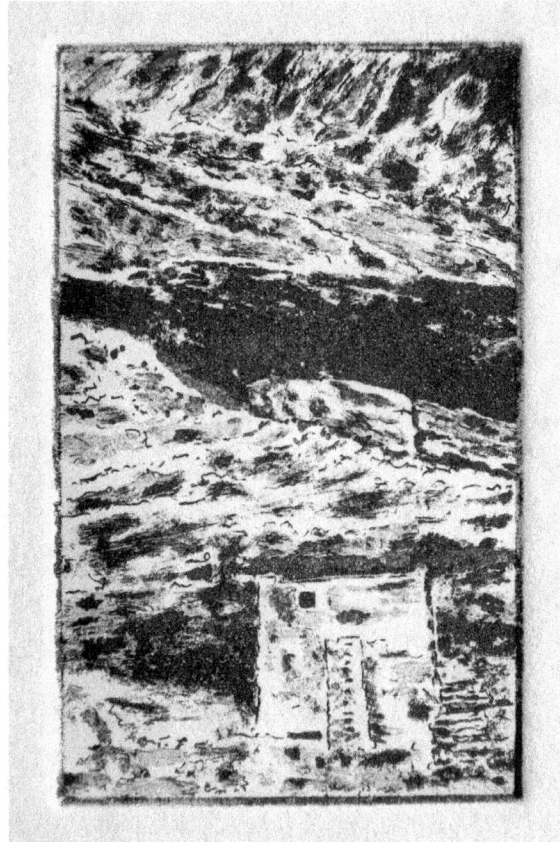

FIGURE 2.10

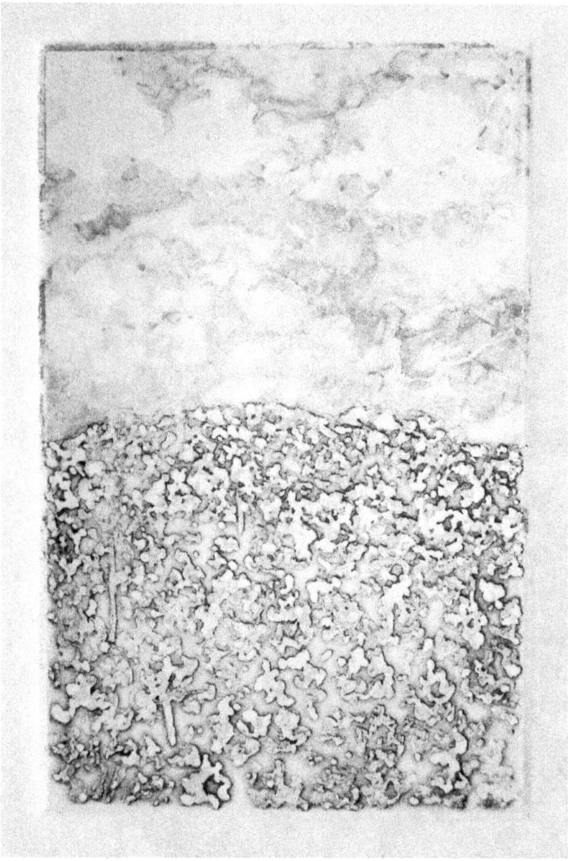

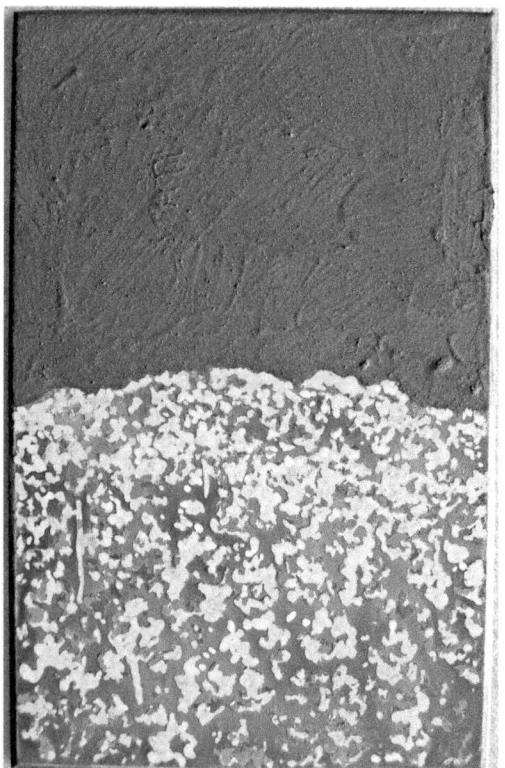

FIGURE 2.11: Print

Three Aquatint Options (Clouds and Hill)

EXAMPLE 3A: PG-11 with No Aquatint

(etchant: 1:1 ferric chloride; 20 minutes)

Examples 3A, 3B, and 3C show three plates with a similar image but with the PG-11 used three different ways. 3A shows PG-11 with no aquatint, 3B shows PG-11 with aquatint underneath, and 3C shows PG-11 with an aquatint on top.

All three plates were etched in 1:1 ferric chloride. They were etched for 9 minutes, then the top cloud portion was stopped out with SO-11 and they were put back in the acid for another 11 minutes for a total etch time (on the bottom) of 20 minutes. With each variation of the technique you get a dramatically different result. Other than what has been noted, no additional work was done on any of the plates.

■   ■   ■

Figure 2.11 shows the print. Figure 2.12 shows the copper plate with the PG-11 applied and no aquatint. Figure 2.13 shows the etched plate with the top portion stopped out with SO-11, to allow additional etching only on the bottom portion.

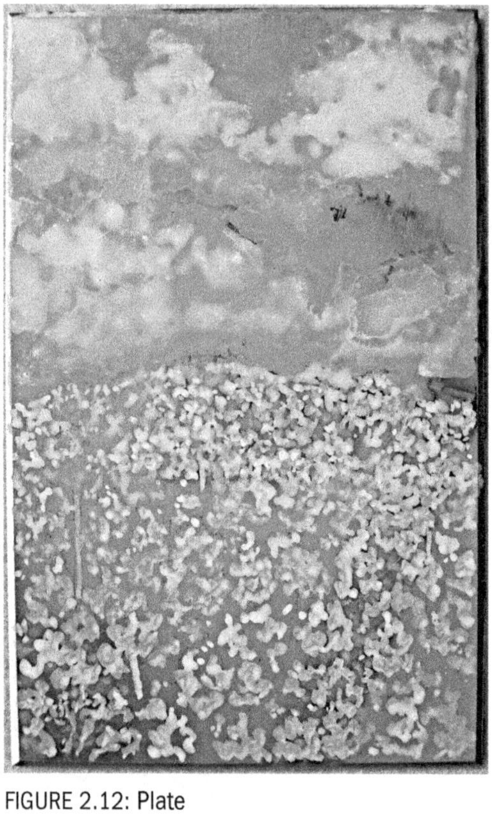

FIGURE 2.12: Plate

FIGURE 2.13: Plate

As can be seen, this technique (permeable ground with no aquatint) is better suited to creating textures than for representational rendering, though it can be a very effective step in a representational rendering if followed by additional aquatint, drypoint, burnishing, etc. (See Example 6A, Figure 2.41.) Areas that are well covered and areas that are left bare both print light, with tones being created in the transitional zones between the two.

EXAMPLE 3B: PG-11 with Aquatint Underneath

(etchant: 1:1 ferric chloride; 20 minutes)

Figure 2.14 shows the print. Figure 2.15 shows the plate with a rosin aquatint and PG-11 on top of the aquatint, before etching. Figure 2.16 shows the etched plate with the top portion stopped out with SO-11.

This, in my opinion, is the technique best suited to creating representational imagery. It is the most predictable and the most likely to give a "what you see is what you get" result.

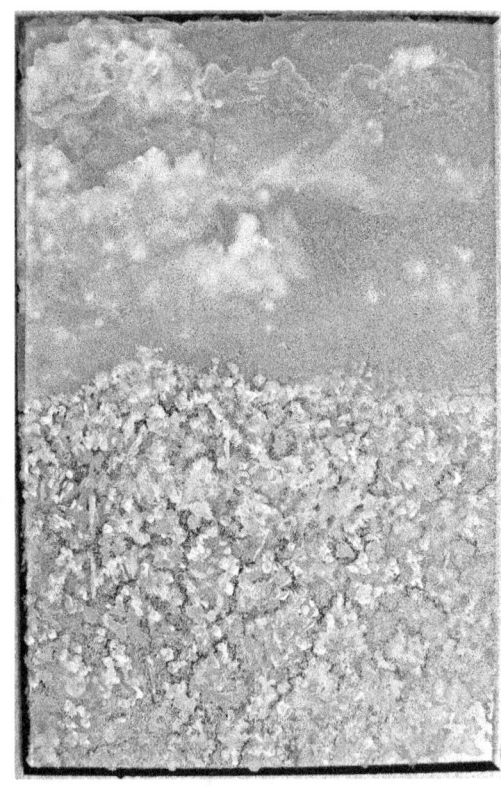

FIGURE 2.15: Plate

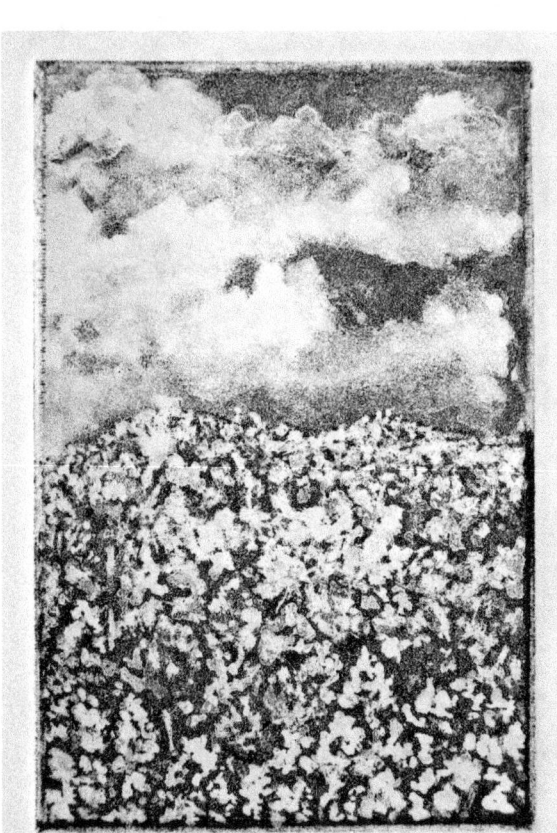

FIGURE 2.14: Print

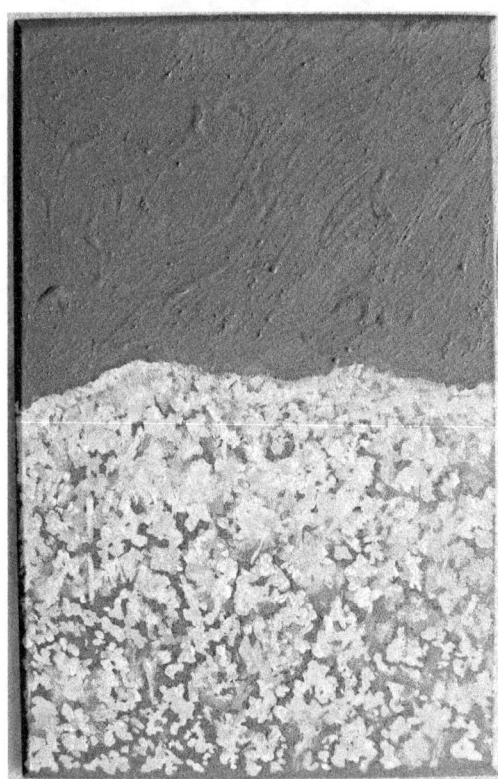

FIGURE 2.16: Plate

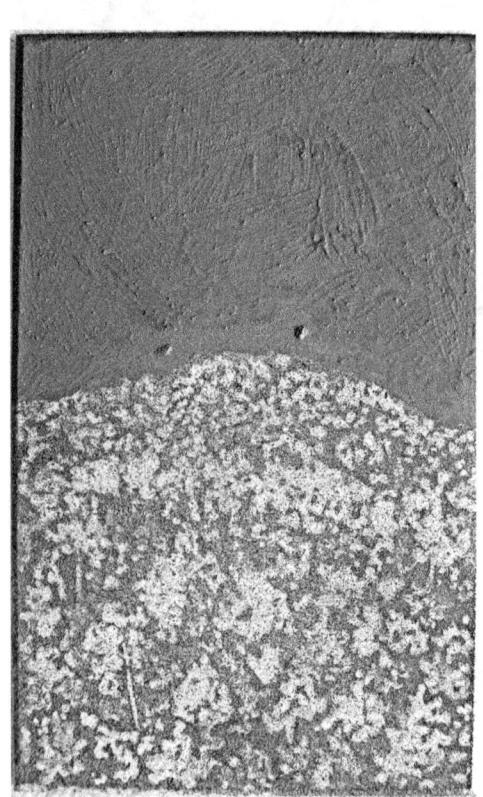

FIGURE 2.18

EXAMPLE 3C: PG-11 with Aquatint on Top

(etchant: 1:1 ferric chloride; 20 minutes)

Figure 2.17 shows the print. Figure 2.18 shows the plate with PG-11 applied, before any etching or spattering. Figure 2.19 shows the plate after etching, with the top portion stopped out with SO-11.

Putting the aquatint on top of the permeable ground gives you the exact opposite of using permeable ground with no aquatint. With no aquatint, tonal contrast is muted; with aquatint on top, it is exaggerated. Places where the ground is very thin, when etched with no aquatint, may be too thin to make a visible difference. However, if they are reinforced by having an aquatint applied on top of them (before being burned off by the acid) they may show up dramatically. Putting the aquatint under the permeable ground represents a more balanced situation between the two extremes but when doing so one still has to remember to keep the permeable ground extra thin because the aquatint significantly reduces permeability.

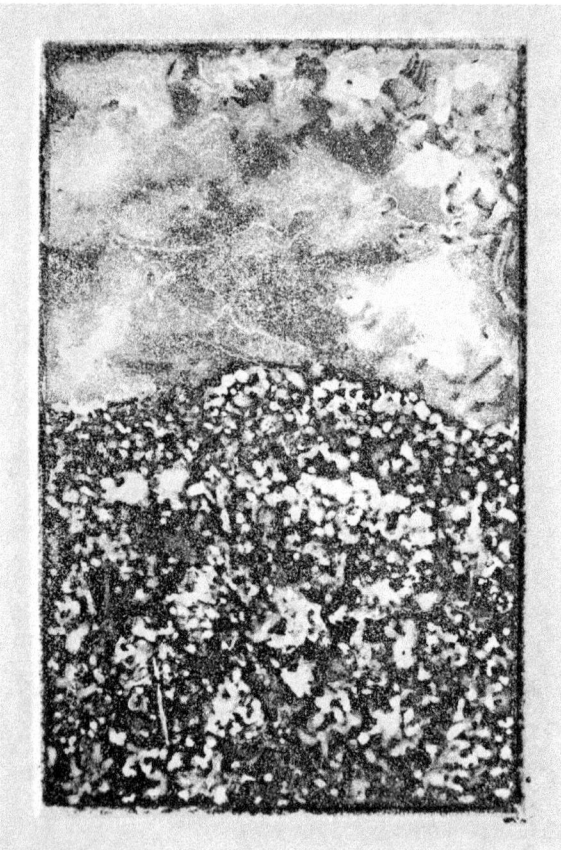

FIGURE 2.19

FIGURE 2.17

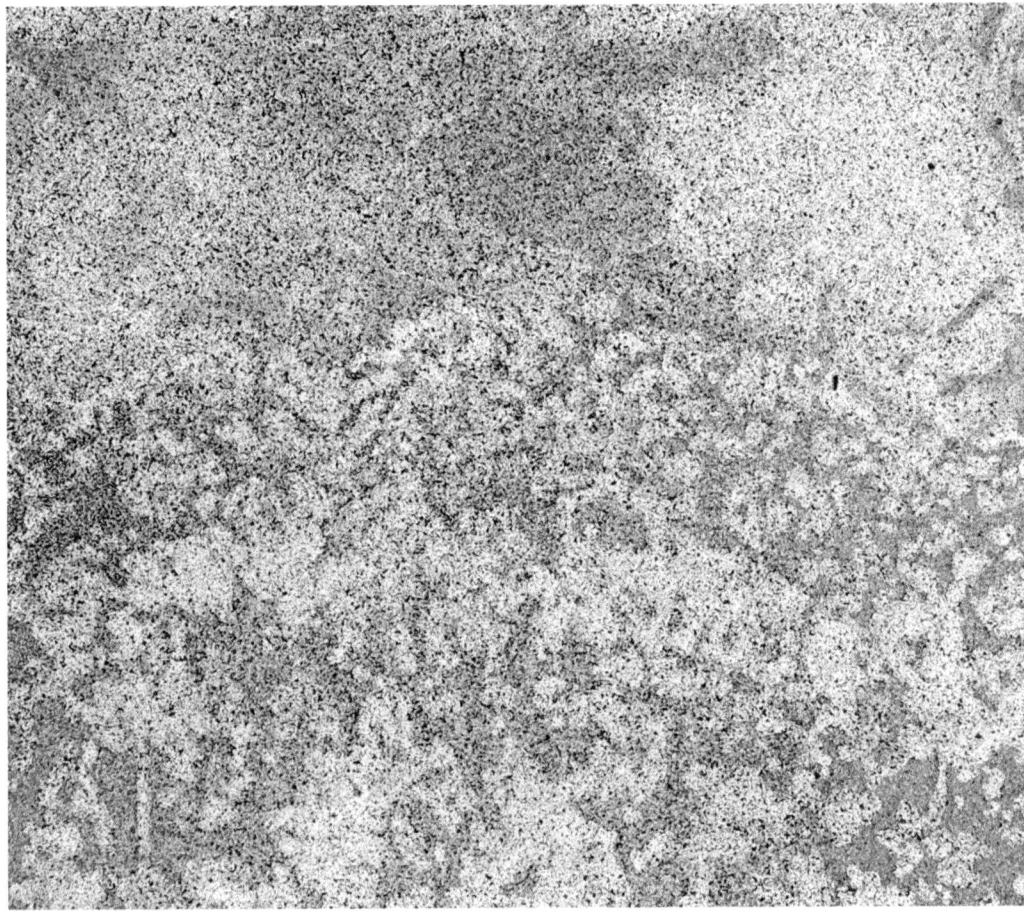

FIGURE 2.20

Figure 2.20 shows a close-up of the aquatint. I placed the aquatint on top of the PG-11 by spattering it with a can of black spray enamel. A rosin aquatint could have been used (see Appendix 3) but this was quicker. The aquatint was applied before any etching took place.

Grass—Single Step

EXAMPLE 4A: PG-11 with No Aquatint

(etchant: 1:1 ferric chloride; 20 minutes)

Figure 2.21 shows the print taken from the plate (Figure 2.23). As is typical of permeable ground with no aquatint, you get a bas-relief look.

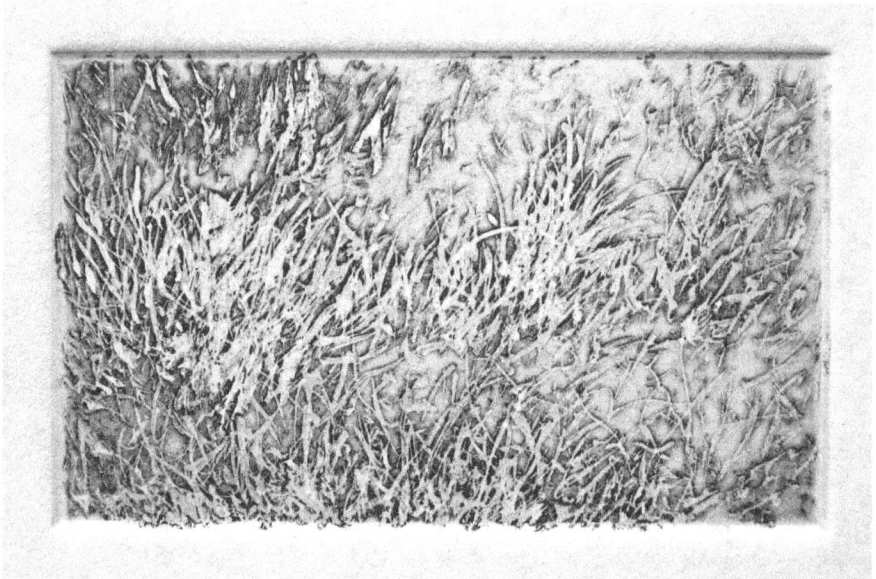

FIGURE 2.21

Figure 2.22 shows the plate, before etching. PG-11 applied with small brushes to the bare copper, no aquatint.

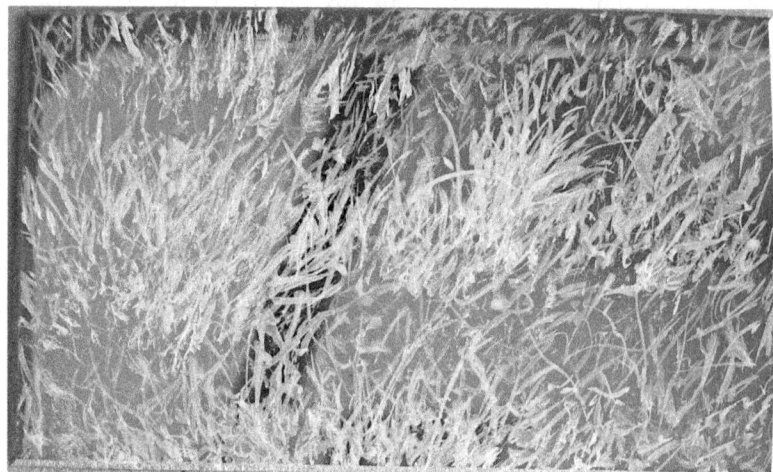

FIGURE 2.22

Figure 2.23 shows the plate after being etched for an uninterrupted 20 minutes in 1:1 ferric chloride. Most of the PG-11 has come off in the acid, but the features haven't been eaten away. This comparison (Figures 2.23 and 2.26) shows how significantly an aquatint under a permeable ground reinforces the permeable ground.

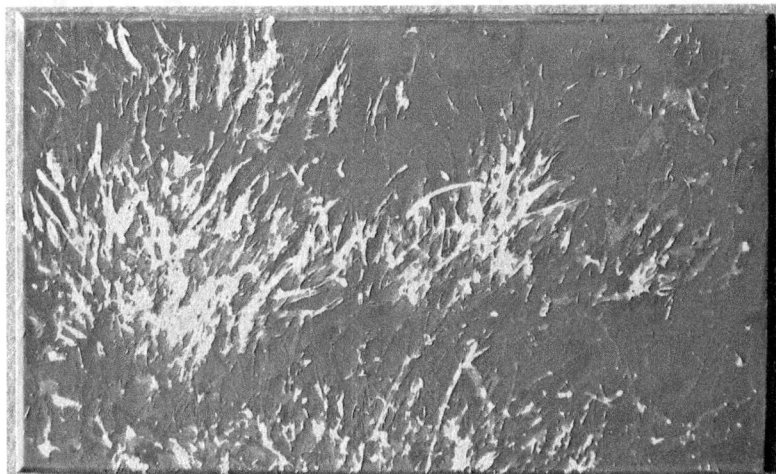

FIGURE 2.23

EXAMPLE 4B: PG-11 on Top of Rosin Aquatint

(etchant: 1:1 ferric chloride; 20 minutes)

Figure 2.24 shows the print from the plate (Figure 2.26). A pretty thoroughly muddled image, which I would blame on contamination in the ground (maybe having dried out and sat around too long). Example 5 is a repeat of this subject, but done with a more complex etching strategy.

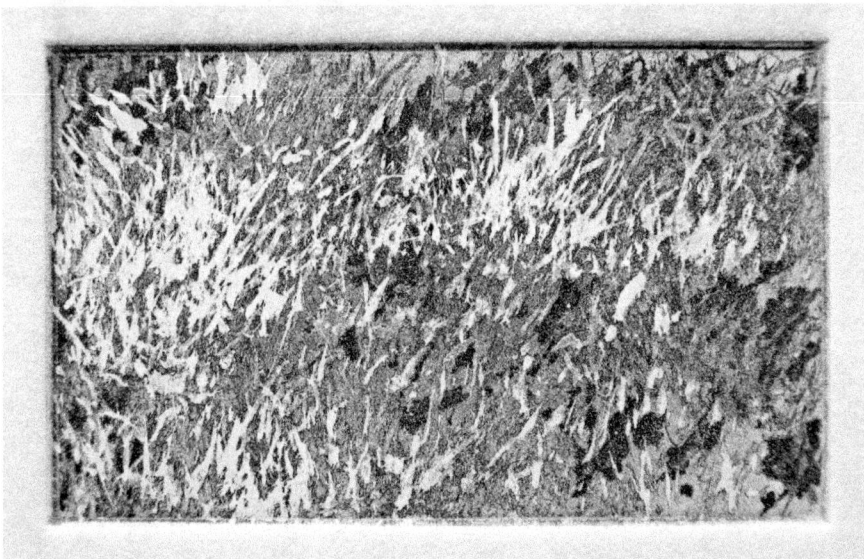

FIGURE 2.24

The plate before etching. The PG-11 is applied on top of a rosin aquatint.

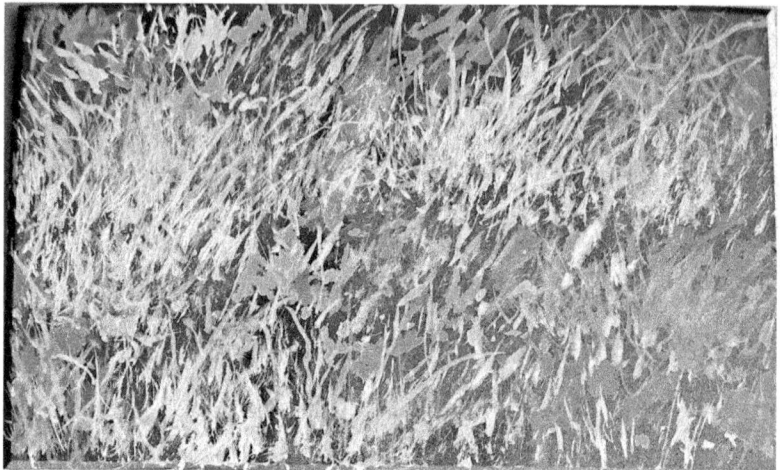

FIGURE 2.25

The plate after a single 20-minute etch in 1:1 ferric chloride. A rosin aquatint strongly reinforces the PG-11. (Compare to Figure 2.23.)

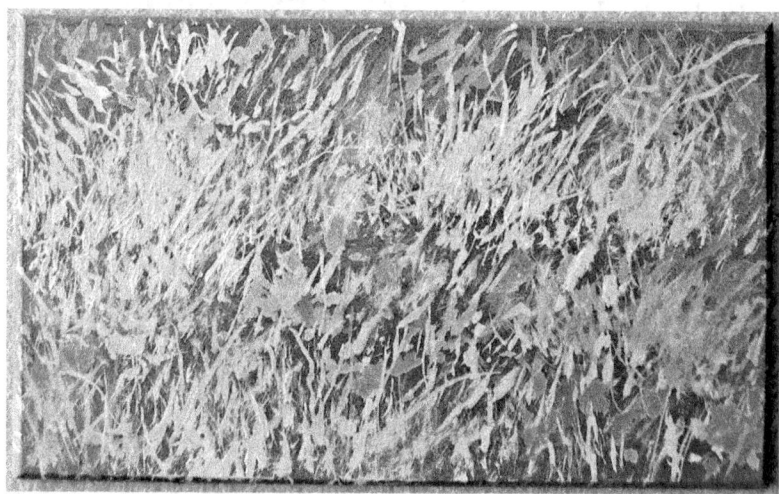

FIGURE 2.26

EXAMPLE 5: Grass—Multiple Steps

(etchant: 1:1 Edinburgh Etch; 20-minute timing chart)

Since I wanted to maintain as much clarity and crispness as possible I used 1:1 Edinburgh Etch. My etching plan for this was as follows: Using PG-11 on top of a rosin aquatint, stopout highlights to be kept white and then step bite six shades of tone, with additional PG-11 applied between each bite to create grass. The bites were timed according to the 20-minute timing chart (see Appendix 2) and were as follows: 10% 0:18 (18 seconds in the Edinburgh Etch to get 10% gray tone); 20% +0:16 (an additional 16 seconds to get 20% tone); 30% +0:30; 40% +0:48; 50% +1:14 (additional one minute 14 seconds); and 60% +1:49. Following are images of the plate through the step biting process.

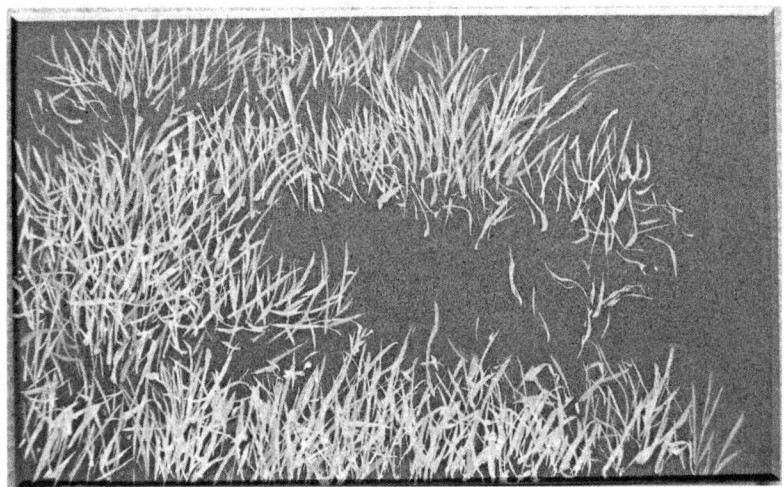

FIGURE 2.27

Figure 2.27 shows the plate with rosin aquatint, PG-11 applied to stop out whites, ready to etch to 10% of tone (18 second etch time).

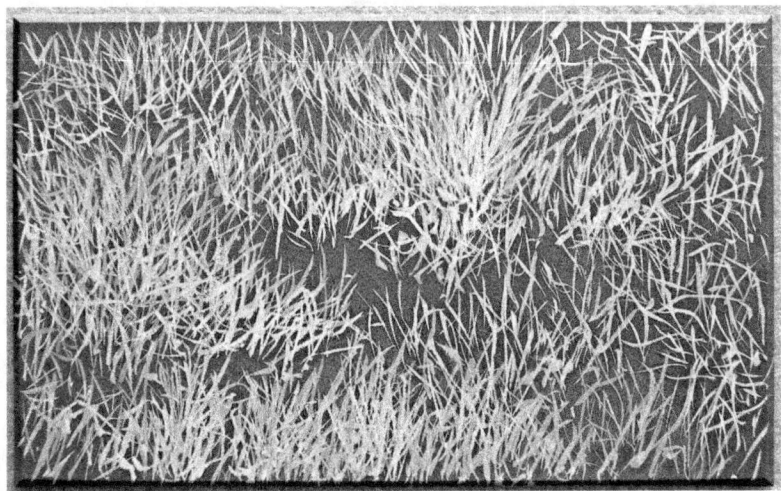

FIGURE 2.28

10% tone etched, more PG-11 applied to stop out the 10% tonal areas, ready to etch to 20% tone (additional 16 seconds etch time).

20% tone etched, more PG-11 applied to stop out 20% areas (blades of grass) and extra PG-11 applied to reinforce previously applied PG-11 and to stop out broader areas that are to remain at 20%, ready to etch to 30% (additional 30 seconds etch time).

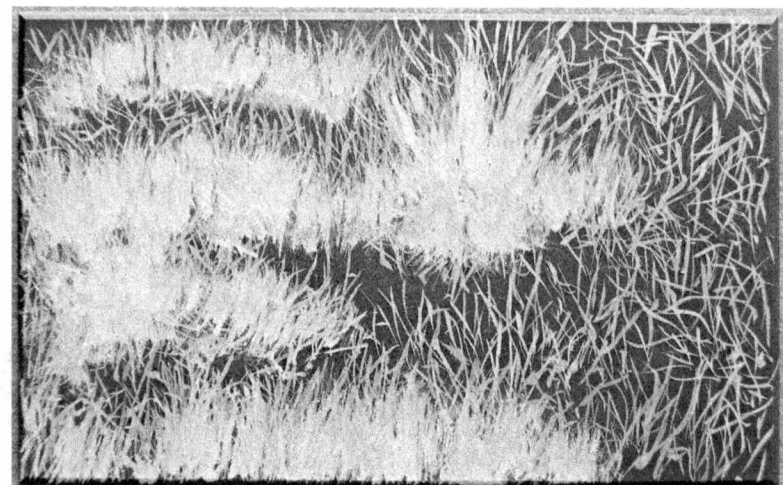

FIGURE 2.29

30% tone etched, PG-11 applied to stop out 30% areas, ready to etch to 40% tone (additional 48 seconds etch time).

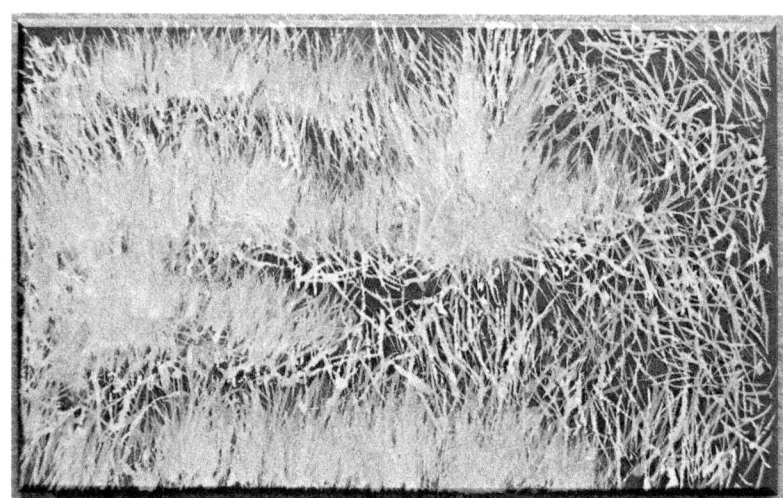

FIGURE 2.30

40% tone etched, PG-11 applied to stop out 40% tone areas, ready to etch to 50% (additional 1 minute 14 seconds etch time).

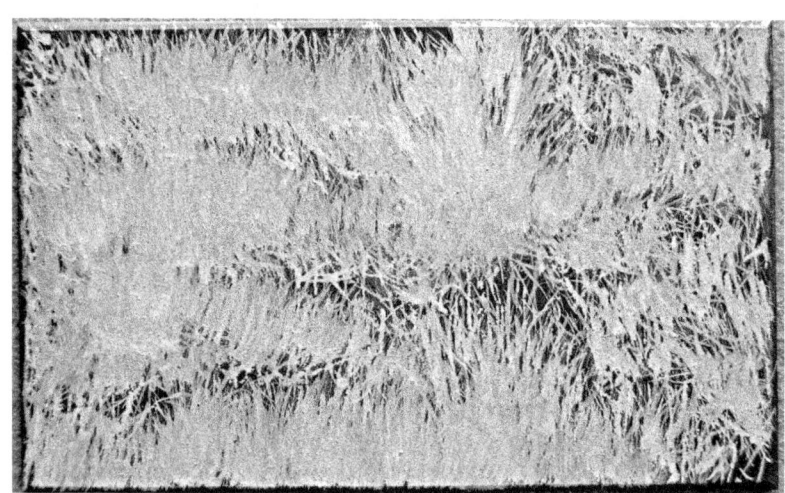

FIGURE 2.31

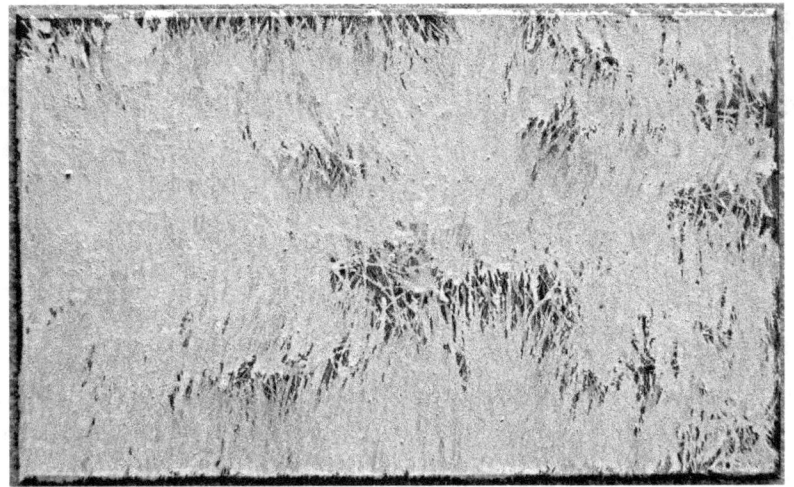

FIGURE 2.32

50% tone etched, 50% areas stopped out with PG-11, ready to etch to 60% (additional 1 minute 49 seconds).

The areas left open on Figure 2.32 received a nominal "60%" etch. However, when I looked at the rosin aquatint under a 10x magnifying glass, the etch looked more like it was at 70 or 80% so I stopped, cleaned the plate, and printed the following proof print.

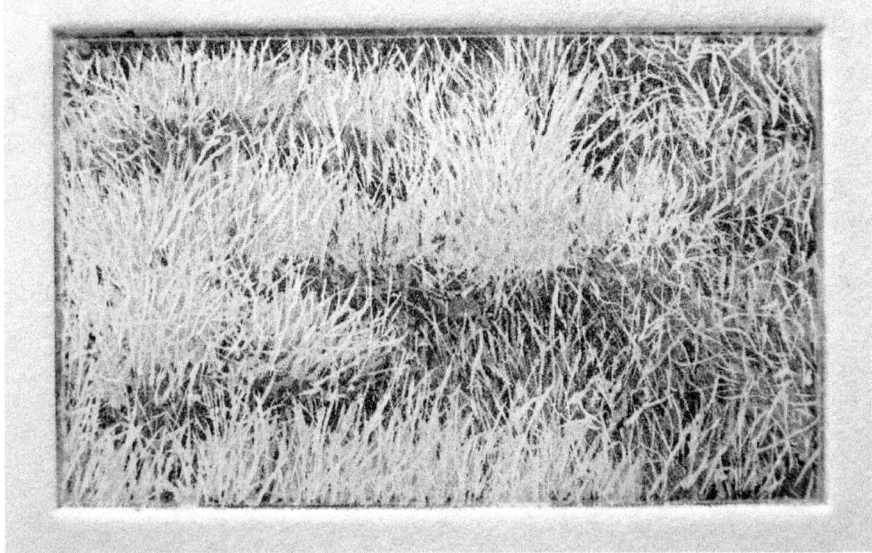

FIGURE 2.33

Print: Not bad for a first proof, but not "there" yet. Kind of ghostly looking.

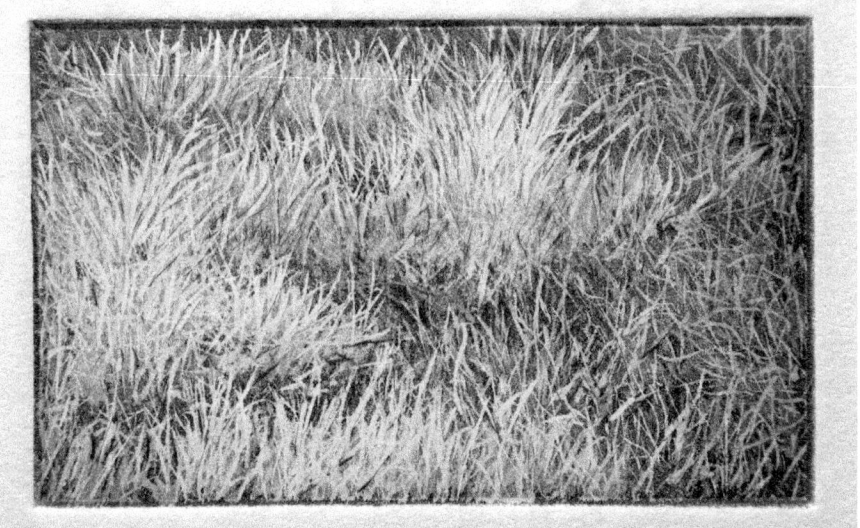

FIGURE 2.34

Print: Better, after some sandpaper, drypoint, and burnishing.

Image Created with No Aquatint Compared to Image Created with Aquatint (Driftwood); Both Reworked—Multiple Steps

EXAMPLE 6A: PG-11 with No Aquatint

(etchant: 1:1 ferric chloride; 30-minute timing chart)

This example has two main parts. Example 6A is the driftwood image done with PG-11 and no aquatint. However, to illustrate the possibility of further developing imagery that has been created with permeable ground and no aquatint, the plate with the bas-relief imagery on it is aquatinted and then burnished to create an altered image. Example 6B is the same driftwood image created with PG-11 on top of a rosin aquatint. The image is also developed further by burnishing.

Both plates were etched in 1:1 ferric chloride with the same timing schedule based on the 30-minute chart (see Appendix 2) with timings equivalent to 30% of tone (1 minute, 35 seconds); 60% (an additional 5 minutes and 48 seconds); 80% (an additional 8 minutes, 49 seconds); and 100% (black) (an additional 13 minutes 48 seconds).

■ ■ ■

This is the bare copper plate with PG-11 applied, ready to be etched in the acid for 1 minute and 36 seconds. Only the lightest (foreground) branch has any stopout applied at this point. The idea is to create some texture.

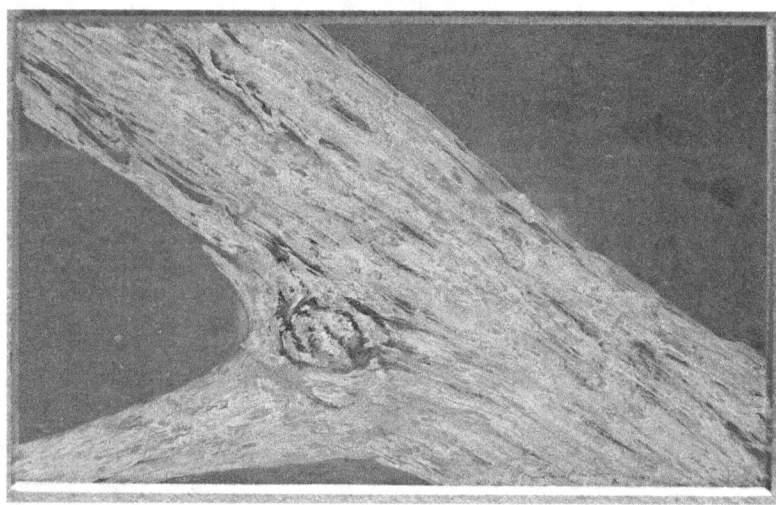

FIGURE 2.35

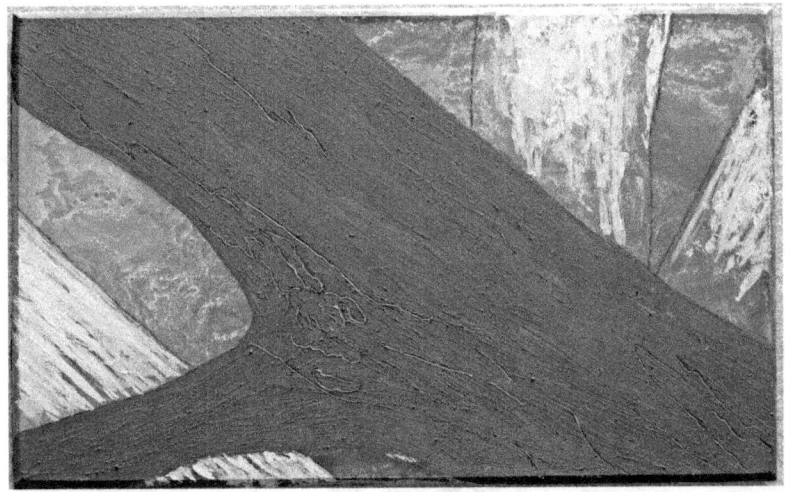

FIGURE 2.36

The plate after 1 minute 35 seconds in the acid. SO-11 has been applied to the foreground branch, to block further etching there except for some lines that have been scraped into it with a hard mechanical pencil to etch as lines for cracks in the wood. Additional PG-11 was applied to background branches for some shading and texture and the plate is ready to be etched for an additional 5 minutes 48 seconds, equivalent to a 60% tone.

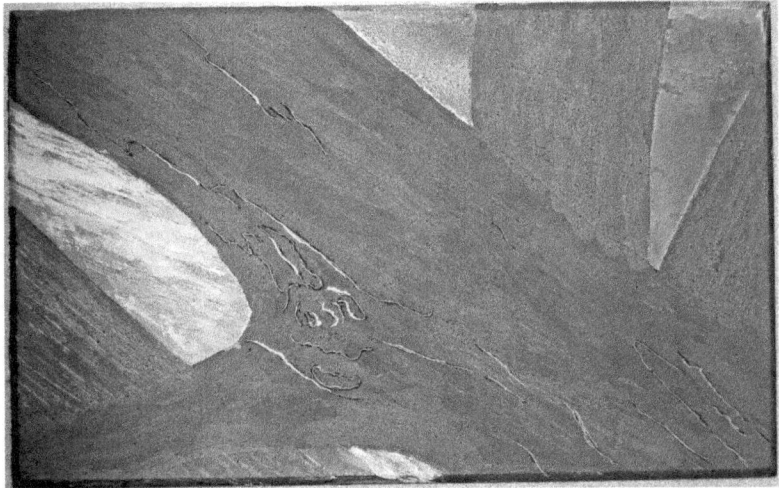

FIGURE 2.37

The 60% etch has been stopped out with SO-11 and some PG-11 has been applied for some wood texture that gets 80%, which is an additional 8 minutes 49 seconds in the acid.

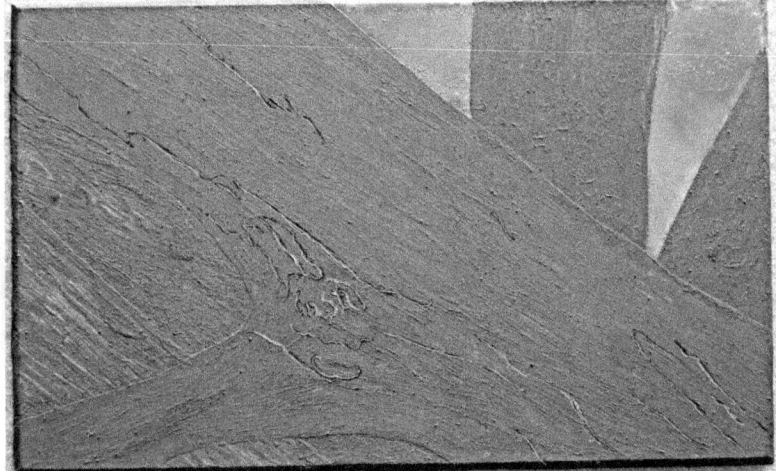

FIGURE 2.38

Here the 80% etch has been stopped out with SO-11. All that is left is to open bite the two remaining background areas to 100%, which is an additional 13 minutes 48 seconds in the acid.

Here is the resulting print. We got some texture and some suggestion of depth.

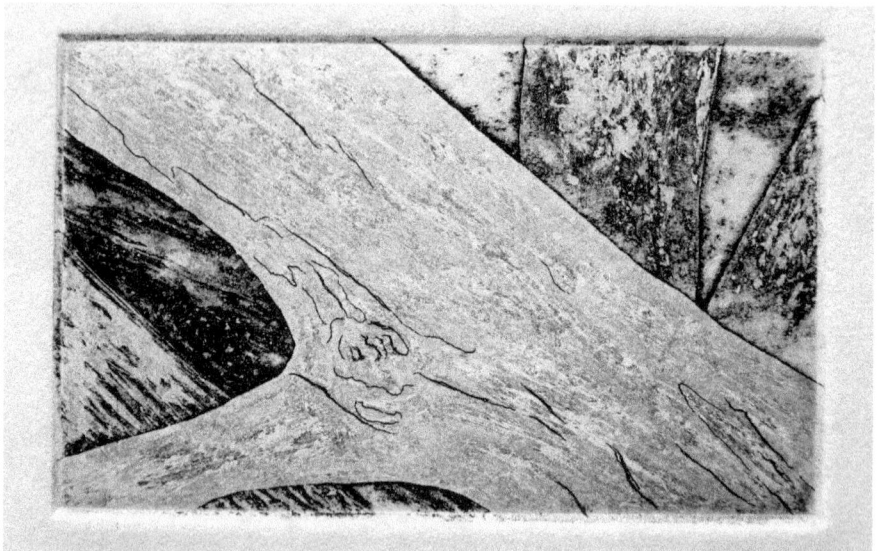
FIGURE 2.39

We can develop the image further with some standard etching techniques: spray can aquatint and burnishing.

This is the resulting print after I cleaned the plate, spattered it with a can of black spray enamel, and etched nominal tones of 20% (foreground branch), 60% (middle ground branches), and 80% (background). No more permeable ground was applied; the tones were etched "flat" over what was already there and stopped out with SO-11.

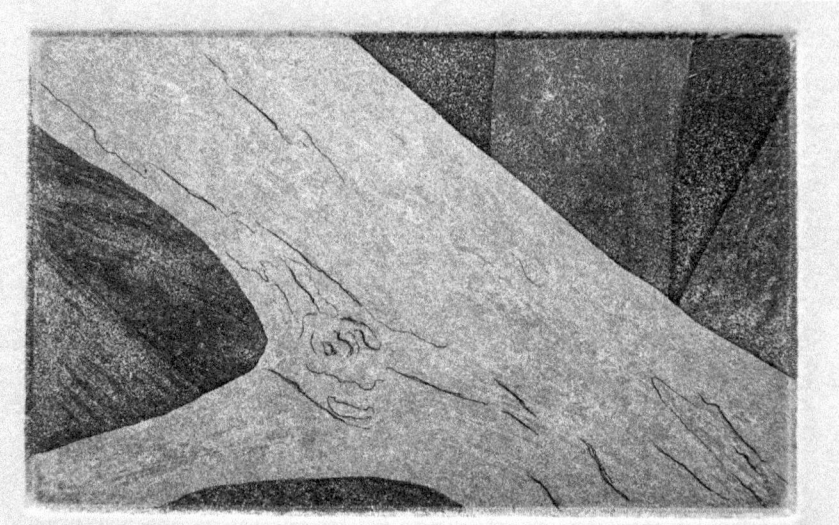
FIGURE 2.40

Figure 2.41 is a print from the plate with the spray can aquatint (Figure 2.40) after some burnishing.

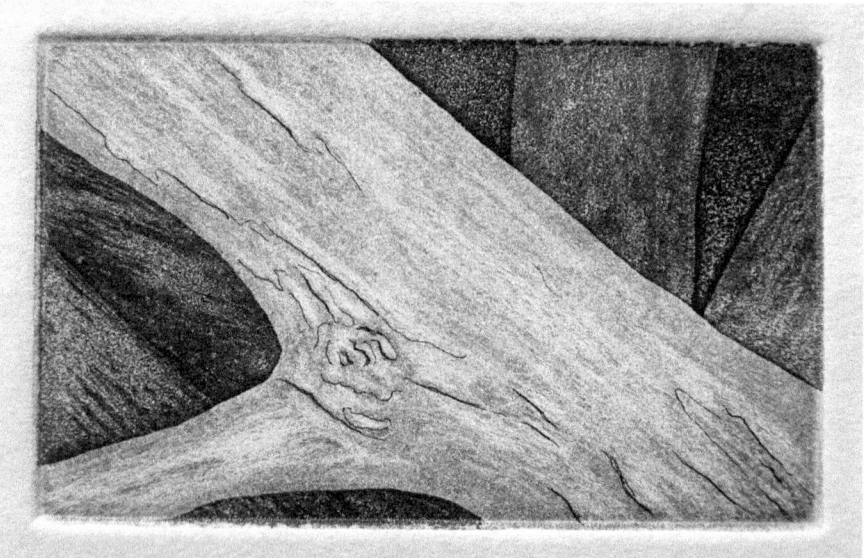
FIGURE 2.41

EXAMPLE 6B: PG-11 on Top of Rosin Aquatint

(etchant: 1:1 ferric chloride; 30-minute timing chart)

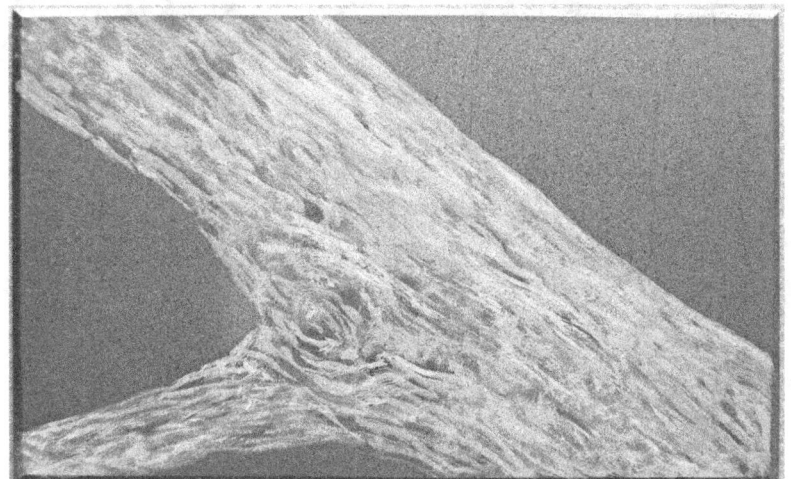

FIGURE 2.42

Copper plate with rosin aquatint. PG-11 applied to foreground branch for first etch, which will be 1 minute 35 seconds in the acid for a tone of 30%.

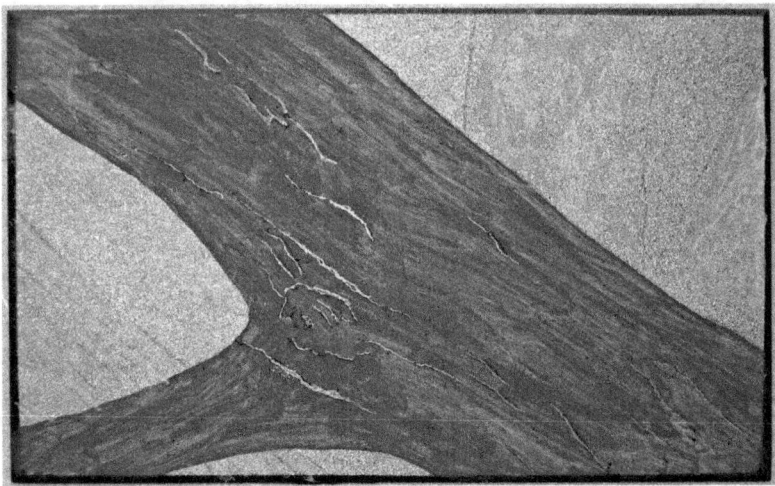

FIGURE 2.43

Plate has been etched to 30%. SO-11 has been applied to foreground branch to block further etching of tone, but lines have been scraped in it to allow etching of cracks in wood. A small amount of PG-11 has been applied to middle ground branches for some modeling. Plate is ready to etch to 60%, which will be an additional 5 minutes 48 seconds in the acid.

The plate, etched to 60%. Some more PG-11 has been added to the middle ground branches and it is now ready to etch to 80%, which will be an additional 8 minutes 49 seconds in the acid.

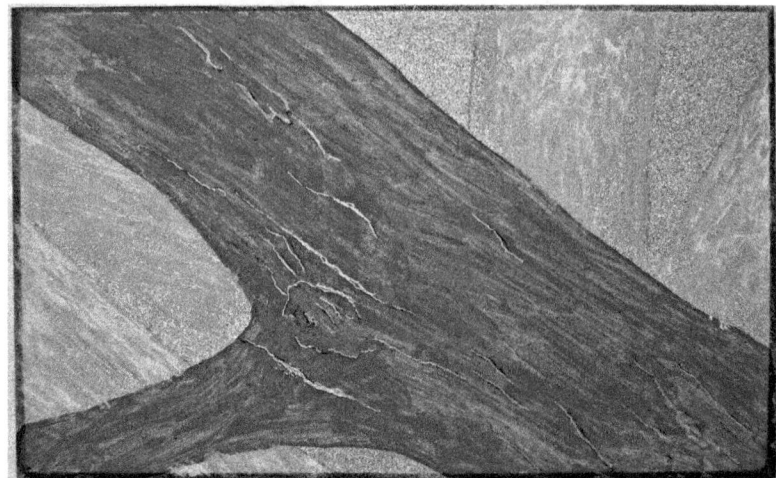

FIGURE 2.44

80% has been etched and stopped out with SO-11. The last step is to etch it to 100%; an additional 13 minutes 48 seconds in the acid.

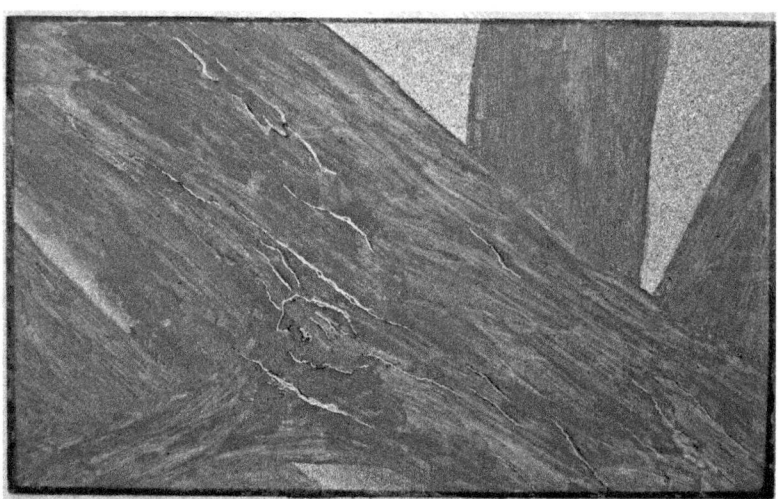

FIGURE 2.45

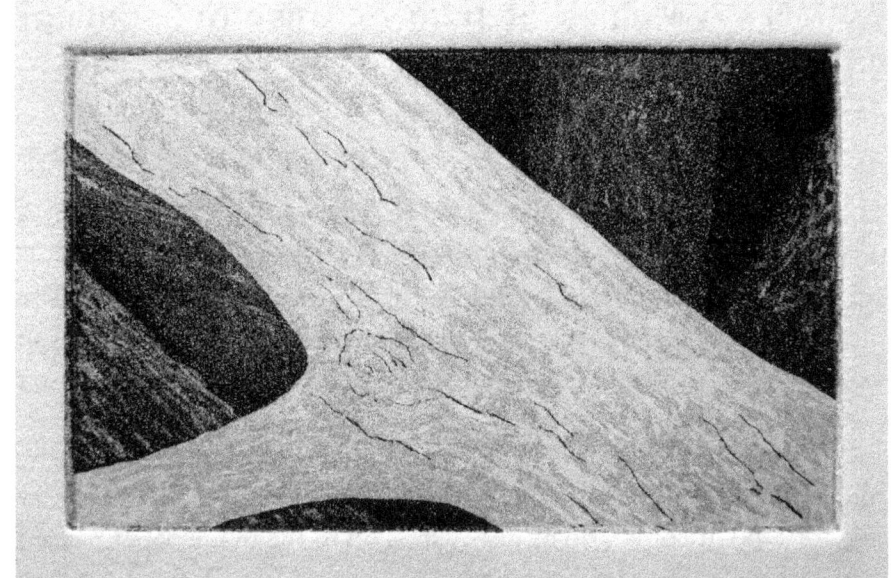

FIGURE 2.46

This print is the result of the previous steps.

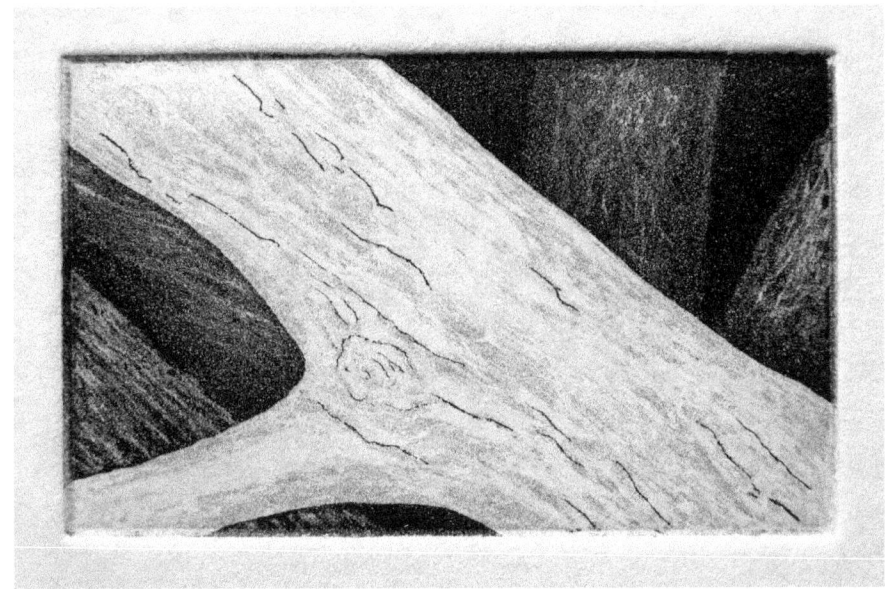

FIGURE 2.47

And this is the result of the previous steps (Figure 2.46) with some burnishing.

EXAMPLE 7: Multiple Step Image Using Nonprinting Reference Lines (Goose)

(etchant: 1:1 Edinburgh Etch; 20-minute timing chart)

This example illustrates a method for getting reference lines on a plate that will not show up in the print. The plan is to take a blank piece of copper, transfer nonprinting reference lines to it, apply PG-11 to create the image, apply an aquatint on top of that to create strong lights and darks, and etch it in two bites in the acid: a short one for the goose and a long one for the dark water.

To get nonprinting lines on the plate I used a transfer paper made by spreading SO-11 thinly on a piece of tissue paper with a plastic spreader (Figure 2.48). It could also be airbrushed on to the tissue paper, waxed paper, or baking parchment paper.

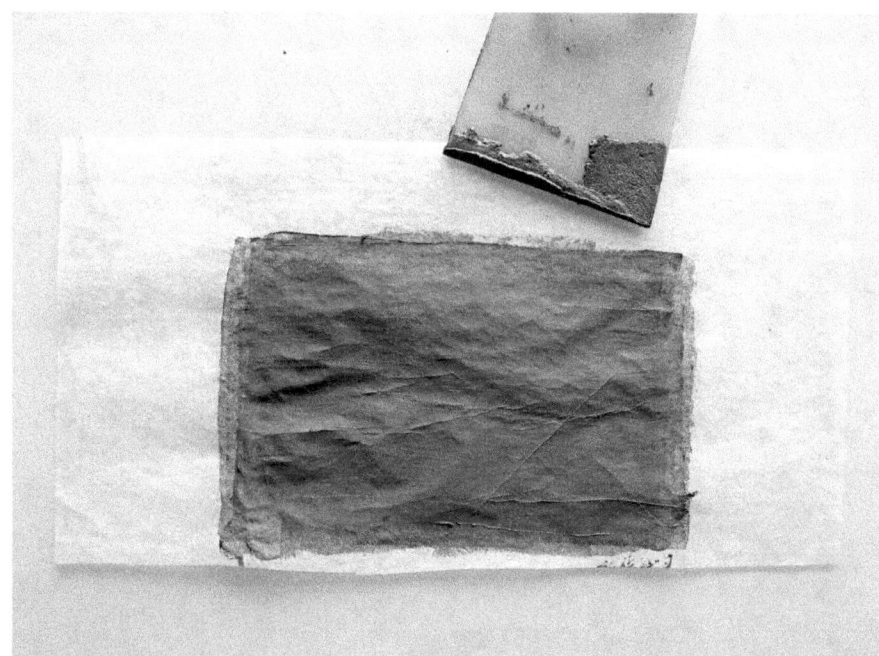

FIGURE 2.48

I laid the transfer paper over the plate with the SO-11 side down and laid a tracing of the goose image (registered to the plate) over that (Figure 2.49). There was also an extra piece of white tissue paper between the tracing paper and the transfer sheet to make the pencil lines on the tracing paper more visible (Figure 2.50).

The tracing paper was flipped, with the pencil lines on the underside so that the image (reversed in the print) would end up oriented correctly. I then traced over the lines in the tracing to transfer lines of SO-11 from the tissue paper to the plate to act as a resist for the oxidizing solution. Before putting it in the oxidizing solution I dipped the

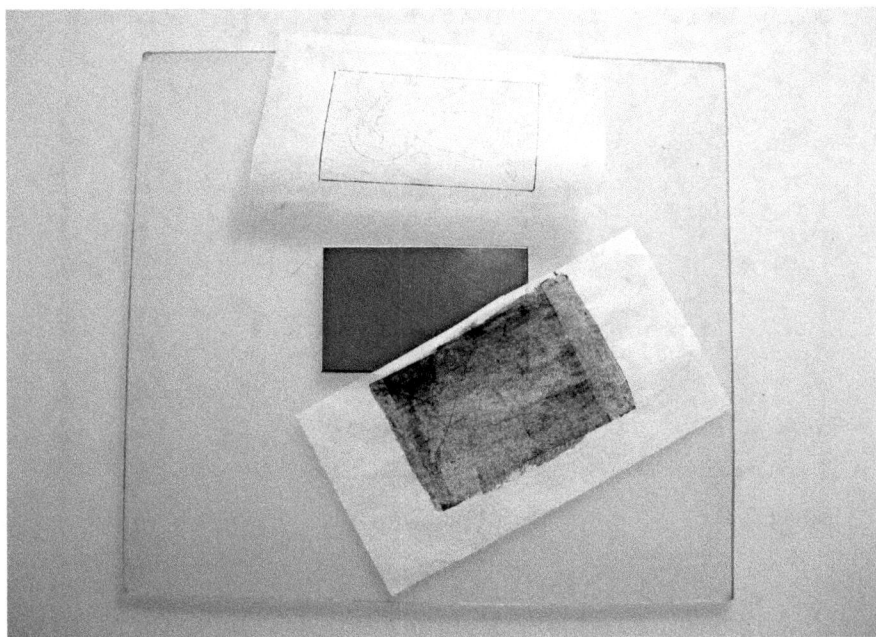

FIGURE 2.49

plate in vinegar to fix the SO-11 and rinsed and dried it. I then put the plate in the oxidizing solution for about 30 seconds, until the copper darkened (see Appendix 1). The copper should be darkened only as much as necessary to make the lines visible. After oxidizing the copper I removed the SO-11 resist to reveal the shiny copper lines under it. When no longer needed, the oxidation can be removed with Brasso or some other metal polish.

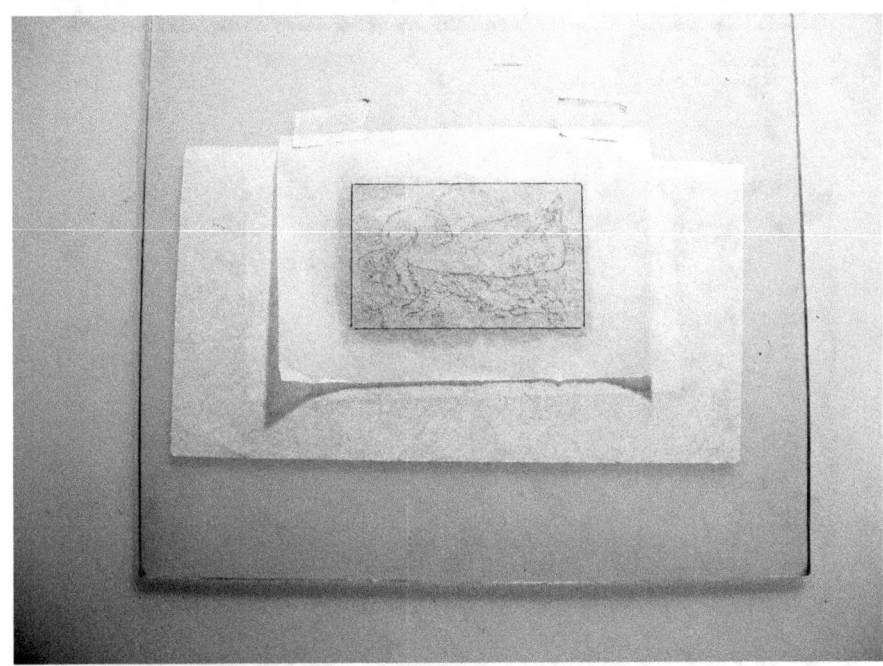

FIGURE 2.50

This is the plate with the SO-11 resist cleaned off, so the bright copper lines show up against the darker oxidized copper. This is one way to get visible reference lines on a plate that don't show up in the print.

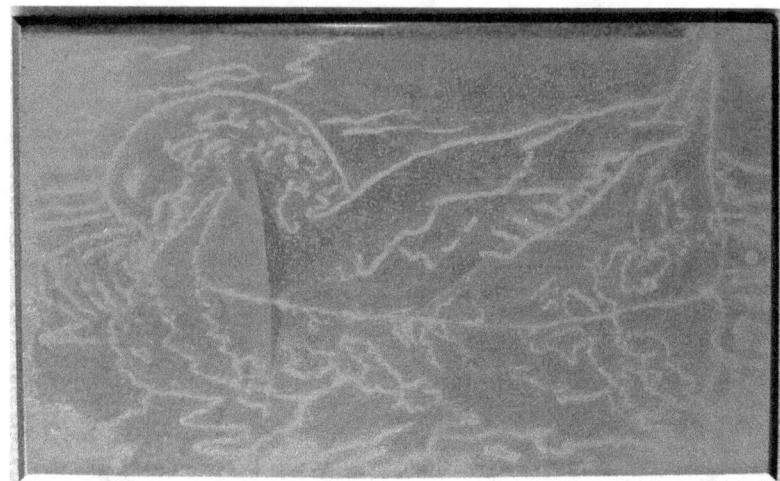

FIGURE 2.51

The plate, no aquatint, with PG-11 applied. I boosted the permeability of the PG-11 for this by adding a small amount of glycerin to it, so that I would get more detail and halftones in the goose. After spattering with black enamel spray can for aquatint, it will be ready for the first etch: 4 minutes 55 seconds for nominal 60% tone.

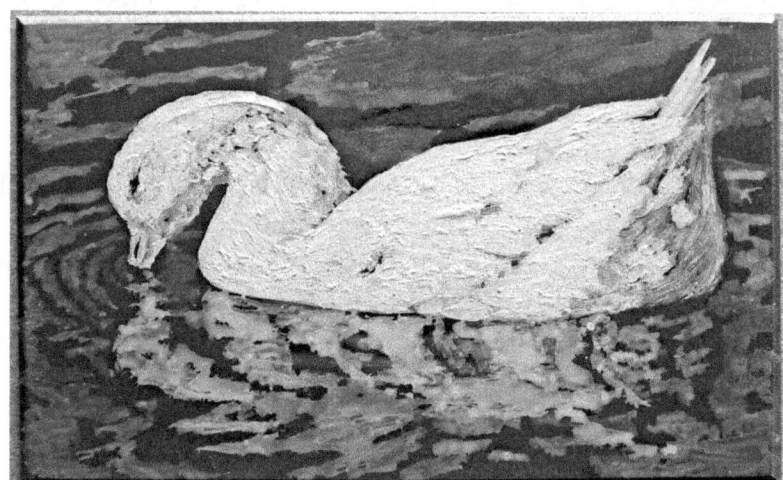

FIGURE 2.52

The plate, spattered, after a 60% etch. Contrary to plan, all the altered PG-11 thinly applied in the water areas broke down completely. The black enamel aquatint that had been on top of it was drifting around in the bottom of the tray. The enamel spatters on bare copper remained in place.

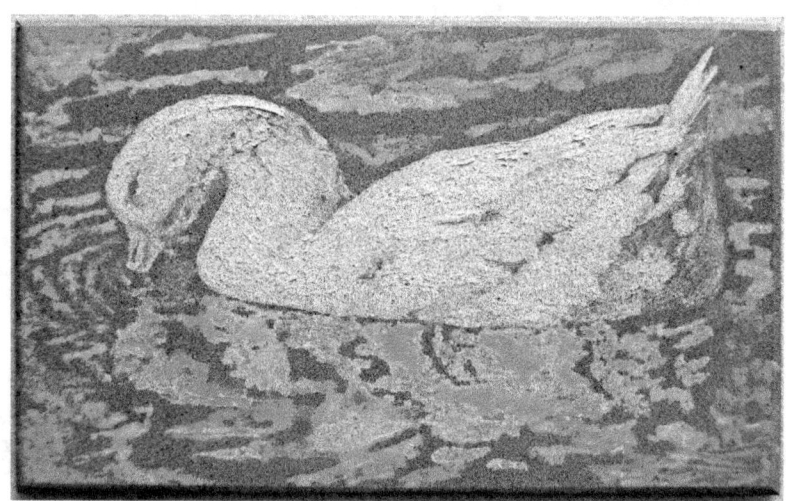

FIGURE 2.53

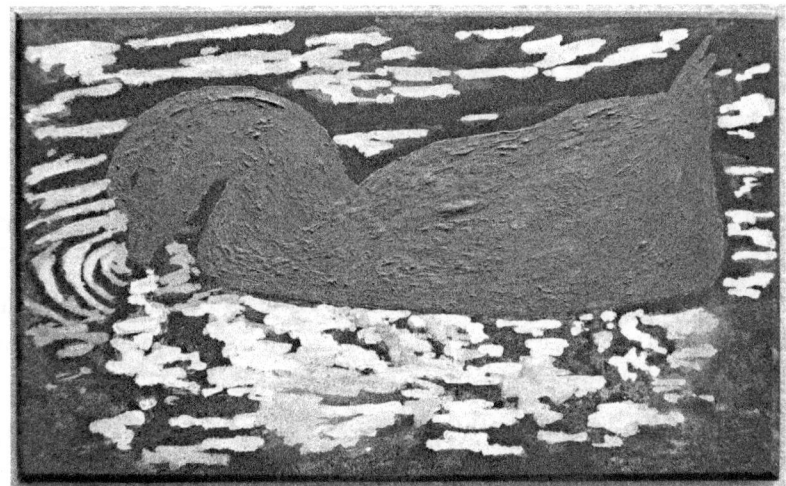

FIGURE 2.54

To block any further etching in the goose, I stopped it out with SO-11 except for the eye and the nostril which I wanted to go to black. To fix the water I spattered again with enamel just enough to prevent flat biting in the open areas but not enough to completely block areas that were still spattered. I then re-applied unaltered PG-11 to the light areas in the water. The plate was now ready to go to 80%, an additional 5 minutes 53 seconds in the acid.

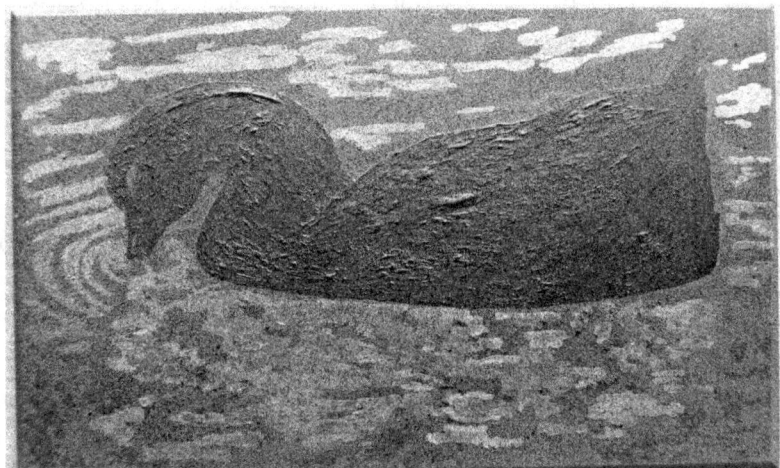

FIGURE 2.55

The plate, etched to 80%. Before going to 100% I wanted to create a slight gradation of tone from lighter foreground water to darker background water, so I added more spray can enamel to pretty much block out the foreground while leaving the background open. I then put it back in the acid for 9 minutes and 12 seconds. Theoretically, it should have been at 100%, but inspection showed that there were some areas that didn't look as deeply bitten as I wanted so I put it back in the acid for an additional 5 minutes.

Figure 2.56 shows the print, resulting from the above steps. An image like this could probably be made more sumptuous by having a 10% aquatint etched on the goose and a 40% or so etched on the water and then burnished to bring back the lights.

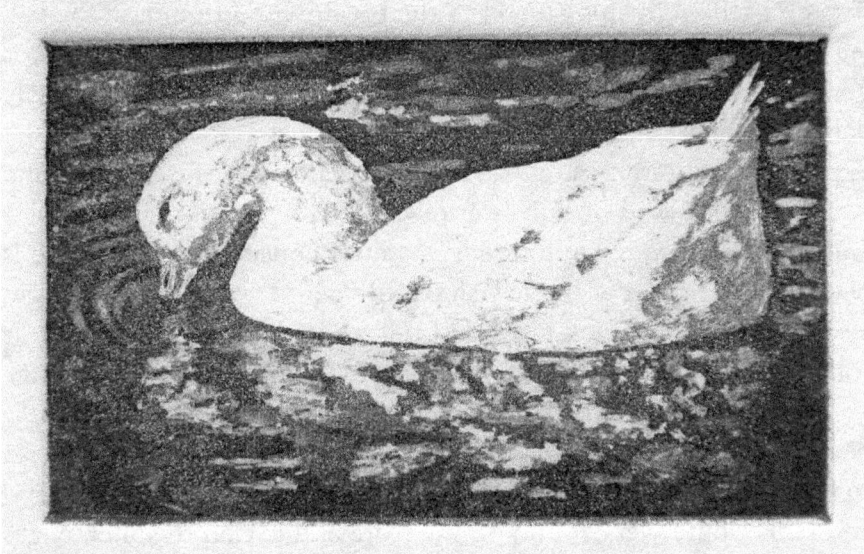

FIGURE 2.56

EXAMPLE 8: Cloud Effects

Following are three examples of progressively looser cloud effects, which I will cover in some detail. All three are PG-11 (Soft, Medium or Regular) on top of a rosin aquatint.

Each artist will develop his or her own variations and innovations related to this technique as well as to the others. These examples and the tools and techniques I used are offered as a point of departure.

Figure 2.57 shows the tools I used for making clouds: a piece of glass for a palette, hemostats to hold wads of cotton and polyester fiber, round brushes, and a cotton swab.

The basic technique is to pick up some ground on a brush and paint it on to the plate. Then while it is still wet, pat it with a wad of cotton or polyester to blend it and soften the edges until it looks like a cloud mass. This is repeated one small area at a time until the desired coverage is achieved. One brush is for applying ground and the other is for applying water and scrubbing when ground on the plate needs to be removed.

I would suggest using the Soft version of PG-11 for clouds. If your darkest tones are in the 50% or lighter range, use a thick application of it to block out areas where no further etching is desired rather than applying a harder (less permeable) ground. When using a harder ground it's easy to stopout too much. If your darkest tones are darker than 50% you should probably use a harder ground (Medium PG-11 or unaltered PG-11, or even SO-11) for blocking out areas.

To apply the ground, take the applicator brush and dip it in water. Then touch the tip of it to a paper towel until excess water is removed. Then mix the remaining water in the brush with ground on the pallet until you have a fairly loose consistency and medium quantity of ground in the brush, and then paint that on to the plate to very roughly define cloud features. Do a small enough area at a time that it doesn't dry before you can blend it. Spritz some water if necessary. To blend it, pat it with a wad of polyester or cotton fiber until the edges blur and it looks "cloudy." For clouds, a wetter consistency of ground is better than a dryer consistency since with a dryer consistency you get a scumbled, patchy look instead of a feathered, blended look. Pat or roll the brush or swab and try to avoid scrubbing as this may damage underlying layers or even the aquatint. Cotton tends to be more absorbent and to compact into lumps, polyester tends to stay springier and to lay down water instead of picking it up, so I use polyester to blend and redistribute wet ground on the plate and cotton to soften edges

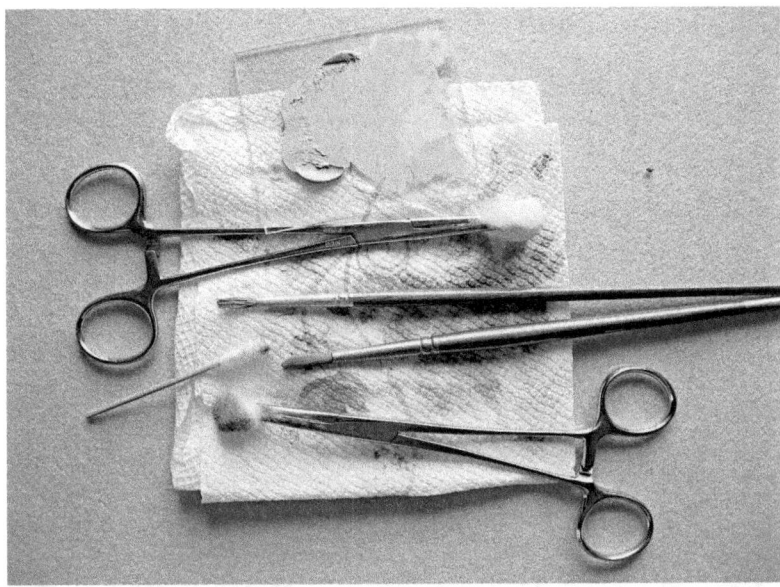

FIGURE 2.57

or pick up wet ground. I use both cotton and polyester dampened by dipping them in water and squeezing out the excess into a paper towel before applying them to the palette or plate. A Q-tip or cotton swab is good for small details.

Work by building up successive layers of ground. Make sure underlying layers are dry, and try to avoid disturbing them. Dip the plate in vinegar to fix existing layers so they will be less likely to be disturbed by additional ground. You can view the plate while working on it with the light glare coming from the copper or with it coming from the ground, and the two views may not look the same. Go by what you see when the light is glaring off of the copper.

Clouds have characteristics that range from harsh and ragged, to misty and ethereal. In these examples I have only used permeable ground. The best cloud effects will be obtained by using permeable ground in combination with other etching techniques, such as applying permeable or nonpermeable grounds with an airbrush, or by creating the basic imagery using permeable ground and then reworking it by covering that with a light aquatint tone and re-introducing lights by burnishing, scrubbing with steel wool or fine (300, 400, or 600) grit sandpaper, or buffing.

EXAMPLE 8A: Cloud Effects—Multiple Steps

(etchant: 1:1 ferric chloride; 20-minute timing chart)

This example uses the Soft, Medium, and Regular (unaltered) variations of PG-11 described in Appendix 5.

Figure 2.58 is a rosin aquatinted plate, with soft PG-11 applied, ready to etch to a 10% tone (18 seconds). The white lines are transferred from a transfer sheet made from tissue paper with titanium white dry pigment rubbed on it, for nonprinting visual reference lines.

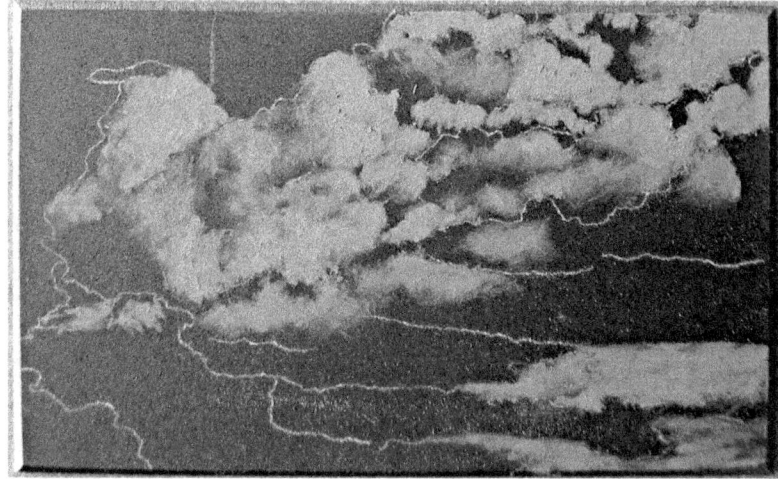

FIGURE 2.58

10% tone has been etched and additional soft PG-11 applied, ready to etch to 40% (additional 1:34). Open sky in upper left corner has been stopped out with SO-11 so it will remain at 10% tone.

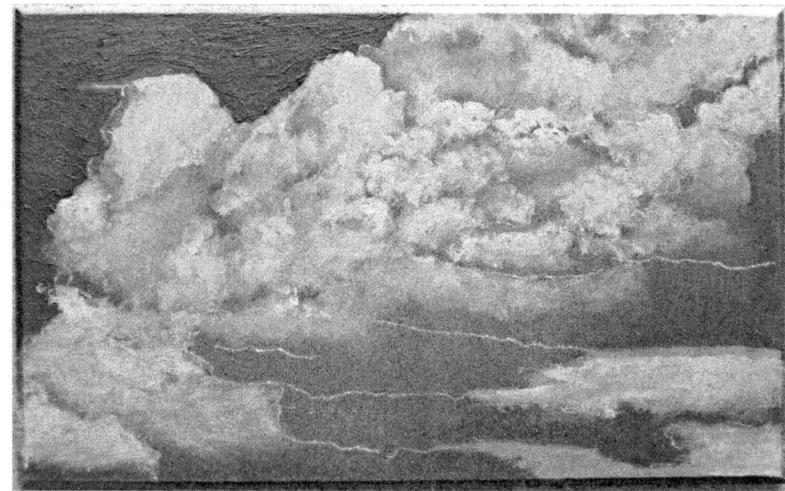

FIGURE 2.59

40% tone etched and all areas to go no darker than 40% stopped out with SO-11. Medium PG-11 applied to ensure a blended edge to the SO-11 and to partially stop out areas to go to 70% (additional 5:35). Ready to etch to 70%.

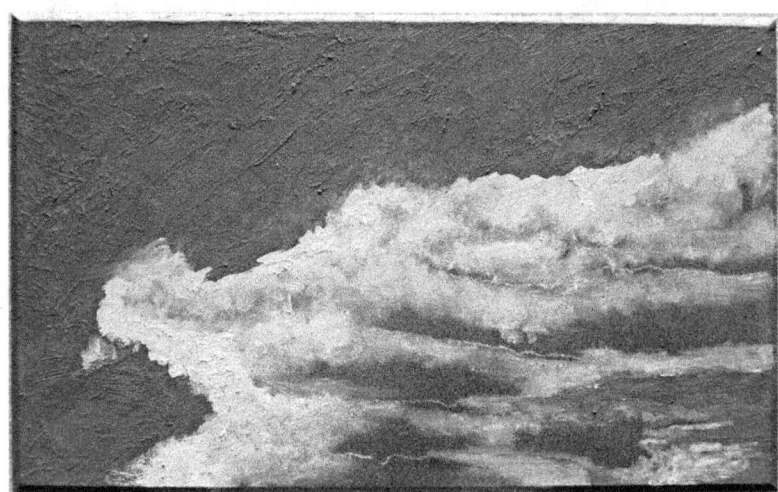

FIGURE 2.60

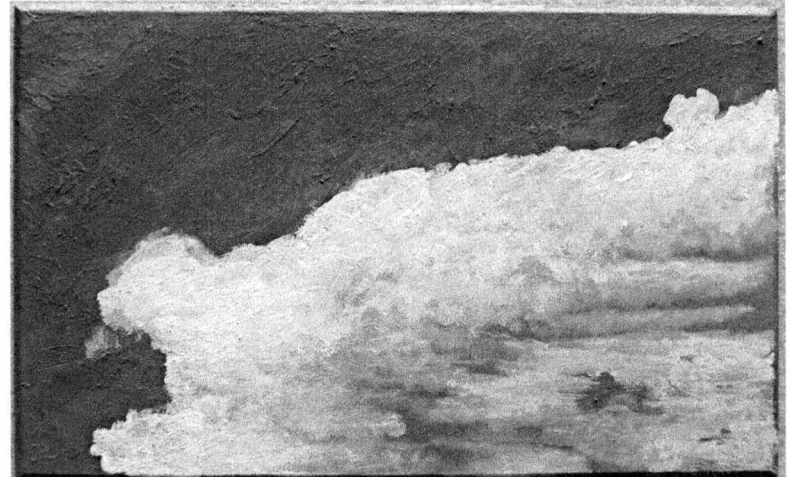

FIGURE 2.61

70% tone etched, ready to go to 100% (additional 12:33). Unaltered PG-11 applied to ensure soft edges and to partially stop out 100% tone areas.

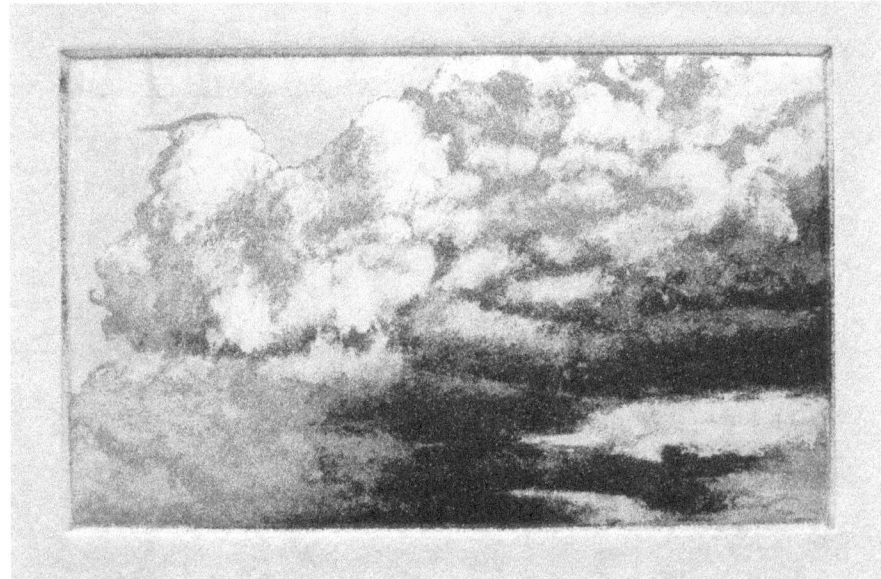

FIGURE 2.62

Print resulting from above steps.

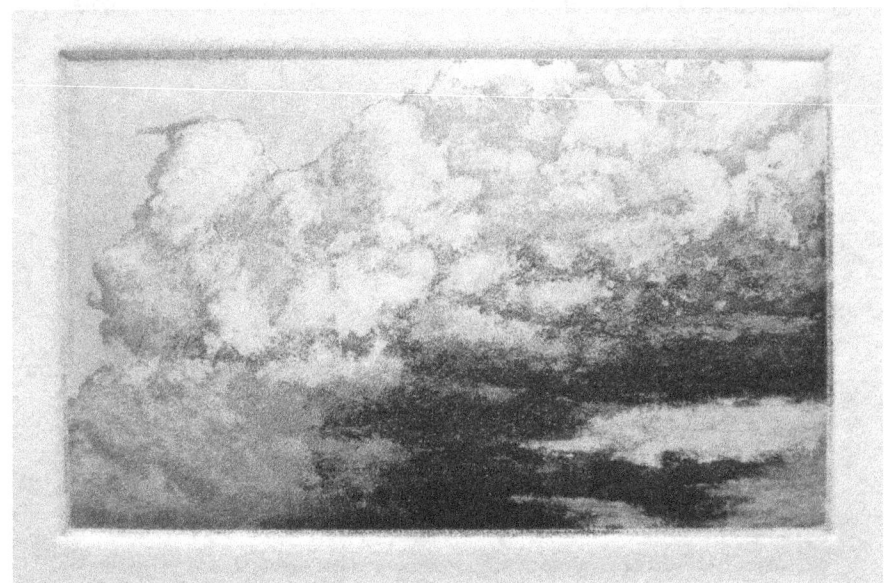

FIGURE 2.63

Print from plate after some scraping, burnishing and sanding.

EXAMPLE 8B: Cloud Effects—Multiple Steps

(etchant: 1:1 ferric chloride; 20-minute timing chart)

The plate, unetched, with ground applied and ready to etch to 10% of tone (18 seconds). Only Soft PG-11 was used for all steps in step biting this plate.

FIGURE 2.64

The plate, more Soft PG-11 applied, ready to etch to 20% tone (+0:16).

FIGURE 2.65

The plate, ready to etch to 30% tone (+0:30).

FIGURE 2.66

The plate, ready to etch to 40% tone (+0:48).

FIGURE 2.67

The plate, ready for the final etch to 50% tone (+1:14).

FIGURE 2.68

The resulting print.

FIGURE 2.69

EXAMPLE 8C: Cloud Effects—Multiple Steps

(etchant: 1:1 ferric chloride; 20-minute timing chart)

The plate, ready to etch to 10% tone (+0:18). As far as the step biting is concerned, this example is a repeat of example B above. This example also uses only the soft variant of PG-11.

FIGURE 2.70

The plate, ready to etch to 20% tone (+0:16).

FIGURE 2.71

The plate, ready to etch to 30% tone (+0:30).

FIGURE 2.72

FIGURE 2.73

The plate, ready to etch to 40% tone (+0:48).

FIGURE 2.74

The plate, ready to etch to 50% tone (+1:14).

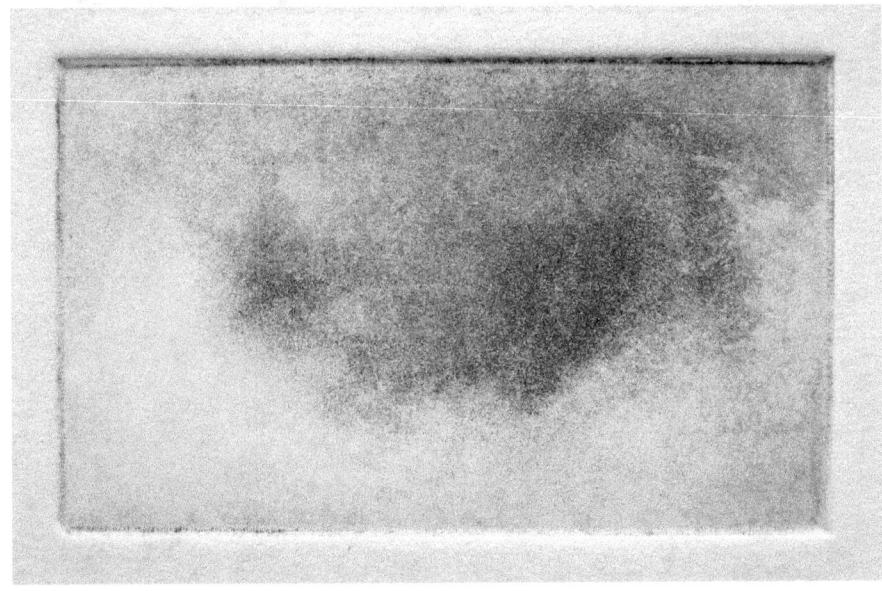

FIGURE 2.75

The print resulting from the above steps. All of these cloud effects could be made softer and more diffuse by the use of sandpaper, steel wool, burnishing, etc.

EXAMPLE 9: Fur—Multiple Steps

(etchant: 1:1 Edinburgh Etch; 20-minute timing chart)

I wanted to keep this example fairly crisp, so I used 1:1 Edinburgh Etch. The stopout is Regular PG-11 on top of a rosin aquatint. The applicator was a ⅛-inch flat watercolor brush with bristles splayed.

This is the aquatinted plate ready to etch to 10% tone (18 seconds). Whites are stopped out.

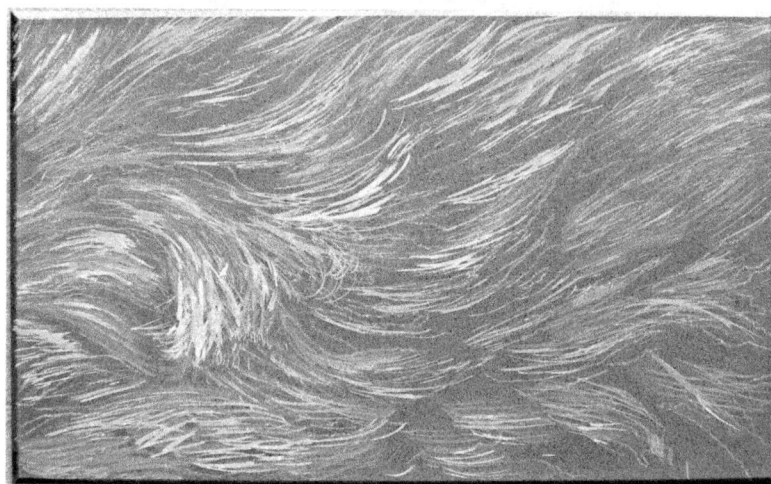

FIGURE 2.76

The plate with more PG-11 added. Ready to etch to 20% tone (+0:16).

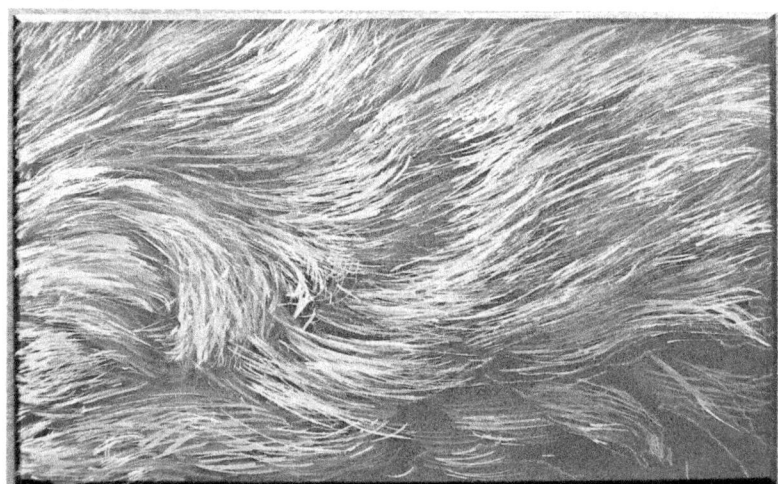

FIGURE 2.77

The plate, ready to etch to 30% tone (+0:30).

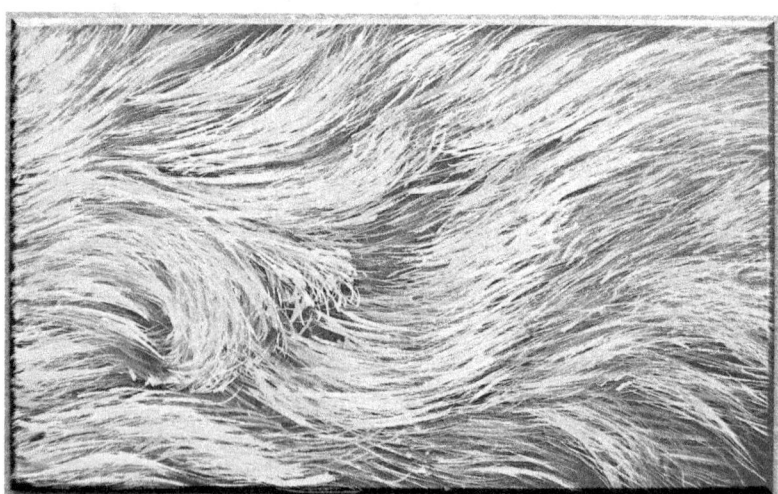

FIGURE 2.78

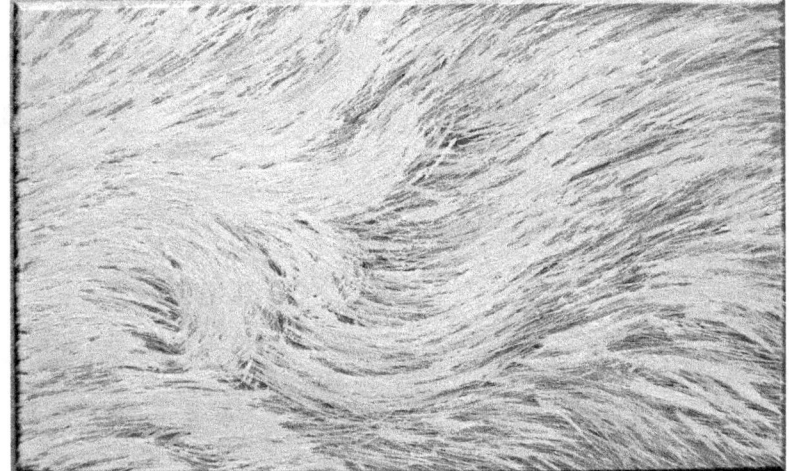
FIGURE 2.79

The plate, ready to etch to 40% tone (+0:48).

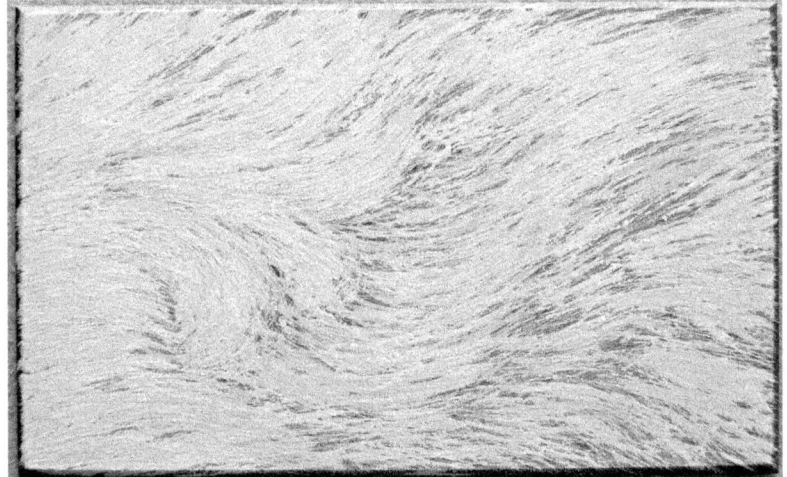
FIGURE 2.80

The plate, ready to etch to 50% tone (+1:14).

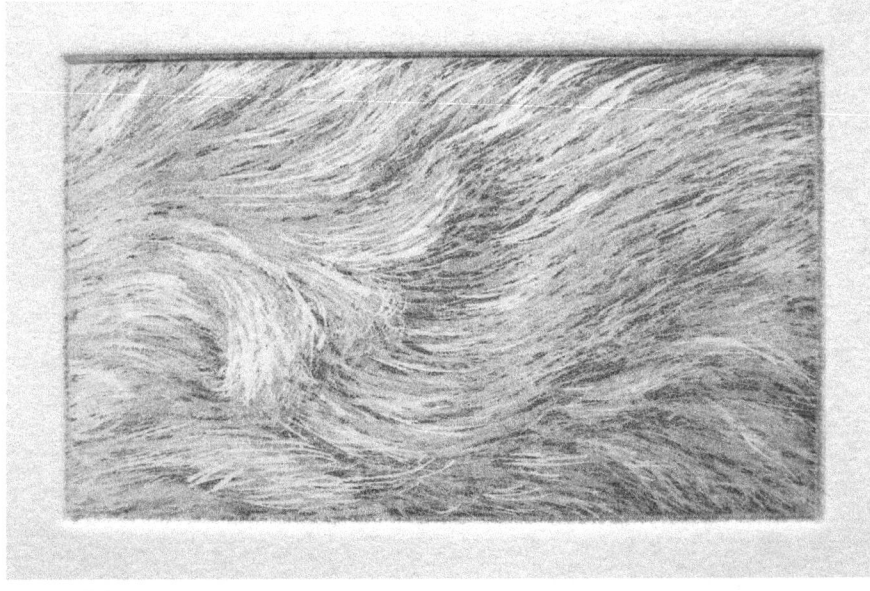
FIGURE 2.81

The first proof print from the plate after step biting. Could stand to look a little bit softer, so I did some additional direct work on it.

Final proof after some dry-pointing, scraping, burnishing, and scrubbing with 220 grit sandpaper.

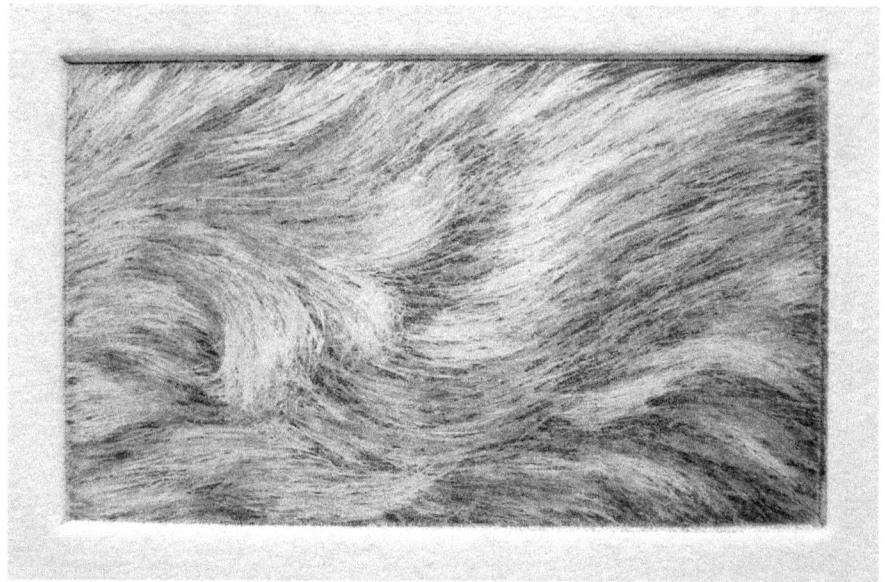

FIGURE 2.82

EXAMPLE 10: Texture and Fine Detail—Multiple Steps (Apple Branch)

(etchant: 1:1 ferric chloride; 20-minute timing chart)

This example includes etched lines used in combination with step biting for the creation of the image. The stopouts used are PG-11 (unaltered) and SO-11. The hard ground used for etching the lines was asphaltum thinned with turpentine.

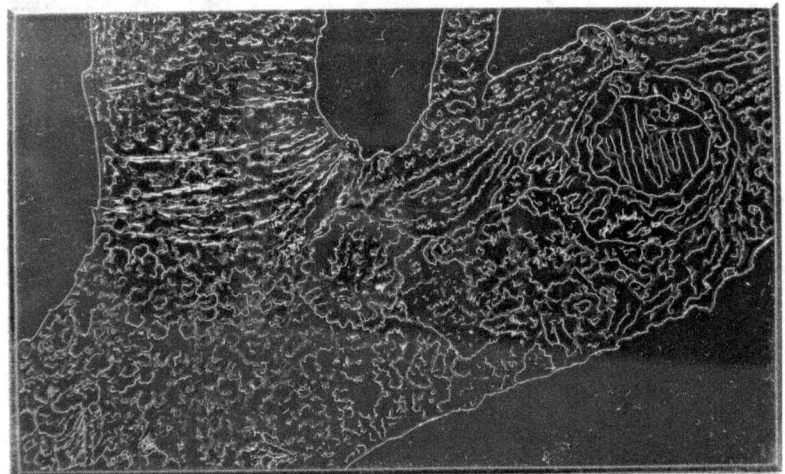

FIGURE 2.83

This is the plate coated with traditional hard ground after the lines have been needled into the ground. I used a graphite transfer from a tracing to get reference lines on to the hard ground. (Make a tracing on tracing paper with graphite lead, place the tracing graphite-side-down on the hard ground and run it through the press to transfer the lines to the plate.) Lines etched for 30 minutes in 1:1 ferric chloride.

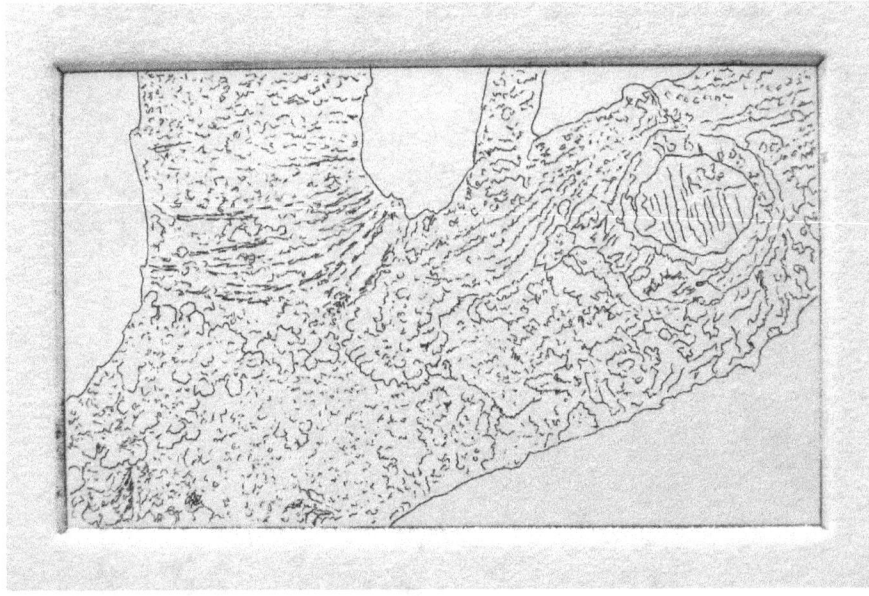

FIGURE 2.84

This is a print made from the above plate after etching the lines.

After etching the lines, a rosin aquatint was applied and everything was etched to 10% tone (18 seconds). The background (which was to stay at a flat 10% tone) was stopped out with SO-11 (two coats) and PG-11 was applied to the lights on the branch. (The lights on the branch were to be burnished to white, and show up against the 10% background tone.)

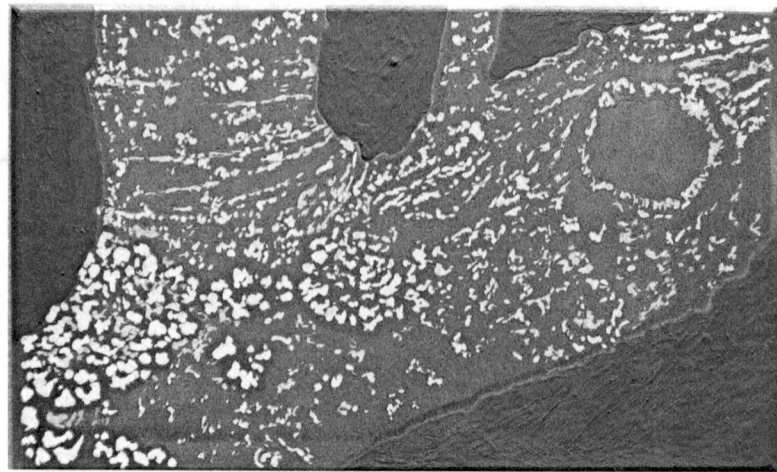

FIGURE 2.85

The plate has been etched to 30% tone (+0:46) and all that is to remain at 30% stopped out. The next etch is to 50% tone.

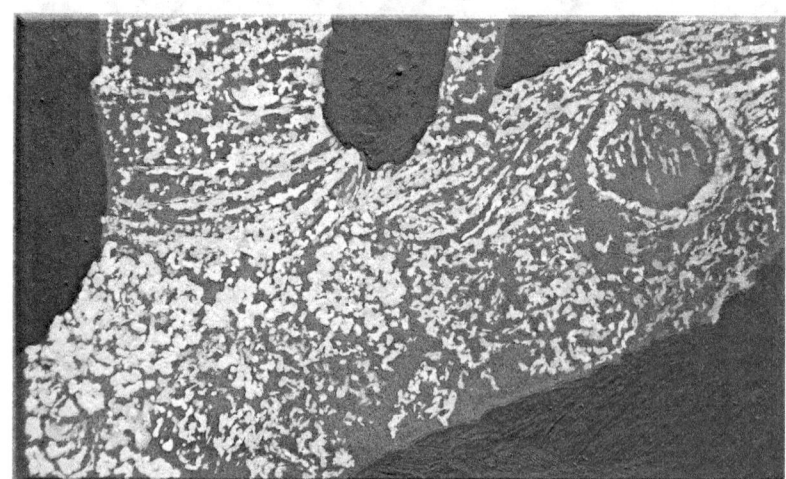

FIGURE 2.86

The plate with 50% tone etched and stopped out (+2:02), ready to etch to 70%.

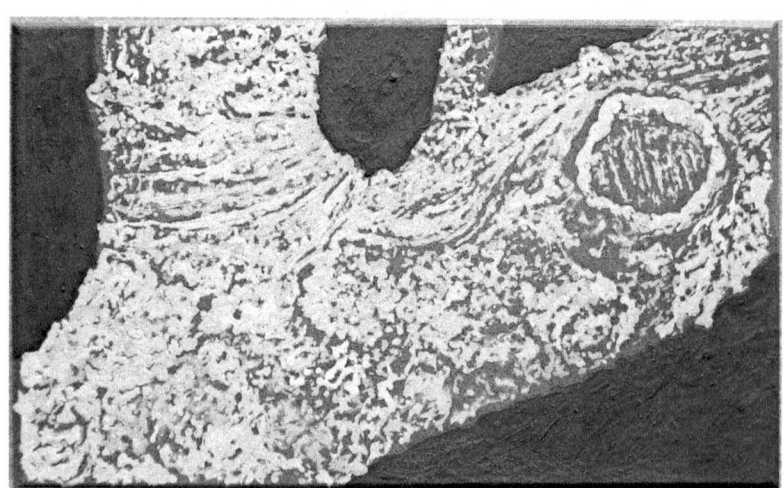

FIGURE 2.87

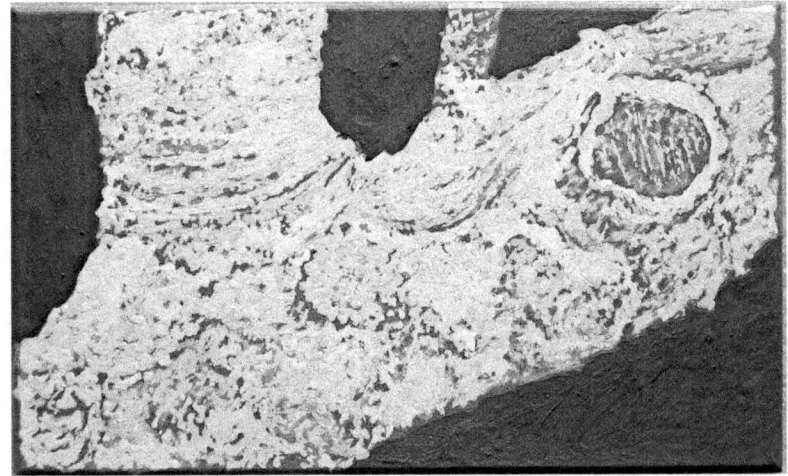

FIGURE 2.88

The plate with 70% tone etched and stopped out (+4:21), ready to etch to 100% (black) tone.

After etching the 100% tone (+12:33, the plate was cleaned and a proof printed.

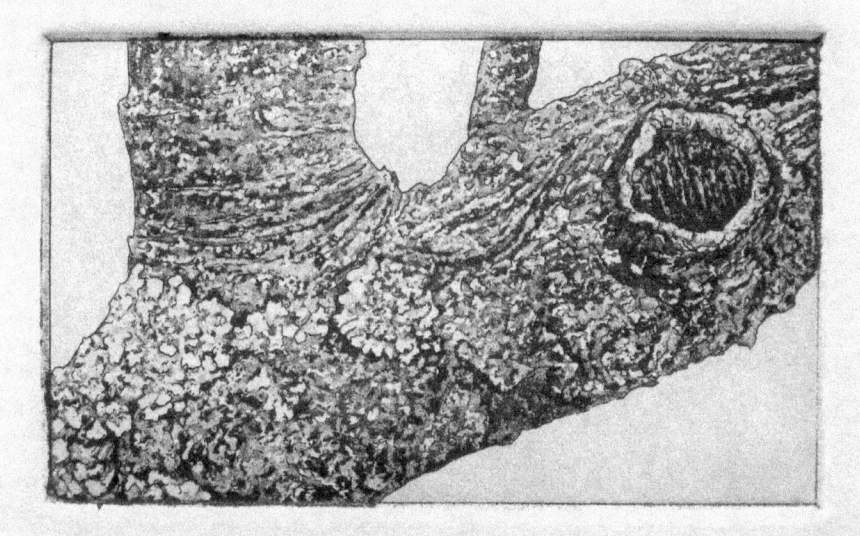

FIGURE 2.89

This is the first proof printed from the plate after the above steps.

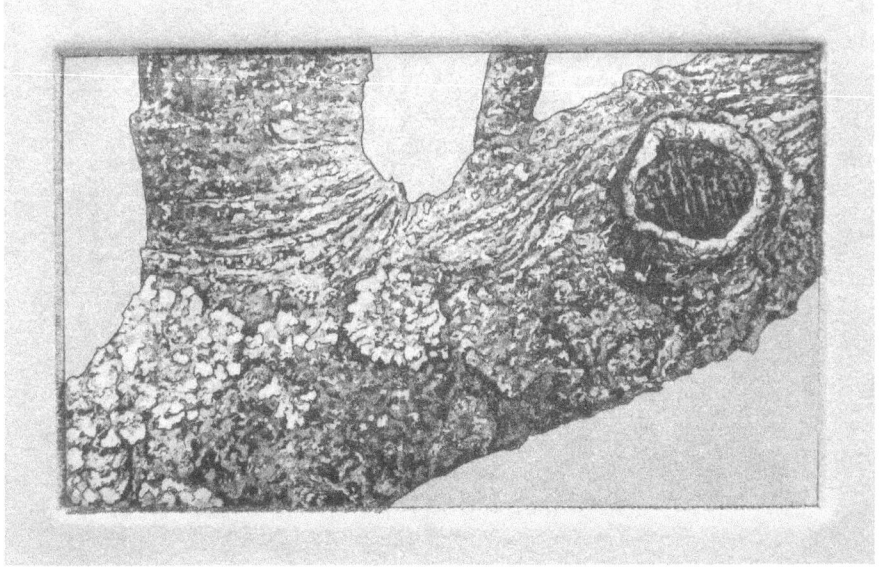

FIGURE 2.90

This is a proof print of the plate after some burnishing.

CHAPTER 3

PG-11 Used As an Adhesive

This chapter focuses primarily on using permeable ground as a sort of adhesive for sticking various materials, some of a particulate nature, to make textures, and some found objects to make shapes, to the surface of the plate. Granular materials (Examples 1–6) can be mixed in with permeable ground and applied as a mixture to the surface of the plate, but I have generally preferred the more random character of the results you get when you paint a wet "field" of watery ground on to the plate and then sprinkle things into it.

As the particles of whatever material you're using land in the thin layer of wet ground they form a meniscus that sucks the surrounding wet ground up around them. When this dries, it effectively holds the particles in place on the plate. It also forms a stopped out pattern of thick ground around each particle and thin ground where the ground was sucked away by the particle. This pattern, different for each different particulate "texturizing" agent, can be etched into the plate as a step in creating an image.

Found objects (Examples 7–11) can also be used, if they can be flattened. This gets into considerations common to soft ground techniques, however; since physical pressure isn't a major component, things that are too soft or juicy to use with soft ground can be used with this technique, although you don't get anywhere near the same amount of detail.

Suppose you are using a fresh green leaf. Basically, you paint or spray a layer of wet diluted PG-11 on to the plate and lay the leaf in it. (For spraying, as an alternative to an airbrush, you can use the type of bottle with a pump sprayer that makes a fine mist used for non-aerosol hairspray. The cheapest ones work best.) If the leaf is flat, no pressure may be required. Most of the time things need to be gently pressed against the plate.

My favorite protective backing film to lay directly on the leaf and wet ground is white vinyl shelf paper with the backing left on, plastic side down. Usually the material on the plate is too uneven for rigid backing so a pad made from layers of cloth, foam rubber, air conditioner filter material, carpet padding, quilting, etc., is necessary. I prefer the ¼-inch thick polyurethane foam sold for cut-to-size air conditioner filter material, so I usually follow the shelf liner with a layer of that.

Follow the padding with a flat layer, like cardboard or wood, and apply some deadweight on top of that: a book or a stack of books, etc.

This means moisture is trapped between non-porous layers, so after a couple hours or overnight with the pressure applied, carefully remove the layers to expose the plate to air and allow the ground to dry. Moisture trapped under things like broad leaves may take a long time to dry. After the ground has finished drying (I would suggest at least overnight) you can do touchup if necessary.

Gaps where stems or other parts are not stuck to the plate can be filled by filling a small brush with diluted ground and touching it to them to allow the ground to flow down and wick along the stem and fill the gap. Small weights, maybe on top of a piece of metal screen or hardware cloth, can be placed on objects that need to be held close to the plate while the ground dries.

Etch the plate with or without the leaf stuck in the ground. You may want to etch for a while with the object stuck to the plate to establish the background areas and then remove the object and etch some more to get internal detail. (See Example 11 "Mimosa Leaves.")

Generally, results will be influenced by things like the version of PG-11 used (Regular, Medium or Soft), the dilution of the ground and how generously it is applied, absorbency and permeability (and solubility) of the particles, evenness and density of the application of the particles, and of course the shape and size of the particles used. A thin layer of wet ground usually works best. If beading is a problem, the plate can be oxidized or a trace amount of hand soap can be added to the diluted ground.

Required tools are minimal. You need a brush (or other applicator) to apply the wet ground, and I usually use my fingers to pick up a pinch of the texture material and sprinkle it on to the plate. Uneven is usually more interesting, but if you want to get it more even, a scatter screen can help. Something like a couple of pieces (or a single piece) of hardware cloth with ⅛- or ¼-inch size mesh. With two pieces you can effectively vary the hole size. Hold it over the plate and drop the particles through it.

The PG-11 has to be diluted to a thin consistency. I usually use the following ratios: Regular PG-11, 1 part to 4 parts water; Medium PG-11, 1 part to 2 parts water; Soft PG-11, 1 part to 1 part water.

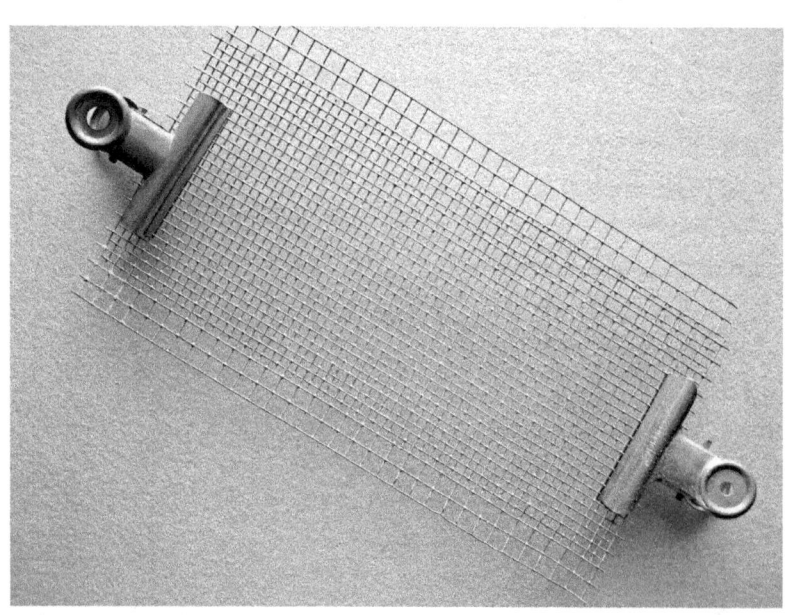

FIGURE 3.1: Scatter Screen

EXAMPLE 1A: Lump Rosin with No Aquatint

(etchant: 1:1 ferric chloride; 20 minutes)

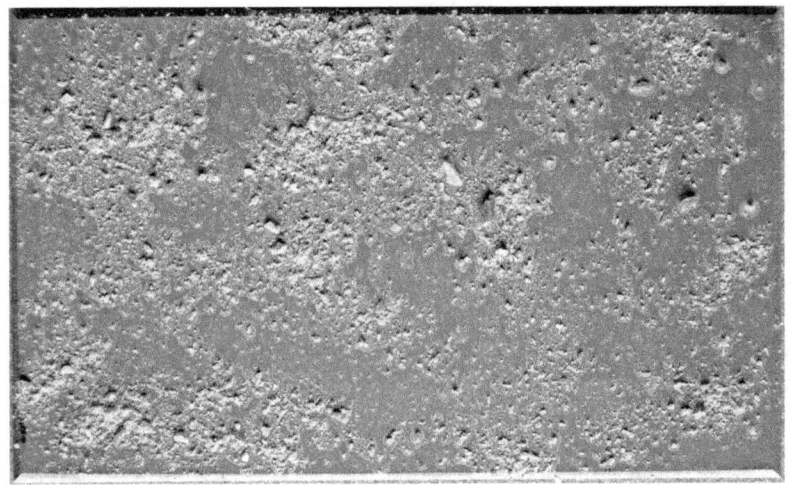

FIGURE 3.2

This is the plate, before etching, with no aquatint on it. The entire plate was coated with a thin wash of diluted (Regular) PG-11. Crushed lump (amber) rosin was sprinkled into the wet ground and the plate was allowed to dry. It was then etched in 1:1 ferric chloride for a single etch of 20 minutes.

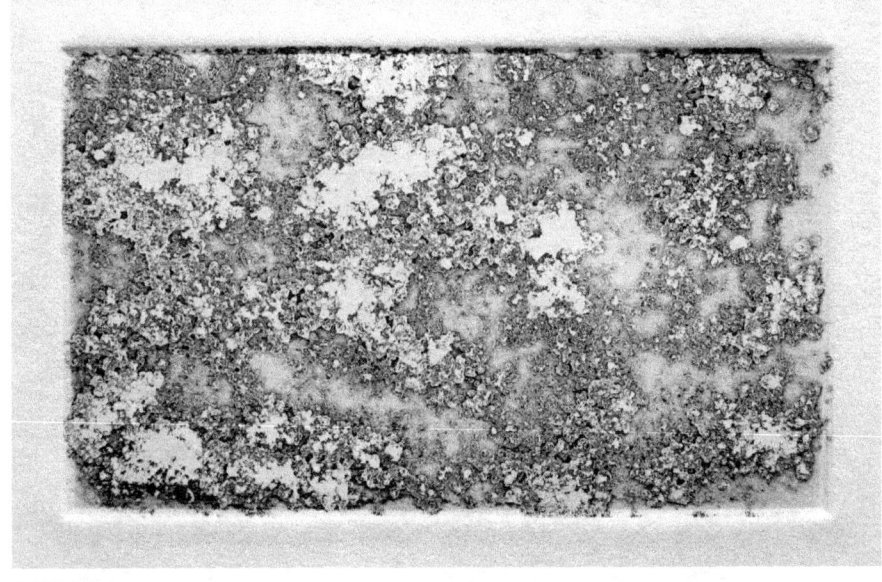

FIGURE 3.3

A print made from the above plate.

EXAMPLE 1B: Lump Rosin with Rosin Aquatint

(etchant: 1:1 ferric chloride; 20 minutes)

Figure 3.4 shows the plate, before etching, with a rosin aquatint on it, coated with diluted (Regular) PG-11 and sprinkled with crushed lump rosin. This was allowed to dry, then it was etched for 20 minutes in 1:1 ferric chloride.

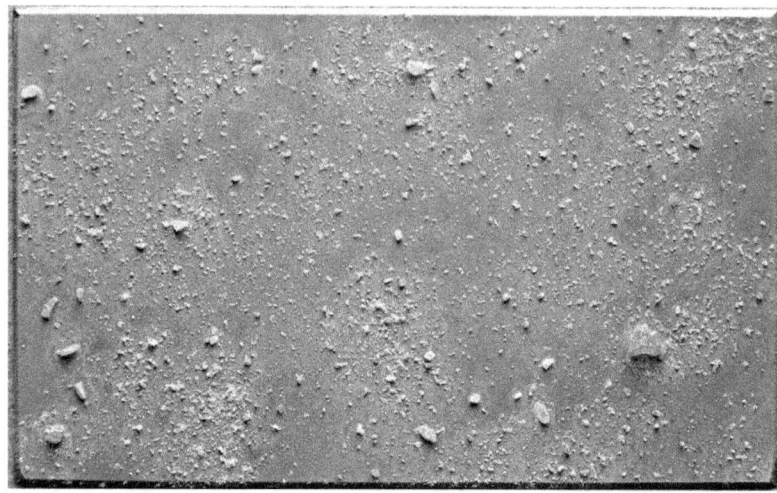

FIGURE 3.4

This is a print, made from the above plate.

FIGURE 3.5

EXAMPLE 2A: Cornmeal with No Aquatint

(etchant: 1:1 ferric chloride; 20 minutes)

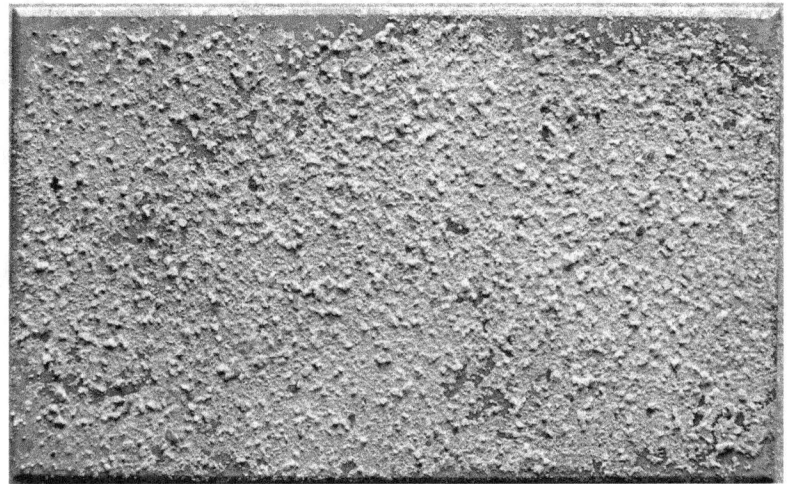

FIGURE 3.6

The plate, with no aquatint, covered with wet ground (Regular PG-11) and sprinkled with cornmeal. The plate is shown after being etched in 1:1 ferric chloride for a single 20-minute etch.

FIGURE 3.7

A print made from the above plate.

EXAMPLE 2B: Cornmeal with Rosin Aquatint

(etchant: 1:1 ferric chloride; 20 minutes)

The plate with a rosin aquatint, covered with wet PG-11 and sprinkled with cornmeal. The picture shows the plate after it was etched in 1:1 ferric chloride for 20 minutes.

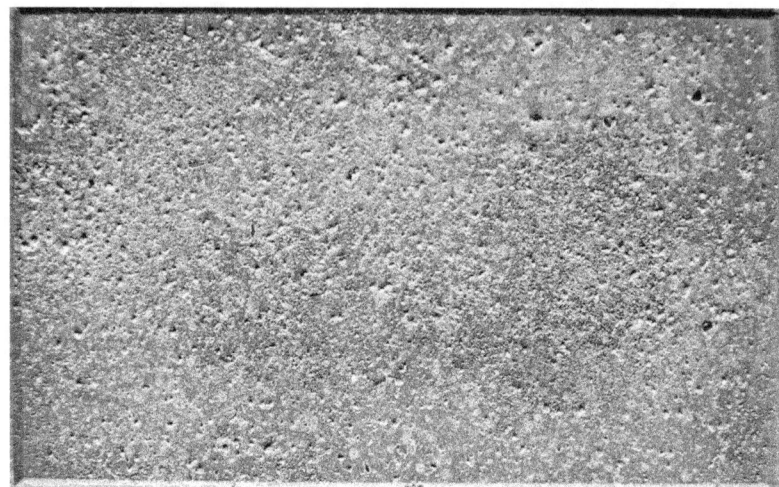

FIGURE 3.8

A print taken from the above plate.

FIGURE 3.9

EXAMPLE 3: Tea Leaves with Rosin Aquatint

(etchant: 1:1 Edinburgh Etch; 20 minutes)

FIGURE 3.10

The plate with a rosin aquatint, coated with watery PG-11 and sprinkled with tea leaves. (After the ground dried most of the tea leaves came off.) The plate was etched in Edinburgh Etch for 20 minutes.

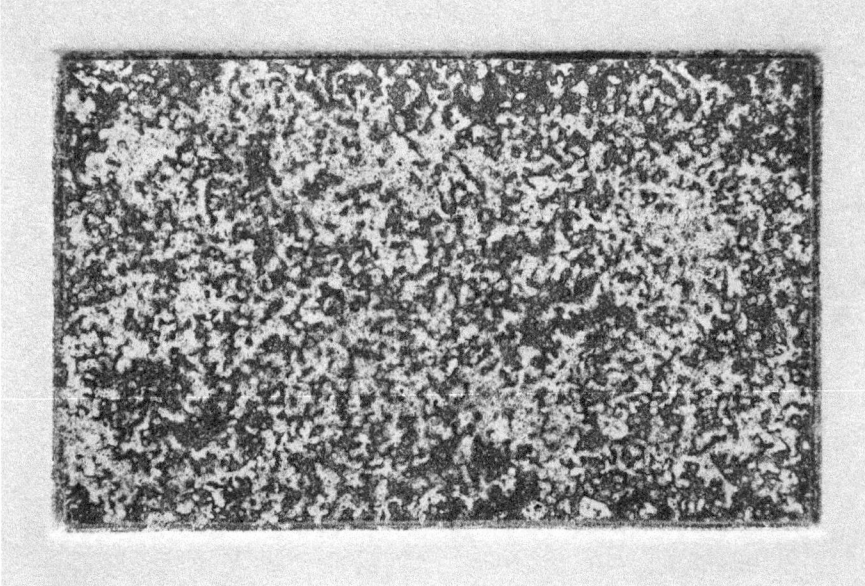

FIGURE 3.11

A print from the above plate.

EXAMPLE 4: Fine Powdered Rosin with Rosin Aquatint

(etchant: 1:1 Edinburgh Etch; 20 minutes)

The plate with a rosin aquatint, coated with diluted PG-11 and sprinkled with fine powdered rosin while the PG-11 was still wet. I used my fingers to sprinkle the powdered rosin, so it landed in clumps. After the PG-11 dried, I blew off the excess powdered rosin with compressed air and etched the plate in Edinburgh Etch for 20 minutes.

FIGURE 3.12

A print from the above plate.

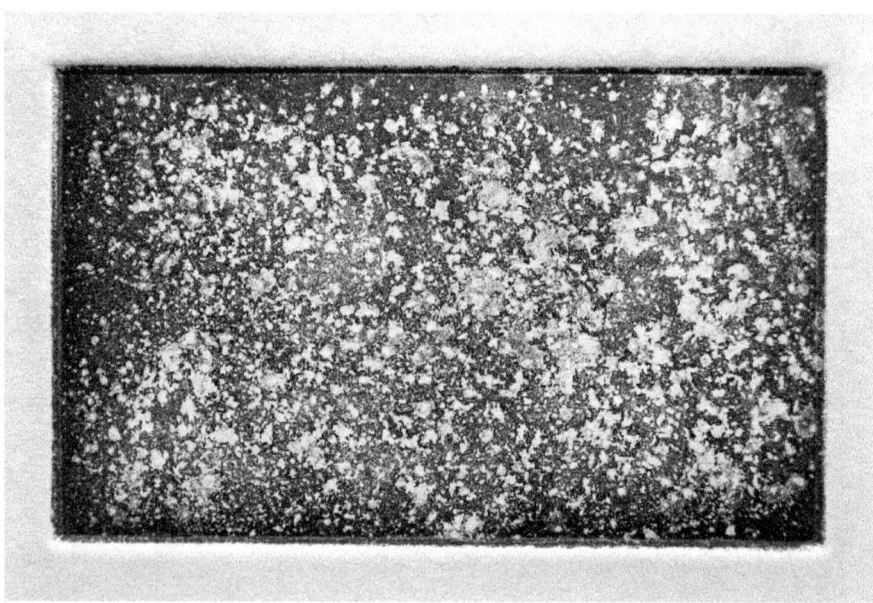

FIGURE 3.13

Predictably, textures made with this technique using materials that have a fairly fine, or even extremely fine, granular consistency tend to produce results that look fairly similar. Differences would be most apparent with plates that use both the thinnest coating of wet ground and the most diluted ground that would be able to hold the particles in place. The particles themselves in most cases provide a 100% stop-out in the spot where they are stuck to the surface of the plate. In most situations this technique is best applied to working on top of an aquatint, where you have the potential to create blacks where you're not creating whites. If you're working on a blank, un-aquatinted plate, applying a very thin and sparse quantity of ground may result in the creation of a sparse amount of imagery for lack of an effective resist. On an un-aquatinted plate consider using an aquatint (rosin or spray) on top of the permeable ground. With PG-11 this works best with the unmodified version of the ground. With the Medium and Soft versions everything tends to come off in the acid.

EXAMPLE 5: Salt and Sugar with Rosin Aquatint

(etchant: 1:1 Edinburgh Etch; 20 minutes)

The plate with a rosin aquatint, coated with a thin wash of PG-11 and sprinkled with salt on the left side, and sugar (coarse, raw) on the right. After the ground dried it was etched in Edinburgh Etch for 20 minutes. Before etching I soaked it in vinegar to set the ground and dissolve remaining grains of salt and sugar. (Water would have dissolved the salt, the sugar, and the ground.)

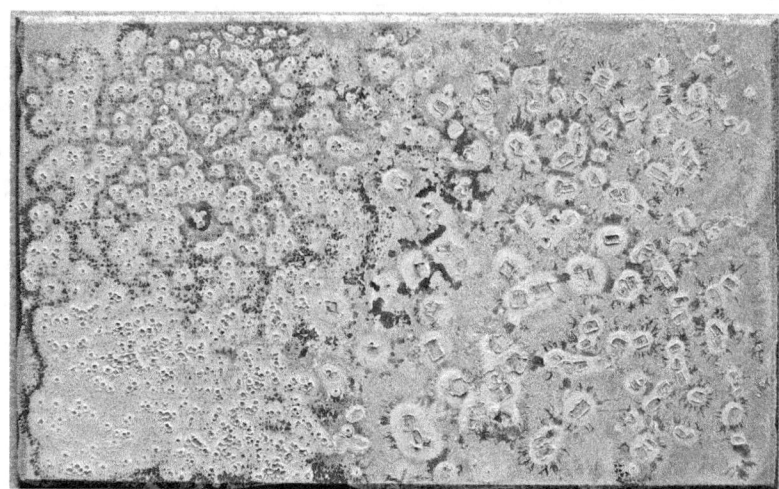

FIGURE 3.14

This is the print resulting from the above plate.

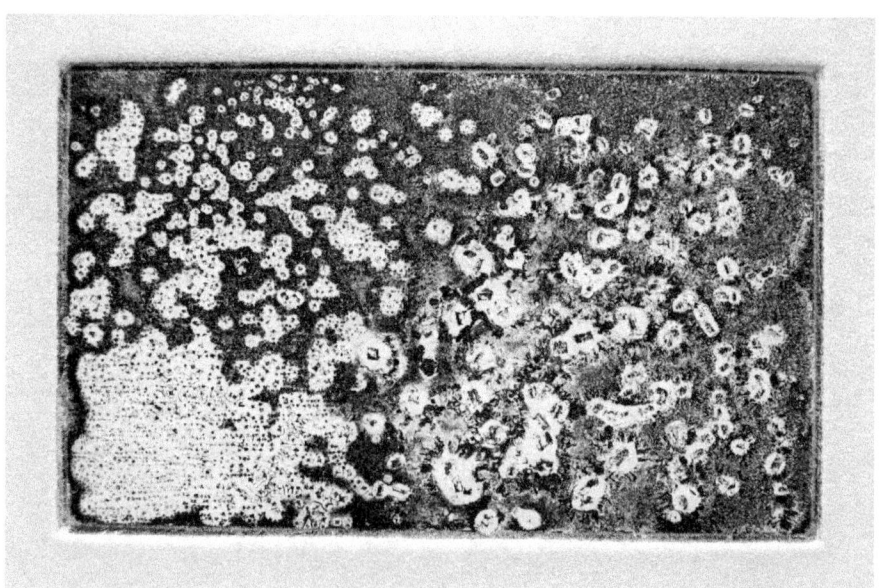

FIGURE 3.15

EXAMPLE 6: Grains of Rice with No Rosin Aquatint

(etchant: 1:1 Edinburgh Etch; 20 minutes)

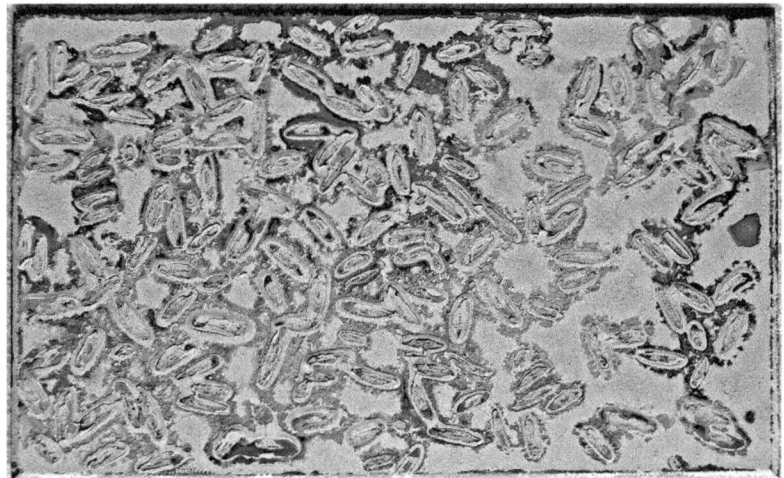

FIGURE 3.16

A bare, un-aquatinted plate, coated with diluted PG-11 (I used the Soft version of PG-11 for this one) and sprinkled with grains of rice. After the ground dried, I blasted the rice off with compressed air and etched the plate in Edinburgh Etch for 20 minutes.

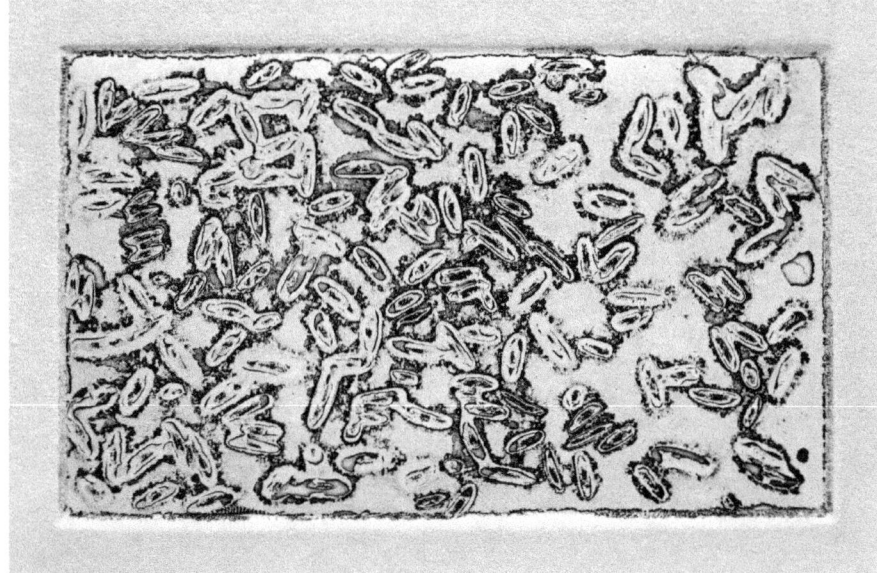

FIGURE 3.17

This is a print taken from the plate above.

EXAMPLE 7: Fabric with No Aquatint

(etchant: 1:1 Edinburgh Etch; 30 minutes)

The plate, no aquatint, coated with wet PG-11 and with fabric laid on it. Moderate deadweight was applied for a couple of hours and when removed additional diluted ground was applied with a brush and allowed to wick down into the fabric. This was allowed to dry.

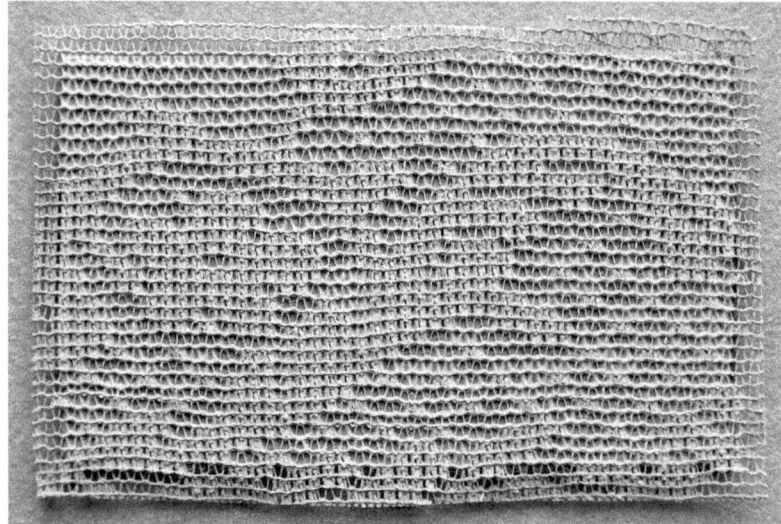

FIGURE 3.18

Once dry, the plate was etched for 20 minutes in 1:1 Edinburgh Etch with the fabric still on the plate. Then the fabric was removed and the plate (shown here) was etched for an additional 10 minutes without the fabric for some additional detail.

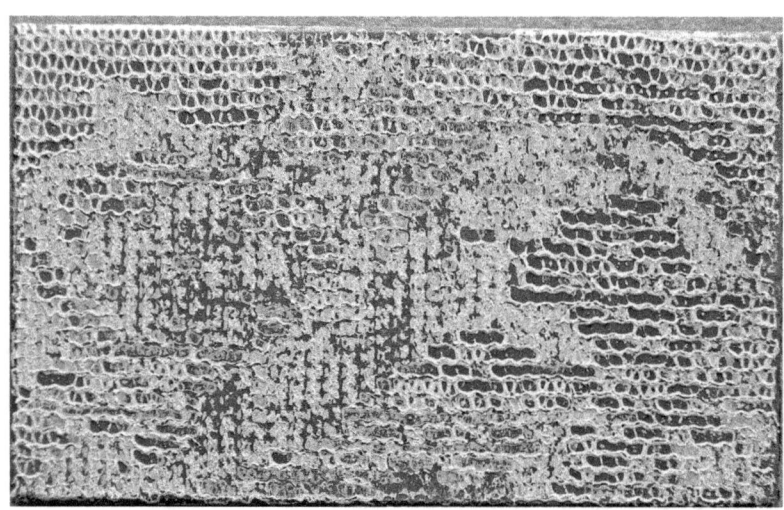

FIGURE 3.19

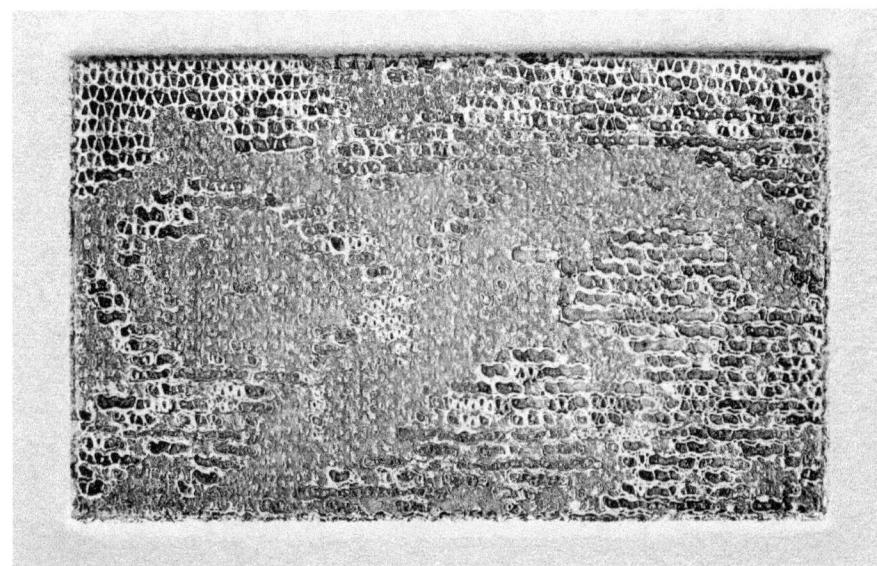

FIGURE 3.20

This is the resulting print. Not at all like what you get with standard soft ground, detail-wise, but maybe useful for when (rotted?) fabric with muted detail is called for.

EXAMPLE 8: Feathers with Rosin Aquatint

(etchant: 1:1 Edinburgh Etch; 20 minutes)

I had to try some feathers to see what kind of detail I could get. This is an aquatinted plate (shown after etching) with a thin wash of regular PG-11 on it, and feathers dropped into it while wet. I applied moderate deadweight. I wanted to see what difference it would make if feathers were left on or removed before etching, so when the ground had dried I removed three of the feathers before putting it in the acid. One came off in the rinse water.

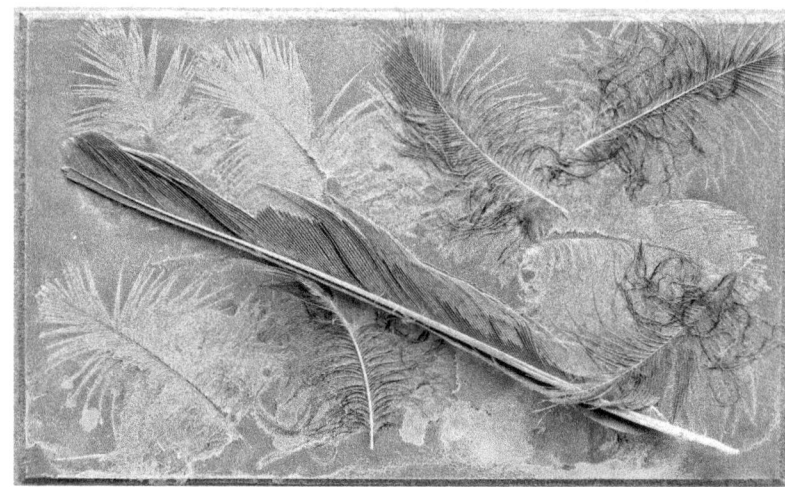

FIGURE 3.21

This shows the print—"Exploding Feathers"? Feathers removed after the ground had dried but before etching are visible but etched darker. Feathers that were attached to the plate during etching stopped out more effectively—too effectively. Maybe they should have all been left on through most of the etch and then completely or partially removed for the last part of the etch to get some detail in the white areas.

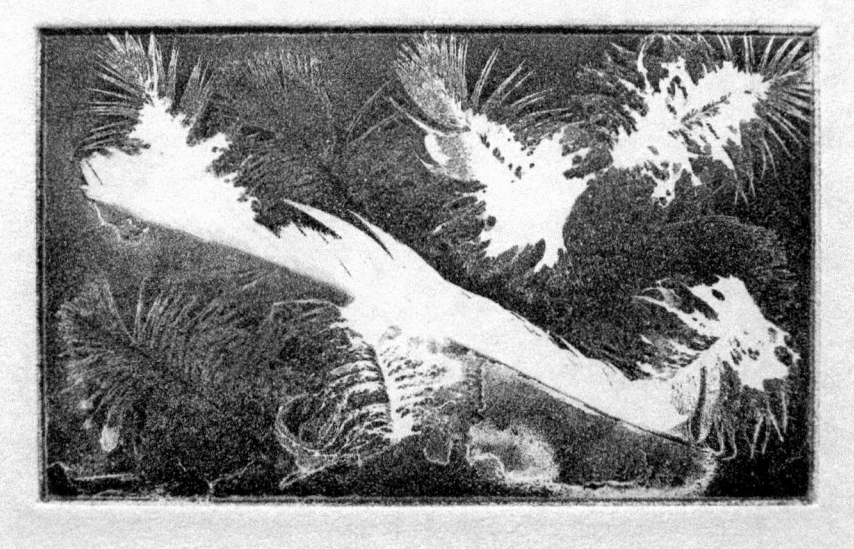

FIGURE 3.22

EXAMPLE 9: Pressed Leaves with Rosin Aquatint

(etchant: 1:1 Edinburgh Etch; 40 minutes)

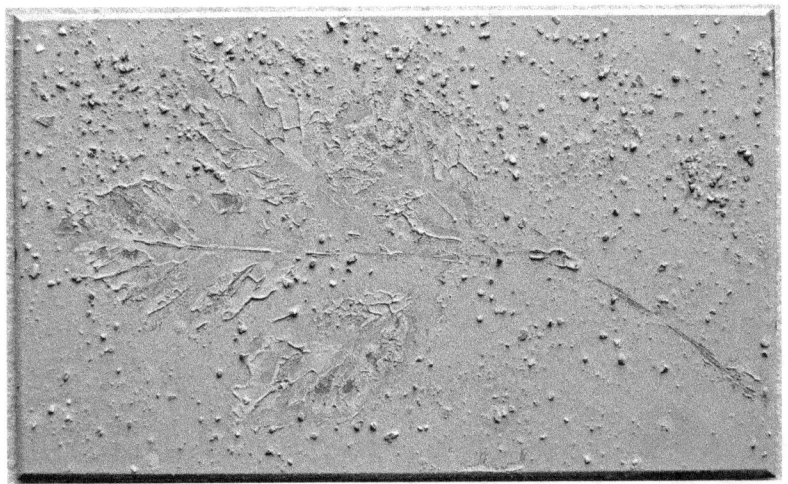

FIGURE 3.23

This was an aquatinted (rosin) plate, coated with diluted Soft PG-11. A twig with four leaves, previously dried and pressed, was laid in the wet ground. Some cornmeal was sparsely scattered in the background area for some texture and minimal deadweight was applied while the ground was drying. When the ground dried, (except, as it turned out, under parts of the leaves) the leaves were removed and the plate was etched.

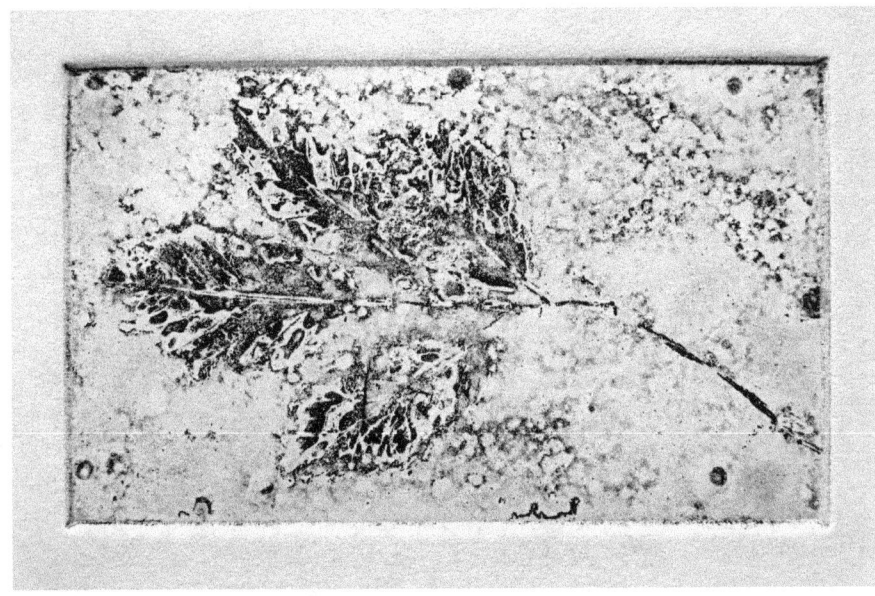

FIGURE 3.24

This is a print from the above plate. This example and the next one (Example 10) are companion pieces. I wanted to try Soft PG-11 with and without aquatint. I actually moved on to a subsequent example after putting them in the acid and was out of the studio when the timer sounded. I think they were in the acid about 40 minutes.

EXAMPLE 10: Queen Anne's Lace Leaves with No Aquatint

(etchant: 1:1 Edinburgh Etch; 40 minutes)

This is the un-aquatinted plate coated with Soft PG-11, with parts of a Queen Anne's Lace plant placed in the wet ground. Moderate deadweight was applied. When the ground was mostly dry, the plant parts were removed. When completely dry, the plate was etched in 1:1 Edinburgh Etch for about 40 minutes.

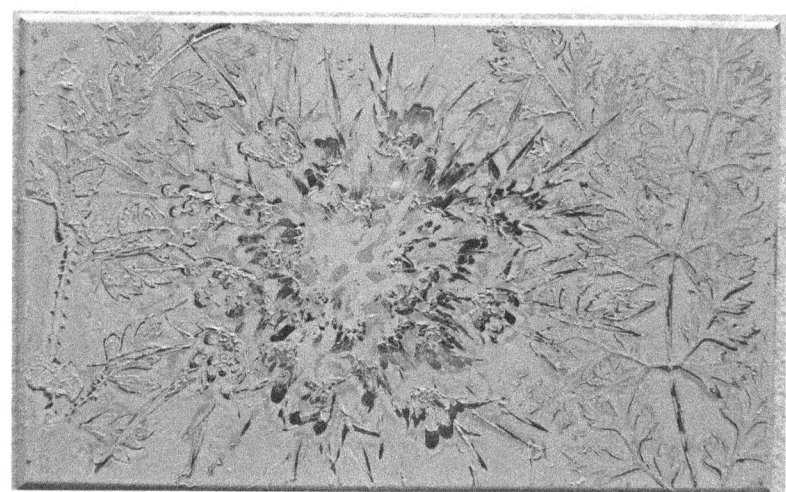

FIGURE 3.25

A print taken from the above plate.

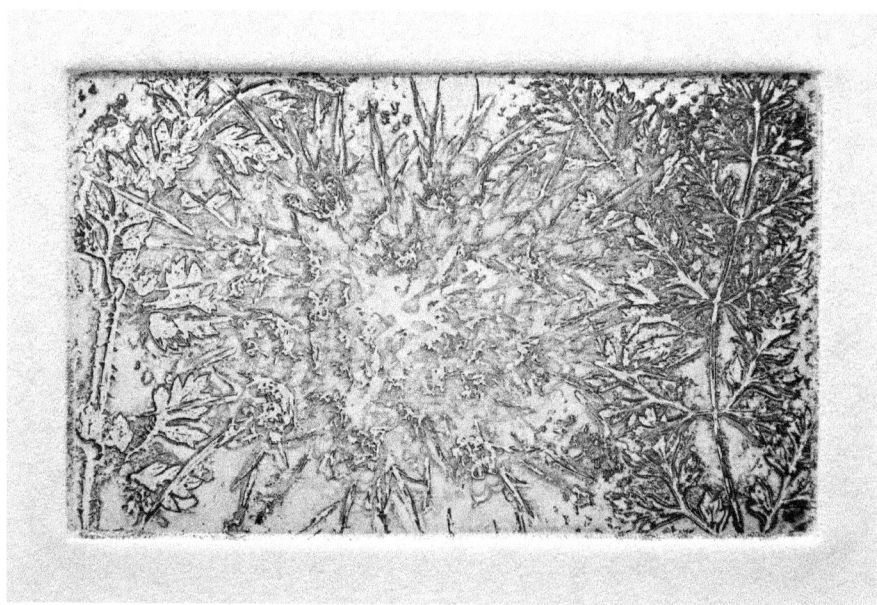

FIGURE 3.26

EXAMPLE 11: Mimosa Leaves with No Rosin Aquatint

(etchant: 1:1 ferric chloride; 40 minutes)

This was the most elaborate and informative of the examples for this chapter, so I will cover it in greater detail.

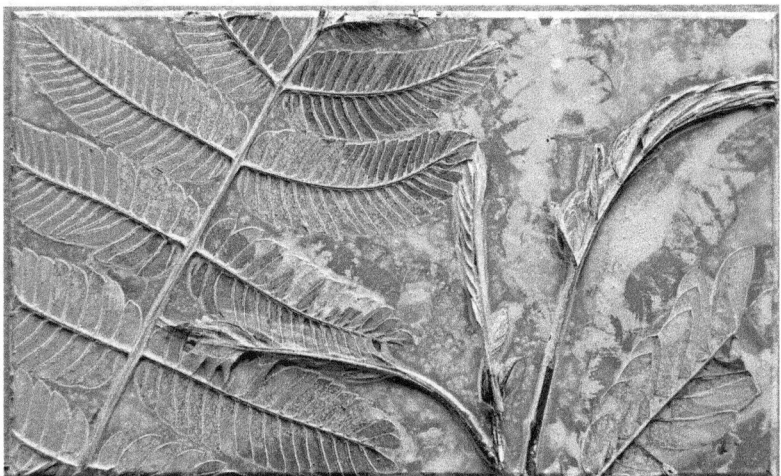

FIGURE 3.27

This is the un-aquatinted plate after having been sprayed with Regular PG-11, having mimosa leaves laid on it, and having been placed under pressure as described in the introduction to this chapter. Some of the leaves that didn't stick to the plate were discarded. The rest were trimmed at the edge of the plate with a razor blade and some touchup was done.

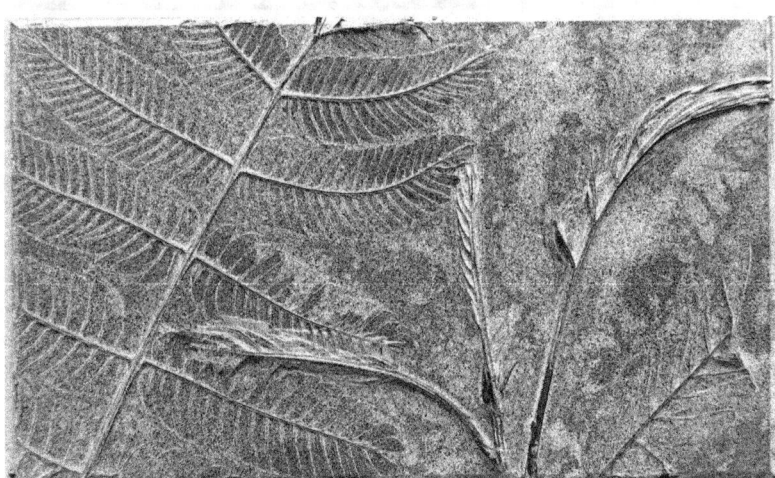

FIGURE 3.28

This is the plate with the leaves still stuck to it after being spattered with black enamel from a spray can. This made it possible to create some darks in the background while leaving the leaves completely stopped out. At this point the plate was etched for a single 20-minute bite in the 1:1 ferric chloride.

After 20 minutes in the 1:1 ferric chloride, I removed the leaves, leaving the dried PG-11 that had been holding them on the plate, and put it back in the acid for another 20 minutes to further darken the background and to etch some detail inside the leaves. I thought the flat-bitten leaves might make an interesting contrast with the aquatinted background, but they ended up looking very similar.

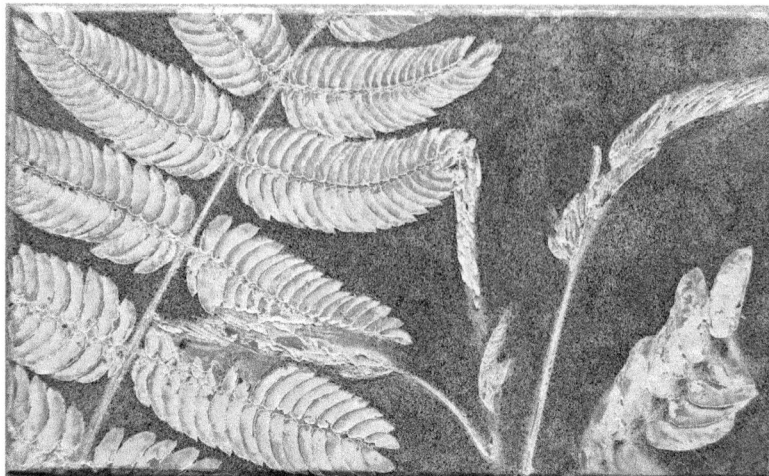

FIGURE 3.29

This is what the plate looked like after the second 20 minutes in the acid. Much of the un-aquatinted PG-11 came off in the rinse water (not in the acid) but the aquatinted (spray can) PG-11 in the background is intact.

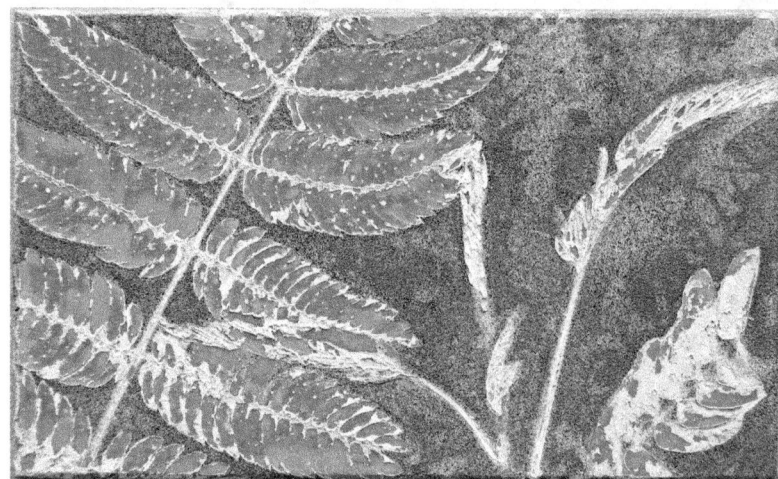

FIGURE 3.30

This is the resulting print from the above steps.

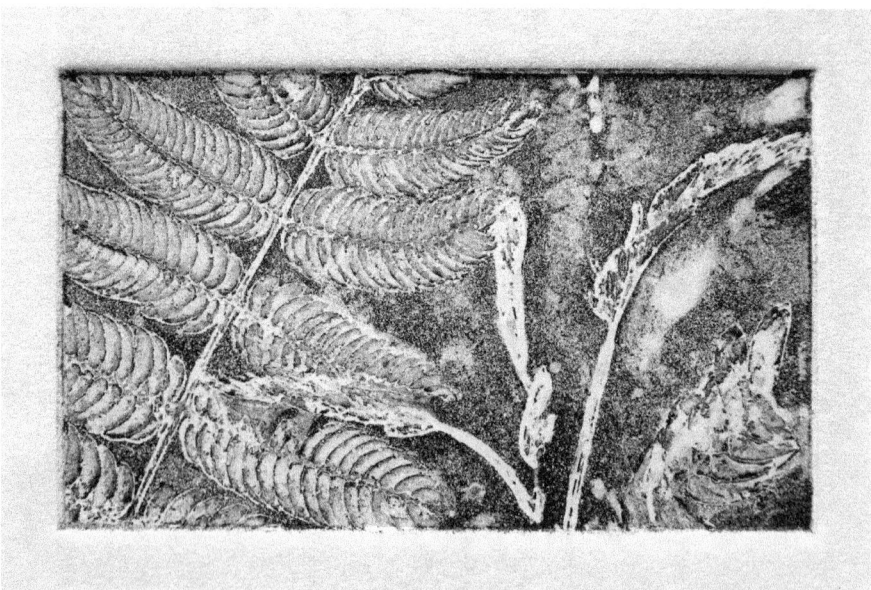

FIGURE 3.31

CHAPTER 4

PG-11 Used Wet in Wet

This is another way to get some interesting textural effects. Basically, you take two liquids and spray or spatter or drip one into the other and see what happens. When the liquids dry, what they leave behind on the surface of the plate acts as a resist for etching imagery into the plate. The liquids may have similar or varying viscosities, compatible or incompatible solvents, and chemical interactions. They may be applied liberally or sparingly. All of these variables will determine characteristics of the patterns formed. This is similar to dropping salt into a watercolor wash to get the textures that technique creates. If a plate has lines or other features etched in it, the patterns will tend to conform to those lines.

The tools I used for spraying and spattering were small spray bottles that make a fine mist, and bristle brushes. For fine spatters I dragged a loaded brush's bristles slowly across the edge of a piece of scrap copper held over the plate and for larger spatters I held a hand palm-up near the plate and slapped the handle of a loaded brush downward against it so the drops would land on the plate.

Control, in this department, is minimal at best but there are a few things you can do to influence the results. Probably the most influential thing is the choice of the liquids. You will find that any given

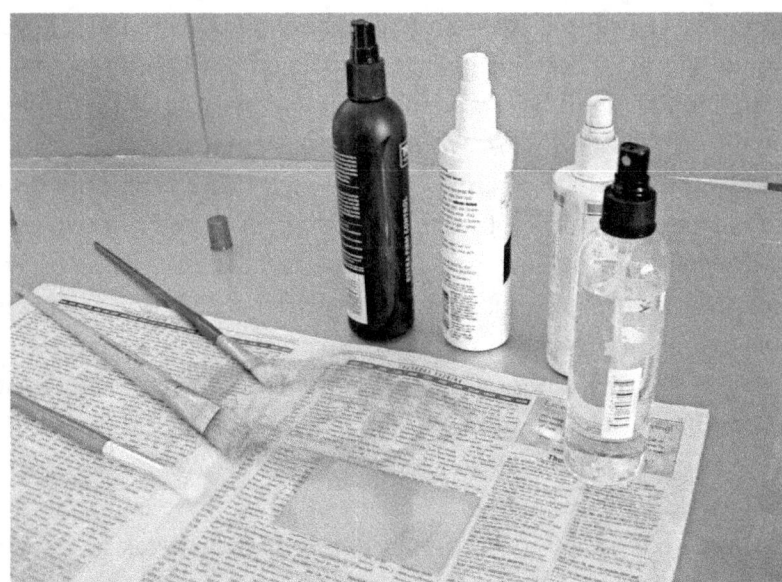

FIGURE 4.1: Tools

combination of liquids has its characteristic result. Beyond that you can influence the degree of spreading and blending by using thicker or thinner solutions to spatter and by how wet the field you spatter them into. Really runny things spread and blend more than thicker more viscous solutions, so that gives you a way to get generally coarser or finer spots.

You can add depth and interest to a pattern by spattering while the field is very wet, allowing that to spread and dry for a while, and then spattering some more (possibly with the same or a different viscosity of the same material, or a different material in the brush) after the field is partially dried so that the new spatters spread less and make a similar but more focused pattern on top of what is already there.

You generally want to avoid flow by having the plate completely level, but some flow can do interesting things. I have an old hair dryer that puts out very little wind and heat, which is good for accelerating drying—another way to limit blending and spreading. Conversely, you can spritz with water or some other solvent to promote or initiate spreading. Most hair dryers put out considerable wind and heat so you have to hold them well away or hold a hand in front of them to keep them from blowing things around too much. Gentle fanning with a piece of paper or cardboard can be good.

The eight examples in this chapter were all done by spraying or spattering diluted PG-11 into some other liquid or the opposite: spattering a liquid into diluted PG-11. Most of the time the PG-11 used was the stock recipe for use in an airbrush: 1 part regular PG-11 to 4 parts water. Specific ingredients used are listed with each example.

All the examples shown are from a combination of liquids applied on top of a rosin aquatint and allowed to dry. If they had been applied to a plate with no aquatint, the patterns would have been similar, but with the same bas-relief look and limited tonal range seen in previous chapters and examples. They could also have had the aquatint applied on top of the PG-11 for exaggerated contrast but I thought that for these eight examples it would be most informative to give them a regular tonal range from black to white.

As always, one has to carefully judge etch times. The only option here, I believe, is to "play it by ear," or rather "by eyeball." I will repeat some of what I said in Chapter 1. You have to base everything on what you see, and what you see happening. In other words, look at the resist you have ended up with on the plate after the liquids have dried and make a professional guess about what's open, what's covered, how thickly and with what, and how long it will hold up in the acid. Etch it for a period of time and then take it out, rinse, dry, and inspect it carefully with a magnifying glass. I etched all of these eight examples for an initial bite of 20 minutes and then put some back in for some additional etch time.

PG-11 on top of an aquatint (seen through a 10x magnifying glass), where it is thin and starting to break down, begins to show minute hints of cracks and fissures indicating that you will get some tone there. Check any open aquatint to see how it's etching and check the edge (bevel) of the plate where the grains of aquatint are most sparse and therefore etch faster than in the middle of the plate. When the aquatint on the edge of the plate is almost completely eaten away, you're probably close to a 100% black in the interior of the plate where there is open aquatint.

If you're etching with plain ferric chloride (as opposed to Edinburgh Etch), copious black runoff coming off of the plate as it etches (visible against the white PG-11) means things are happening fast and fairly normal etch times can be used, whereas little or no black runoff means not much is happening and etch times should be extended, perhaps radically. These are the indicators I used in etching these plates, and you will notice the etch times varied widely.

All eight plates were etched in 1:1 ferric chloride.

EXAMPLE 1: PG-11 Spattered into Wet Methyl Cellulose Paste

(etchant: 1:1 ferric chloride; 20 minutes)

This is the plate prior to etching. The plate was painted with a medium layer of water with just a trace of methyl cellulose paste in it, which has a dramatic detergent effect. Then watery PG-11 was spattered into it sparingly as it dried. Methyl cellulose paste is highly permeable and like glycerin can be mixed with PG-11 to boost permeability.

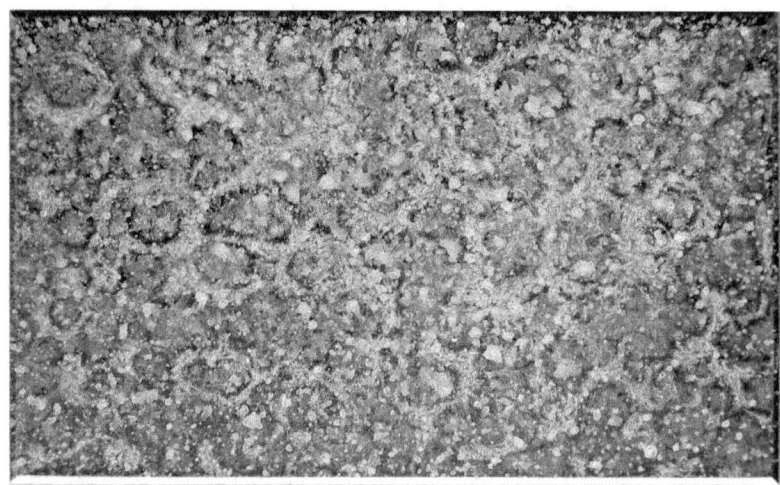

FIGURE 4.2

This is a print taken from the above plate.

FIGURE 4.3

EXAMPLE 2: Kerosene Sprayed into Wet PG-11

(etchant: 1:1 ferric chloride; 40 minutes)

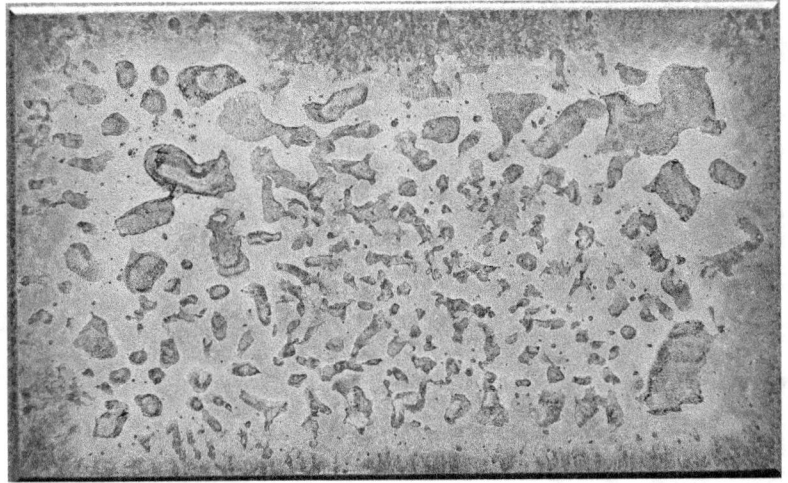

FIGURE 4.4

The plate painted with a medium layer of wet PG-11 into which kerosene was sprayed. This is an example of incompatible solvents. The kerosene forms segregated pools in the PG-11 and takes much longer to dry than the PG-11.

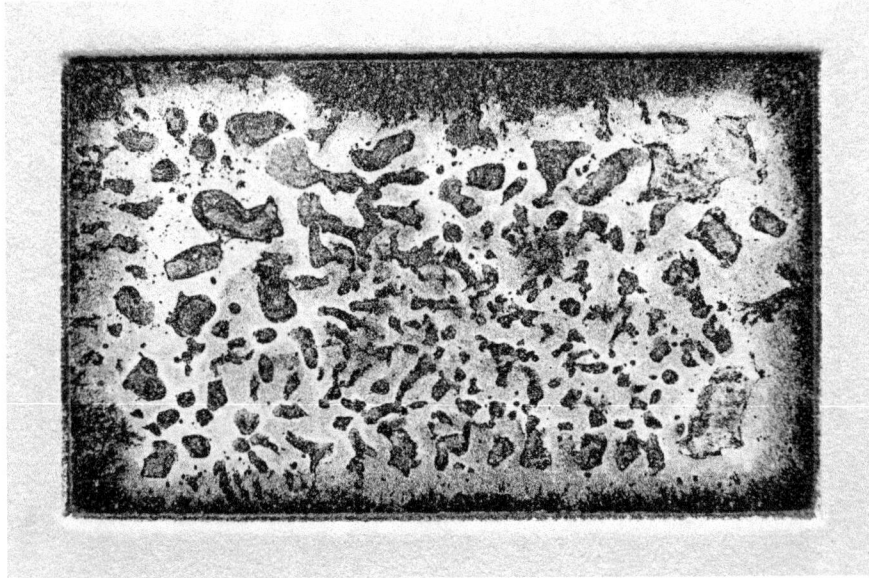

FIGURE 4.5

A print made from the above plate.

EXAMPLE 3: Asphaltum and Kerosene in Wet PG-11

(etchant: 1:1 ferric chloride; 60 minutes)

The plate, ready to etch. It was painted with a layer of diluted PG-11 into which asphaltum thinned with paint thinner and turpentine was spattered, and that was spritzed with a small amount of kerosene from a sprayer.

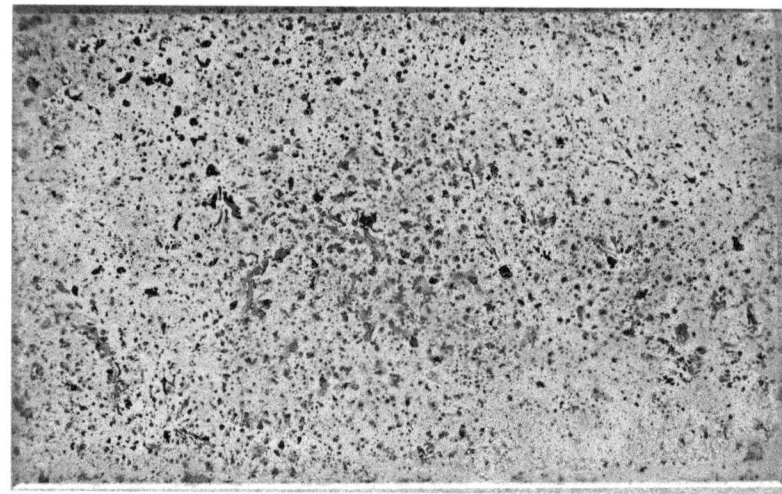

FIGURE 4.6

A print from the above plate, after a 60-minute etch.

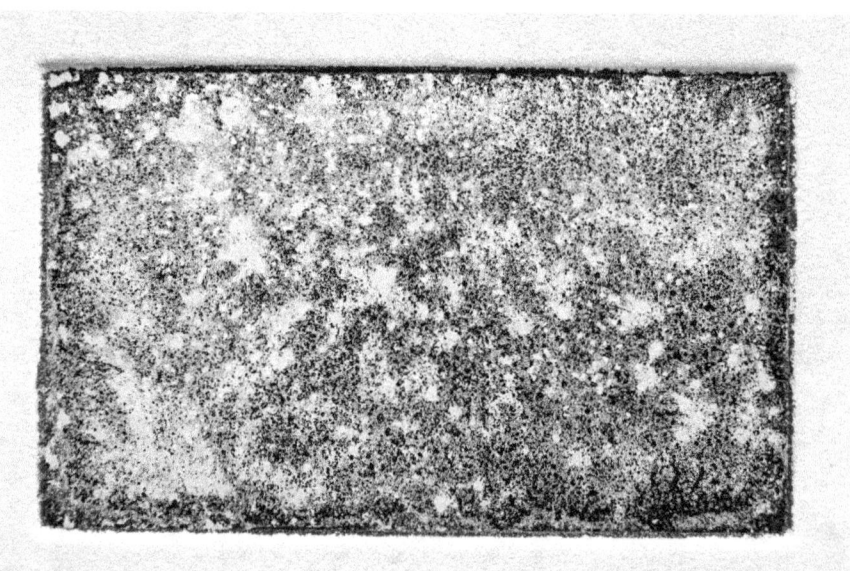

FIGURE 4.7

EXAMPLE 4: Salt and Vinegar Sprayed into Wet PG-11

(etchant: 1:1 ferric chloride; 20 minutes)

FIGURE 4.8

The plate, painted with a medium layer of wet PG-11 and sprayed with a salt and vinegar solution (from a regular utility spray bottle) while still wet. The vinegar, being acidic, caused the wet PG-11 to congeal. This was allowed to dry and then etched for 20 minutes.

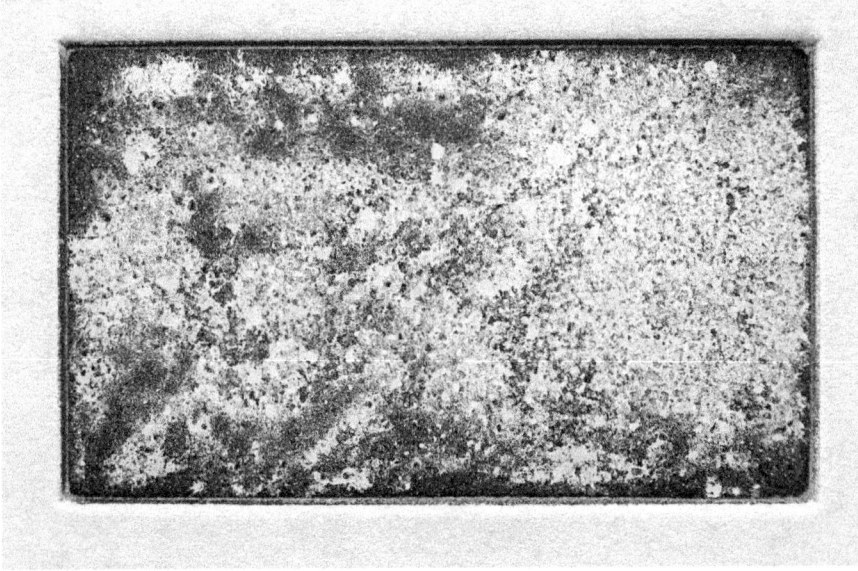

FIGURE 4.9

A print of the resulting image.

The plate before etching. It was painted with a medium layer of diluted PG-11, into which was spattered spirit ground while it was still wet. The spirit ground was made of powdered rosin dissolved in 70% isopropyl rubbing alcohol. The spirit ground tended to make the PG-11 bead up and dry fairly thick in places. That plus the residual glazing from the spirit ground necessitated the long (60-minute) etch time.

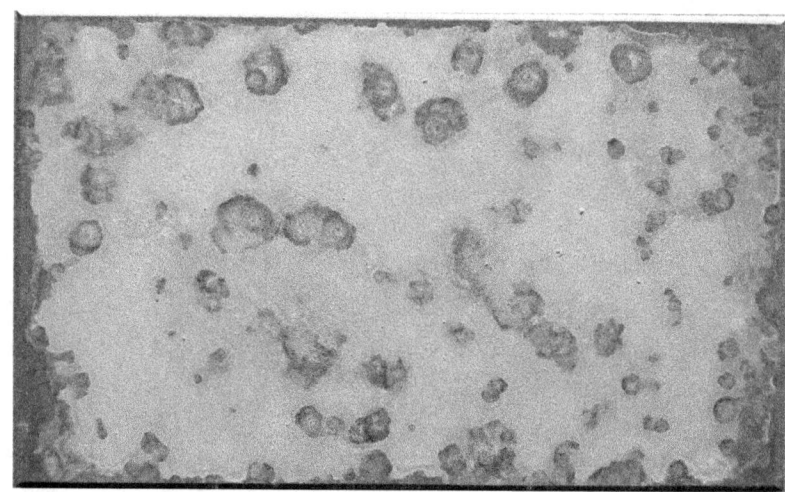

FIGURE 4.10

This is a print made from the above plate.

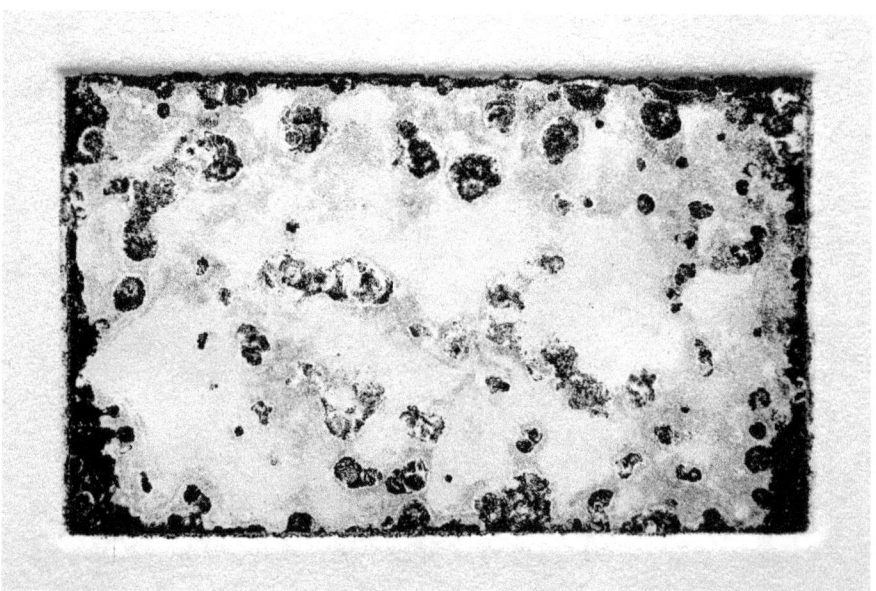

FIGURE 4.11

EXAMPLE 6: PG-11 Spattered into Wet Baking Soda Solution

(etchant: 1:1 ferric chloride; 20 minutes)

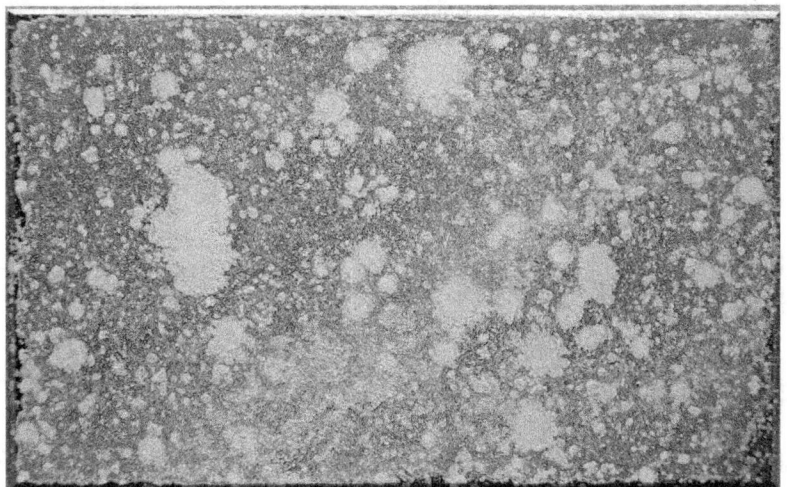

FIGURE 4.12

The plate ready to be etched. It was painted with a saturated solution of baking soda dissolved in water, and into that was spattered diluted PG-11. This was allowed to dry, then etched for 20 minutes. The plate bubbled vigorously for a few seconds upon being put into the acid.

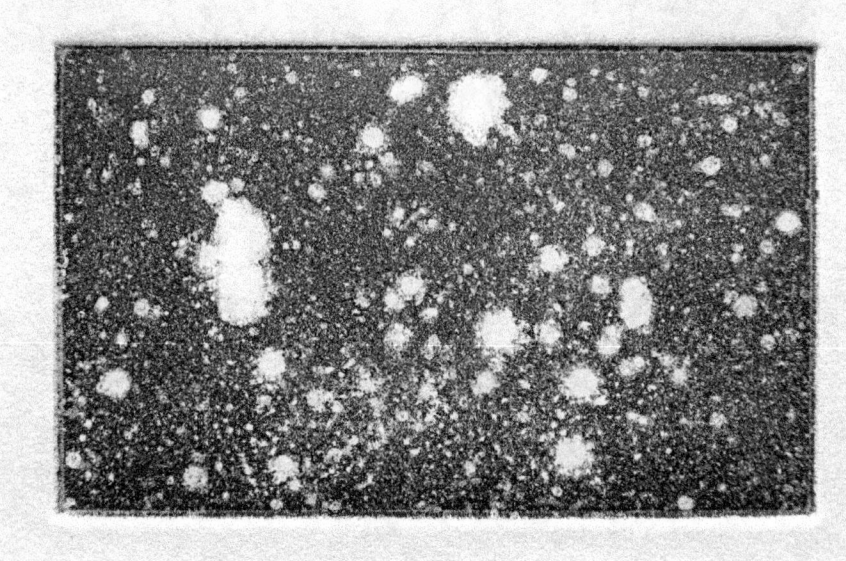

FIGURE 4.13

A print of the imagery created by the above process.

EXAMPLE 7: PG-11 Spattered into Wet Borax Solution

(etchant: 1:1 ferric chloride; 30 minutes)

The plate, painted with a saturated solution of Borax (the laundry booster) dissolved in water and then spattered with diluted PG-11 while wet. This was allowed to dry and the plate was etched for 30 minutes.

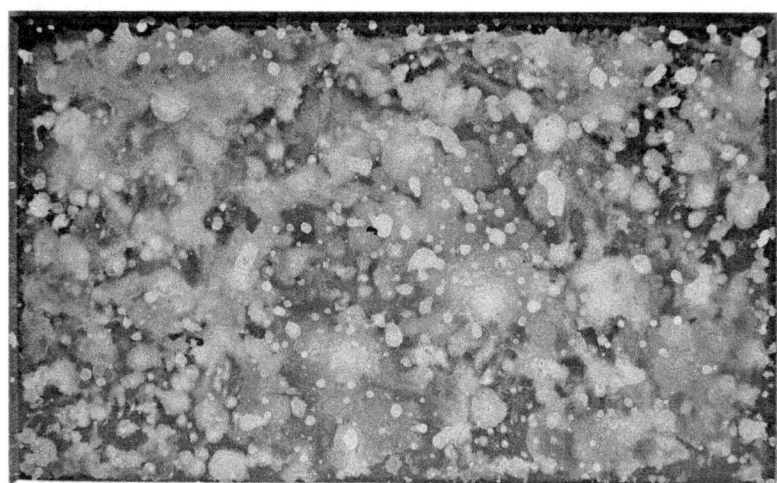

FIGURE 4.14

A print of the image created by the above procedure.

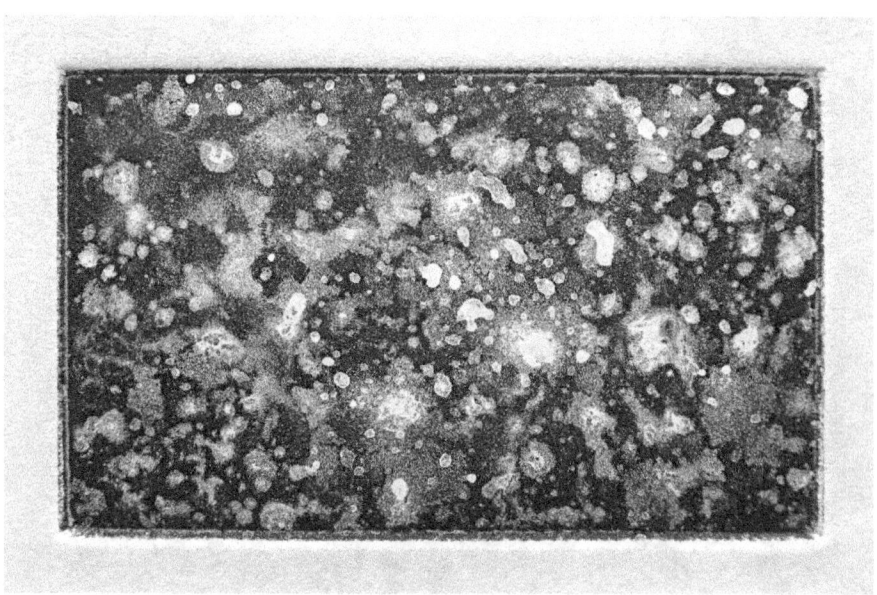

FIGURE 4.15

EXAMPLE 8: PG-11 Spattered into Dish Soap

(etchant: 1:1 ferric chloride; 30 minutes)

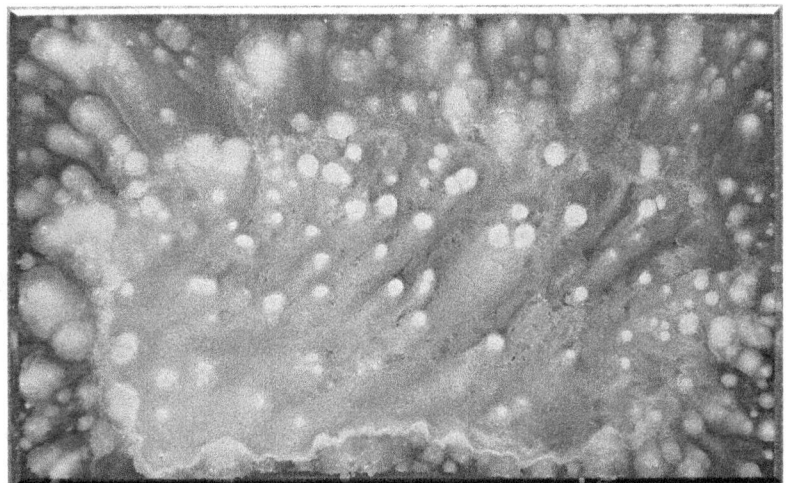

FIGURE 4.16

The plate, ready to etch. It was painted with a film of water that had a trace amount of dish soap in it and then spattered with diluted PG-11. The PG-11 I used for this one was a bit thicker than the others, to somewhat mute the amount of blending and spreading. The plate wasn't completely level while drying so the solutions flowed and pooled toward the bottom of the plate. When dry it was etched for 30 minutes.

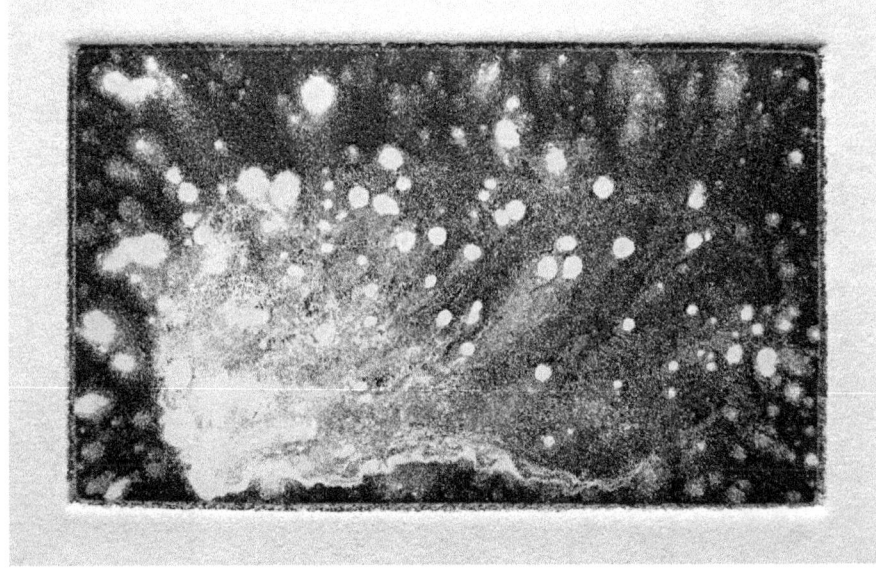

FIGURE 4.17

A print of the resulting image.

CHAPTER 5

PG-11 and SO-11
Used As Soft Ground

Most of the time when people use soft ground they are trying to get imagery that is strong and clear and has as much detail as possible. Strength, clarity, and detail are more the strong suits of nonpermeable grounds whereas permeable grounds are more into soft and fuzzy. All four of the grounds discussed in this book (SO-11, PG-11, PG-11 Medium, and PG-11 Soft) can be used as soft grounds. They range in permeability from SO-11, which is virtually impermeable, gives clear impressions, and behaves pretty much identically to traditional asphaltum-based soft grounds (not surprising since it actually is an asphaltum-based soft ground) to PG-11 Soft, which is very soft and permeable and will, generally speaking, only give very muted results.

I wanted to explore and illustrate this range of effects for these four grounds as well as some general guidelines for using them. The general guidelines are the same as those for using any soft ground. You need an optimal balance between, on the one hand, having a thick enough layer of ground on the plate to make the acid do what it's supposed to, and on the other hand, having a thin enough layer of ground on the plate that the objects or materials you press into it can penetrate the ground effectively to create the desired imagery.

What usually works best is to apply a thin layer of ground to the plate and to press things into it with just enough pressure to create detailed imagery, but not enough to obliterate the ground. This has to be done by cautiously experimenting until you have the right press pressure for the physical hardness or softness of the ground and the thickness of the film of ground on the plate, as well as for the characteristics of whatever you're pressing into the ground.

To apply the ground, I tried spraying it on with a spray bottle, but tended to get it too thick and most of it went everywhere but on the plate. I tried brushes, including a foam (poly) brush, and by diluting with extra water I was able to get semi-usable results with the SO-11, but the PG-11 pulled away from the edge of the plate and wouldn't dry evenly. So I got out my airbrush and that eliminated the problems. I was able to spray on a very thin coat, dry that with a hair dryer, turn the plate and spray on some more from a different angle, dry that, etc., until I had a fairly opaque, even coating on the plate. I have included two examples of plates (Examples 2 and 3) where the ground was applied with a 1-inch poly brush. For all the others the grounds were applied with the airbrush. The grounds were diluted approximately 1 part ground to 3 or 4 parts water, and went through the airbrush without being strained at 20 psi.

Blankets used for pressing the imaging materials into the soft grounds were a ¹⁄₁₆-inch sizing catcher, a ¼-inch felt cushion, and a ⅛-inch woven pusher. To set the pressure, I applied my usual print pressure and, depending on the softness of the ground being used, reduced that by fractions of a turn of the pressure screws as noted by each image. Since print pressures and pressure screws vary, this will only give an approximate idea for where to set the pressure in any particular case.

First are the four fabric comparison plates, using pieces of the same open-weave material to press into four plates with the four grounds on them.

Then there is a somewhat random selection of additional images. Each grounded plate was laid on the press bed, the material was laid on it, then it was covered with a piece of thin gray cardboard (smooth side down) that was hinged to the press bed with masking tape along the leading edge, then the blankets were laid down and this was run through the press. The two PG-11 Soft plates additionally had a piece of parchment paper (a non-stick baking paper from the wax paper and aluminum foil section of the grocery store) inserted between the materials and the cardboard. I was hoping that the ground wouldn't stick to it, but some did.

Finally there is a comparison of the four grounds, each used with a tracing paper overlay, which is a standard technique for creating lines.

All were etched in 1:1 ferric chloride for 20 minutes except for the fabric example with PG-11 Soft (Figure 5.5) which I took out after 15 minutes because the ground was starting to come off.

Plate preparation was not particularly consistent. For most of them I scrubbed with scouring powder until they held a film of water, then rinsed and dried and scrubbed with a clean dry paper towel. I found that the SO-11 has a tendency to lift off of the plate slightly when removing the materials after preparing the plate this way. I experimented with oxidizing two of the plates to see if the ground would adhere to an oxidized plate better than a shiny copper one. There may have been some difference, but it wasn't dramatic. What seems to work best is vinegar. Immediately before applying any of these four grounds (especially the Medium and Soft variants of PG-11 when applied with an airbrush), clean the plate by dunking it in vinegar or a salt and vinegar solution, then rinse, dry it, and scrub with a clean dry paper towel.

The vinegar bath applies throughout the process as well. To repeat some of what was said in Chapter 1, SO-11 and Regular PG-11 are stable after drying on a plate but the Medium and Soft variants of PG-11 are less so. If you're using the Medium or Soft variants for soft ground work, you have about 12 hours after they dry on the plate before the glycerin starts to separate from the compound and causes the film of ground to detach from the plate. This can be avoided by dipping the plate in a vinegar bath after the ground has dried. This stabilizes the film of ground on the plate. It has a slight effect on the performance of the ground, causing the ground to be a bit tougher and less permeable, but if this is a disadvantage at all it is a negligible one. Repeated immersions in vinegar over a period of days don't seem to have any added effects beyond the effects of the initial immersion.

The best protection against having the ground lift is to test the ground on the plate before investing time and effort in creating lines or imagery. To test the ground after it has been applied to the plate and allowed to dry, immerse the plate in vinegar for 10 to 20 seconds. If the ground is not properly adhering to the plate it may start flaking off in the vinegar. Take it out of the vinegar and rinse it off in water. If it doesn't start coming off in the water, you can further test it by hitting it with a jet of water from a spray bottle. If it can survive being hit with a gentle jet from a spray bottle, it's probably okay. Usually some will come off if hit with a vigorous jet from a spray bottle.

With SO-11 and PG-11, a spray can or airbrush aquatint could be applied, after pressing the materials, to reinforce the ground and promote contrast in the image, but with PG-11 Medium and PG-11 Soft the ground breaks down too fast for a spray aquatint on top of it to be very effective.

There was no aquatint, step biting or reworking used with any of these examples.

EXAMPLE 1: A Comparison of SO-11, PG-11, PG-11 Medium, and PG-11 Soft Used As Soft Ground

(etchant: 1:1 ferric chloride; 20/15 minutes)

This is a sample from the fabric used on all four plates (also for Example 7 in Chapter 3). It is the piece that was used for the SO-11 plate below (Figure 5.2). For this example I omitted pictures of the plates, since the plates look very much like the prints.

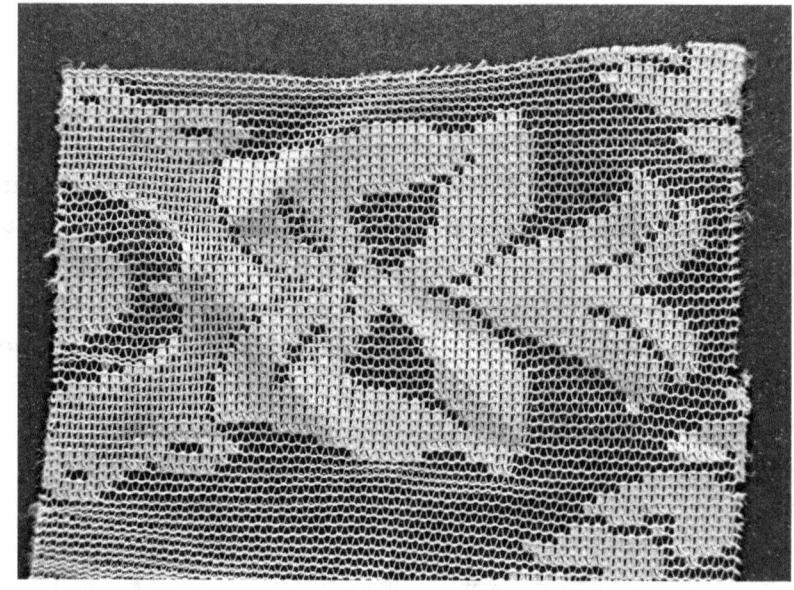

FIGURE 5.1

This is a print from the plate grounded with SO-11. Transfer-pressure was print pressure minus ¼ turn of the pressure screws. Etch time was 20 minutes in 1:1 ferric chloride.

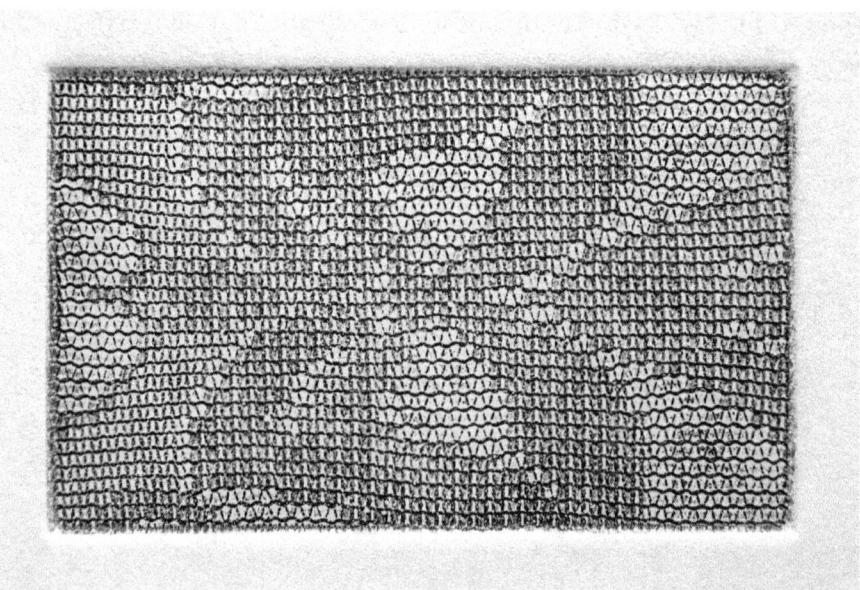

FIGURE 5.2

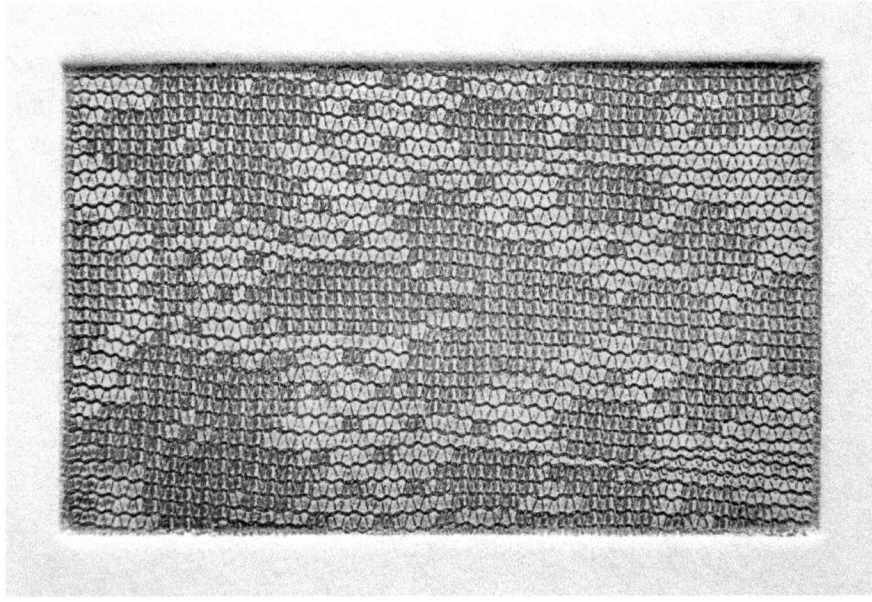

A print from the plate grounded with PG-11. Transfer pressure was full print pressure. (Actually, it was more than full print pressure, because of the thickness of the fabric and cardboard.) Etch time: 20 minutes in 1:1 ferric chloride.

FIGURE 5.3

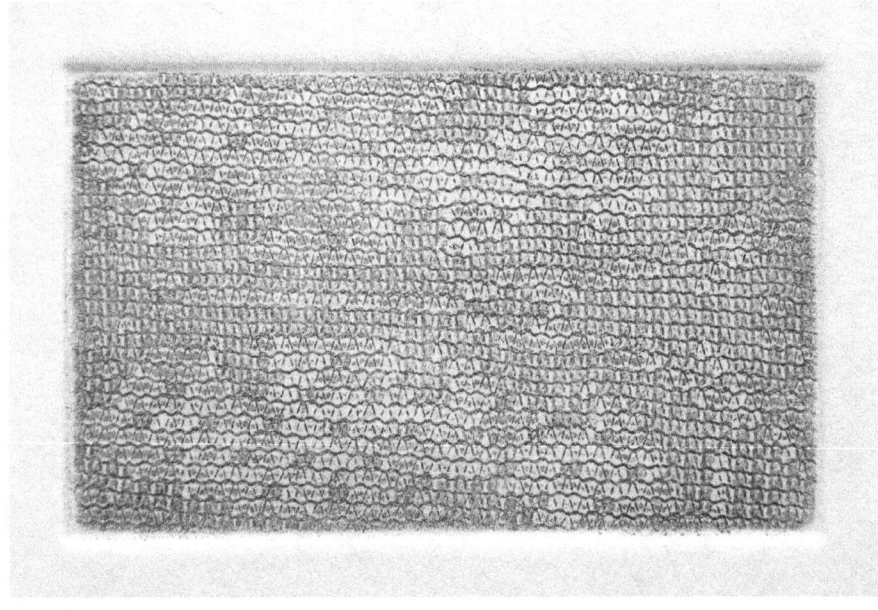

A print from the plate coated with PG-11 Medium. Transfer pressure was print pressure minus ⅜ turn of pressure screws. Etch time was 20 minutes in 1:1 ferric chloride. Imagery is losing contrast.

FIGURE 5.4

A print from the plate coated with PG-11 Soft. Transfer pressure was print pressure minus ½ turn of the pressure screws. Etch time was 15 minutes in 1:1 ferric chloride, at which point the ground started flaking off. Imagery has low contrast.

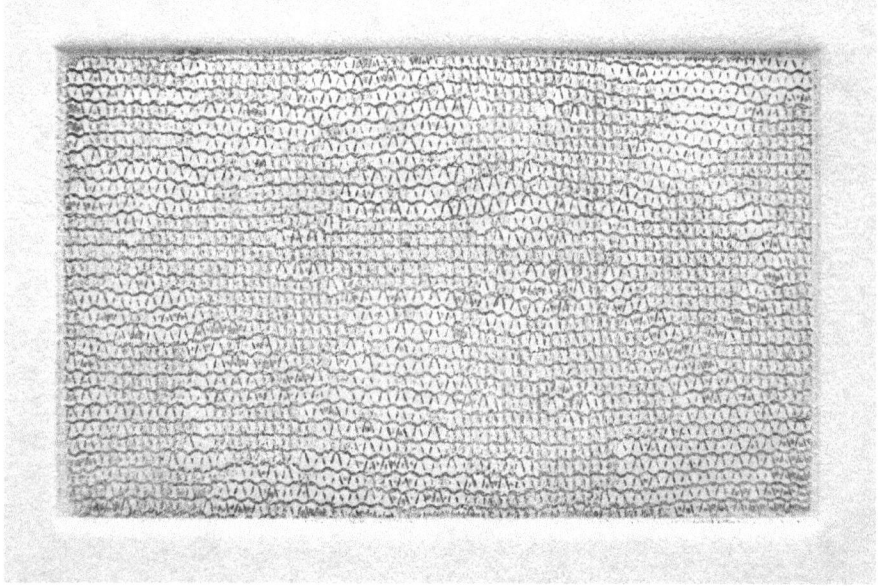

FIGURE 5.5

EXAMPLE 2: SO-11 with Grass Seeds

(etchant: 1:1 ferric chloride; 30 minutes)

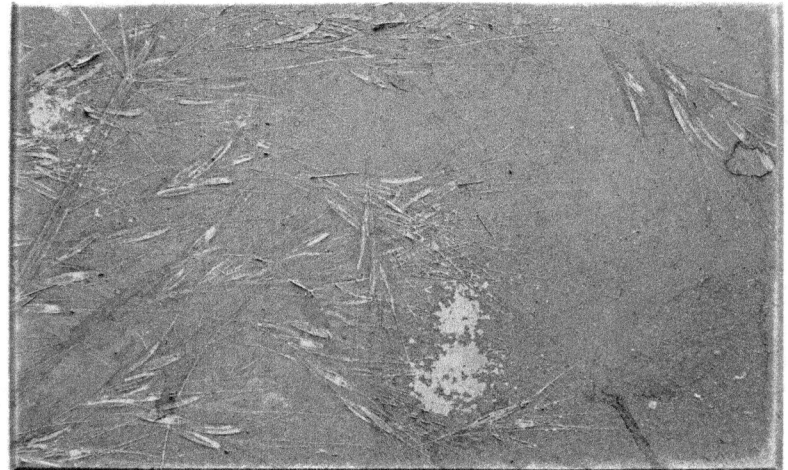

FIGURE 5.6

The plate, oxidized and coated with diluted SO-11 using a 1-inch poly brush. The patches on the left, lower center, and right of the plate are places where the ground was thicker and stuck to the cardboard backing. Transfer pressure was print pressure minus ⅛ turn of the pressure screws. I etched it in 1:1 ferric chloride for 20 minutes, took it out and noticed deposits in some of the etched areas, so I cleaned it in a salt and vinegar solution and etched it for an additional 10 minutes.

The resulting print.

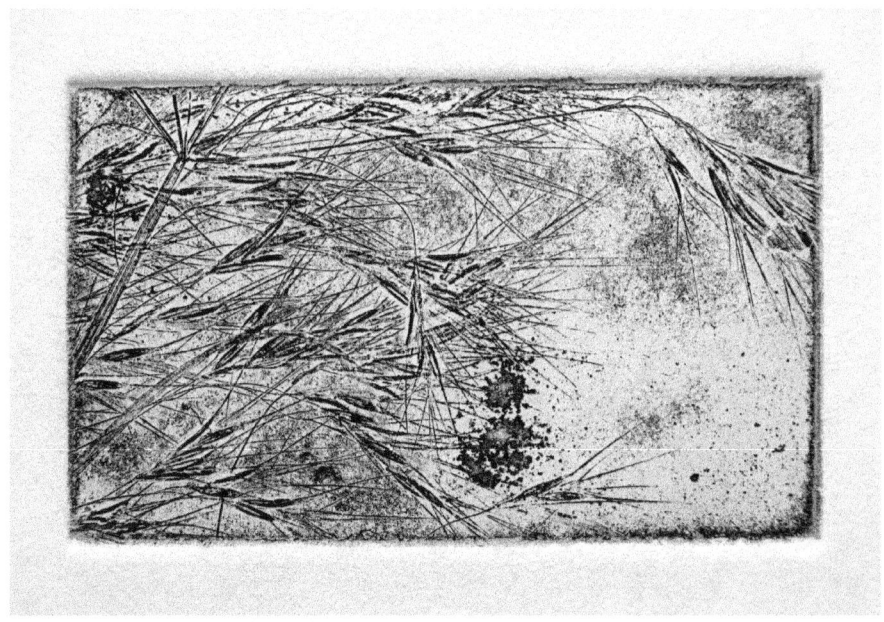

FIGURE 5.7

EXAMPLE 3: SO-11 with Leaves

(etchant: 1:1 ferric chloride; 20 minutes)

The oxidized plate coated with SO-11. I thinned the ground with some additional water, applied it with a 1-inch poly brush, and this time got it on more evenly. Transfer pressure was print pressure minus ⅛ turn of the pressure screws. I etched it in 1:1 ferric chloride for 12 minutes, took it out and cleaned it with salt/vinegar solution, and put it back in the acid for another 8 minutes.

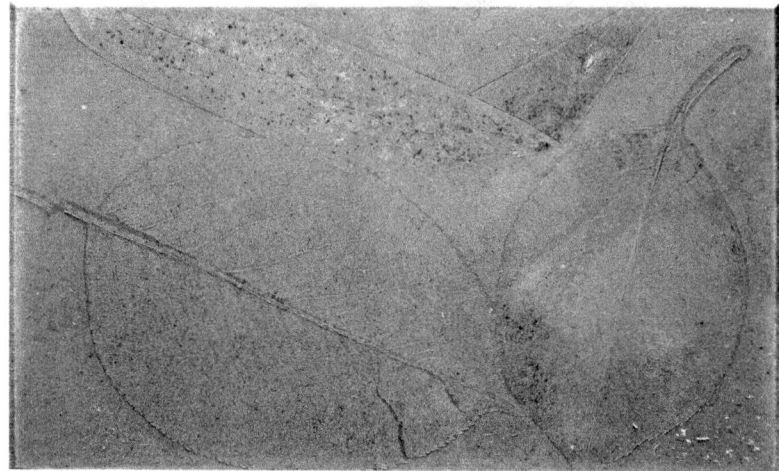

FIGURE 5.8

This is the resulting print.

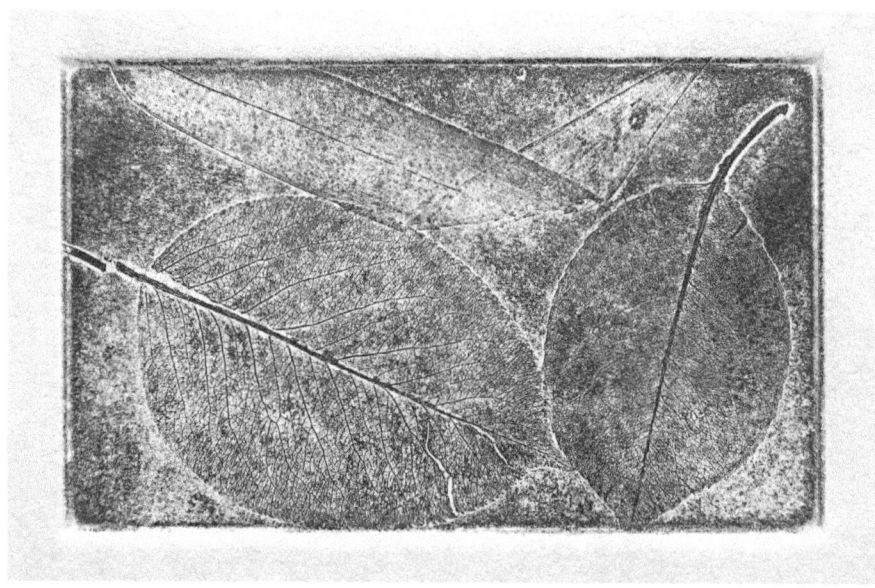

FIGURE 5.9

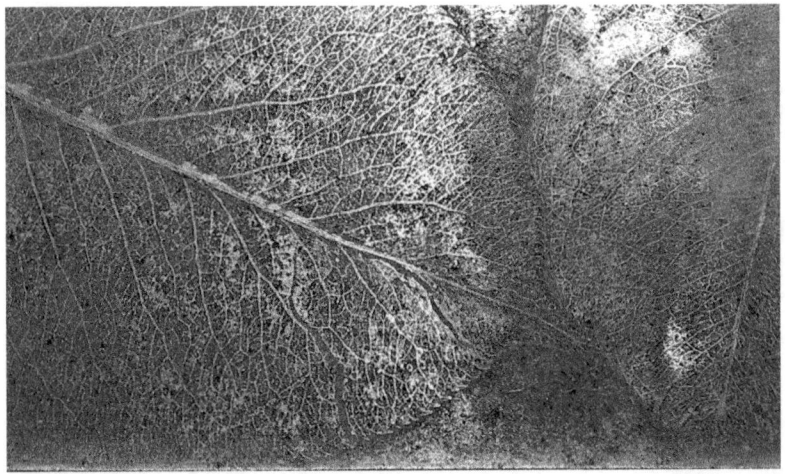

FIGURE 5.10

This is an enlarged section of the plate before etching, showing the high level of detail in the impression after running it through the press.

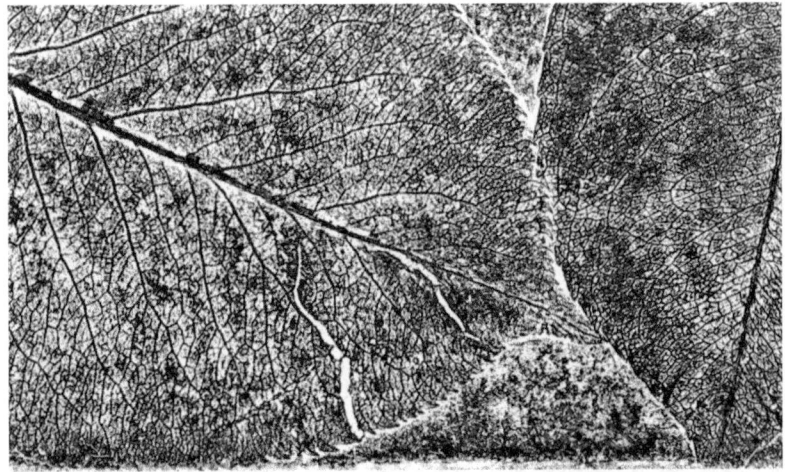

FIGURE 5.11

This is the corresponding section of the resulting print.

EXAMPLE 4: PG-11 with Grass Seeds

(etchant: 1:1 ferric chloride; 20 minutes)

The plate, coated with PG-11 with grass seeds pressed into it. Transfer was at full print pressure (PG-11 is the physically hardest of the four grounds) and it was etched in 1:1 ferric chloride for 20 minutes.

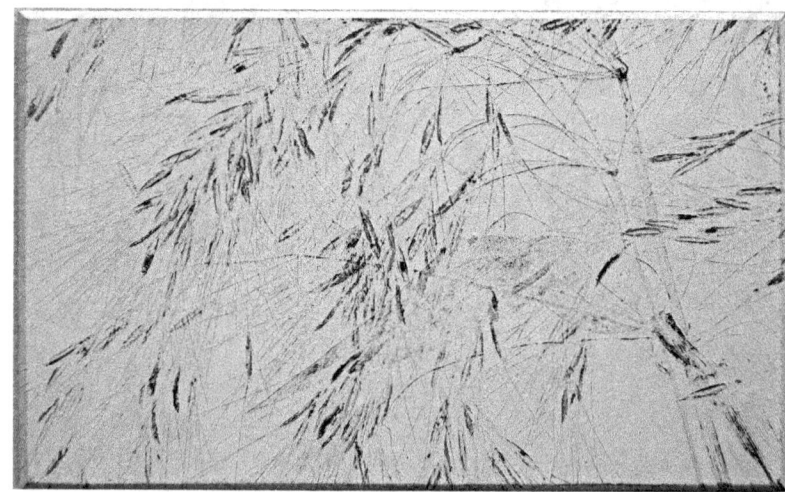

FIGURE 5.12

The resulting print.

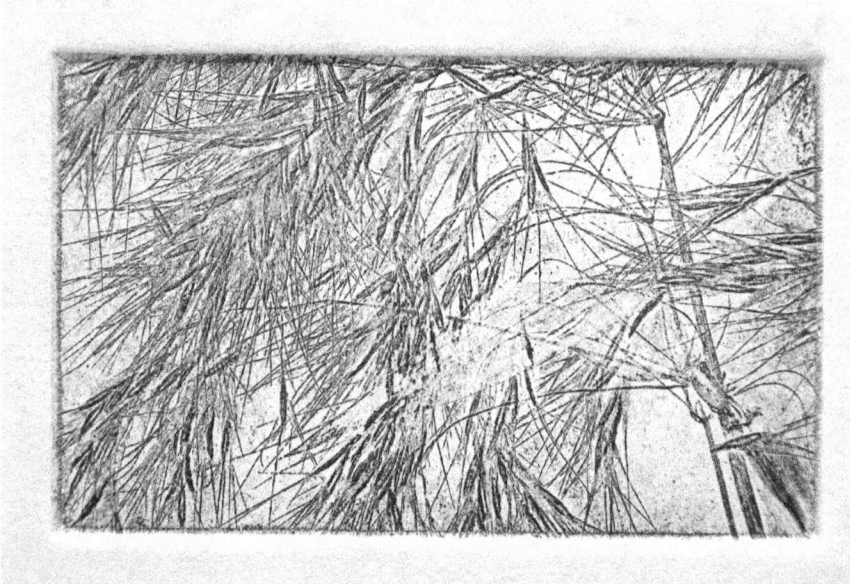

FIGURE 5.13

EXAMPLE 5: PG-11 Medium with Leaves

(etchant: 1:1 ferric chloride; 20 minutes)

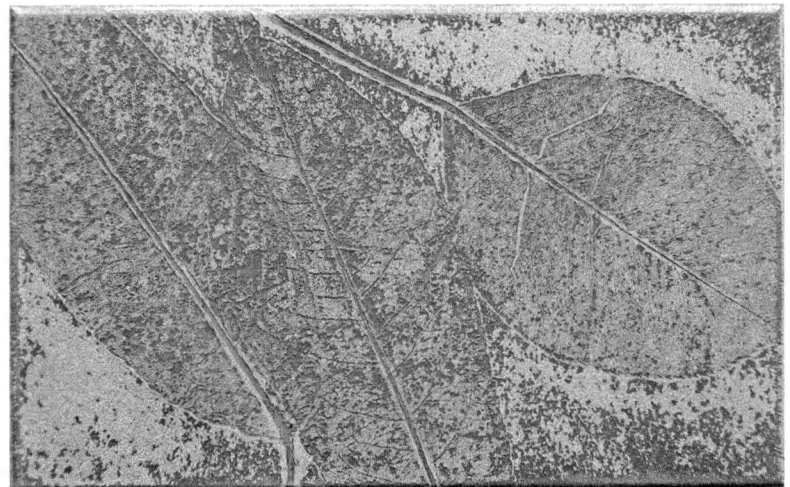

FIGURE 5.14

This is the plate with leaves pressed into PG-11 Medium ground after being in the acid for 20 minutes. Much of the ground came off in the rinse water. Transfer pressure was print pressure minus ⅜ turn of the pressure screws.

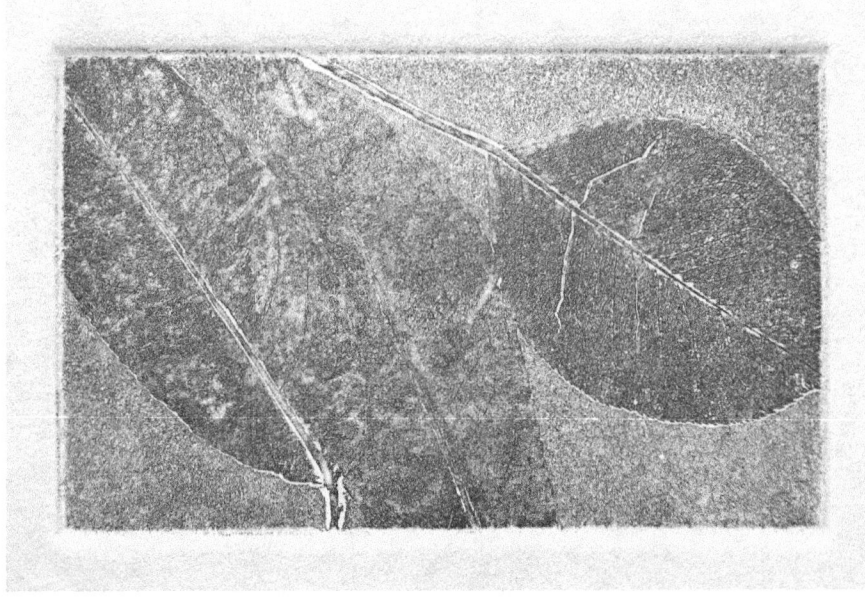

FIGURE 5.15

This is the resulting print.

EXAMPLE 6: PG-11 Medium with Grass Seeds

(etchant: 1:1 ferric chloride; 20 minutes)

The plate, before etching, coated with PG-11 Medium after pressing grass seeds into it. Transfer pressure was print pressure minus ⅜ turn of the pressure screws.

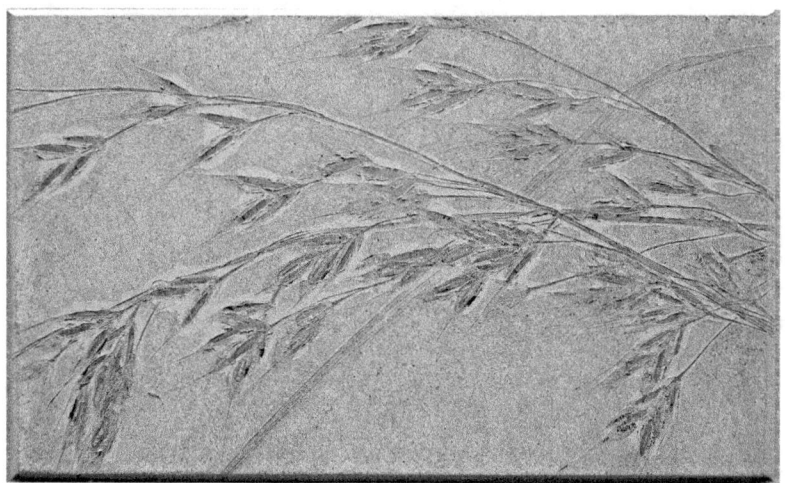

FIGURE 5.16

The plate after 20 minutes in 1:1 ferric chloride. Some of the relatively soft PG-11 Medium has broken down in the acid and come off in the rinse water.

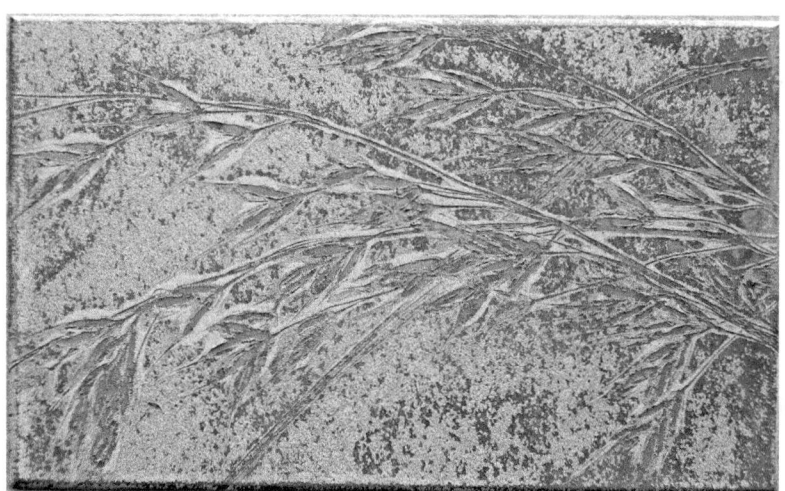

FIGURE 5.17

The resulting print.

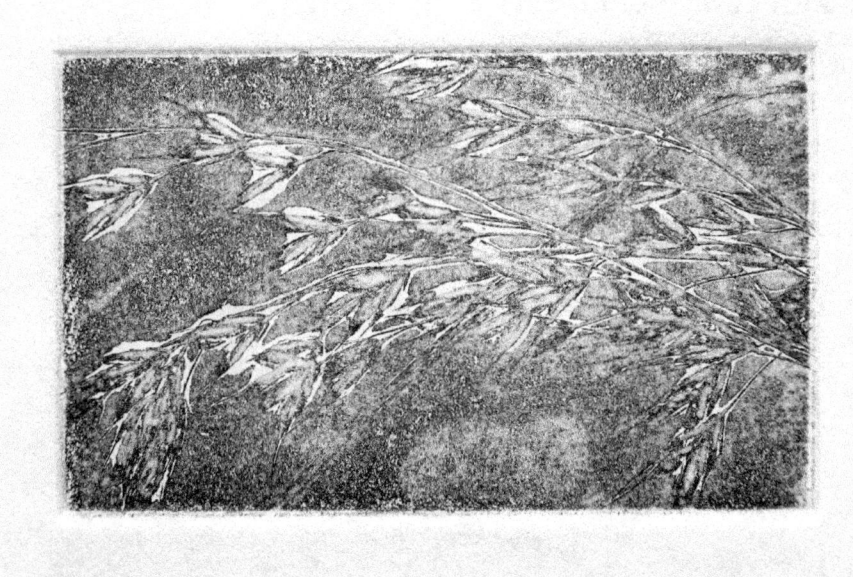

FIGURE 5.18

EXAMPLE 7: PG-11 Soft with Feathers

(etchant: 1:1 ferric chloride; 20 minutes)

The plate before etching, coated with PG-11 Soft with feathers pressed into it. (The feathers have been removed.) Transfer pressure was print pressure minus ½ turn of the pressure screws.

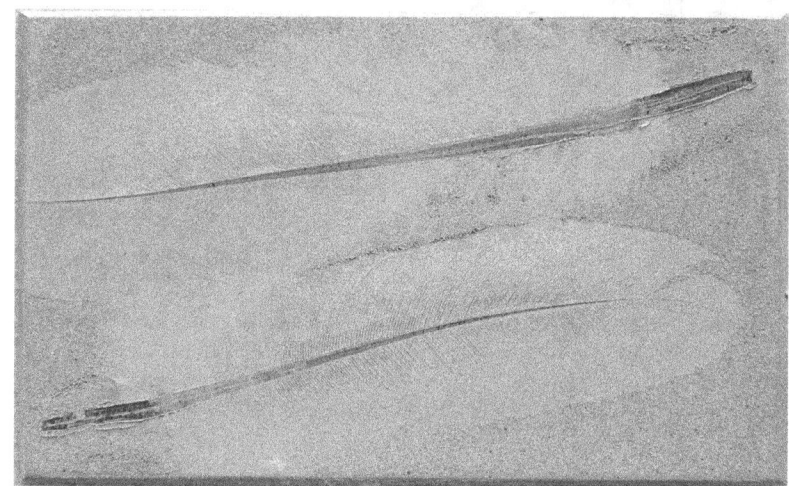

FIGURE 5.19

The plate after 20 minutes in 1:1 ferric chloride.

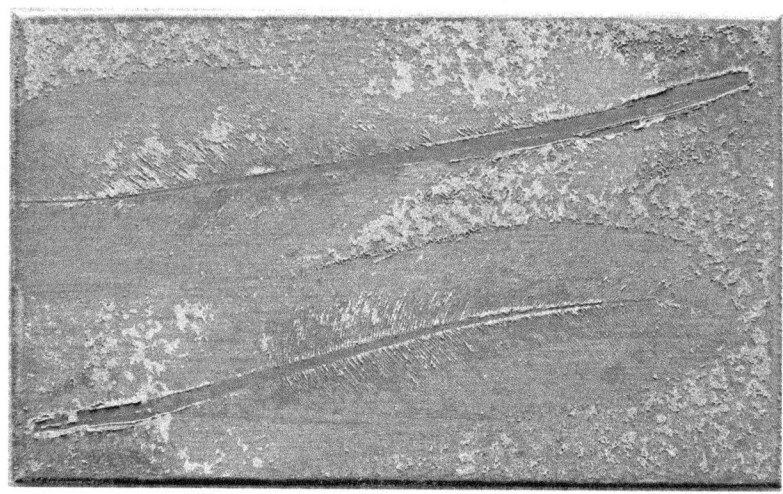

FIGURE 5.20

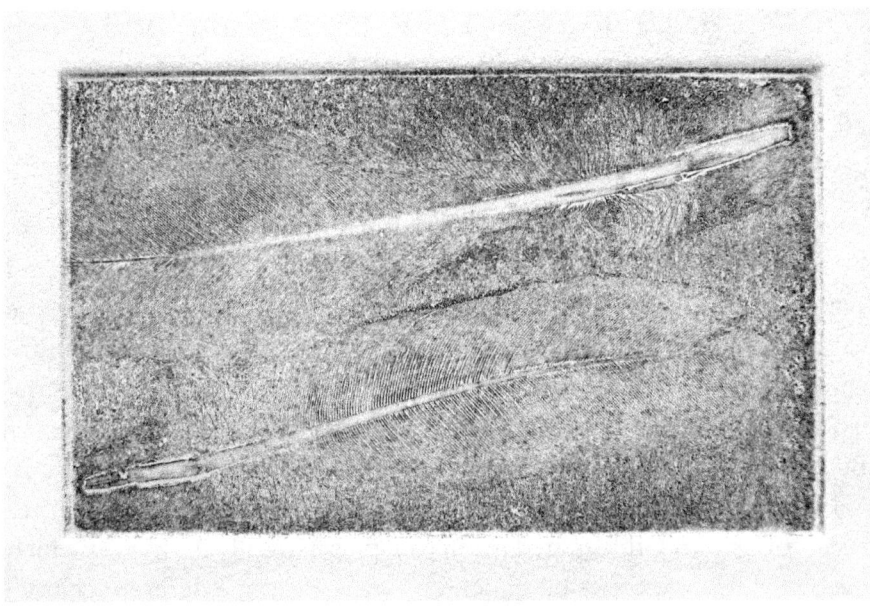

The resulting print. As is characteristic with the Soft version of PG-11, much of the imagery has melted into the background. More of the feathers could have been saved if it had been put in the acid for 5 or 10 minutes, then the feathers stopped out with SO-11, and the plate put back in the acid for the remaining time on the background.

FIGURE 5.21

EXAMPLE 8: SO-11, PG-11, PG-11 Medium, and PG-11 Soft Used with Tracing Paper Overlay

(etchant: 1:1 ferric chloride; 20 minutes)

I wanted to explore how well these four grounds work when used with the standard soft ground technique where a thin layer of soft ground is applied to a plate and then a piece of tracing paper is laid over the ground and pencil lines are drawn on the tracing paper. The pressure from the point of the pencil moving over the tracing paper presses the paper into the ground, causing perforations in the ground and lifting of the ground, which allows the acid to etch the copper and create lines. With a traditional soft ground overlay, using a traditional asphaltum-based soft ground, the etched result (the print) usually looks very much like pencil lines or tones on paper, even reflecting the different characteristics of hard, medium, or soft drawing pencils.

SO-11 comes closest to this, but all four of these grounds yield results that look more like charcoal than like graphite. All four work well and are easy to use, but are quite different.

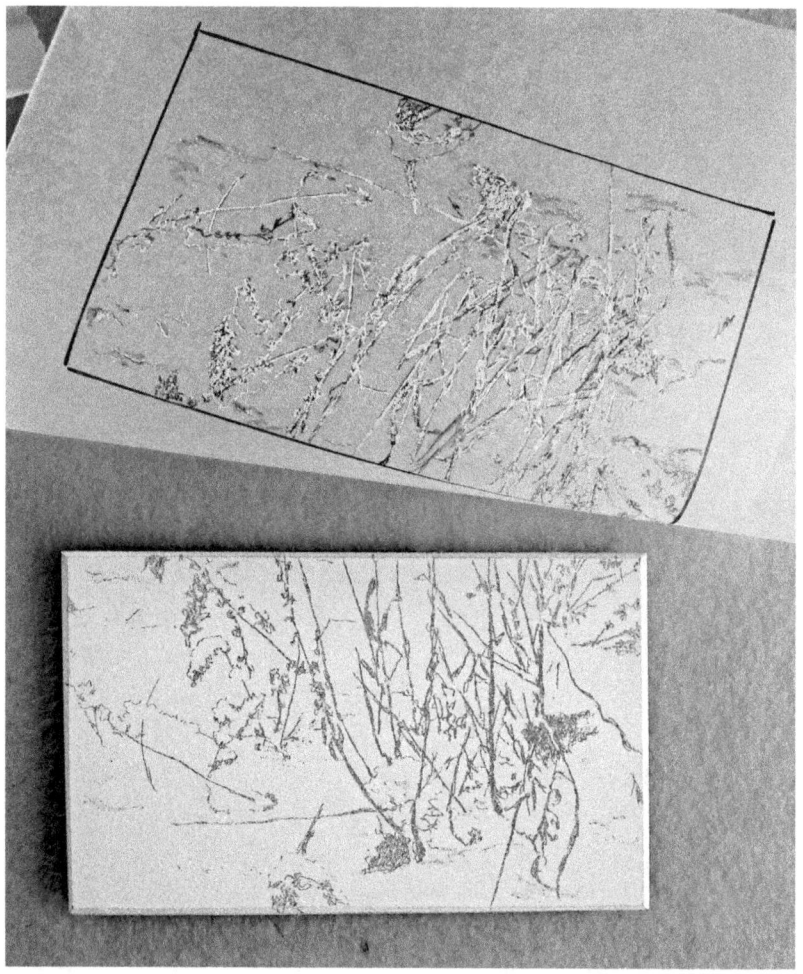

FIGURE 5.22: The plate with PG-11 and the overlay.

EXAMPLE 8A: SO-11 Used with Tracing Paper Overlay

(etchant: 1:1 ferric chloride; 20 minutes)

SO-11 is the least permeable of the four. A thin coat is all that is needed to block the acid and since it's fairly soft it is responsive to the pressure from the pencil point. I found that it can leave trace amounts of something on the plate where it appears to have been removed, that block etching, so when you take your plate out of the acid there are shiny flecks in the lines where no etching occurred. To prevent this you can immerse the plate in a salt and vinegar solution prior to putting it in the etchant.

With SO-11 used this way, fairly firm pencil pressure is called for. The printed lines are softer in character than lines needled in hard ground, but can be etched strongly with relatively little chance for foul bite. Since it is a dark brown color, if you have a previously drawn image on the tracing paper that you're using for visual reference, the graphite lines of the drawing may not be adequately visible against the dark brown ground, particularly if you've flipped the tracing paper so the graphite lines are on the underside of it, so you may need to insert a sheet of white tissue paper between the plate and the overlay. This will make the lines on the tracing paper overlay visible—you can trace over them and the ground will transfer to the tissue paper.

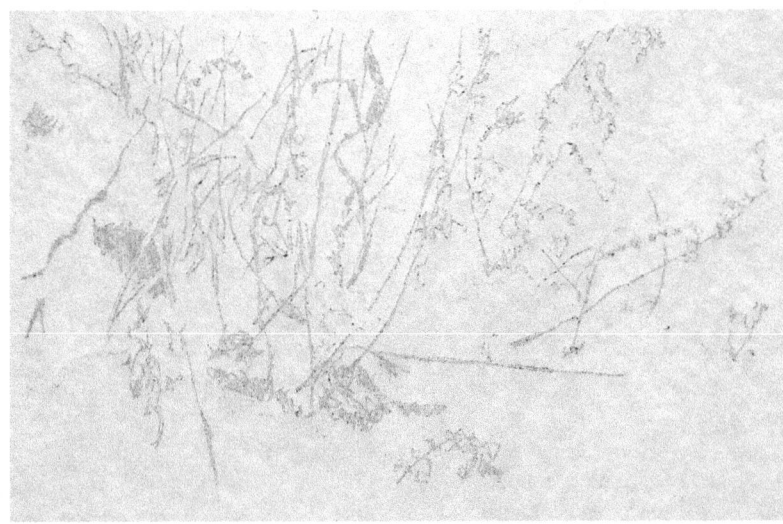

FIGURE 5.23

This shows the SO-11 that was transferred to a piece of white tissue paper that was laid between the plate and the tracing paper overlay. The amount of ground that transfers is sparse compared to the other three grounds.

This is the plate, coated with SO-11, after transferring lines from the overlay. At this stage it was placed in 1:1 ferric chloride for a single 20-minute etch.

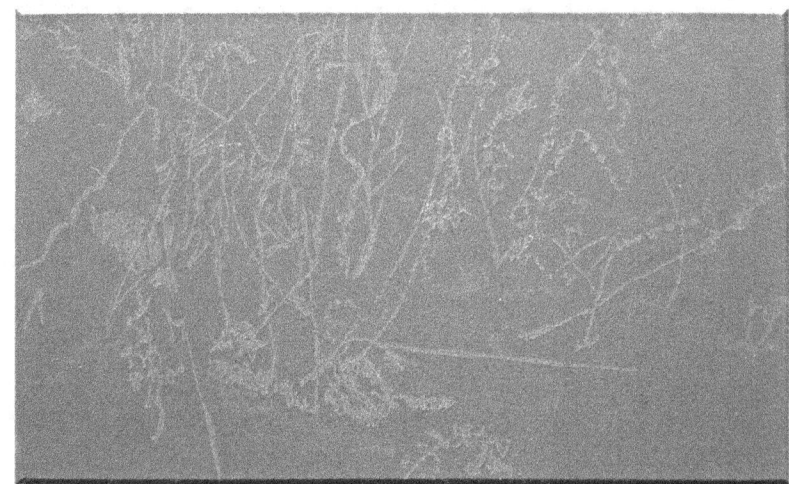

FIGURE 5.24

The resulting print. The lines are sparse, which would generally indicate the need for more aggressive pencil pressure during the line transfer/tracing process and/or a longer etch time.

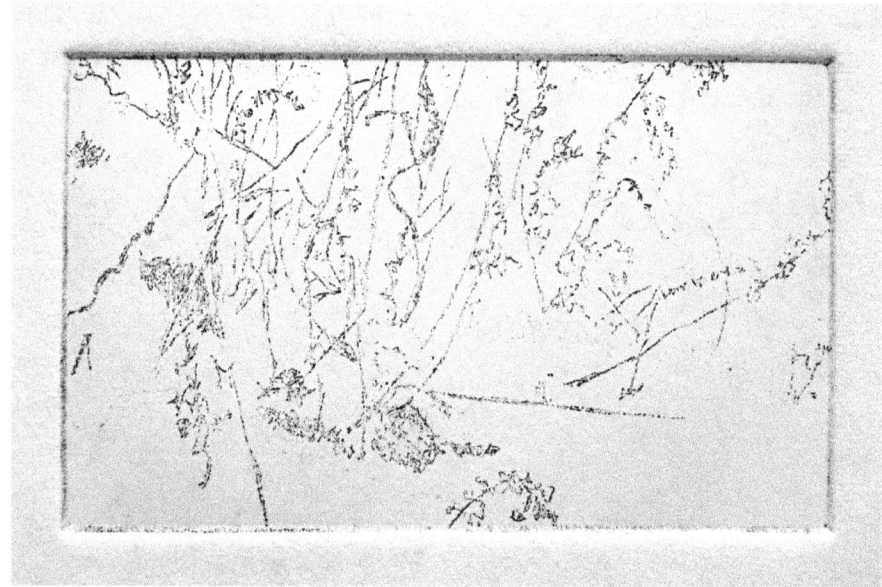

FIGURE 5.25

EXAMPLE 8B: PG-11 Used with Tracing Paper Overlay

(etchant: 1:1 ferric chloride; 20 minutes)

PG-11, though physically harder than SO-11, is permeable and therefore a slightly thicker base coat is needed on the plate to prevent foul bite. This means you don't get as much fine detail, but you can get good detail and you can etch strong, dark lines. It adheres well to the tracing paper and lifts cleanly off of the plate, so moderate pencil pressure is called for.

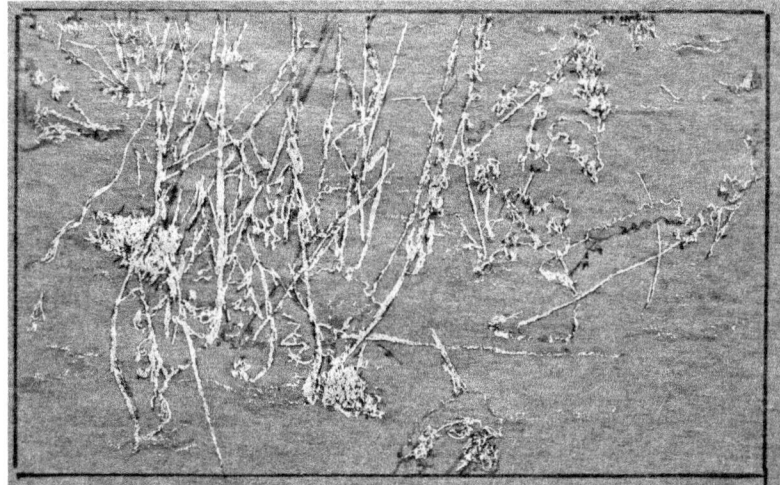

FIGURE 5.26

The back side of the tracing paper overlay with PG-11 transferred to it from the plate—missed lines show black.

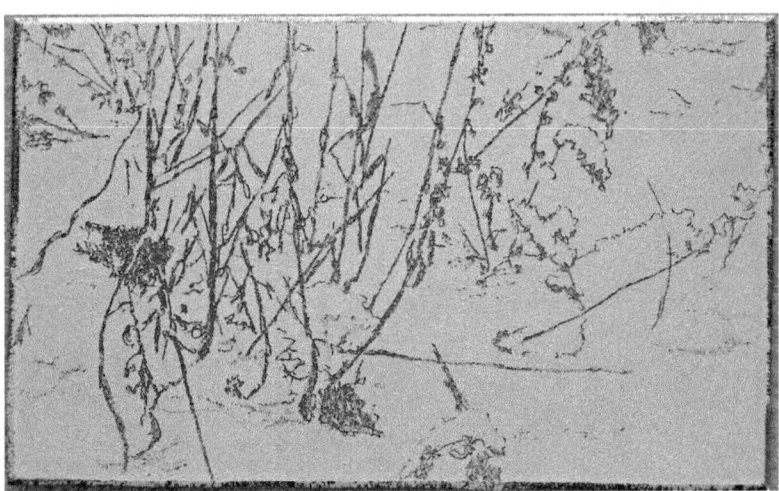

FIGURE 5.27

The plate, with lines transferred. It was etched in 1:1 ferric chloride for a single 20-minute etch.

The resulting print.

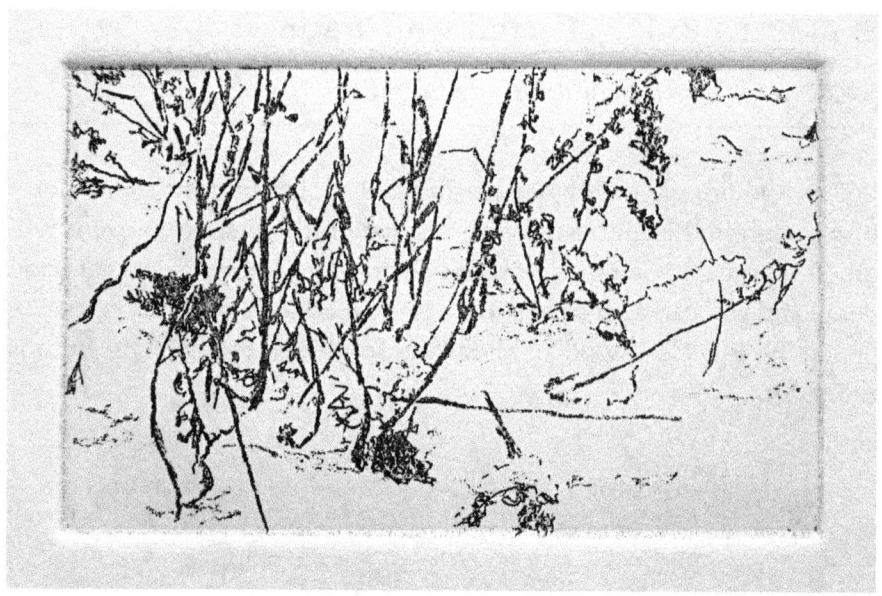

FIGURE 5.28

EXAMPLE 8C: PG-11 Medium Used with Tracing Paper Overlay

(etchant: 1:1 ferric chloride; 20 minutes)

PG-11 Medium is soft enough that light pencil pressure is good. It comes off in fat-looking lines on the back of the tracing paper and makes a broad impression in the ground, so you want to use a thin, soft paper overlay. On the plate this means there is a margin of thin ground adjacent to the actual perforated line that etches to create the printed line. This is a permeable ground, so a thin area of it will etch if left in the acid long enough.

For comparison purposes all four of these plates were left in the 1:1 ferric chloride for 20 minutes. What happened in this case was that when I cleaned the ground off of the plate there was a "halo" of oxidized patina along the edge of each line. I scrubbed all four plates vigorously with Brasso and this patina came off and none of it showed up in the print. Only the perforated and etched lines showed up in the print, though this thin ground along the edges of the lines would have to have had the effect of softening the edges of the printed lines.

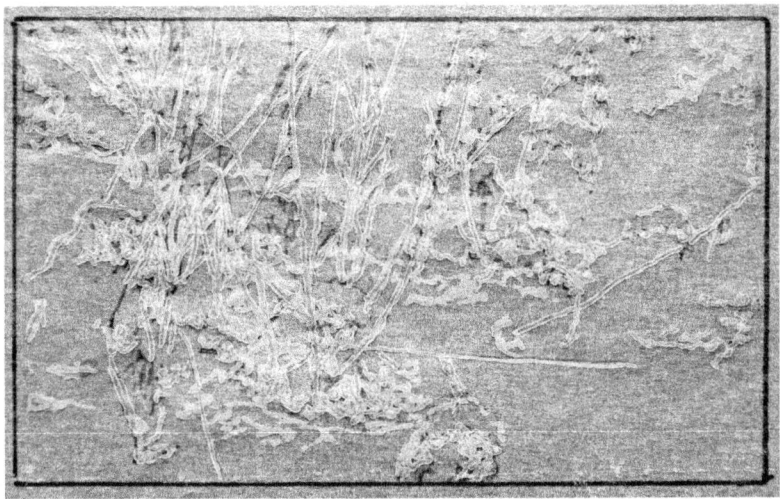

FIGURE 5.29

Back side of tracing paper overlay after transferring lines. Notice the extra ground along the edges of lines that transferred to the overlay.

The plate, after transferring lines from the overlay. Ready for a 20-minute etch in 1:1 ferric chloride.

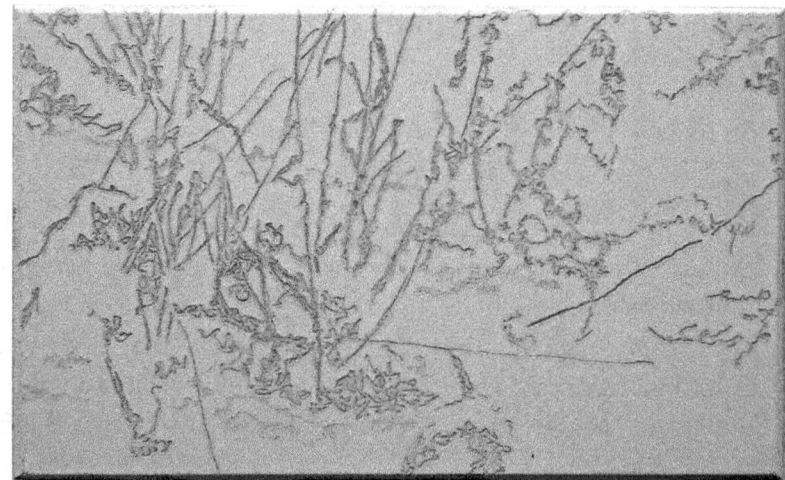

FIGURE 5.30

The print.

FIGURE 5.31

EXAMPLE 8D: PG-11 Soft Used with Tracing Paper Overlay

(etchant: 1:1 ferric chloride; 20 minutes)

PG-11 Soft is so soft it's almost too soft to use for this, but you can lay a tracing paper overlay on it and pencil over it without the paper sticking to the ground too much in the places where it's not supposed to stick. (As described in Chapter 1, these grounds can be slightly hardened by immersion in vinegar, however this was not done with any of these examples.) The lines of ground that end up on the back of the tracing paper are much wider than the lines (perforations in the ground) that are created by them on the plate and, as with the Medium version, there is a wide halo of oxidation along each line.

This plate, like the others, was in the acid for 20 minutes and I thought the oxidation along the edges of the lines had etched enough that it would print, but after Brassoing it the lines printed cleanly. Twenty minutes is a long time in the acid for Soft PG-11 and this was being conducted during a summer heat wave. The temperature of the acid was 78°F, but other than the oxidation haloing along the lines, there was no sign of foul biting. This would of course all be affected by how thick a layer of ground was applied to the plate in the first place.

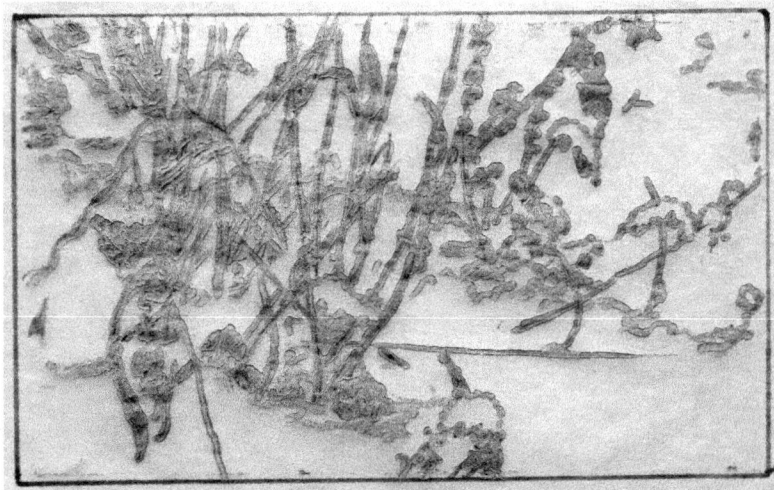

The back side of the transfer sheet, showing ground transferred from the plate.

FIGURE 5.32

The plate, showing lines impressed in the ground. Ready for a 20-minute etch in 1:1 ferric chloride.

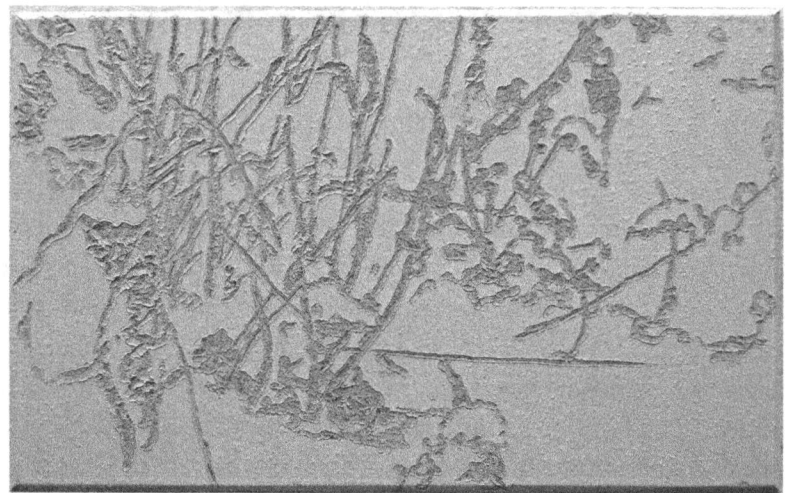

FIGURE 5.33

The resulting print.

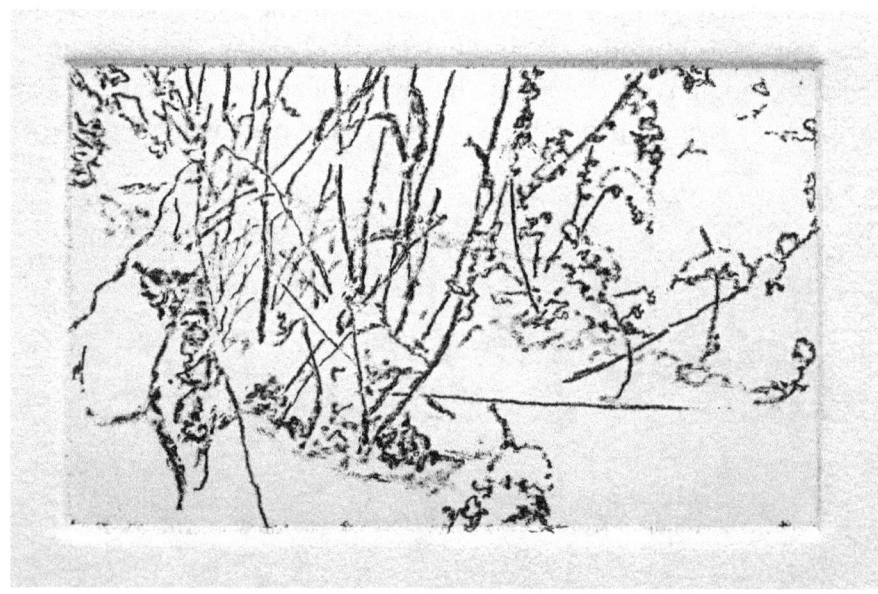

FIGURE 5.34

Generally speaking I would say that SO-11 or PG-11 are appropriate for strong foreground imagery and PG-11 Medium and Soft maybe for lighter, less distinct middle or background elements with shorter etch times.

CHAPTER 6

Larger Illustrations

This gallery of larger images is included as a resource for additional information about actual usage of these grounds. In doing this series of images I used PG-11 and SO-11 whenever possible, even in situations where I might normally have used a traditional nonpermeable ground, just to see what would happen. I had fun doing them and on the whole, was pleased with the results.

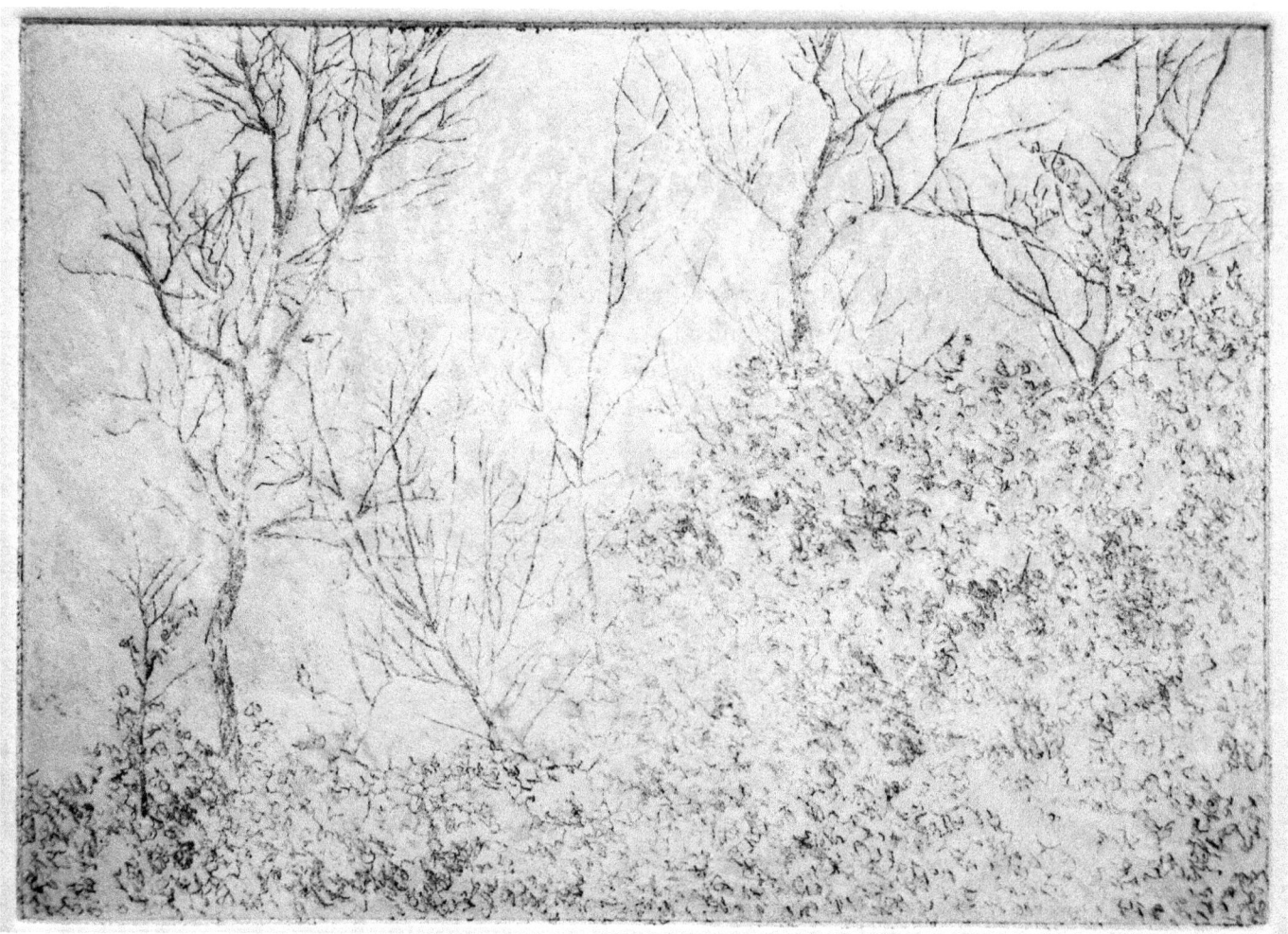

"Winter Trees," etching by
Richard Stauffacher.

1. Winter Trees (Soft Ground Lines)

(Plate size: 5x7 in. Etchant: 1:1 ferric chloride.)

This plate was supposed to be a "one-bite wonder." It didn't work entirely according to the plan I had, but I think I still ended up with an interesting image.

The initial concept was an image of trees in falling snow, with a very faint line of trees and pasture grasses in the background, more distinct but softly rendered trees and a honeysuckle thicket in the foreground all seen through falling snow.

The plan to make this happen was to airbrush the plate with a medium-thin layer of PG-11 Soft. Once that dried and was immersed in vinegar to make it a little bit tougher and no longer water soluble, Step Two was to lay a tracing of the background material over it and lightly pencil trace the background lines and tones into the soft ground. Step Three was to lay the tracing of the foreground material over the plate and transfer the lines more strongly by pressing down harder with the pencil to create stronger lines in the ground. The PG-11 Soft was

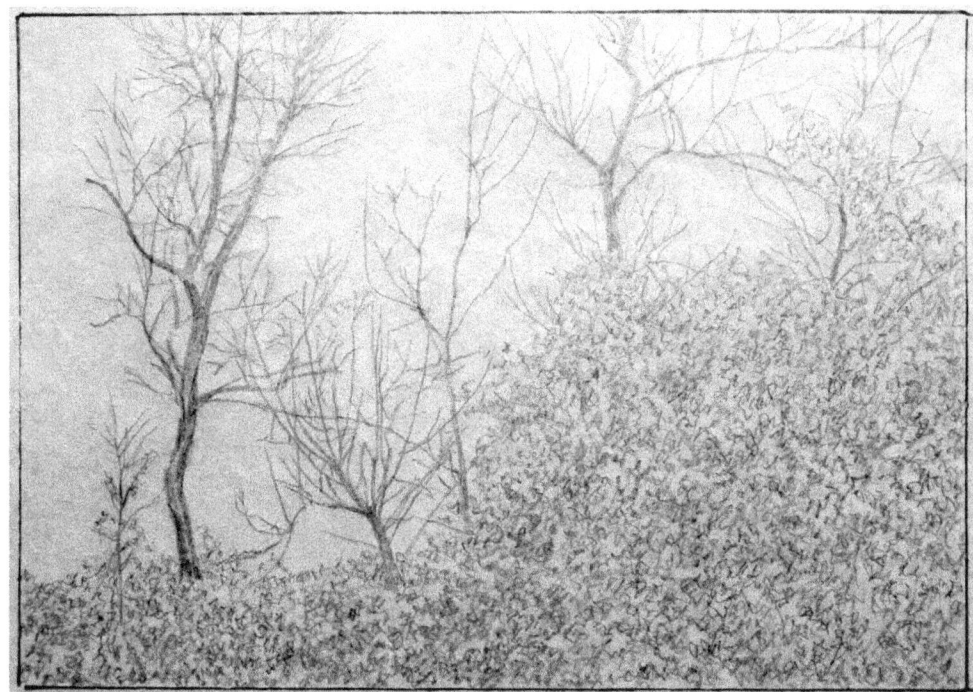

FIGURE 6.1: Pencil tracing
of foreground material

dark enough that it made the lines on the tracing overlays hard to see when placed over it, so I placed a sheet of white tissue paper under the tracings (an "underlay") to enhance the visibility of the pencil lines on the tracings. Lastly I spattered the plate with unaltered (white) PG-11 from a bristle brush to make the falling snow and spritzed it with a fine spray of water to blur the edges of the spatters.

So, the background lines would etch lightly because they were impressed lightly in the ground, the foreground material would etch strongly because those lines were impressed strongly in the ground, there would be some overall gray tone because I would leave it in the acid long enough for the acid to begin to penetrate the layer of softened ground all over, and the snowflakes would be created by the unaltered (less permeable) dots of PG-11 blocking the acid and leaving white spots. All in one bite!

Figure 6.2 shows what the plate looked like when it was ready to be etched.

To etch the plate, I put it in 1:1 ferric chloride. I was planning on a 20-minute etch, but after being in the ferric chloride for 20 minutes it didn't look like much was happening, so I put it back in for an additional 20 minutes after which some pitting and minor erosion of the ground (signs of acid penetration) could be seen, so I cleaned and proofed the plate.

Figure 6.3 is the proof. The background material is not significantly visible, the foreground material is lighter than expected, the falling snow didn't materialize, and the white "bloom" in the central area of the image was caused by the vinegar or the rinse water.

FIGURE 6.2

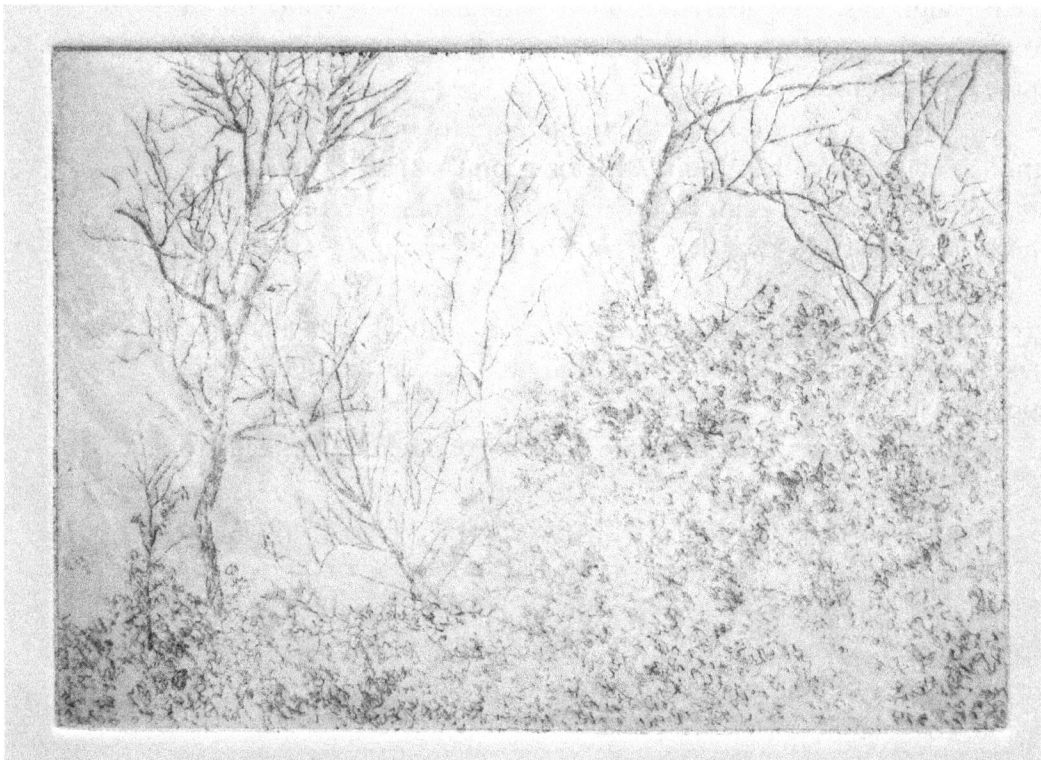

FIGURE 6.3

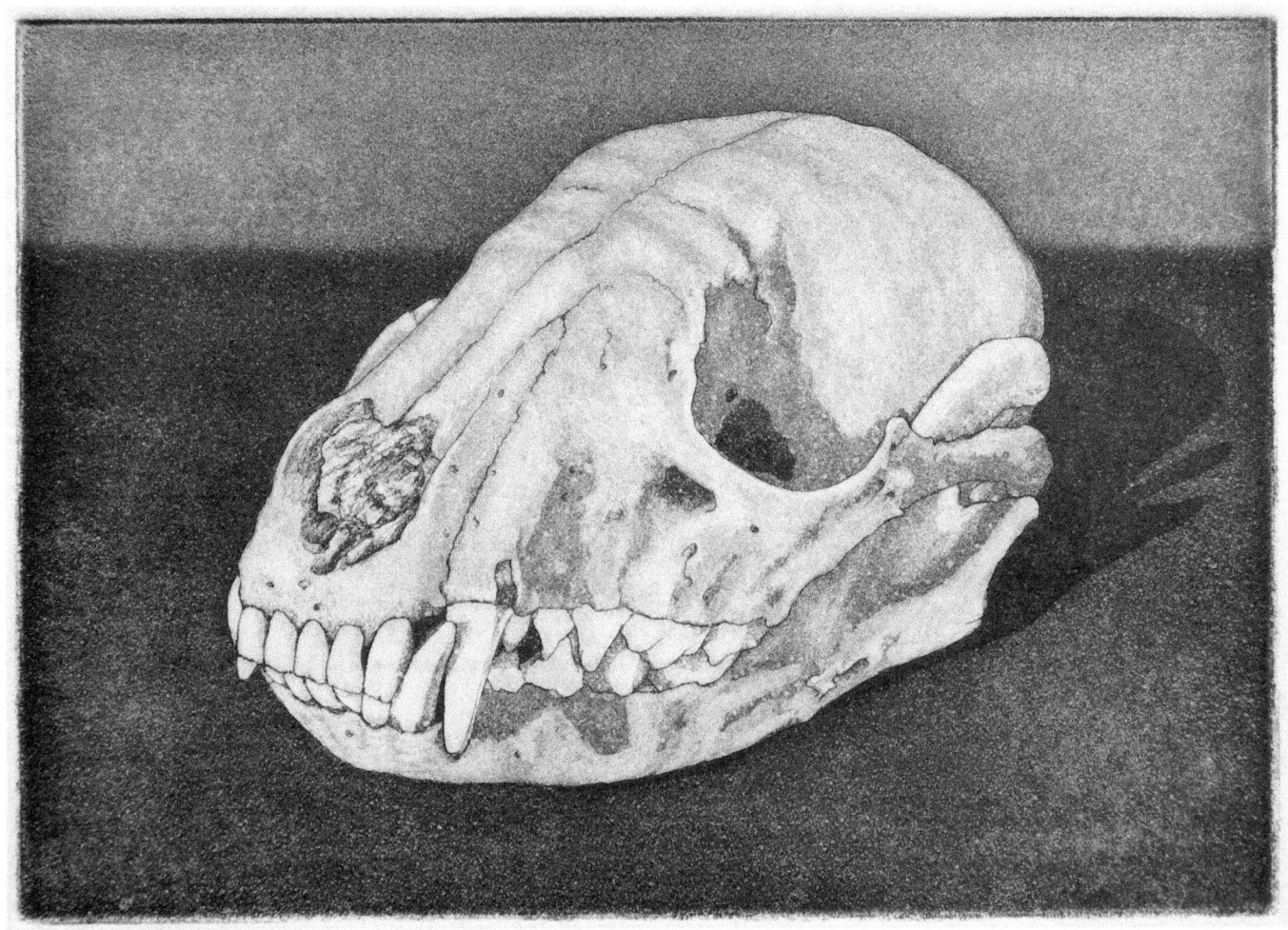

"Susan's Skull," etching by Richard Stauffacher.

2. Susan's Skull

(Hard Etched Lines, Soft Ground Texture, Adhesive Texture, Aquatint)

(Plate size: 5x7 in. Etchant: 1:1 ferric chloride. Target percentages of tone are based on the 20-minute timing chart.)

This image was executed pretty much the same way I would have done it using traditional asphaltum-based nonpermeable grounds, except that I used permeable grounds to see how they would compare and how well they would work, generally. I used a long series of steps as described below.

First I etched lines (Figure 6.4). I airbrushed the plate with a coating of Regular PG-11, allowed it to dry, and immersed it in vinegar. I then transferred visual reference lines to it from a tracing overlay registered to the plate, using a transfer sheet made from a piece of tissue paper with gray dry pigment (a mixture of titanium white and lampblack)

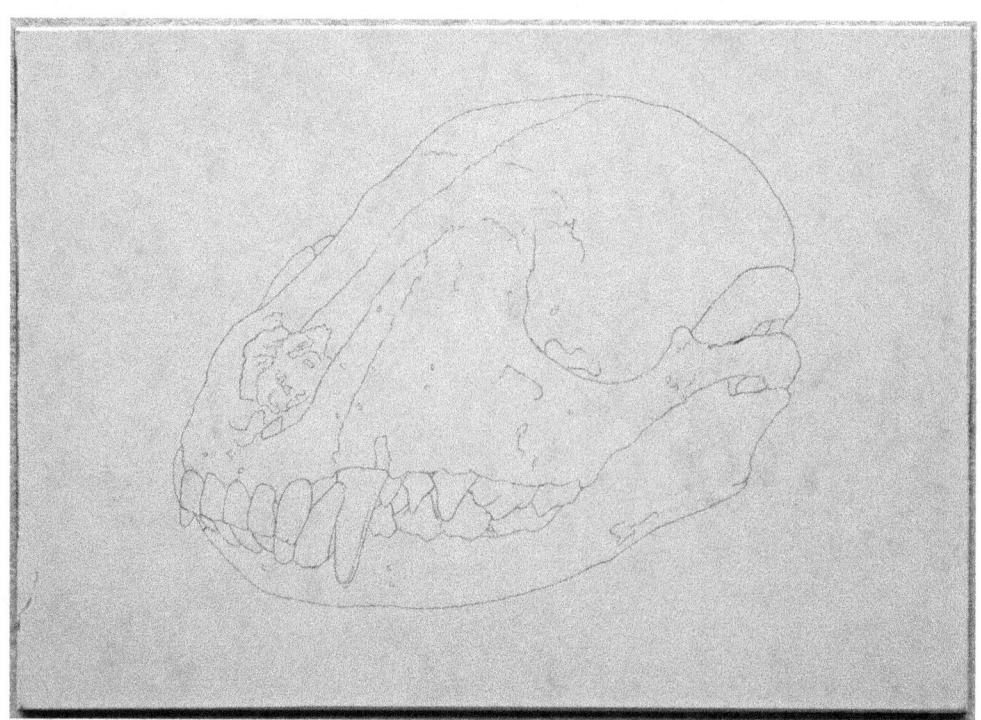

FIGURE 6.4

rubbed on it. I used very light pencil pressure which transferred the pigment to the ground, but didn't make an impression in the ground. Once the visual reference lines were transferred, I needled the lines in the ground with an etching needle. I wanted clean "hard ground lines," not "soft ground lines." This worked very similarly to needling lines in an asphaltum hard ground, except that I was unable to do a "graphite line transfer" by running it through the press, because PG-11 doesn't dry hard enough for that. By the same token, it is very easy to needle lines cleanly, resulting in fewer lines with gaps or missing ends. Chipping and flaking is not a problem.

Having established the contours with etched lines, I moved to the background. I wanted something that wouldn't attract attention, but that was more interesting than just a flat aquatint so I airbrushed a very thin layer of SO-11 on the plate and made a fine soft ground texture by laying a piece of smooth paper on it and running it through the press.

I stopped out the central image with SO-11 and etched the plate to 50% tone across the top quarter of the image, and 80% on the remaining three-quarters of the plate (Figure 6.5). (Actually, though the timing chart called for 3 minutes and 6 seconds in the acid for a 50% tone and an additional 7 minutes and 42 seconds for an 80% tone, inspection of the plate after 3 minutes and 6 seconds in the acid revealed that not much was happening, so I doubled the 50% time to 6 minutes and 12 seconds, and tripled the 80% time to an additional 23 minutes and 6 seconds. The point being that visual inspection trumps timing charts.)

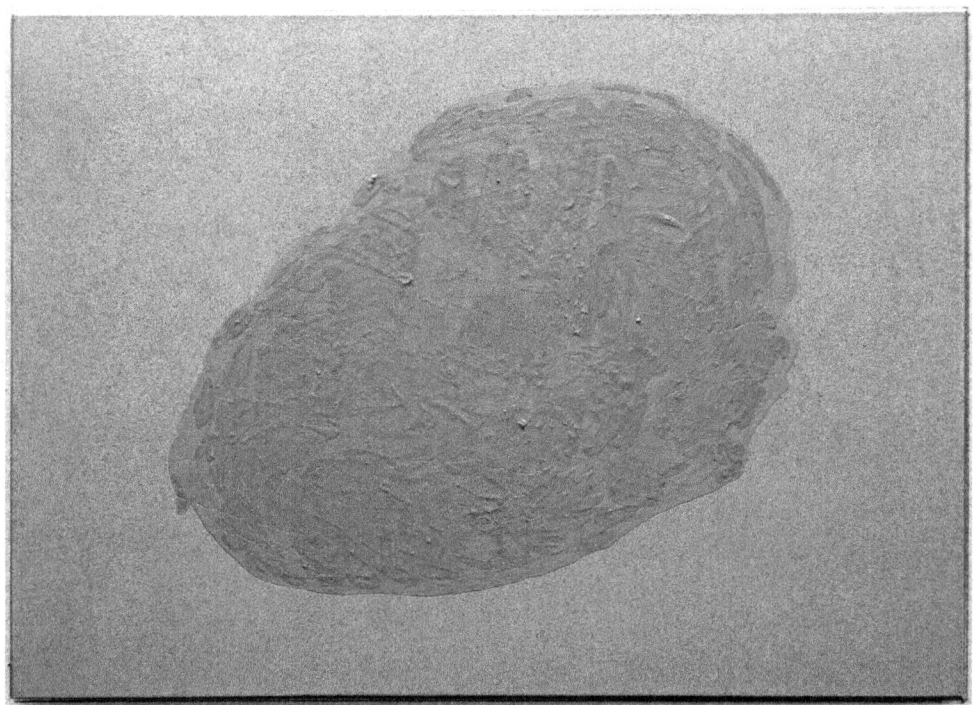

FIGURE 6.5

Figure 6.6 is a state proof print of the plate. I was surprised to see the very faint mottling on the skull, which was stopped out with several layers of SO-11. I used frequent immersions in vinegar during all of this process, and did so between pressing the soft ground texture and stopping out the skull. It must have been etched by the vinegar.

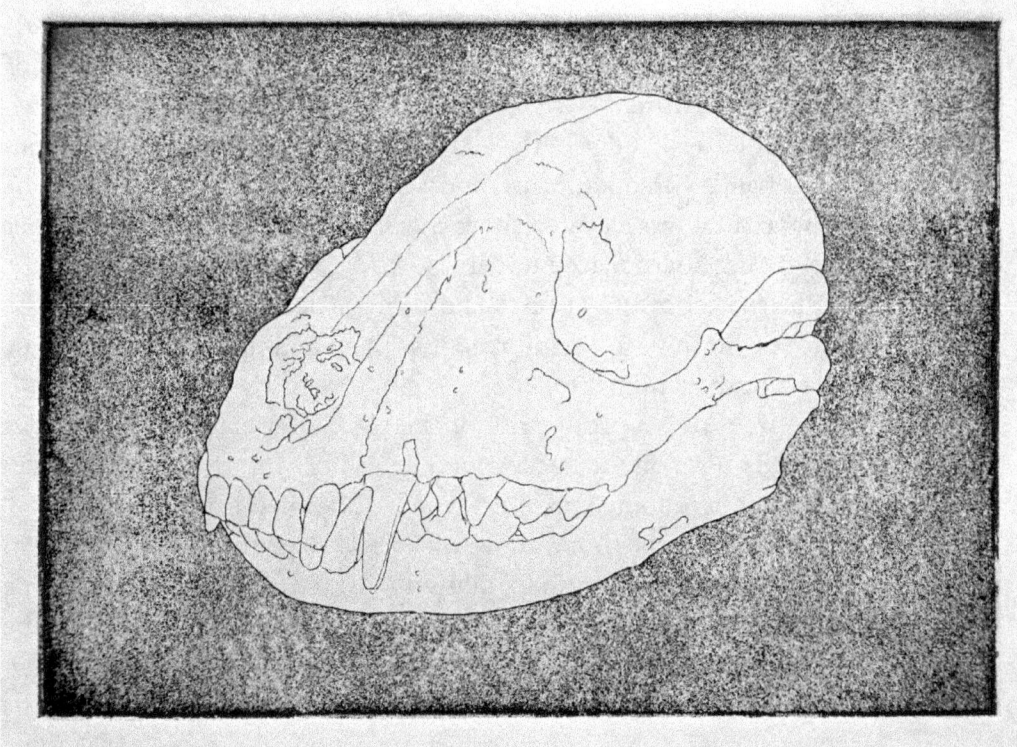

FIGURE 6.6

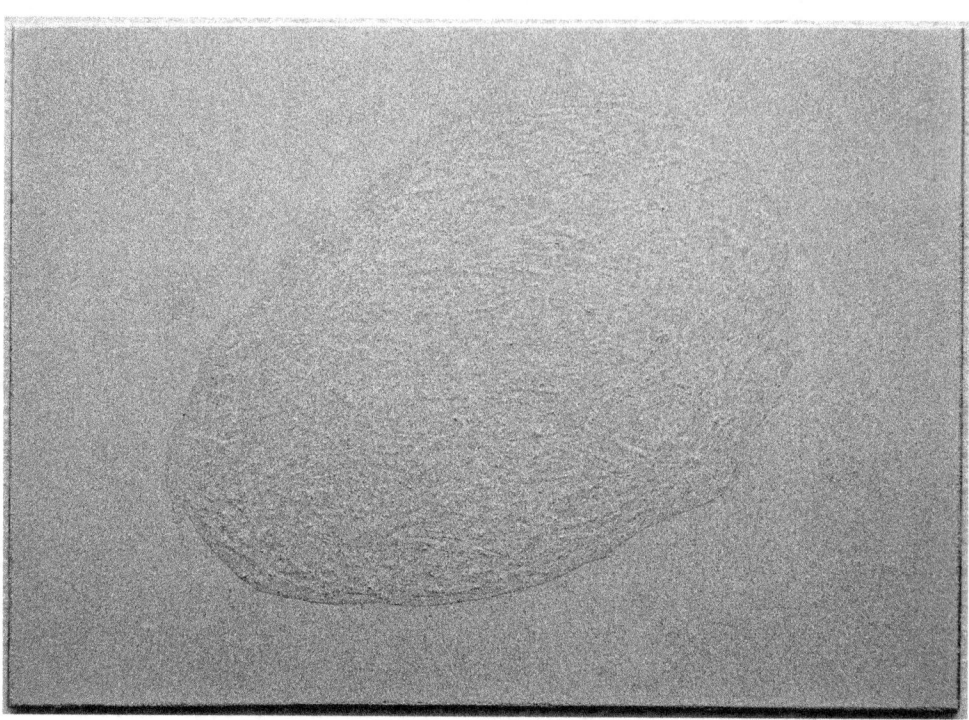

FIGURE 6.7

The soft ground texture wasn't bad, but I wanted more of a soft tone instead of much texture, so I stopped out the skull with SO-11 and applied an aquatint on top of it. I used an airbrush aquatint with PG-11 for the resist material (see Figure 6.7).

Figure 6.8 is a close-up, to more clearly show the coverage and dot size of the airbrushed PG-11.

In Figure 6.9 I re-applied the etch times from the chart: 3 minutes 6 seconds for 50% tone across the top, and 7 minutes 42 seconds for 80% tone across the bottom, this time to a fairly normal aquatint instead of soft ground texture.

I wanted a soft edge between the two tones, so when I stopped out the top band with an airbrush and SO-11, I used as a mask a piece of mat board that was elevated above the plate by the thickness of another piece of mat board placed under it.

The spatter of PG-11 on the bottom portion of the plate was looking a little bit thin, so I reinforced it with an additional light spatter of SO-11 before etching it to 80%.

Figure 6.10 is a proof print of the plate after etching the aquatint described above on the background. It's a little bit too dark, but I plan to do some scrubbing with steel wool and some burnishing later.

I wanted to try to get more of a "bony" texture on the skull, so I applied a very thin wash of diluted PG-11 and dusted it with some flour. I let this dry, then immersed it in vinegar to fix it so it wouldn't be water soluble. When I blew compressed air on it to dry it after rinsing it in water, some of the chunks of flour came off, creating the dark spots (copper showing) visible across the top portion of Figure 6.11. Most of

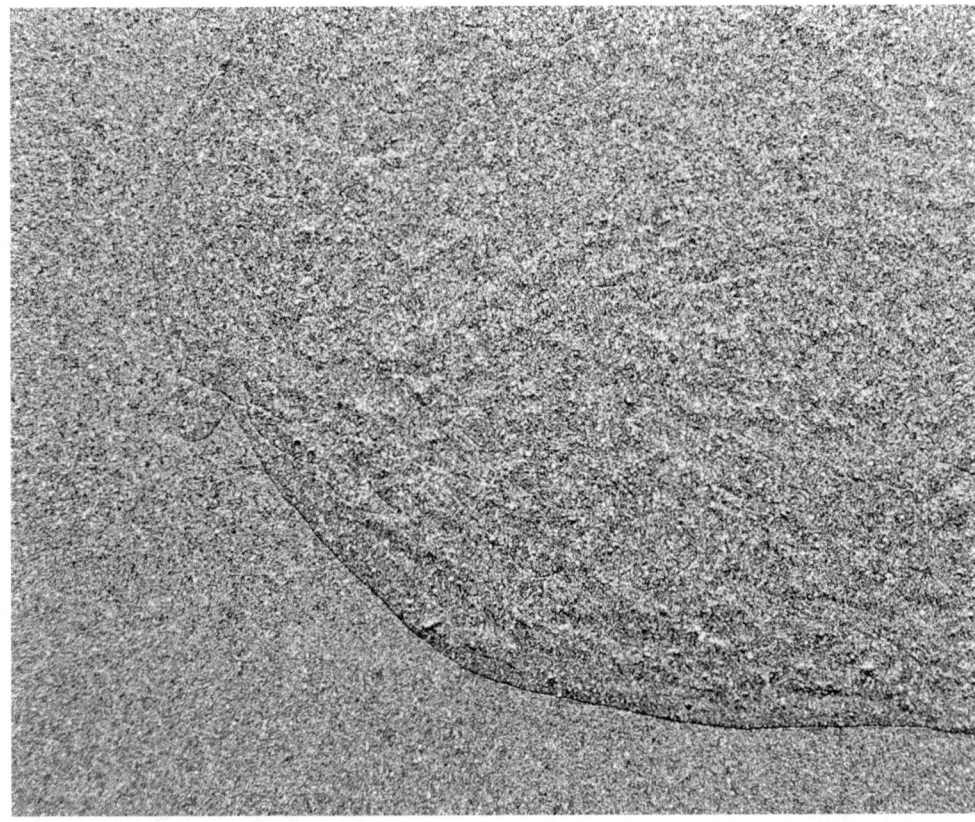

FIGURE 6.8

it stayed on and I was only planning a light etch, so I went ahead and used it. I only wanted the texture on the bone, not on the enamel of the teeth so I stopped them out with SO-11. (See Figure 6.11.)

Figure 6.12 is a state proof of the plate to this point. I etched the

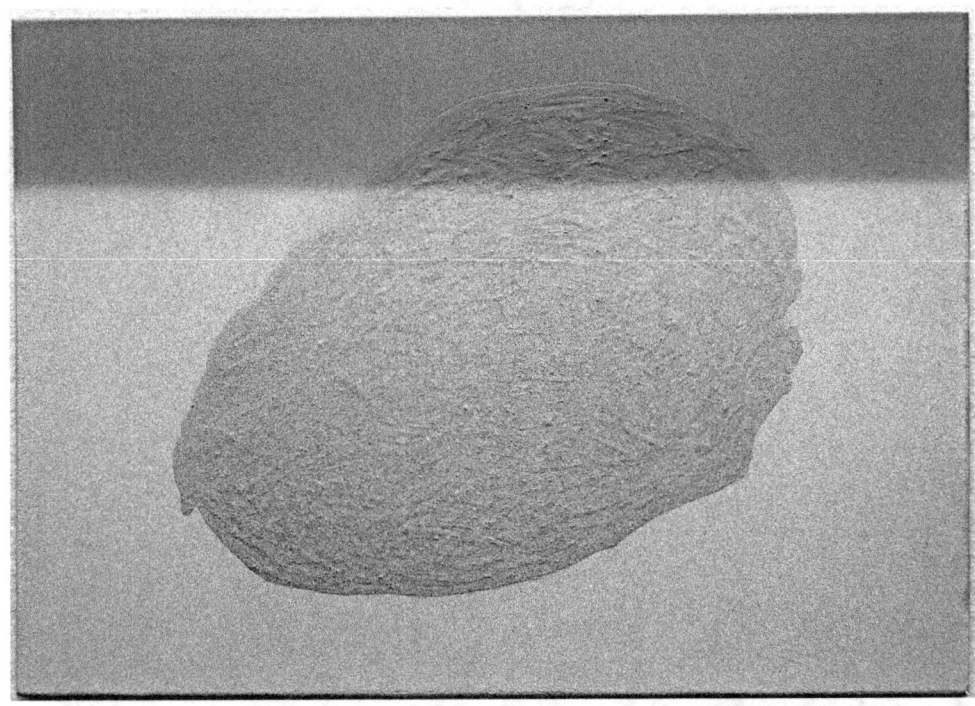

FIGURE 6.9

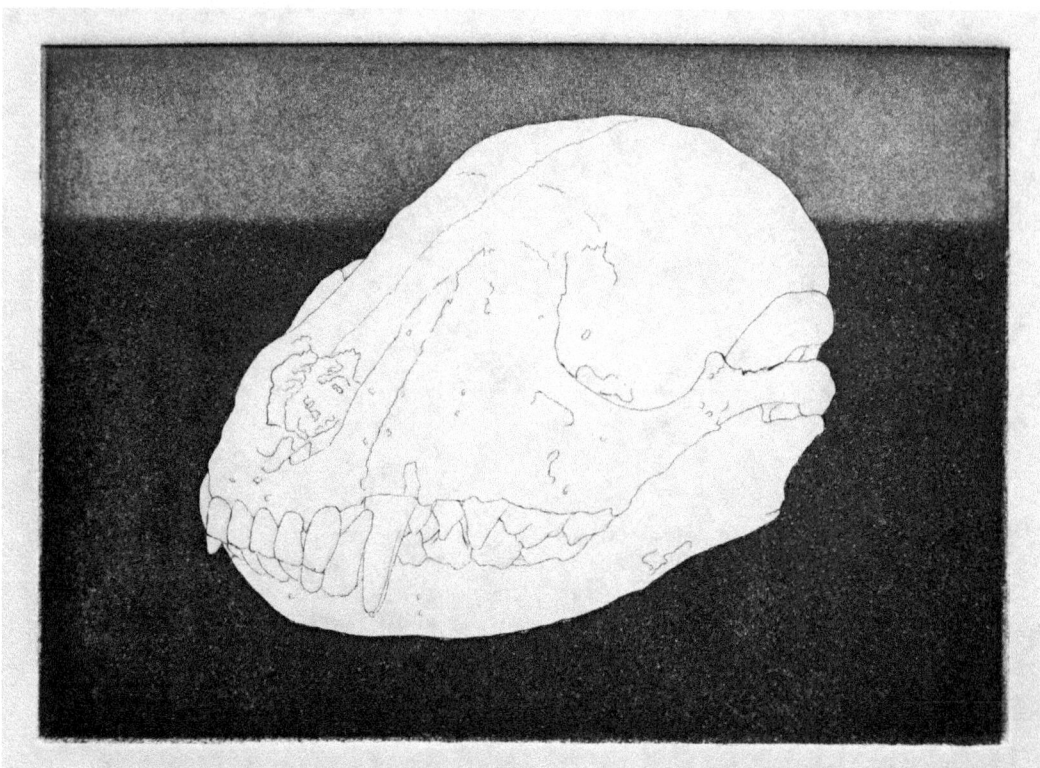

FIGURE 6.10

bone texture to 40% tone (1 minute 52 seconds), planning to cover this with an aquatint for shadows and modeling on the skull and teeth.

Time for some shadows. I decided I wanted shadows of 20%, 50%, 80%, and 100% tone. This would include the shadow falling on the surface behind the skull, so I did my scrubbing with steel wool and bur-

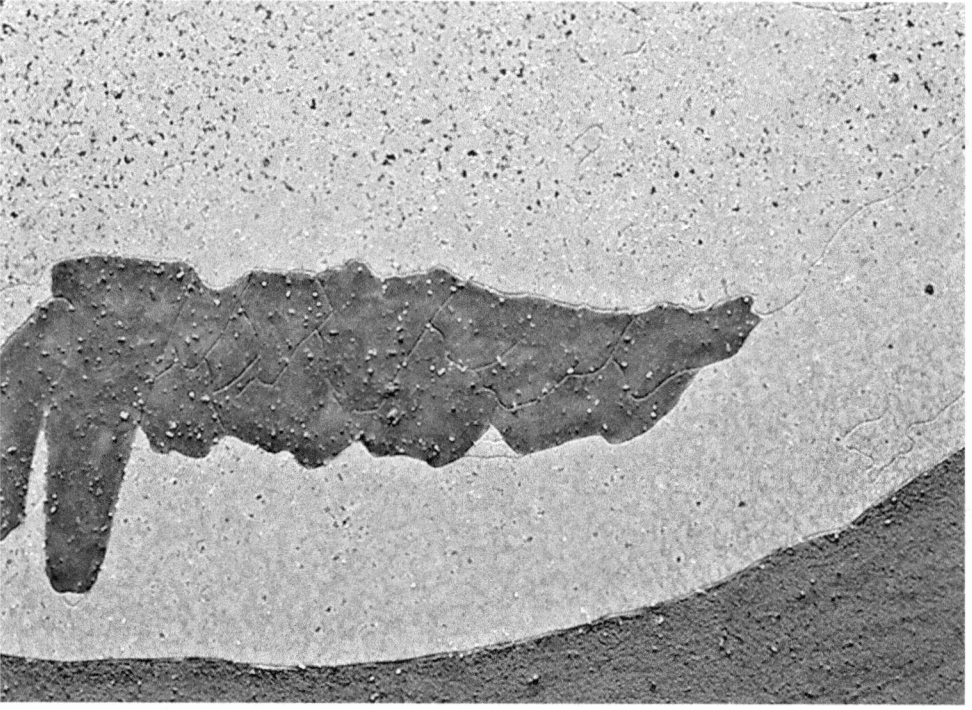

FIGURE 6.11

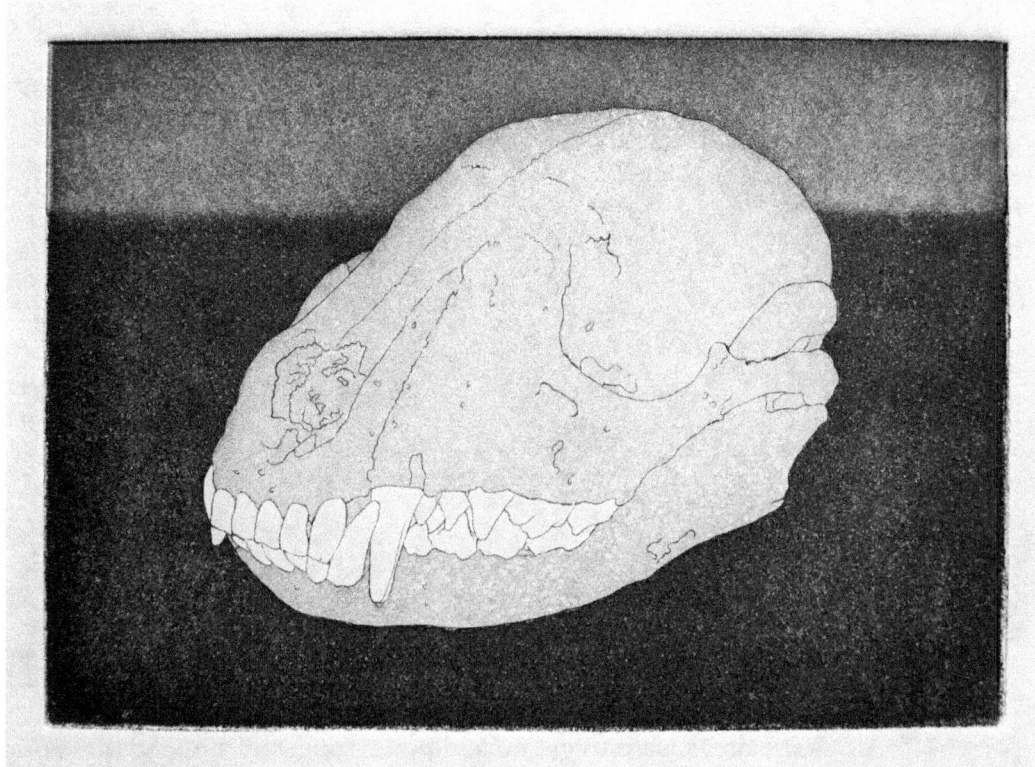

FIGURE 6.12

nishing on the background tones since I didn't want to do any of it after the shadow was there. I spattered everything again with airbrushed PG-11 and transferred visual reference (nonprinting) lines from a tracing to locate all the shadows, using a gray dry pigment underlay transfer sheet. Then I stopped out the unaffected areas with SO-11. (See Figure 6.13.)

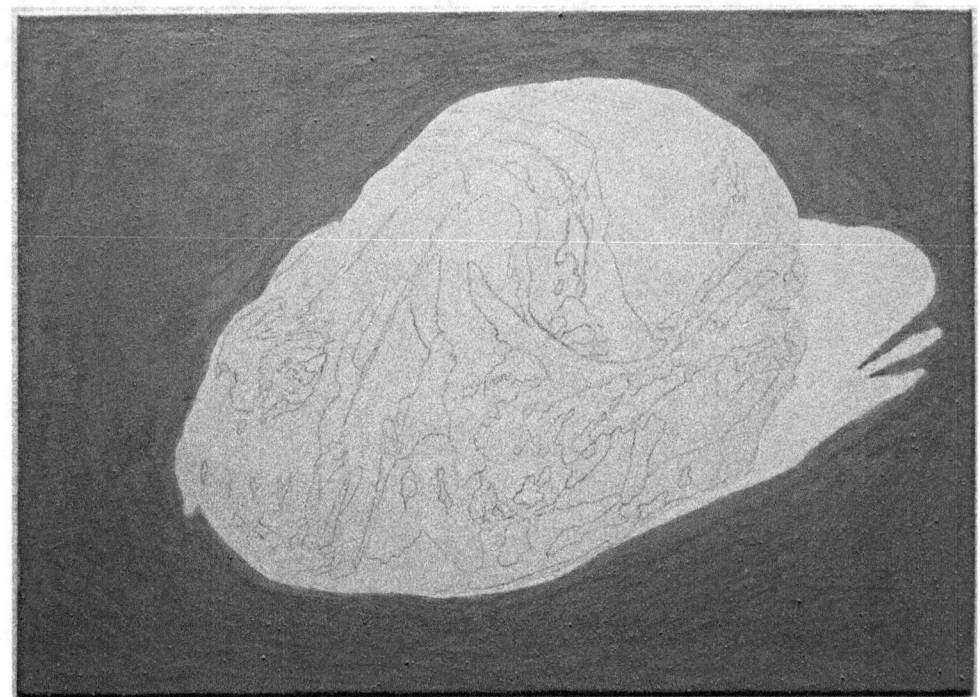

FIGURE 6.13

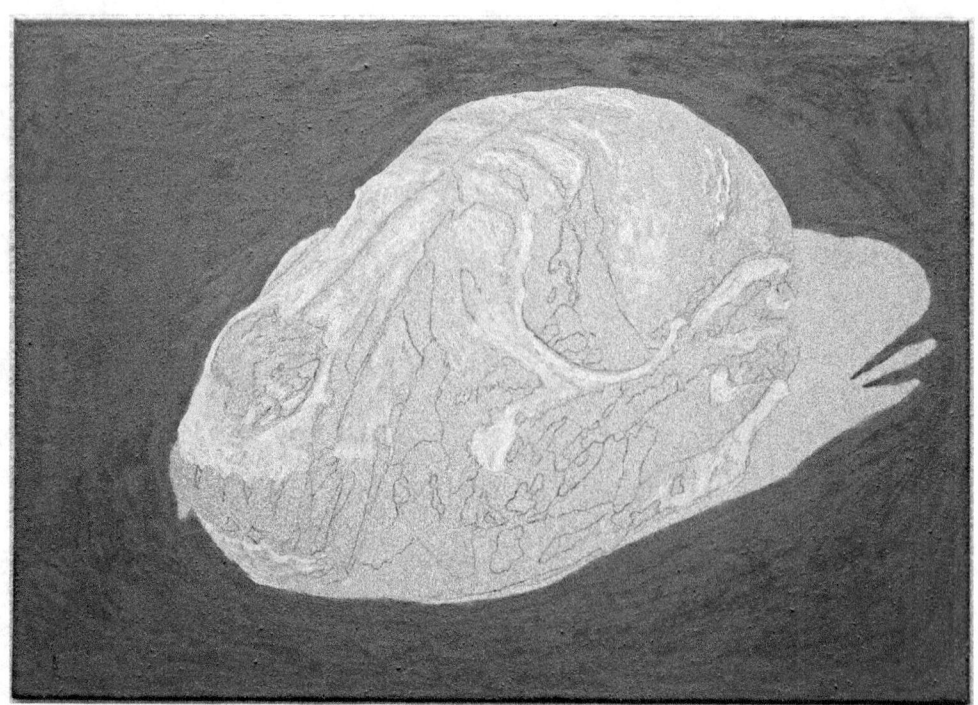

FIGURE 6.14

Some areas were to get no additional tone, so I stopped these out with PG-11 Medium before etching the 20% tone. Figure 6.14 is the plate, ready to etch to 20% tone.

More PG-11 Medium (SO-11 on teeth). Ready to go to 50% tone (Figure 6.15).

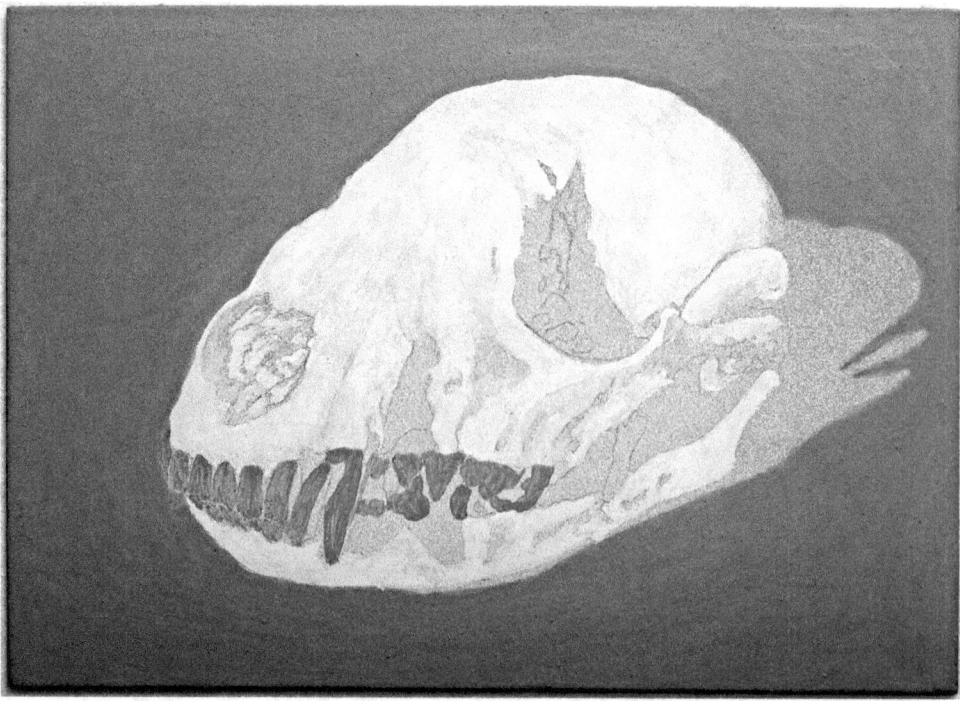

FIGURE 6.15

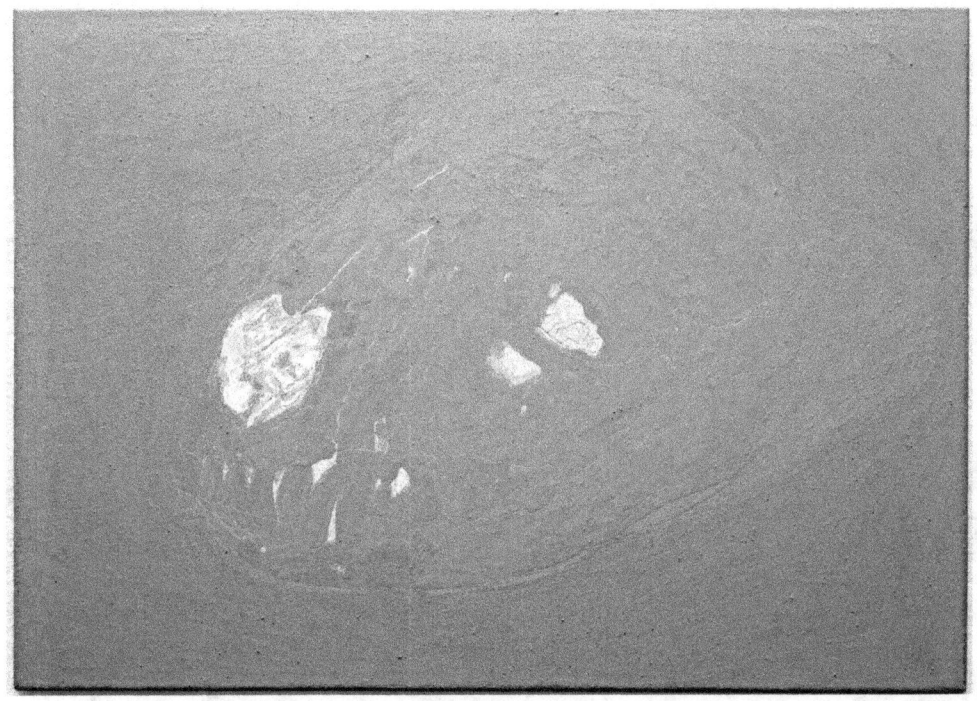

FIGURE 6.16

The plate, stopped out with more PG-11 Medium and SO-11. Ready to go to 80% tone (Figure 6.16).

The plate, ready to be etched to 100% (black) tone (Figure 6.17).

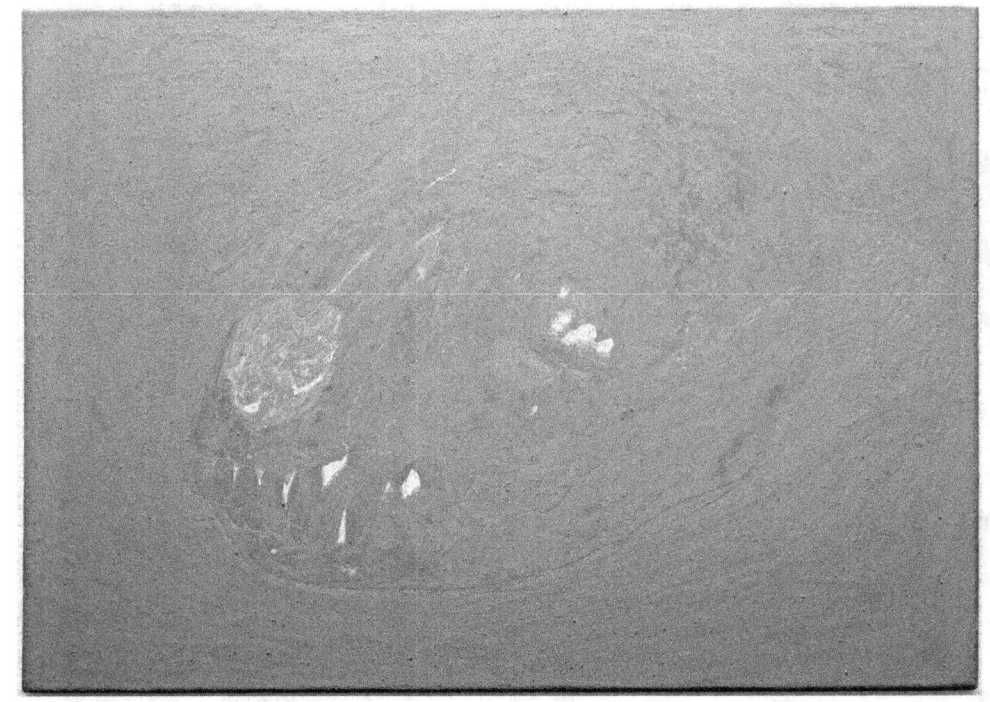

FIGURE 6.17

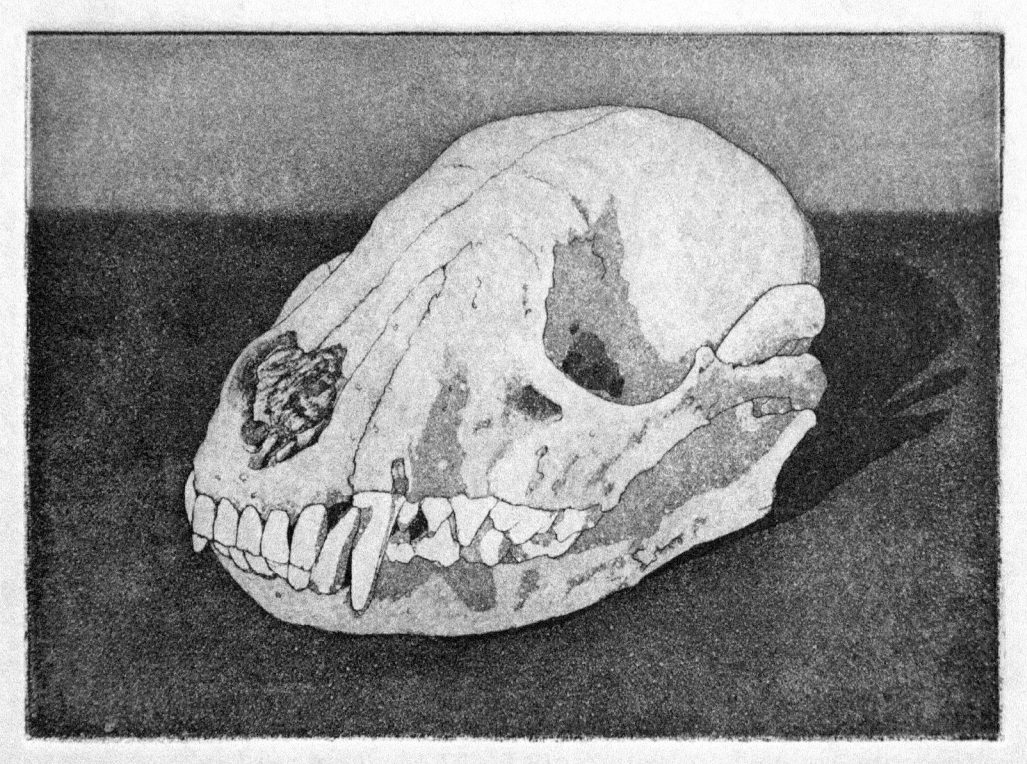

FIGURE 6.18

Figure 6.18 is a state proof print of the plate, after the above steps. All that's left is some burnishing and maybe some drypointing. Figure 6.19 is a proof print of the completed plate.

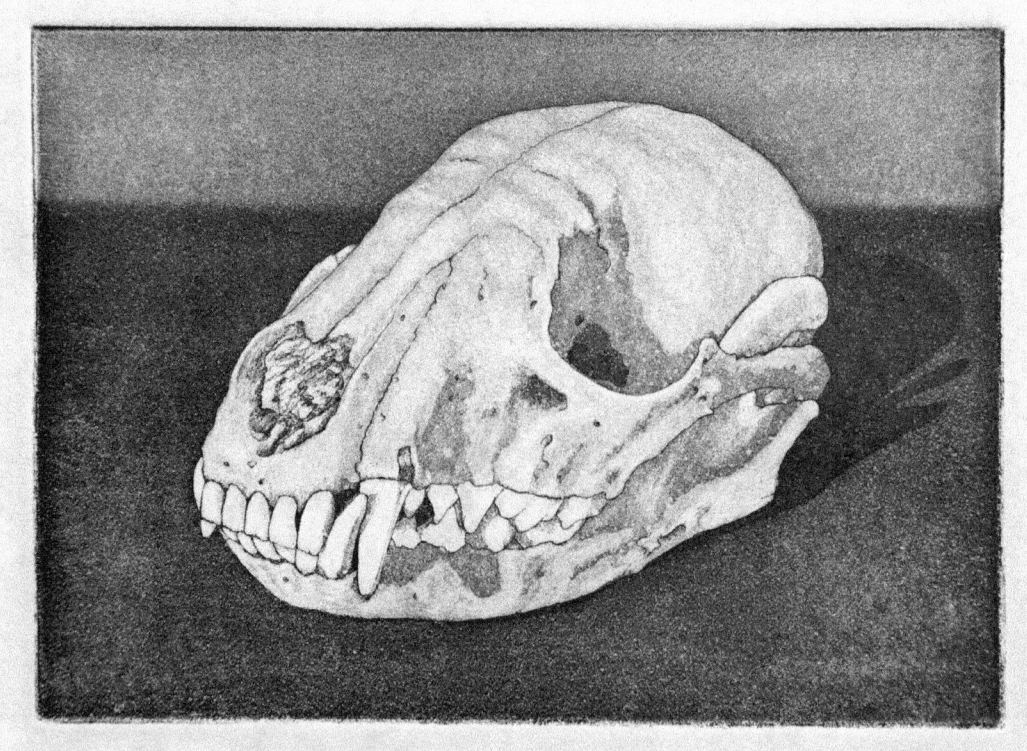

FIGURE 6.19

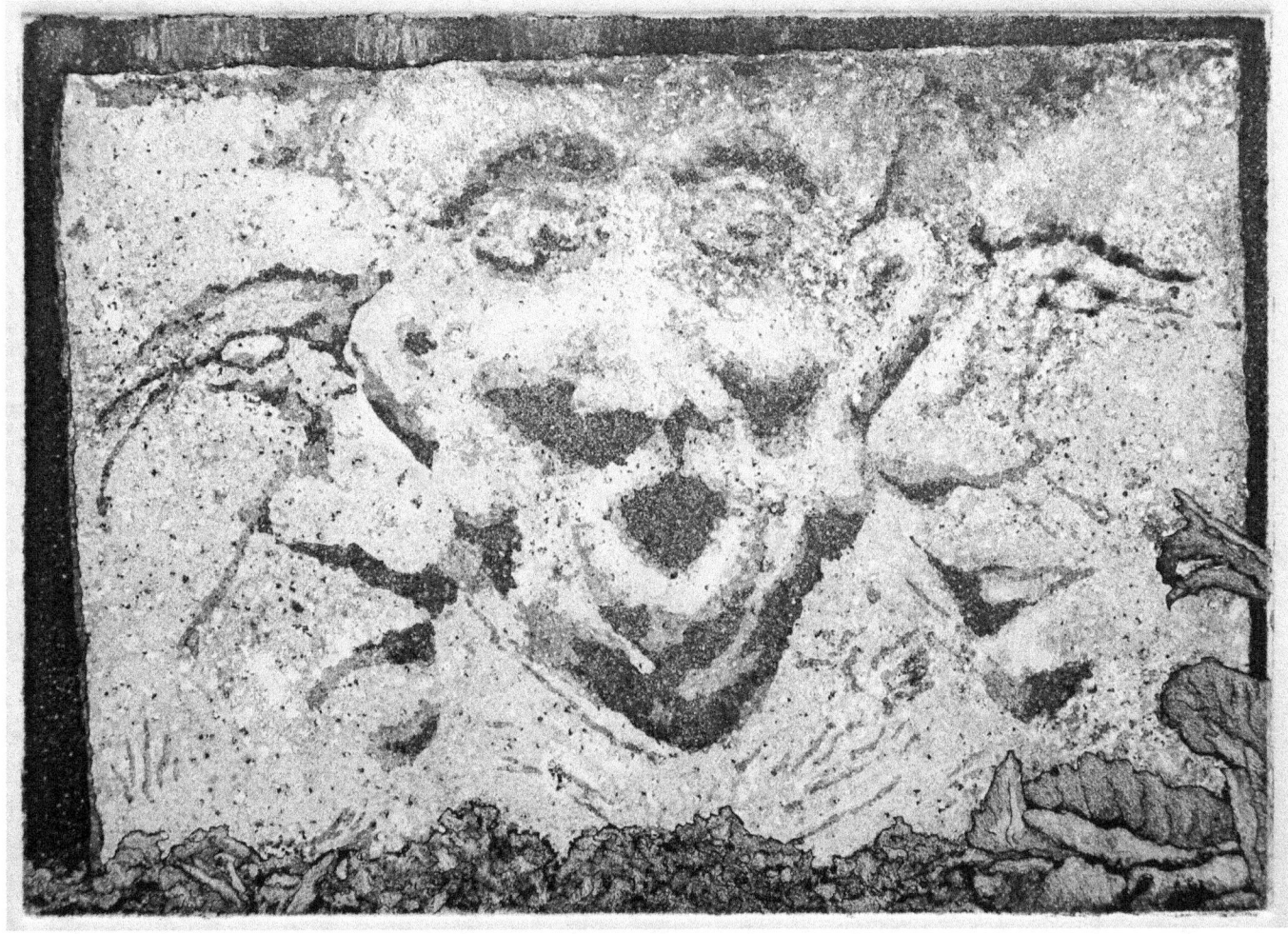

"Trio," etching by
Richard Stauffacher.

3. Trio (Hard Etched Lines, Adhesive Texture, Lift Ground, Aquatint)

(Plate size: 5x7 in. Etchant: 1:1 ferric chloride. Target percentages of tone are based on the 20-minute timing chart.)

This is an etching of a concrete plaque from my neighbor's garden. I thought it was a good subject for featuring textures. My plan was to use etched lines to define the plaque and the leaf debris across the bottom, but to only use tones to define the faces.

I airbrushed a coating of PG-11 onto the plate shown in Figure 6.20, transferred reference lines to it from a tracing using a gray dry pigment transfer sheet, needled the lines, and etched them for 20 minutes.

I decided to do the plaque first and then the material around the edge of the plate. Figure 6.21 shows the plate (after etching the lines) with the peripheral material stopped out with SO-11 and the center left open to receive the basic texture. I dipped the plate in vinegar to

FIGURE 6.20

clean the exposed copper and to set the SO-11 so that it wouldn't be water soluble.

I thought maybe a mixture of crushed lump-rosin and cornmeal would serve as a texturizing agent, so I wet the area (no aquatint) with thinned PG-11 and sprinkled the rosin and cornmeal into it and allowed it to dry (Figure 6.22).

FIGURE 6.21

FIGURE 6.22

The plate is shown here (Figure 6.23) after a 20-minute etch in 1:1 ferric chloride. I was surprised at the extent to which the ground broke down. There may have been something in the brush I used to apply the diluted PG-11 with.

Figure 6.24 is a state proof print of the plate up to this point. So far everything looks about as planned.

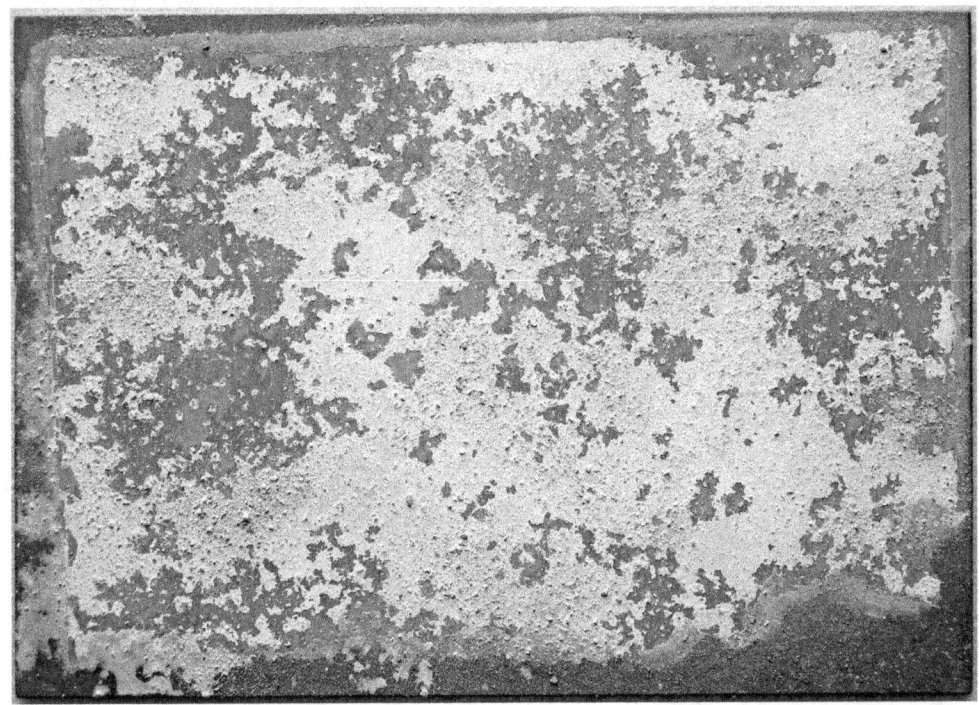

FIGURE 6.23

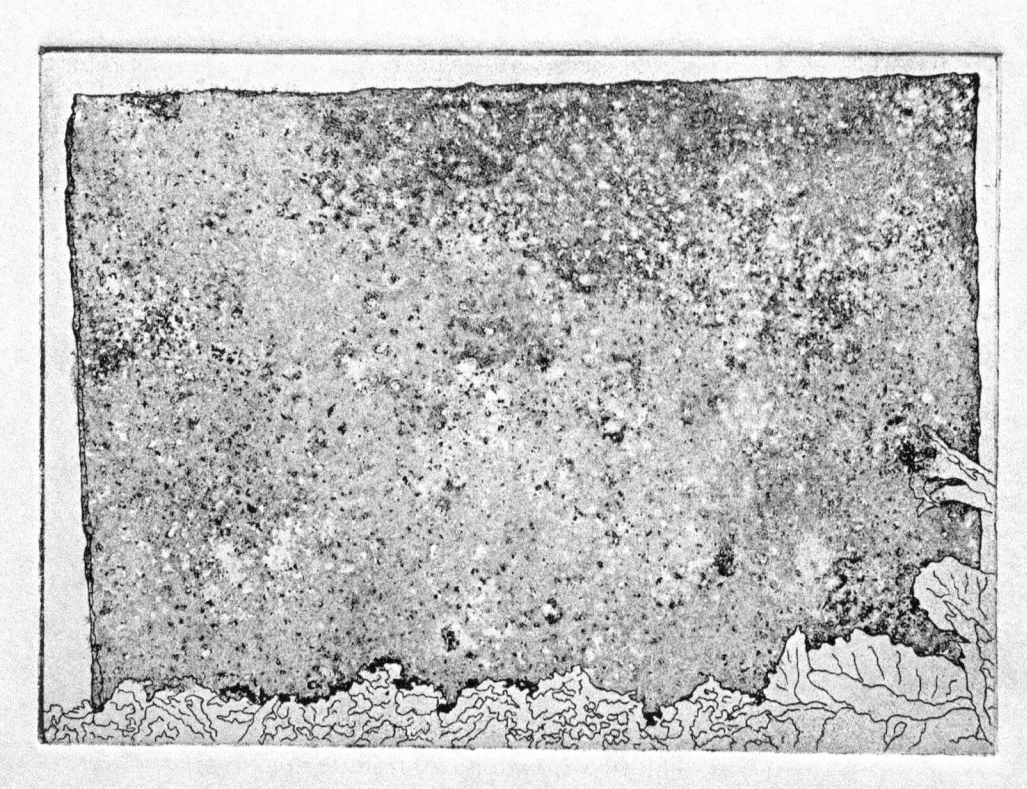

FIGURE 6.24

I decided to use a traditional lift ground to create the faces. Figure 6.25 is the plate with white reference lines transferred from a tracing via a dry pigment (titanium white) transfer sheet on to the bare etched copper. Then I applied the lift medium (dark) which was Eagle Brand Fat Free Sweetened Condensed Milk (an idea posted on MTSU Bulletin Board), thinned with water and with some Bone Black dry pigment added to make it more visible.

I usually like to use a soft ground for lifts. I coated this one with a fairly thin coating of soft ground made from Senefelder's asphaltum, Vaseline, and turpentine. Figure 6.26 is the plate after the ground was lifted with a jet of water from a utility spray bottle.

Some of the white reference lines for darker tonal areas are visible.

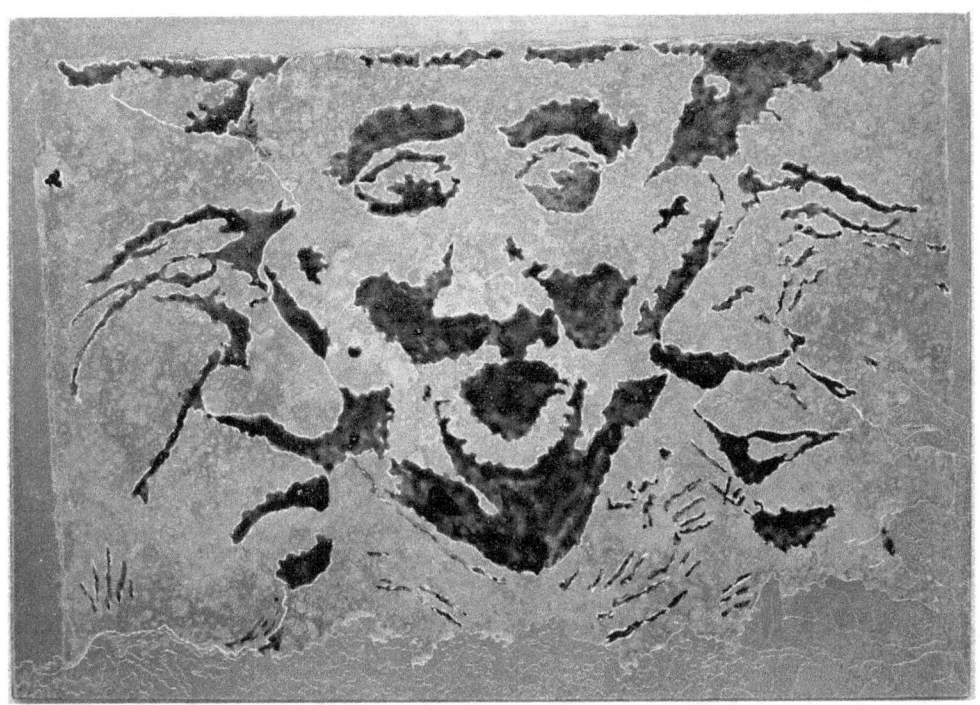

FIGURE 6.25

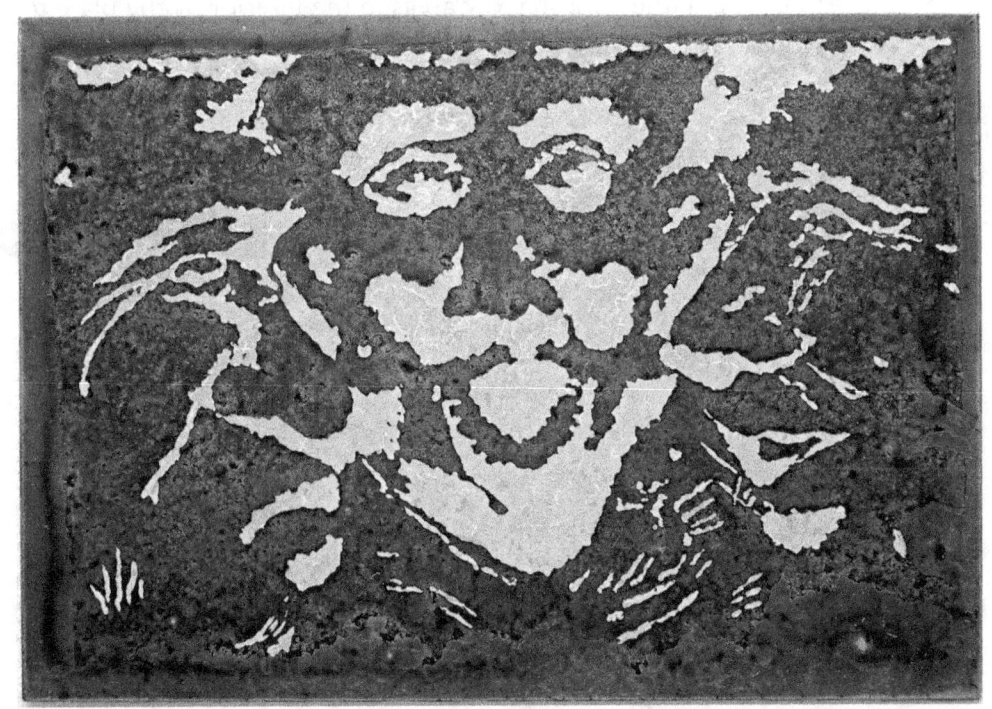

FIGURE 6.26

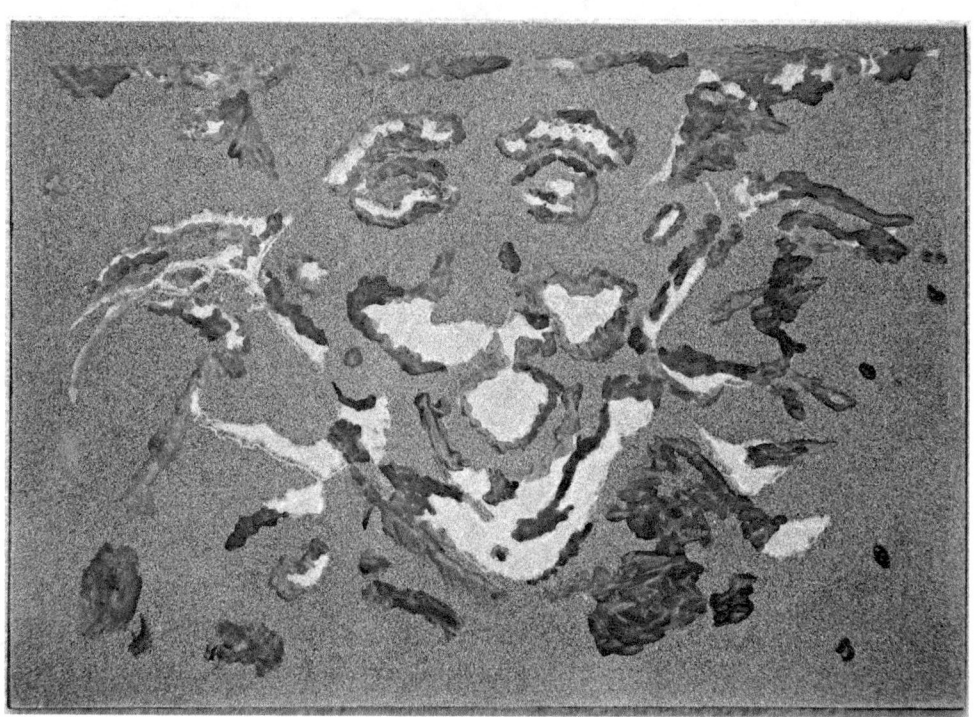

FIGURE 6.27

For an aquatint I spattered the plate with PG-11 from an airbrush. I only wanted two tones: 50% (3:06 in the acid) and 80% (7:42 additional). Figure 6.27 is the plate spattered, etched to 50%, and SO-11 applied to leave only the 80% areas open.

After etching the dark shadow areas in the interior of the plate to 80%, I focused on the periphery. Figure 6.28 is the plate with the central

FIGURE 6.28

FIGURE 6.29

area stopped out with two layers of SO-11 and spattered with PG-11 for an aquatint on the border areas. This gets a 20% etch (34 seconds). I plan to step bite additional tones of 40%, 60%, and 100%.

Figure 6.29 shows the plate, ready to etch to 40% (additional 1:18).

Figure 6.30 shows the plate with 40% stopped out and ready to etch to 60% (+3:03 in acid).

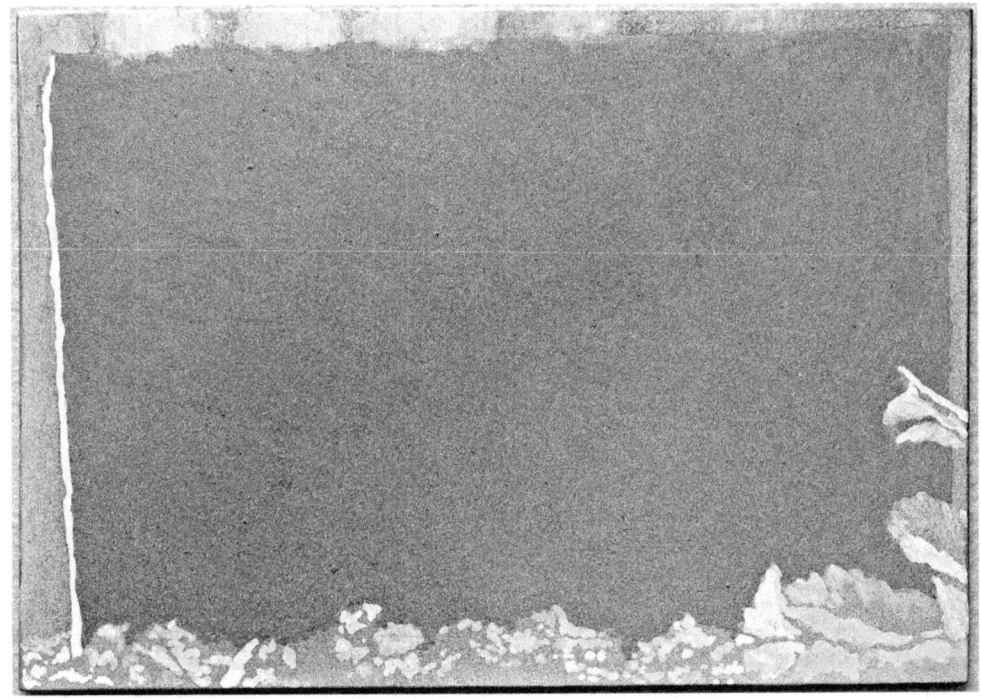

FIGURE 6.30

FIGURE 6.31

Figure 6.31 shows the plate ready to go from 60% to 100% (additional 15:05). The PG-11 aquatint was looking a bit scant, so I spattered some more on before doing the final etch.

Figure 6.32 shows a state proof print, after etching the faces and border imagery.

Another proof print after some scraping, burnishing, and drypointing (Figure 6.33).

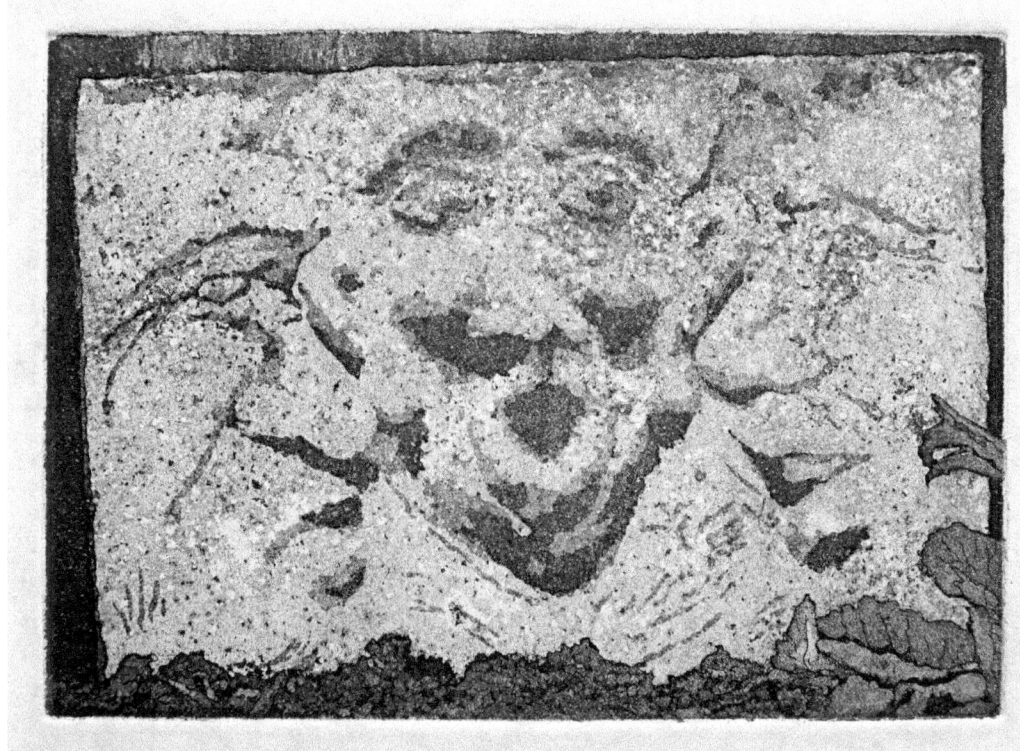

FIGURE 6.32

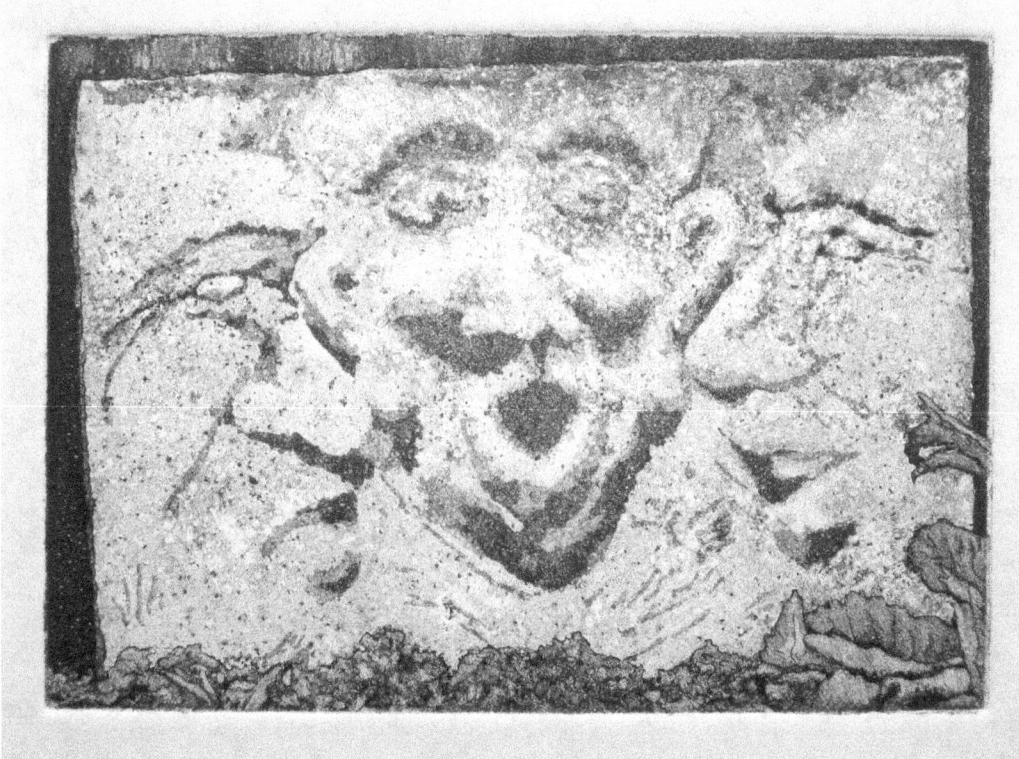

FIGURE 6.33

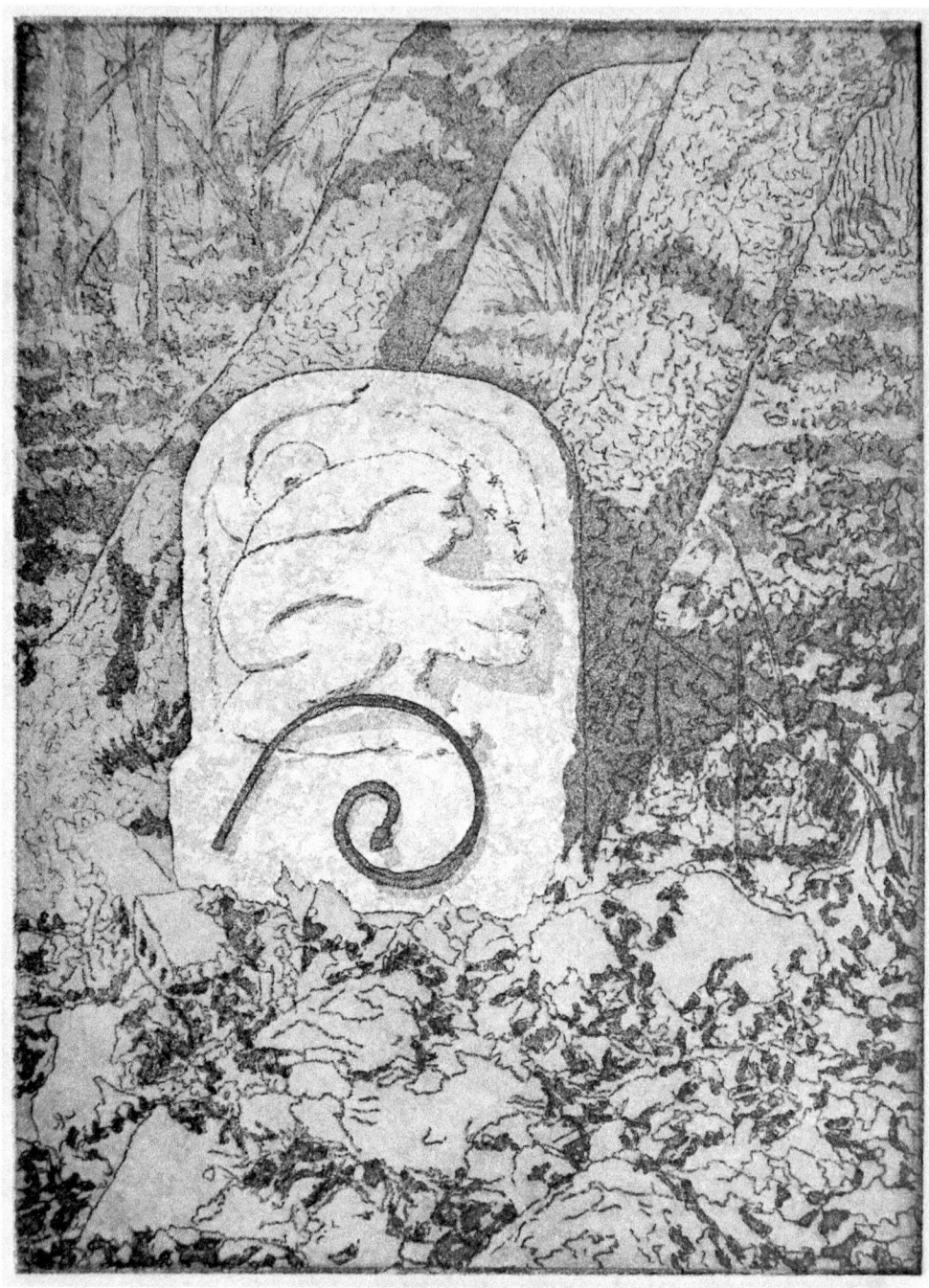

"Water Carrier," etching by Richard Stauffacher.

4. Water Carrier (Soft Ground Lines, Adhesive Texture, Lift Ground, Aquatint)

(Plate size: 5x7 in. Etchant: 1:1 ferric chloride. Target percentages of tone are based on the 20-minute timing chart.)

The first step in etching this image was to coat the plate with a medium-thick coating of PG-11 Medium, using an airbrush. The lines were created with a tracing paper overlay. (I traced the lines in pencil from a photograph on to tracing paper, then turned the tracing paper over and laid it on the coated plate. I then went back over the lines with a pencil to impress the lines into the ground on the plate so they would etch.)

Figure 6.35 is the line proof printed from the plate (Figure 6.34) after the lines were etched for 15 minutes in 1:1 ferric chloride.

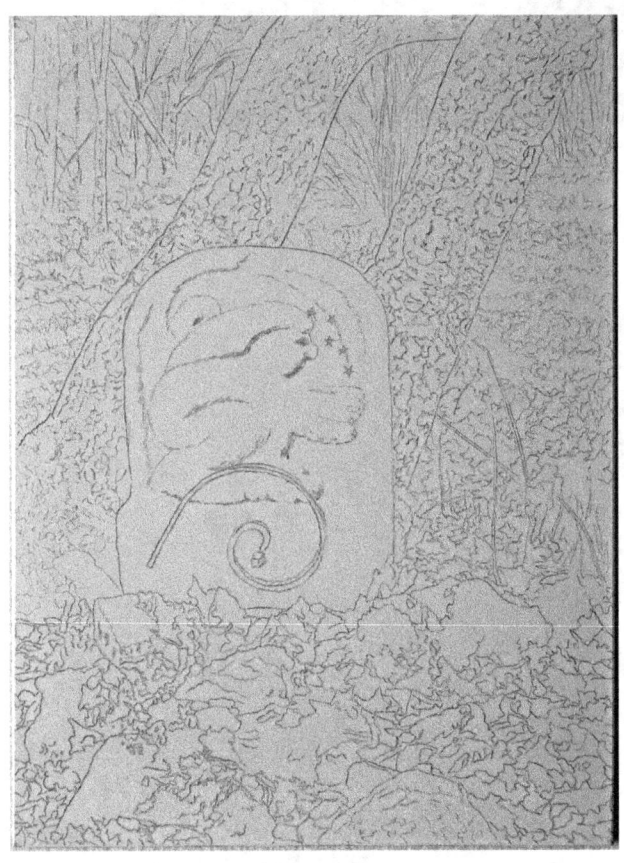

FIGURE 6.34

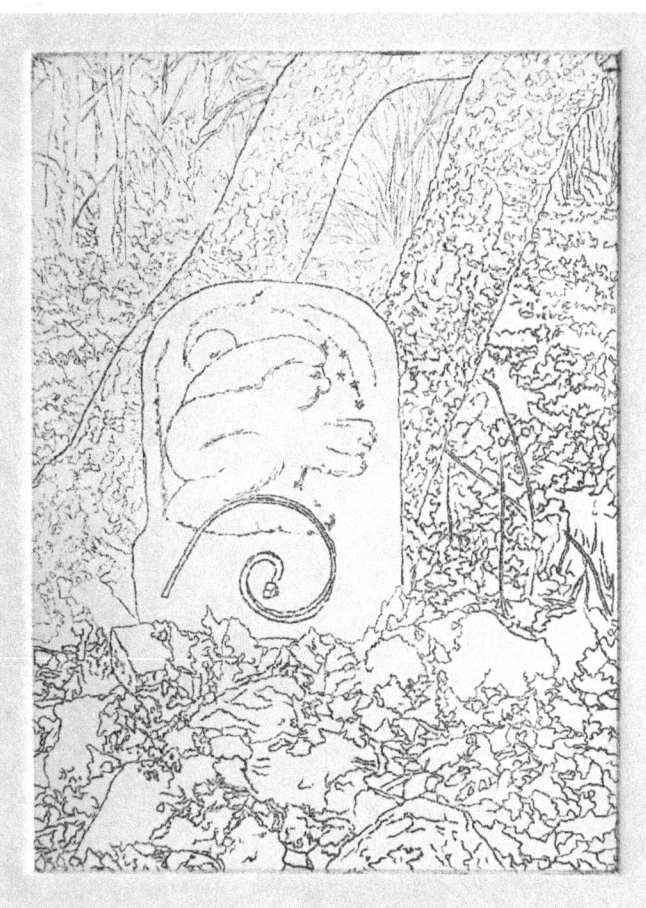

FIGURE 6.35

The next step was to apply some texture to the sculpture. I used the same method and materials as in the previous image, "Trio," except that I ground the mixture of crushed rosin and cornmeal a bit finer. I painted some diluted PG-11 on to the area to be textured and sprinkled some rosin and cornmeal into it after stopping out the rest of the plate with SO-11 and dipping it in vinegar so that the diluted PG-11 would not dissolve the SO-11 stopout.

I etched this texture to a nominal 40%, which was 1 minute and 52 seconds in the acid (Figure 6.36).

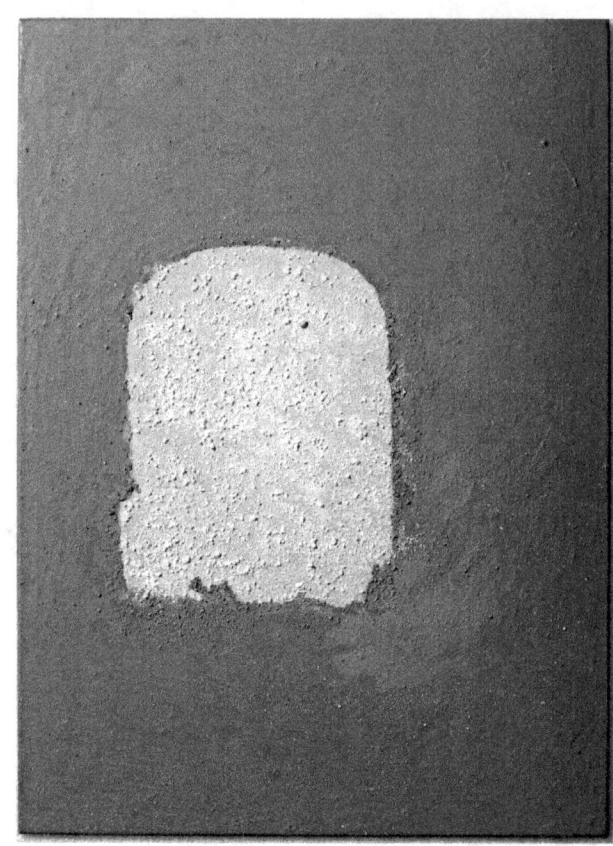

FIGURE
6.36

Figure 6.37 is a proof print of the plate at this stage, with lines and the 40% texture on the sculpture.

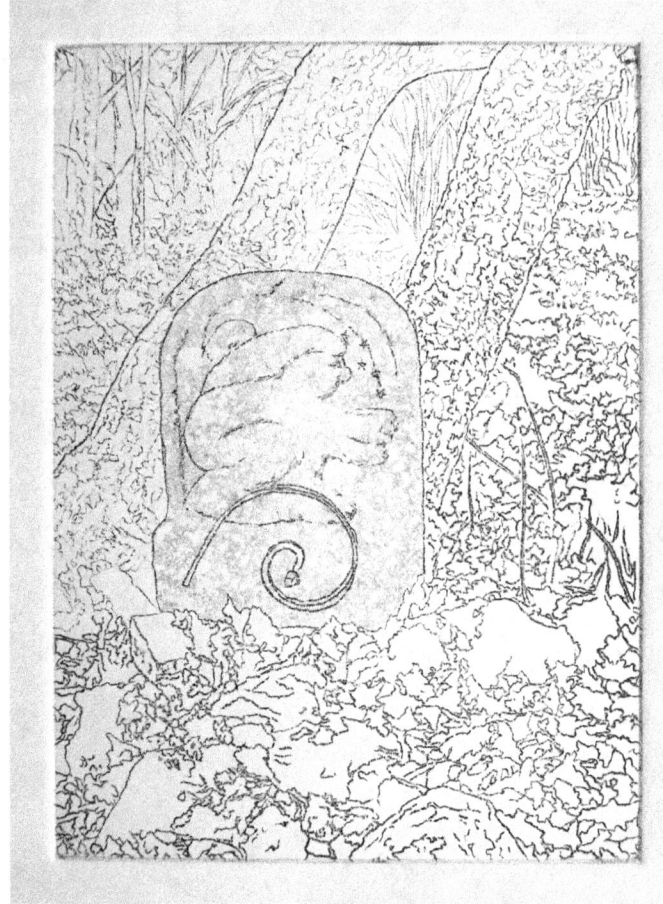

FIGURE
6.37

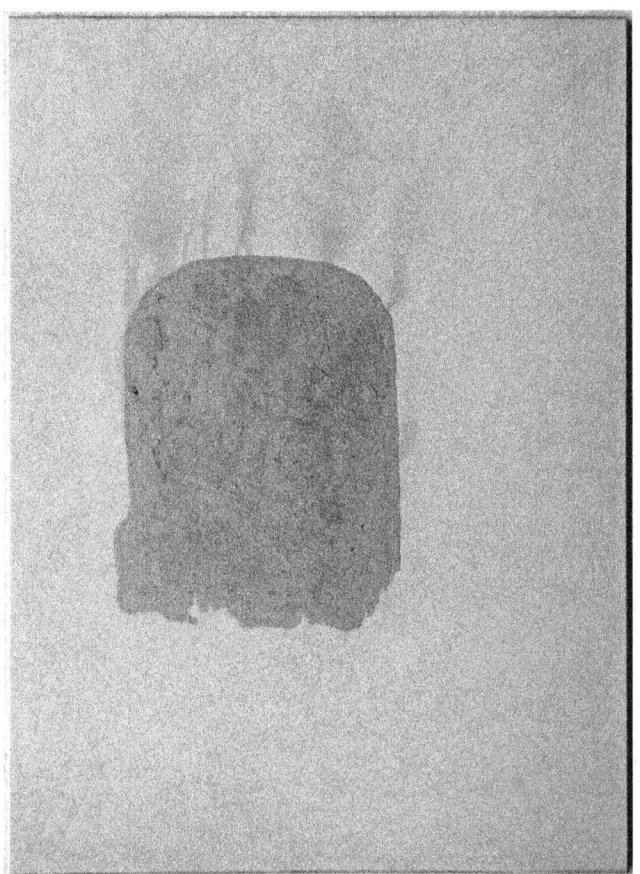

Next I wanted to apply a flat 40% tone over all the non-sculpture part of the plate, so I stopped out the sculpture with SO-11 and spattered the plate with PG-11 from an airbrush. I etched this in 1:1 ferric chloride for 1 minute and 52 seconds for a nominal 40% tone.

The ominous-looking discoloration was caused by trace ferric chloride draining from the stopped out area during rinsing.

FIGURE
6.38

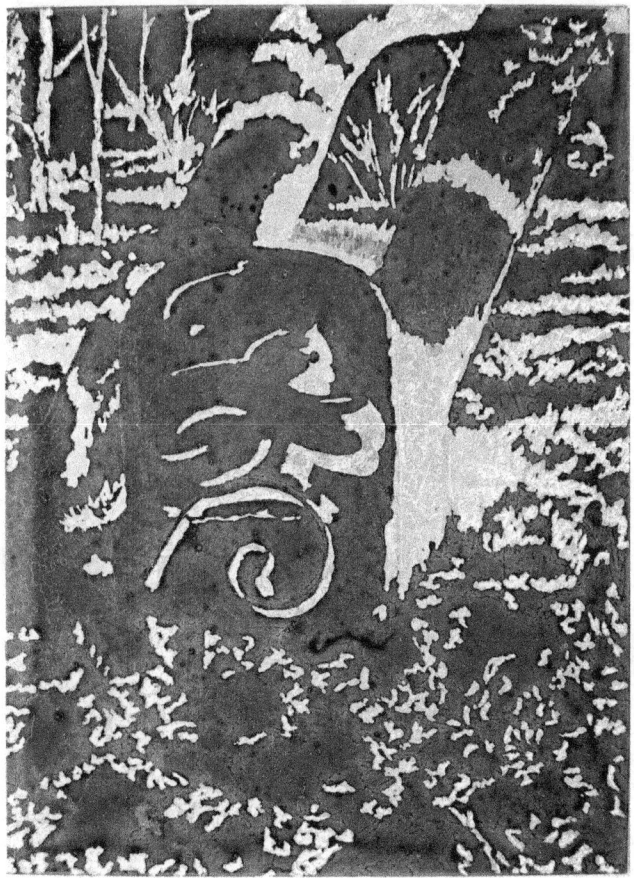

I wanted some detailed dark shadow areas, so again, as in "Trio" above, I transferred reference lines and tones to the plate with a titanium white dry pigment transfer sheet, applied sugar lift medium (condensed milk with bone black pigment in it), coated it with a thin layer of asphaltum-based soft ground and lifted it with a water jet from a spray bottle.

The plate is seen here with the areas to print as dark shadows lifted (the light areas on the plate) and the rest of the plate (the dark areas) covered with the asphaltum soft ground. (What you see is the opposite of what you will get.)

FIGURE
6.39

To etch the dark shadows I spattered the plate with PG-11 from an airbrush, this time with 10 lbs. of air pressure instead of the usual 20 lbs., for a slightly coarser spatter. I put the plate in the acid for 1 minute and 52 seconds, for an additional nominal 40% of tone on top of the 40% of tone that was already there. One might expect that would make an 80% tone, but inspection of the plate suggested that it wasn't that dark, so I decided to go darker, but only in the foreground and not on the sculpture.

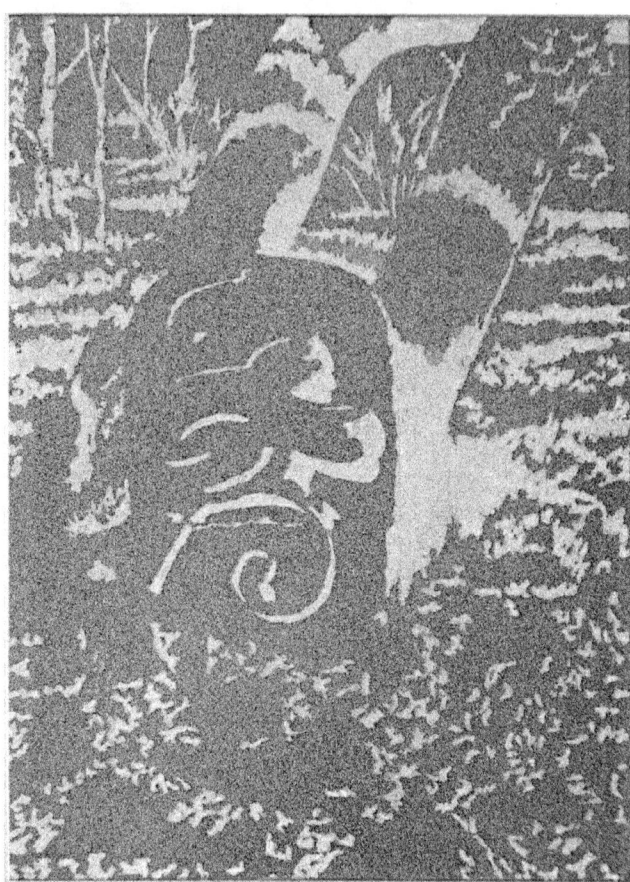

FIGURE 6.40

So, I stopped out the open areas on the sculpture with SO-11 and with the airbrush sprayed additional PG-11 on the plate, mostly in the top portion, fading it to the middle of the plate to give me a smoothly graded tone that would be lighter at the top (where enough PG-11 was added to the existing spatter to completely block the plate out) and darker toward the bottom of the plate (where it was left open, having only the initial application of spatter).

I then put the plate in the acid for 5 minutes and 35 seconds, which is what the 20-minute chart calls for to darken a 40% etch to a 70% etch.

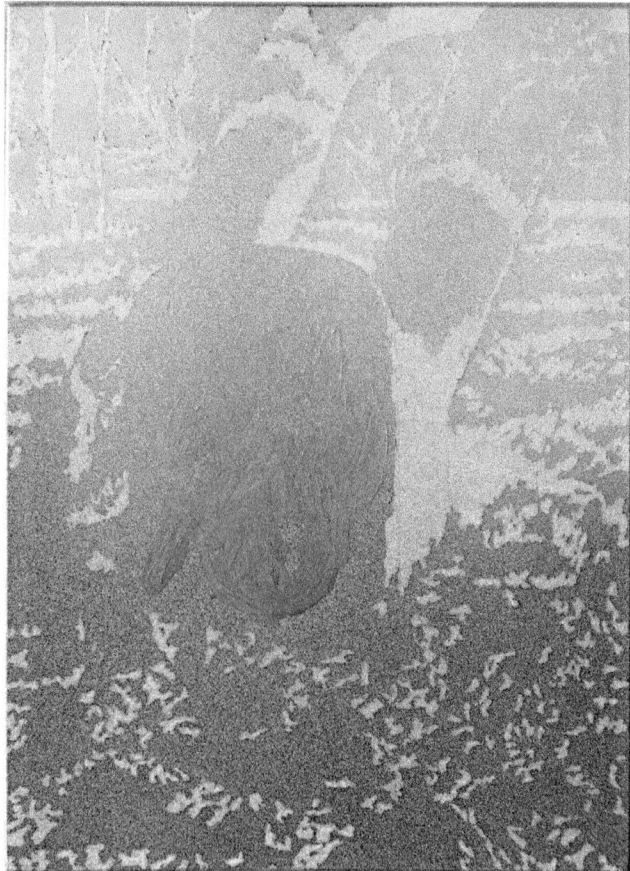

FIGURE 6.41

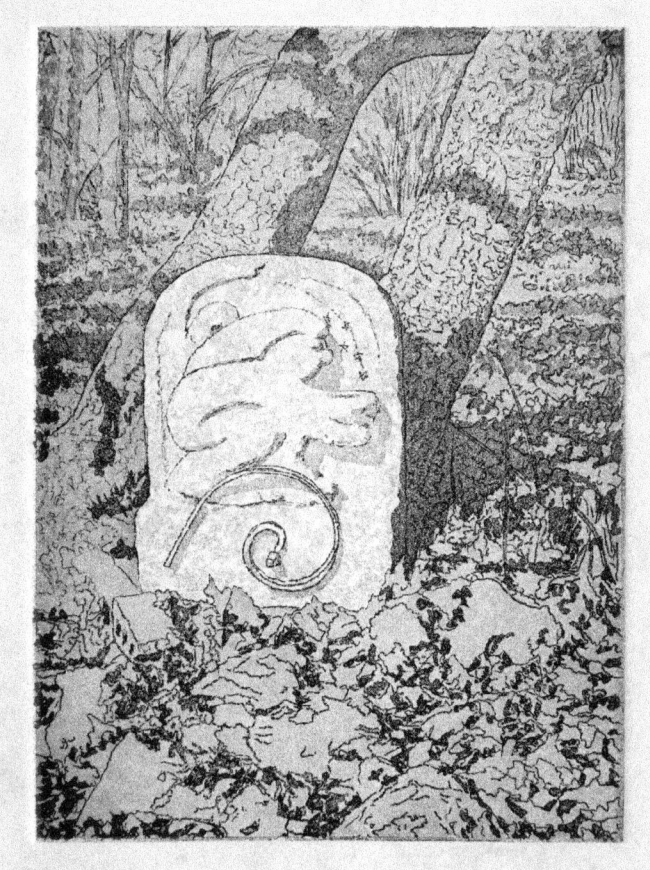

This is a state proof of the plate after the above steps. It's almost complete, but a couple of things are missing. The swirl at the base of the sculpture is wrought iron and needs some dark tone on it, and there is a line missing from the sculpture. So I put a patch of PG-11 Medium on the sculpture in which I could make a pencil overlay line, and stopped out everything else except the wrought iron swirl. Then I spattered the swirl with PG-11 for some tone and put it in the acid for 6 minutes.

FIGURE
6.42

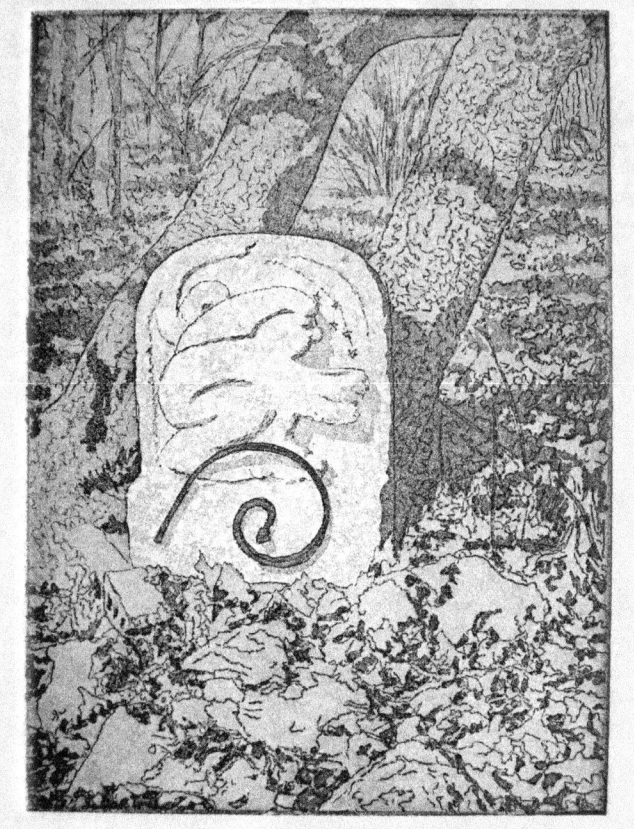

This is the final proof. The sculpture has the line, and the swirl looks like wrought iron.

FIGURE
6.43

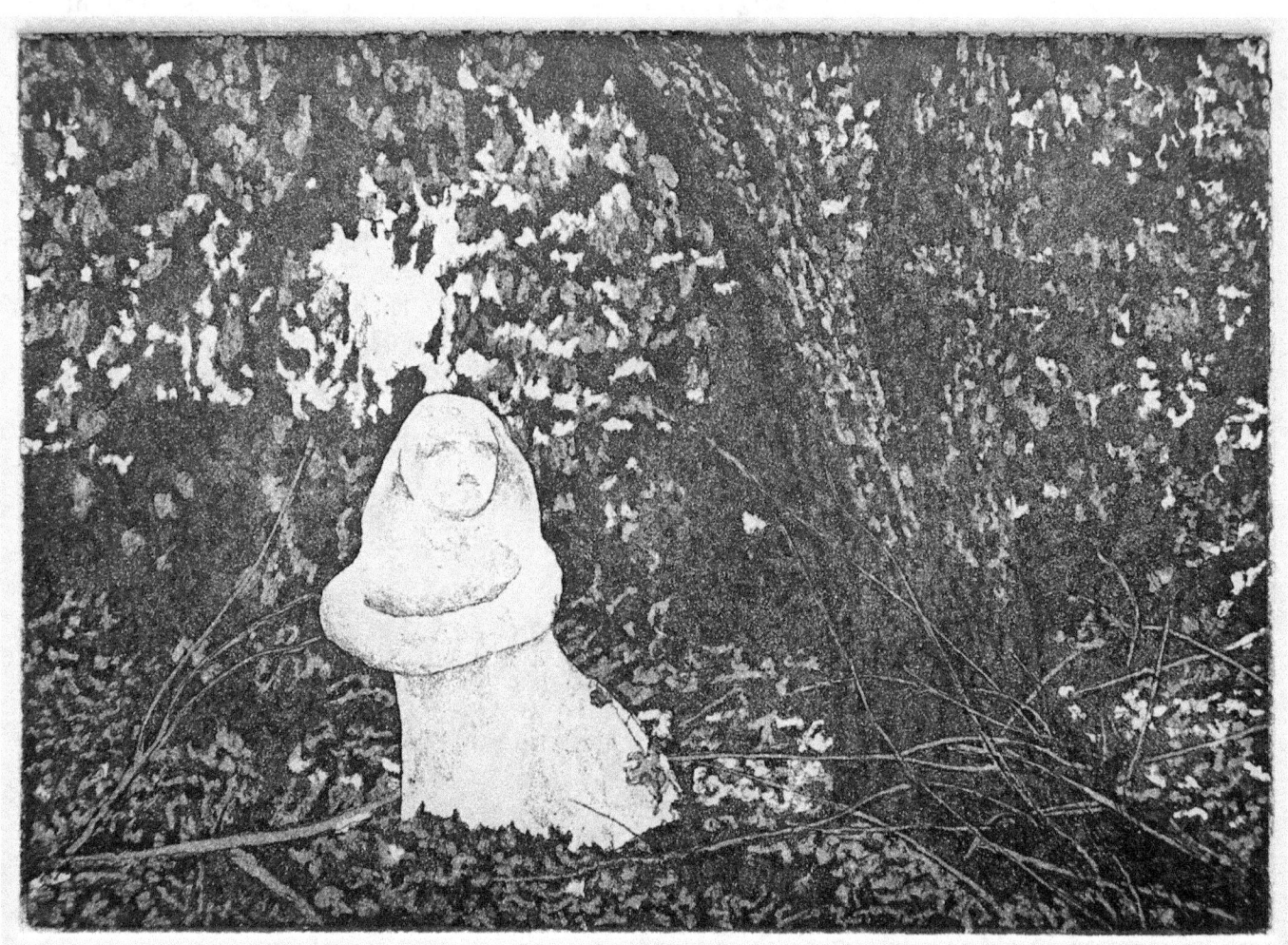

"Birdbath," etching by
Richard Stauffacher.

5. Birdbath (Soft Ground Lines and Tones, Aquatint)

(Plate size: 5x7 in. Etchant: 1:1 ferric chloride. Target percentages of tone are based on the 20-minute timing chart.)

Figure 6.44 shows the line tracing I worked from to create the lines as well as the tones on the figure.

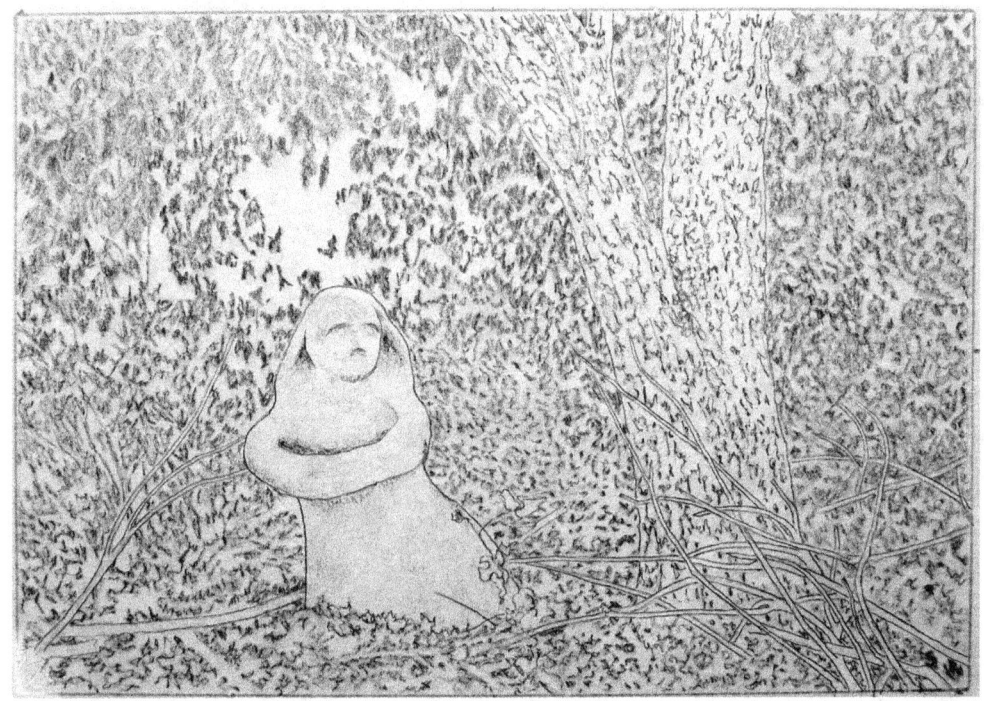

FIGURE 6.44

Figure 6.45 is the grounded plate with the lines impressed in the ground. I wanted the lines to be fairly strong and distinct, so I applied a thin airbrushed layer of SO-11. The dark brown color of the SO-11 made the lines on the tracing hard to see, so I airbrushed a thin layer of PG-11 on top of the SO-11, which dried to a light gray against which the lines on the tracing were clearly visible. I then laid the tracing on top of the plate and drew over the lines with the same pencils I used to make the tracing: a 0.5 mm HB lead for the contours, a .046 in. (1.1684 mm) lead for the "leaf" motif, and a 4B drawing pencil for the shading on the statue.

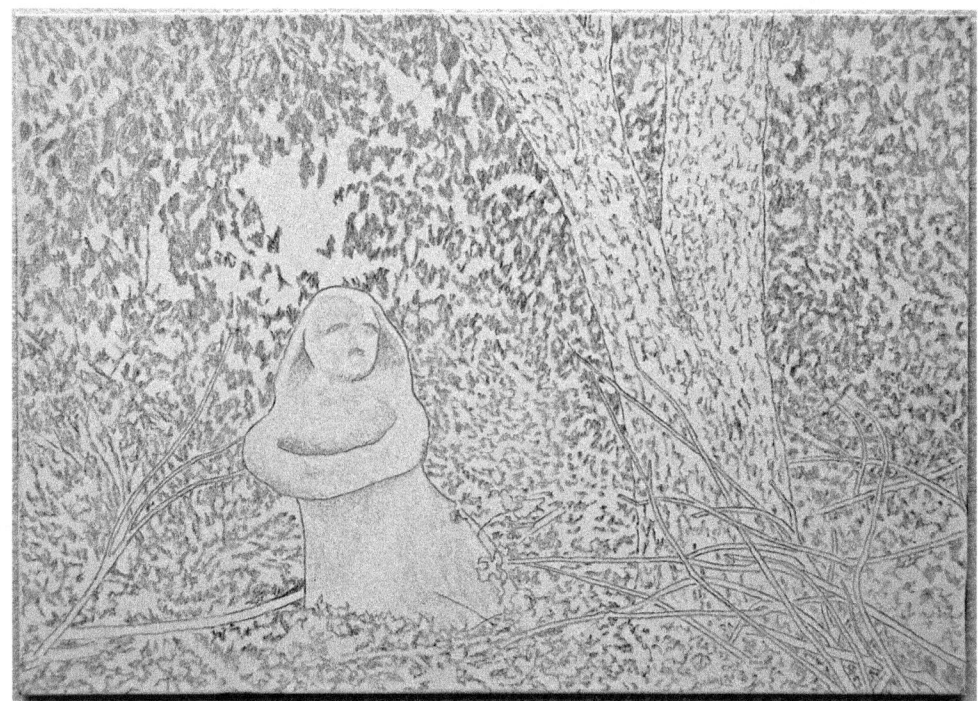

FIGURE 6.45

Figure 6.46 is a proof print of the plate after the lines had been etched for 15 minutes in 1:1 ferric chloride.

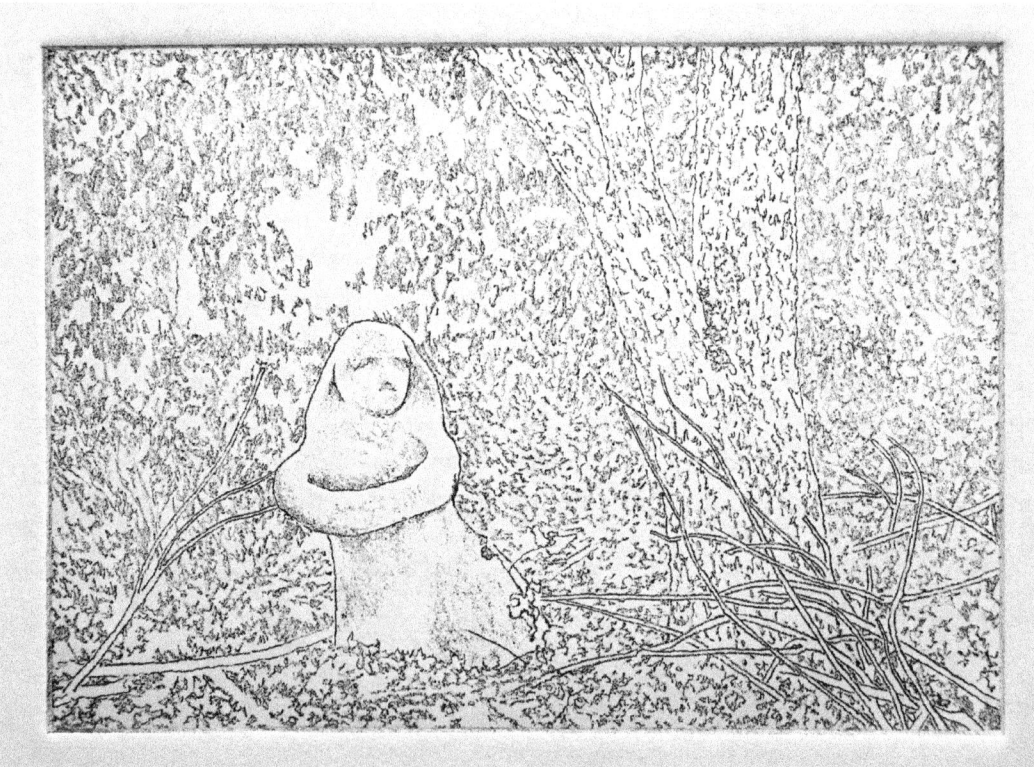

FIGURE 6.46

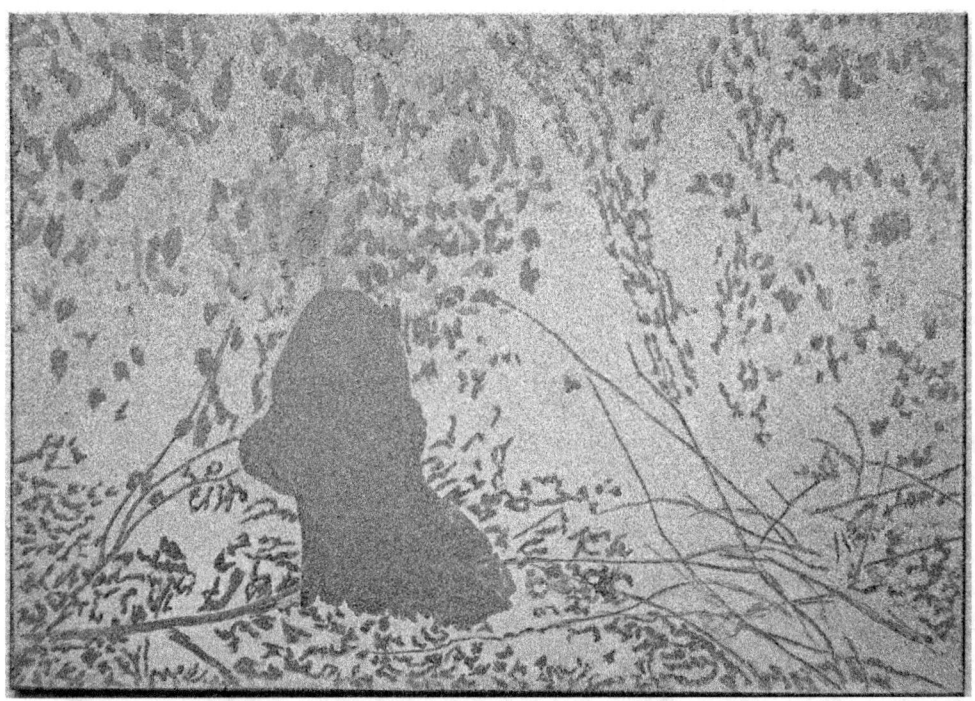

FIGURE 6.47

After etching the lines, I cleaned and proofed the plate (Figure 6.47) and then spattered the plate with PG-11 from an airbrush for an aquatint. I put the plate in the acid for 18 seconds to etch a 10% tone over everything. I then stopped out everything that was to print at 10% tone ("whites") with SO-11 and put the plate back in the acid for an additional minute and 34 seconds for a 40% tone, and stopped out everything that was to get 40% tone.

The plate (Figure 6.47) has the 10% and 40% tones etched and stopped out, ready to go to 70% tone. I was working here from tracings. I made three tonal tracings: one for "white" (10%), one for "medium" (40%), and one for "medium dark" (70%), which I transferred to the plate at each step using a transfer sheet made of tissue paper and lampblack dry pigment. There would also be a "dark" (90%), which didn't have a tracing because it would be whatever was left open after stopping out the 70%.

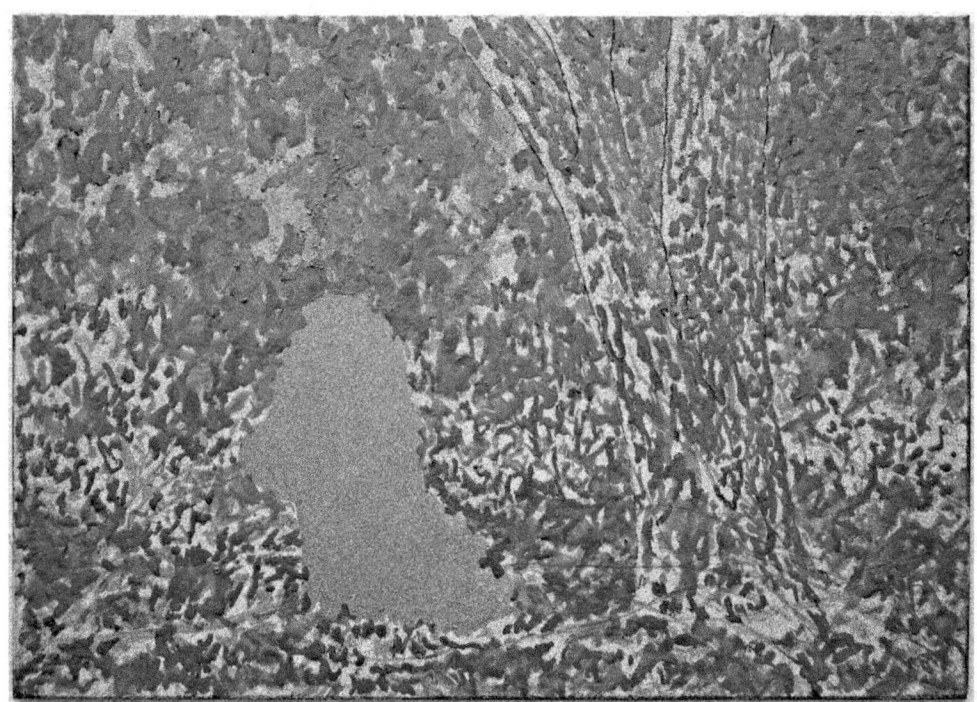

FIGURE 6.48

Figure 6.48 is the plate near the end of the tonal (aquatint) step biting process, ready to be etched to 90% tone. Tones of 10%, 40%, and 70% have been etched and stopped out. I ended up improvising broadly on stopping out the 70% because I realized I was going to have way too much 90% if I went strictly by the tracing.

Figure 6.49 shows a proof print from the plate, after the above steps.

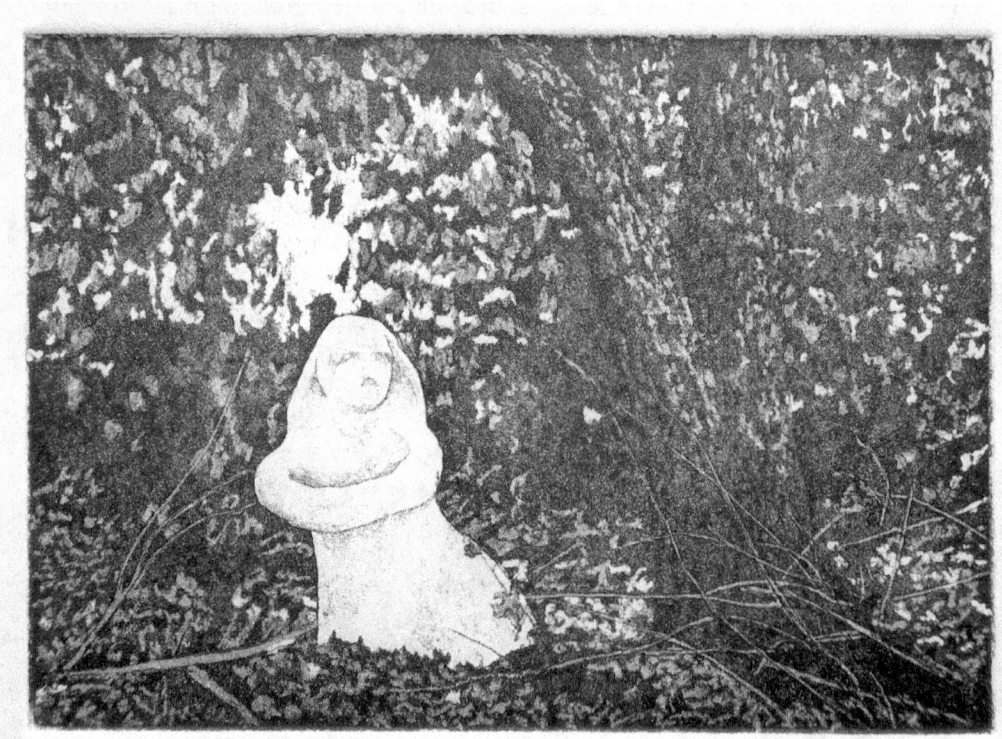

FIGURE 6.49

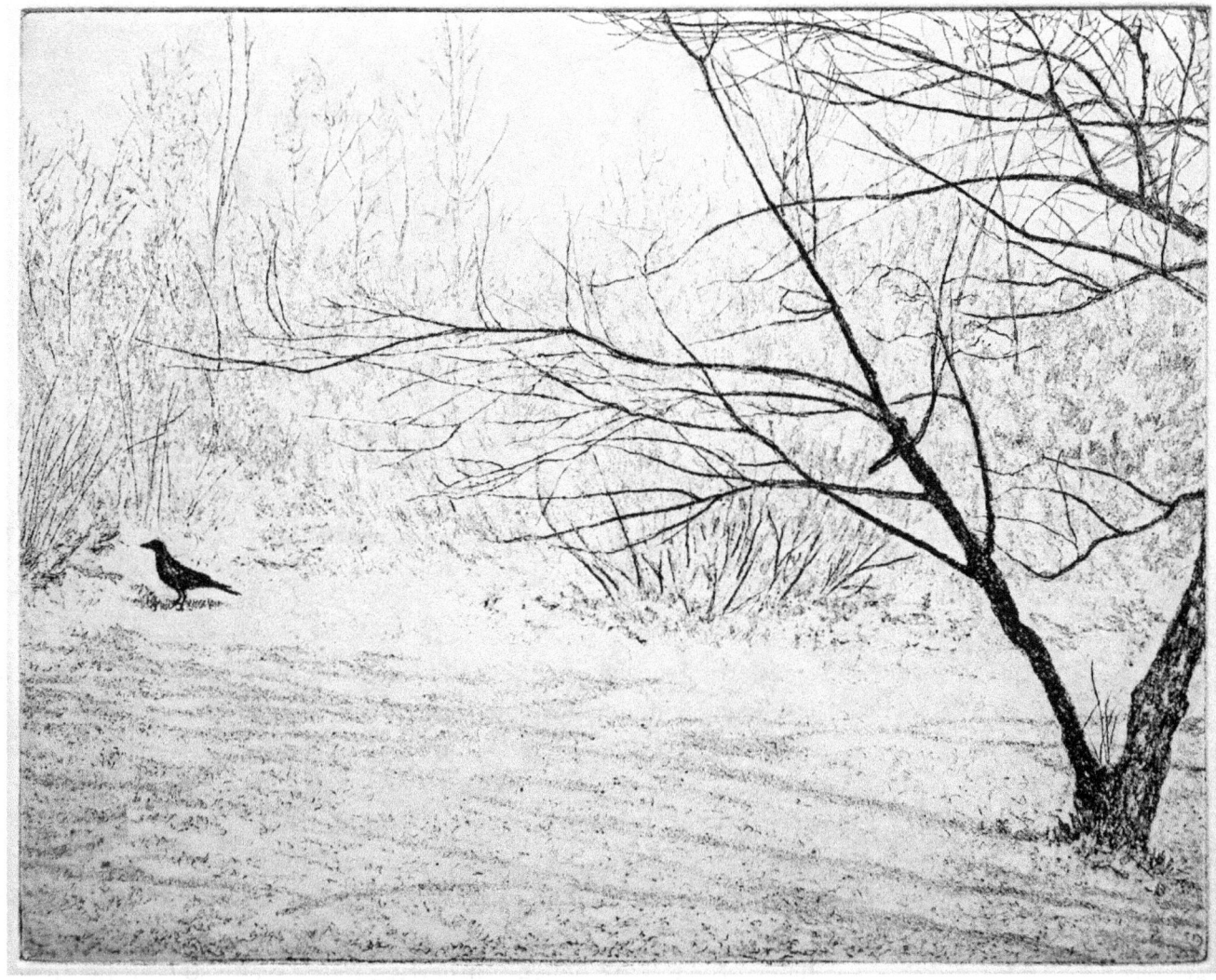

"Winter Crow," etching by
Richard Stauffacher.

6. Winter Crow (Soft Ground Lines)

(Plate size: 8x10 in. Etchant: 1:1 ferric chloride.)

I wanted to explore the soft ground technique of creating lines and tones by using paper overlays. Basically, you coat the plate with a thin layer of a soft ground and then lay a piece of paper over it and draw on the paper. The pressure from the pencil point presses the paper into the ground (creating places where the acid can get through) and some of the ground sticks to the paper and is lifted off of the plate, creating more openings for the acid to get through and etch the copper. Instead of the sharp, crisp, etched lines resulting from an etching needle and hard ground, this method results in more of a charcoal effect.

Accurate registration of the various tracings in relationship with the plate is important since you can't see lines already etched on the plate when you're drawing on the overlay to create more lines or tones.

Figure 6.50 shows the registration system I used. (Here I was

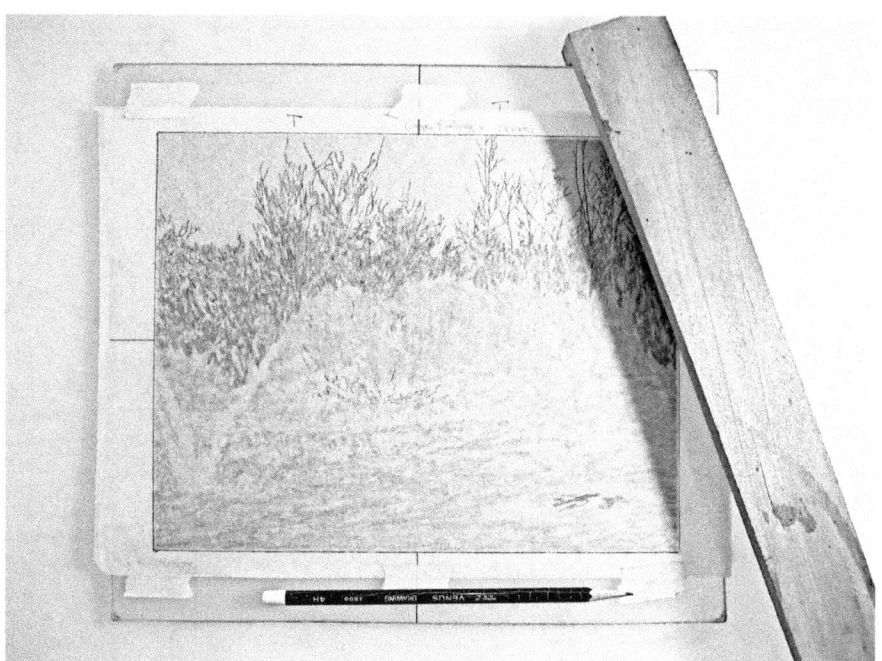

FIGURE 6.50

transferring the lightest lines and tones to the plate, using a 3H mechanical pencil with 0.5 mm lead, and a 4H drawing pencil.)

I mounted everything on a piece of clear plastic. I made a mark on the back of the plate to identify the top edge and then traced the perimeter of the plate on to the plastic with a fine point Sharpie pen. I similarly traced the plate perimeter on each of the tracing paper overlays and the photograph I was working from. On each of the overlay tracings I marked the top with a "T" at the top on the right side. I flipped the tracings when transferring to the plate (so that the image would be back to the original orientation when printed from the plate) so by putting the "T" on the right side I had a visual cue. If the "T" was on the right side, the image hadn't been flipped; and if it was on the left side, it had been flipped.

Another reason to flip the tracings is because as you draw over the lines with a pencil, the lines are darkened and you can see which ones you have traced over and which ones you haven't. Also if you find that you need to use the tracing a second or third time, you can erase the graphite on the back side and still have the original lines on the front side ready to be re-used.

Besides tracing the perimeter of the plate on the plastic base, photograph, and each overlay, I carefully measured the center point of each side on the plastic base, laid a ruler across vertical and horizontal centers and drew registration lines across all four margins. Using a light table, I carefully transferred the registration lines to the photograph and each of the tracings from the plastic base. These registration lines in the margins were what I relied on to locate everything except the plate, for which I used the perimeter outline on the plastic base. I secured the plate to the base with two small loops of masking tape, sticky side out, near the bottom of the plate. This system seemed to work well enough.

I was interested in experimenting with things like the effect of drying time on the grounds, effects from using different kinds of pencils, effects from using different kinds of papers between the tracing and the ground (underlays), and which applications of grounds work best (thick, thin, combinations, etc.).

Figure 6.50 shows the "grays" tracing, partially transferred. Figure 6.51 is the tracing for the "darks." I wanted to ensure a visible difference between the grays and the darks so I used an underlay of baker's parchment with the gray transfer and an underlay of tracing paper with the darks transfer. Baker's parchment is a non-stick material, so it doesn't lift any of the ground off of the plate during line transfers. This gives a very muted result, since the acid can only get through perforations made by pressure, and none from ground removal. In my experience, baker's parchment lifts ground the least; tissue paper and tracing paper are almost equal, with tissue paper lifting slightly less than tracing paper; and waxed paper lifts the most, giving the darkest results. For transferring the darks I used a 3H 0.5 mm mechanical pencil and a 4H drawing pencil, the same as for the grays.

Visibility is also a major issue with underlays. If you lay a tracing with dark lines on a plate coated with a dark ground, the lines tend to disappear. A light-colored sheet of something between the tracing and the dark ground makes the lines visible.

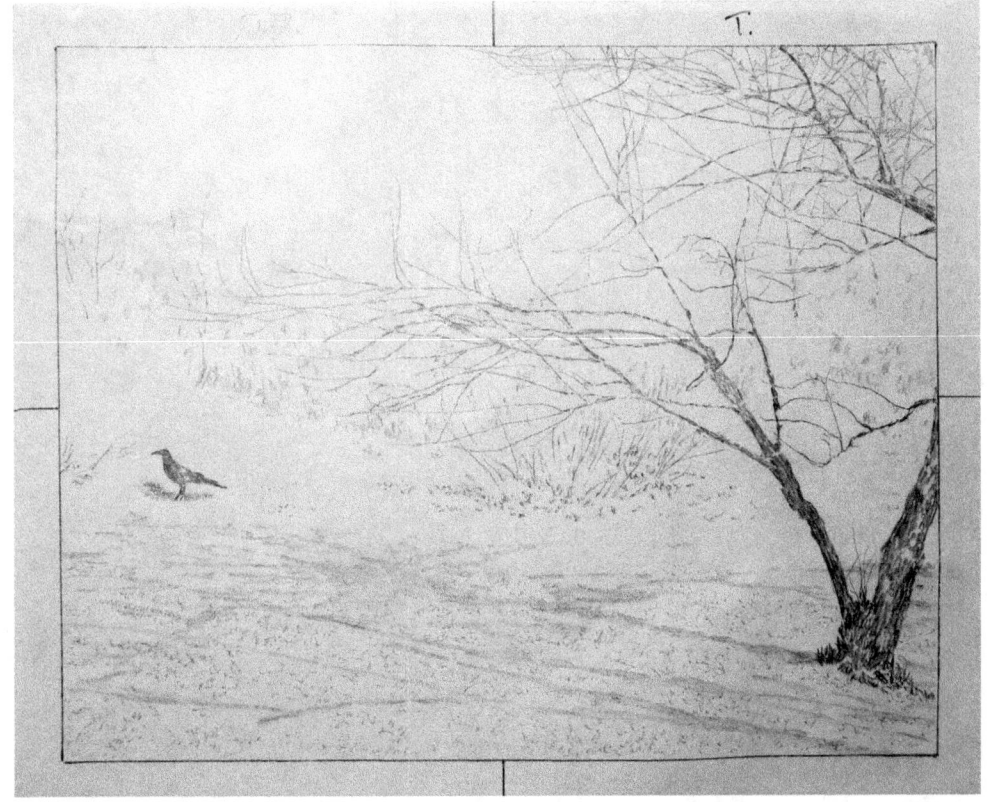

FIGURE 6.51

I airbrushed the plate with SO-11, let dry and immersed in vinegar, and by the time I got around to doing the line transfers it had been on the plate for three full days. I etched it on the morning of the fourth day. I wouldn't recommend waiting that long because all soft grounds I've had experience with harden over time, but this seemed like an opportunity to see how this would behave.

There were quite a few interesting highlights in the photograph I was working from, so I wanted to see if I could capture some of them by transferring ground onto the plate from a sheet of paper (an underlay) with an overlay (a tracing) on top of it: a "stopout transfer." These would show up as "whites." My underlay for this was a piece of waxed paper with a layer of PG-11 airbrushed on to it. PG-11 adheres less strongly to surfaces than SO-11, so it transferred well from the waxed paper to the plate.

Figure 6.52 is the "whites" tracing paper overlay.

Figure 6.53 is the plate (attached to its clear plastic base, with register marks) after all the above steps. I used a 0.5 mm mechanical pencil with HB lead and medium to light pressure to transfer the white lines from the "whites" tracing.

At this stage I put the plate in the acid for 20 minutes. During and after the 20-minute bite it didn't look like much was happening so I put it in for two additional 10-minute bites for a total etch time of 40 minutes, then cleaned it and printed a proof.

Figure 6.54 is the first proof print from the plate after the steps

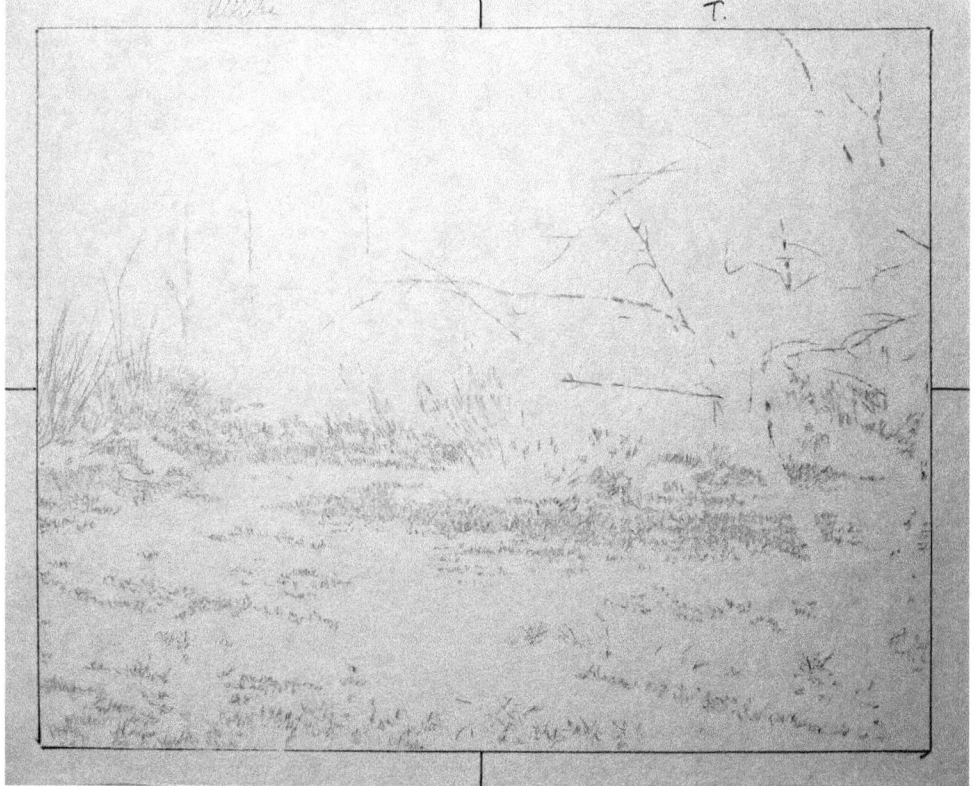

FIGURE 6.52

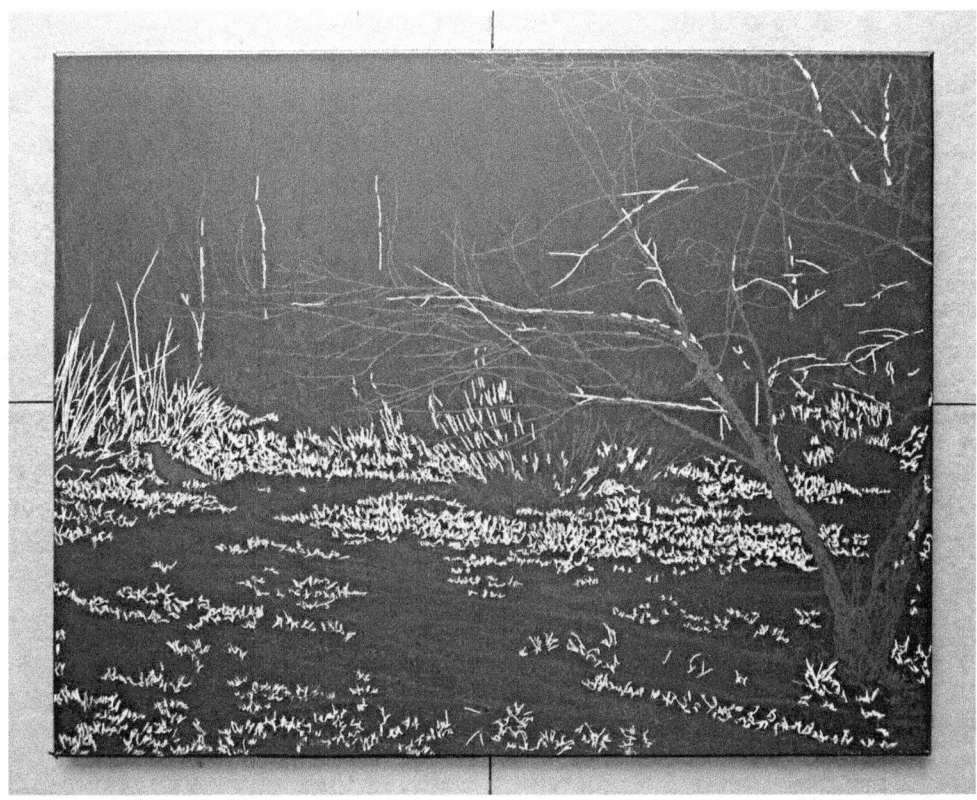

FIGURE 6.53

described above. Not a total failure, but not what I was looking for. The baker's parchment did too good a job of muting the lines and the grays were hardly more than plate tone. Also, the darks weren't nearly

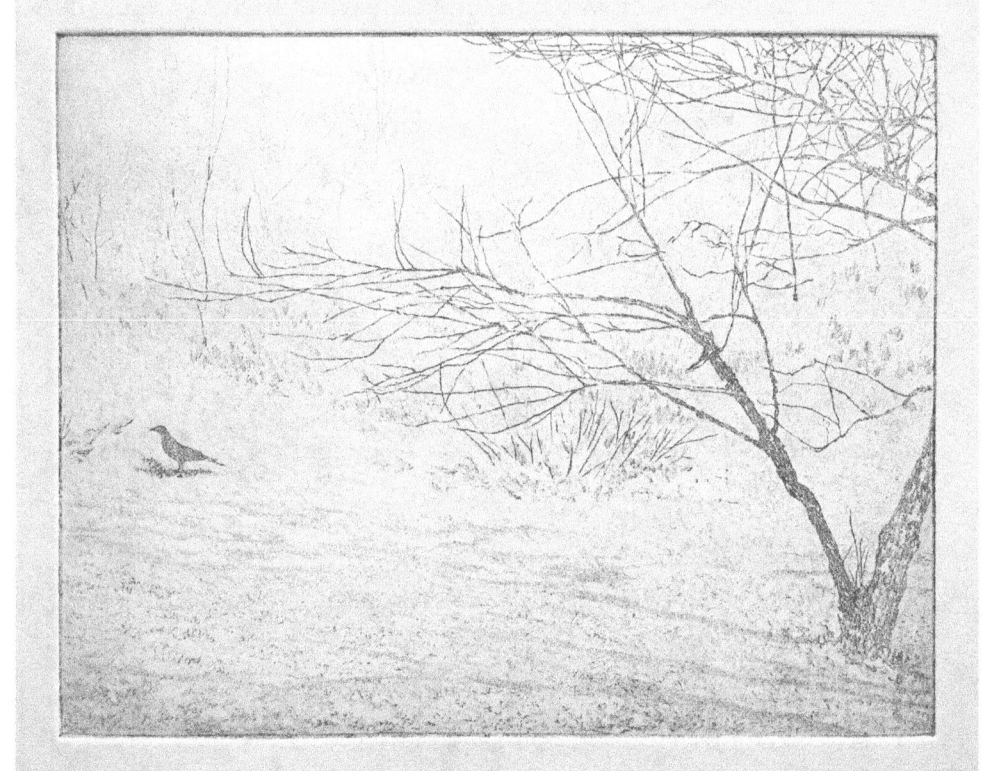

FIGURE 6.54

as strong as planned. Since most of the tones didn't happen, the whites had nothing to contrast with so they also didn't happen.

Not much to do but do it over. I erased the graphite from the backs of the three tracings (whites, grays, and darks) and coated the plate with a thin layer of SO-11. After it dried I immersed it in vinegar for 20 seconds and then "whitewashed" it with a thin coating of PG-11 to make the lines on the tracings more visible and then dipped that in vinegar.

As shown on the plate (Figure 6.55), I modified and retraced the grays with a tissue underlay, redid the darks (partially) with a tracing paper underlay, and redid the whites, abandoning the idea of highlights in favor of using them as additional darks with a tracing paper underlay. I then etched it for 20 minutes, an additional 10 minutes, and another 10 minutes. The background trees looked like they might be dark enough, so I stopped them out with SO-11 from the airbrush and etched on for three more 20-minute bites. It just didn't seem to be doing much. I cleaned and proofed the plate.

Figure 6.56 is the second proof print from the plate. The image has been bumped in the right direction, but the darks still lack a bit of punch.

I wondered if temperatures were a factor. I'd been using this ferric chloride all summer and now it was fall, with a couple of frosts; maybe the acid was getting a bit slow. So I tested it and found that it was taking about three times as long to etch as had been normal.

I got some fresh ferric chloride, airbrushed another coating of SO-11 on to the plate and redid some of the main darks with the tracing overlay and an underlay of waxed paper. I etched it for two 20-minute bites.

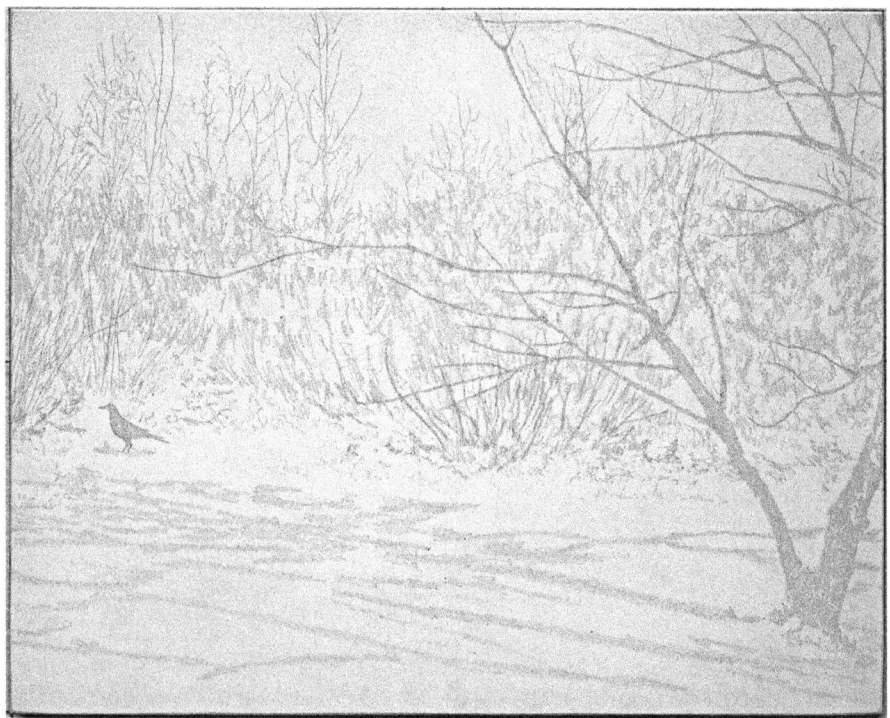

FIGURE 6.55

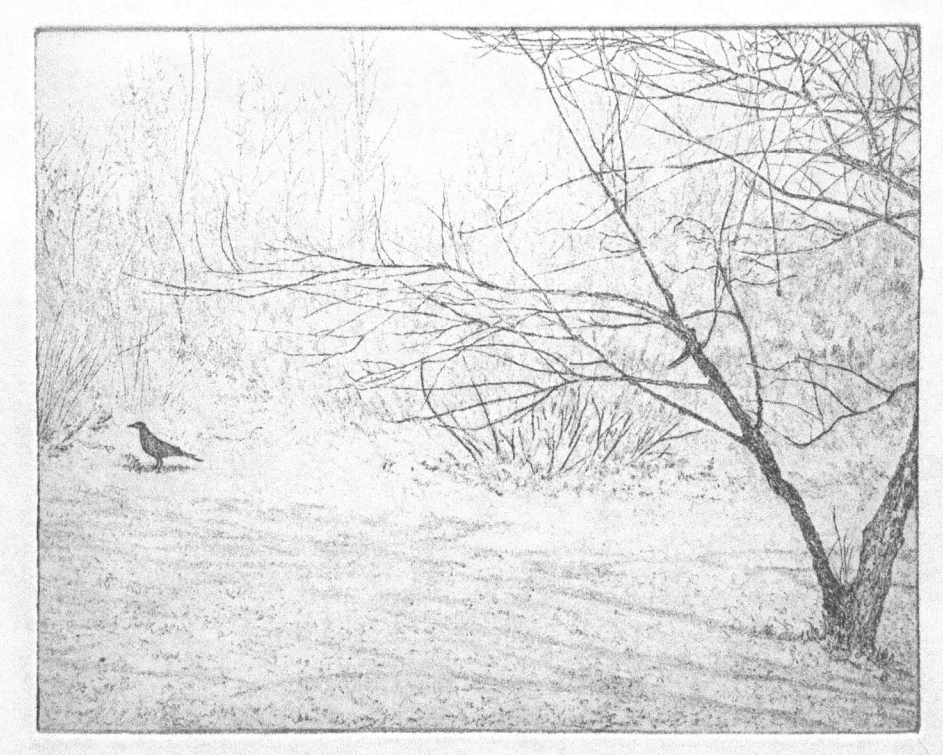

FIGURE 6.56

Figure 6.57 is the third proof print. This was more like what I was after.

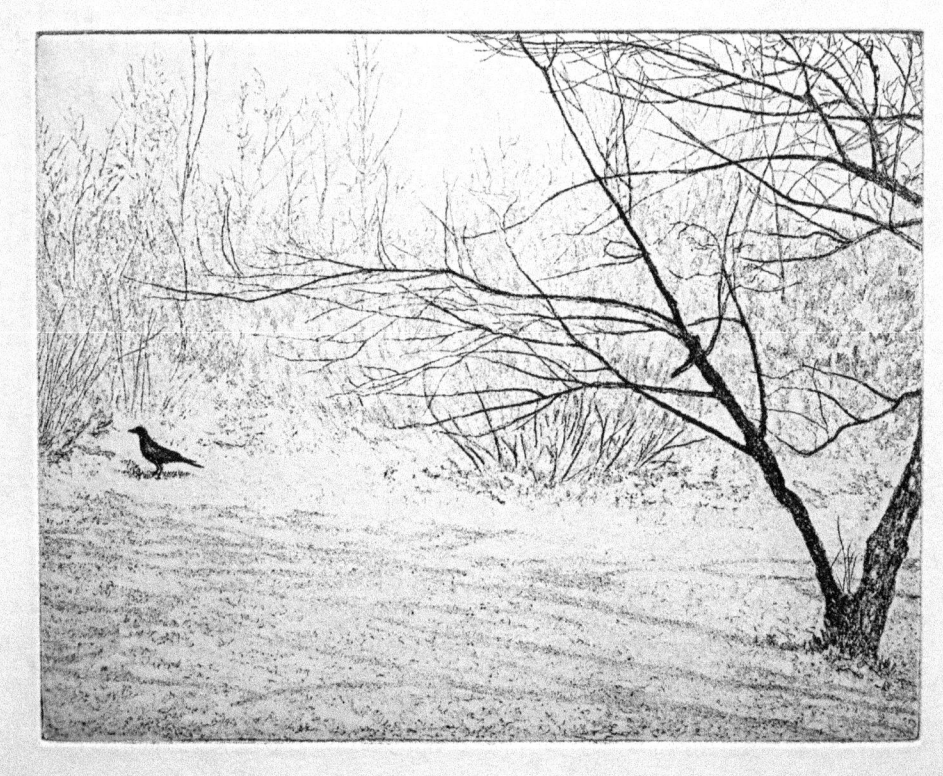

FIGURE 6.57

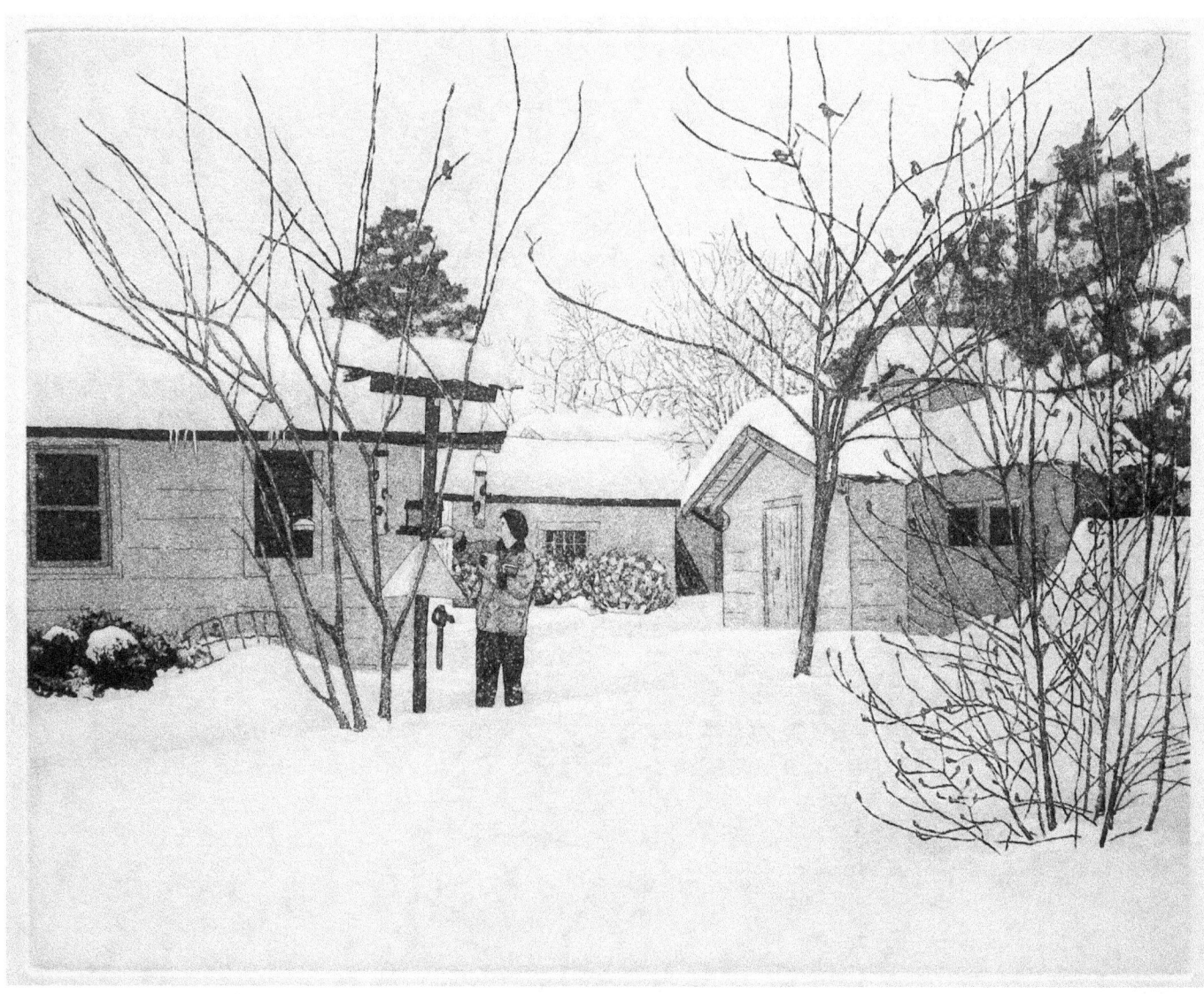

"Martha's Feeder," etching by
Richard Stauffacher.

7. Martha's Feeder (Soft Ground Lines, Hard Etched Lines, Aquatint)

(Plate size: 8x10 in. Etchant: 1:1 ferric chloride; 20-minute timing chart.)

For this plate I used four tracings—for organizational purposes and to be able to re-establish imagery on the plate at any time during production if necessary—since there were many times when the grounds made it hard to see what was already etched on the plate when adding new material.

Figure 6.58 is the tracing for background trees. Lines are to be created by impression in soft ground.

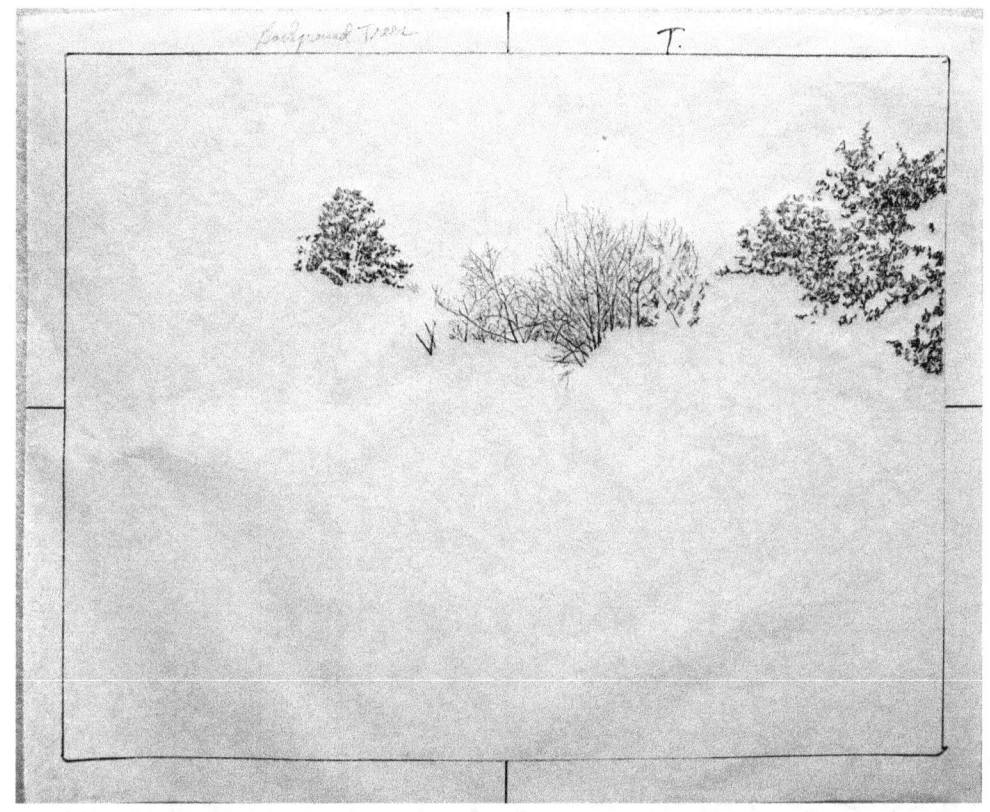

FIGURE 6.58

The tracing for middle ground material. Lines are to be created by dry pigment transfer sheet, followed by needling in the ground.

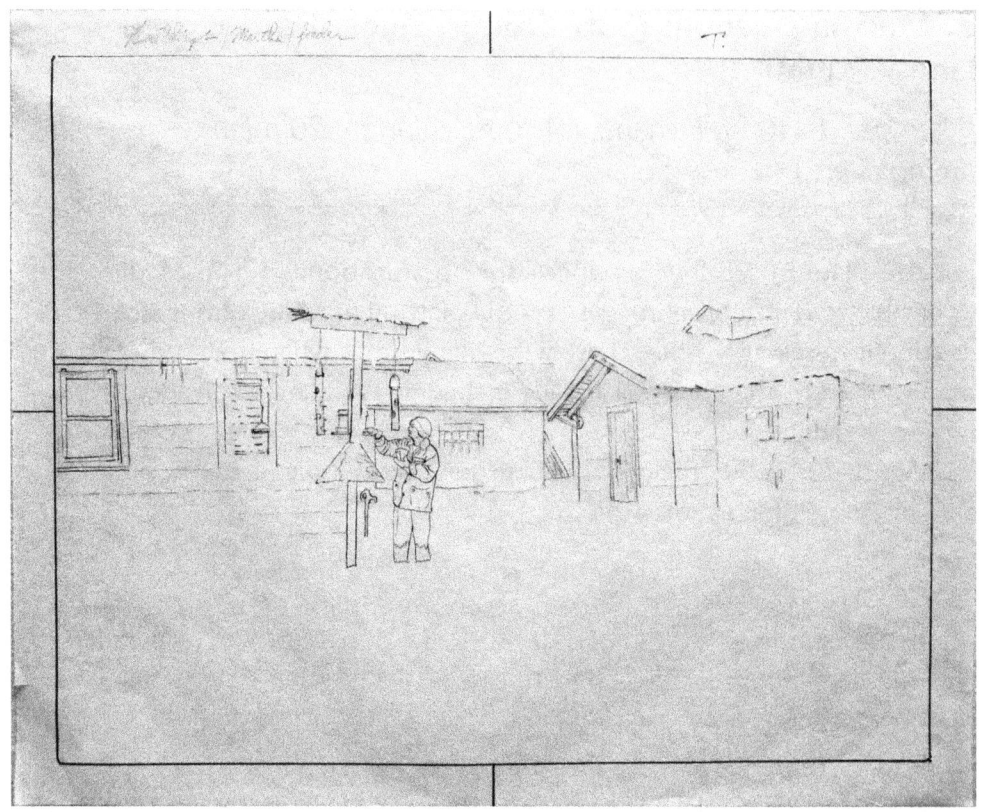

FIGURE 6.59

The tracing for foreground trees. Lines are to be created by soft ground impression.

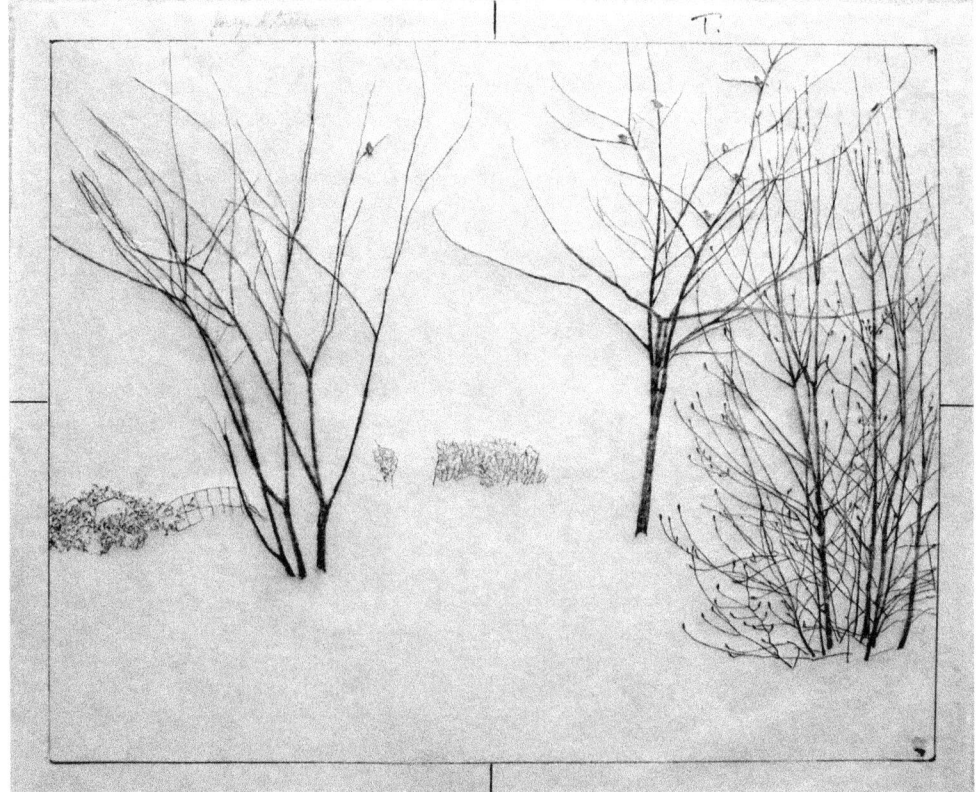

FIGURE 6.60

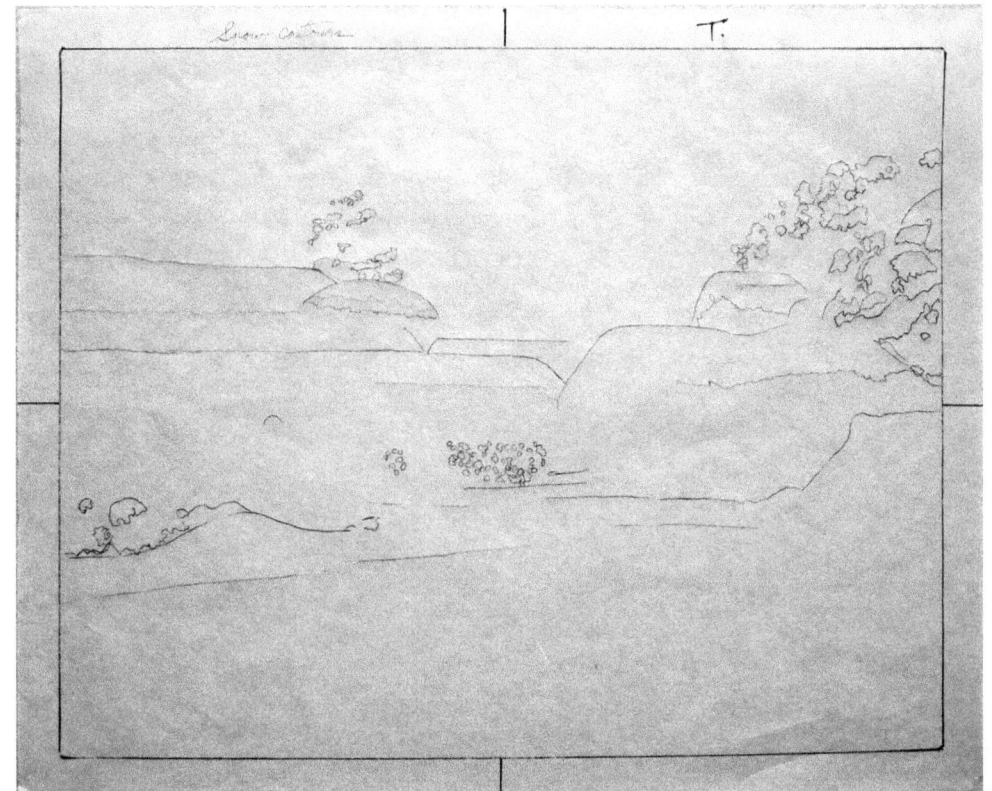

FIGURE 6.61

The tracing for snow contours. Nonprinting lines; reference only.

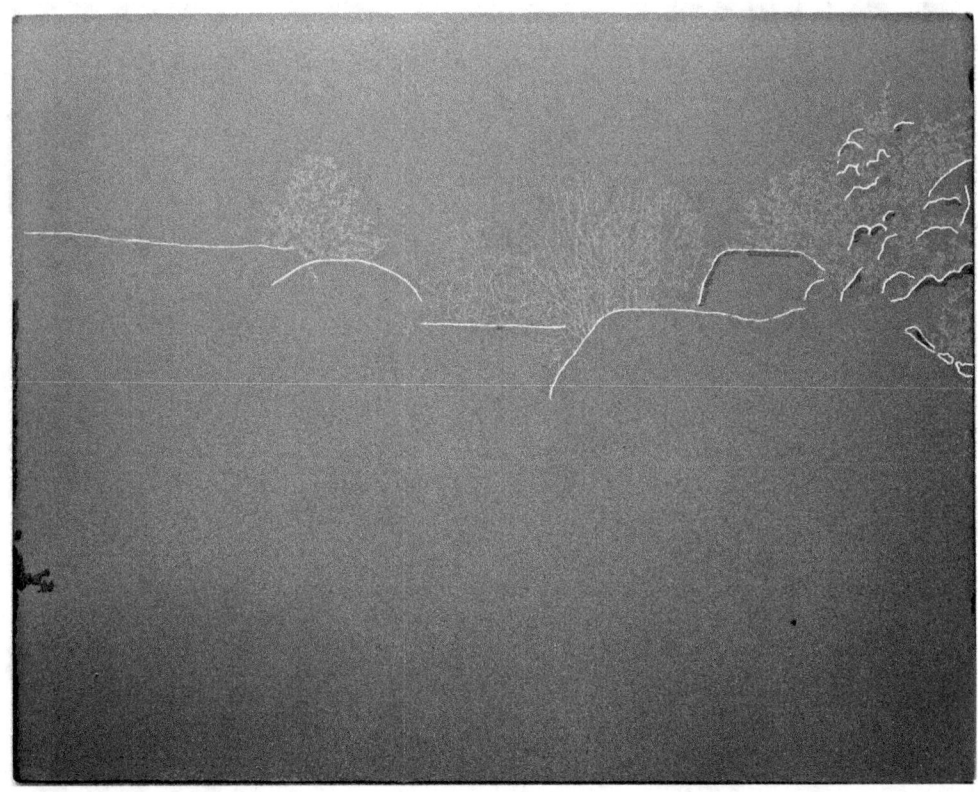

FIGURE 6.62

The first step. I impressed the lines for background trees using the tracing and a tracing paper underlay. I transferred the snow contour lines to the plate with a white dry pigment sheet to avoid having any of the tree lines penetrating snow contours. Wherever tree branches intruded into snow areas, I stopped them out to prevent their etching and appearing in the print.

The plate was coated with SO-11, applied with an airbrush. Lines were etched 15 minutes.

Step two: middle ground lines. I transferred the middle ground lines from the tracing using a light gray dry pigment transfer sheet and light pencil pressure. These lines were to be needled, for hard crisp lines. I also transferred reference lines from the foreground trees, using a light green dry pigment transfer sheet to help avoid needling lines through the tree trunks, which were to come next. (Both sets of lines show as white lines in this black and white image.)

I needled these lines and etched them for 20 minutes.

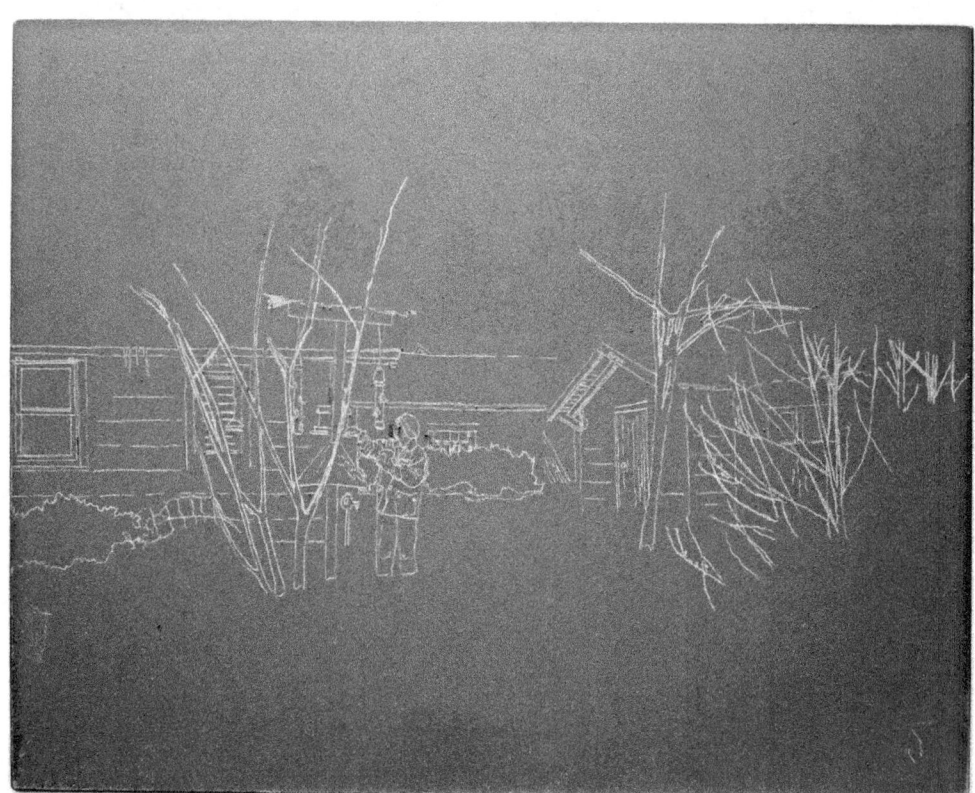

FIGURE 6.63

Step three was to transfer the foreground lines, using soft ground impression. I etched these for 15 minutes, touched up the ground and etched them for an additional 10 minutes for a total etch time of 25 minutes.

Between each of these three steps I cleaned the plate, re-coated it with SO-11 and dipped it in vinegar for 20 seconds.

I then proofed the plate.

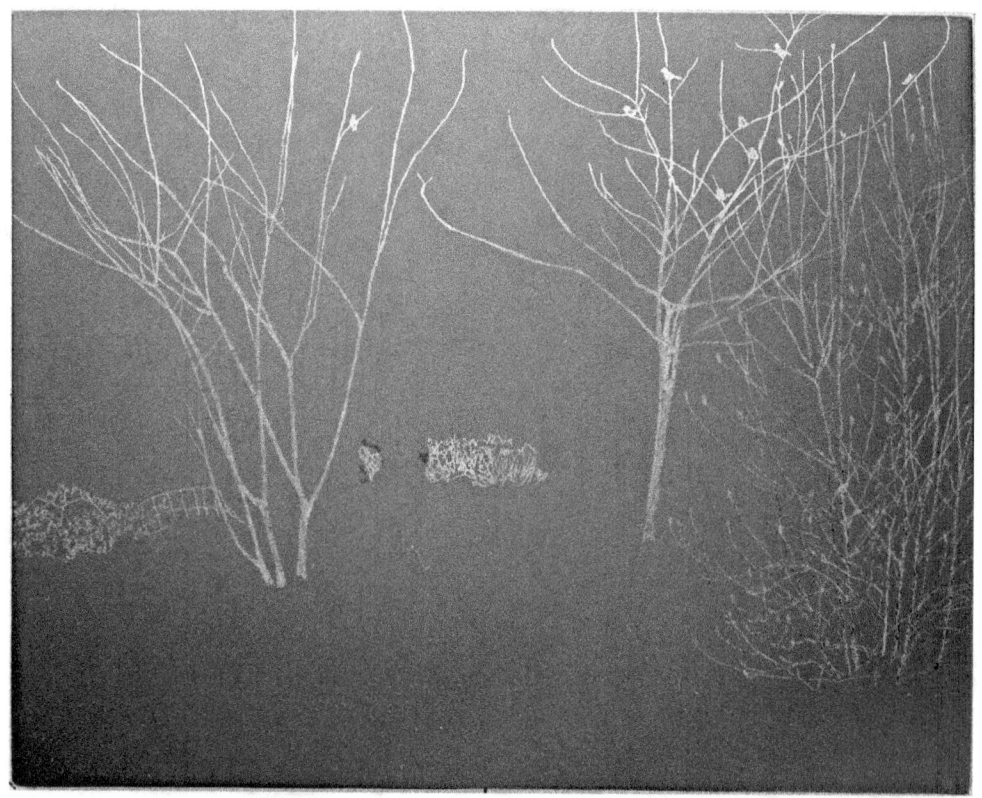

FIGURE 6.64

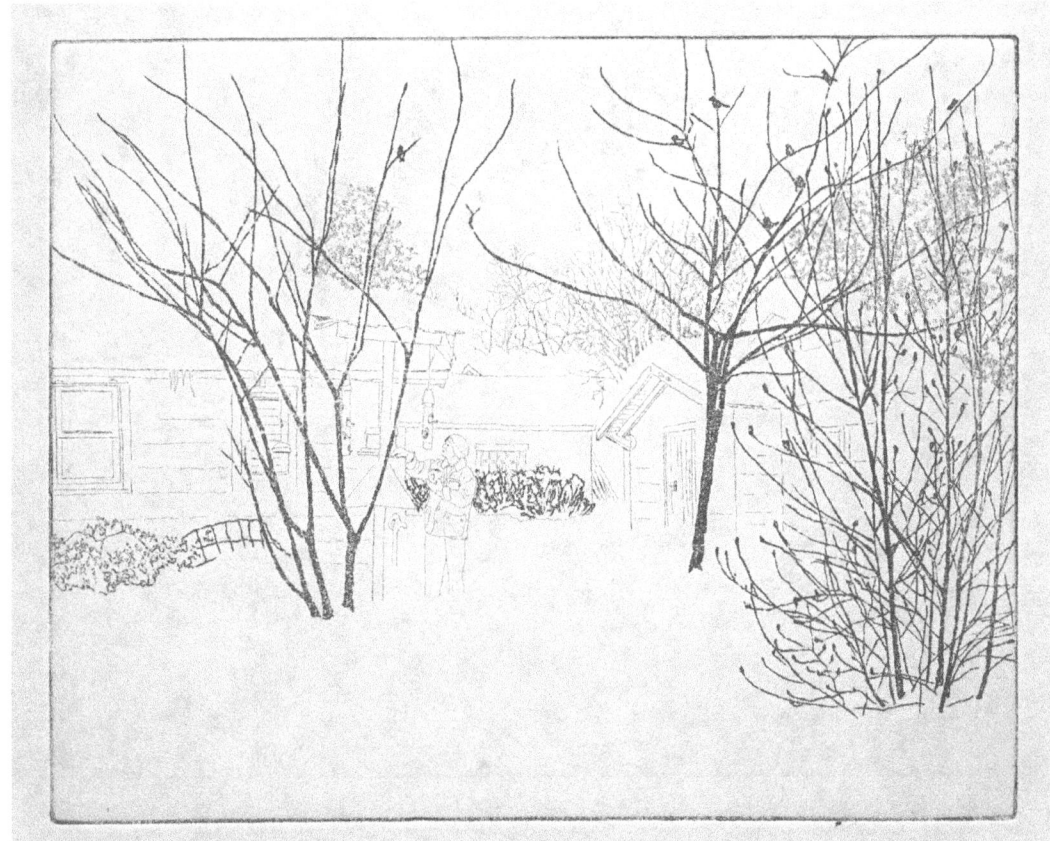

FIGURE 6.65

This is the first proof, showing the lines created by the three above steps.

FIGURE 6.66

Step four was to create tones by step biting an aquatint. This is the plate, spattered with PG-11. The discoloration, caused by dipping it in vinegar and rinsing it, didn't show up in the print. The white lines are from a dry pigment sheet, to guide the stopping out of the snow.

This was the lightest (10%) etch, which was 18 seconds in the acid and applied to the entire plate.

The sky (10%) is stopped out, and the rest of the plate is ready to go to 20% tone: an additional 16 seconds in the acid.

FIGURE 6.67

The snow, which gets 20% tone, is stopped out with SO-11. The 30% tone, which is an additional 30 seconds in the acid, has also been etched and stopped out (the wall and door of the small building) and it is ready to go to 40%: an additional 48 seconds etch time.

The major tree branches are stopped out as well, to keep them from getting too dark.

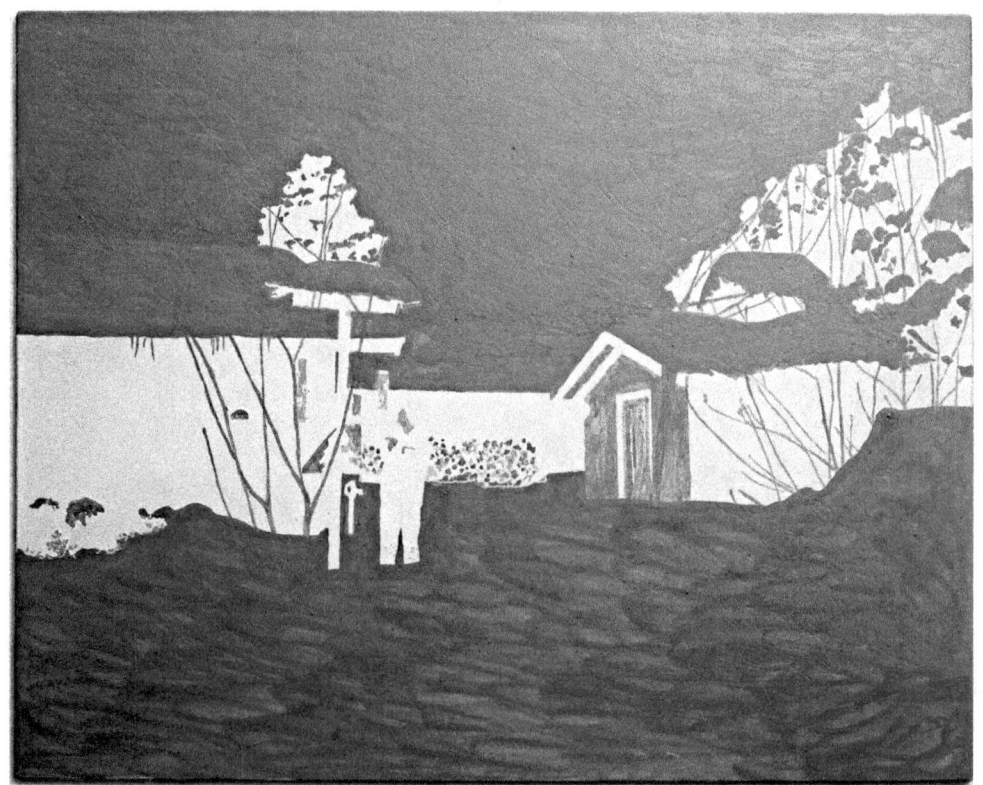

FIGURE 6.68

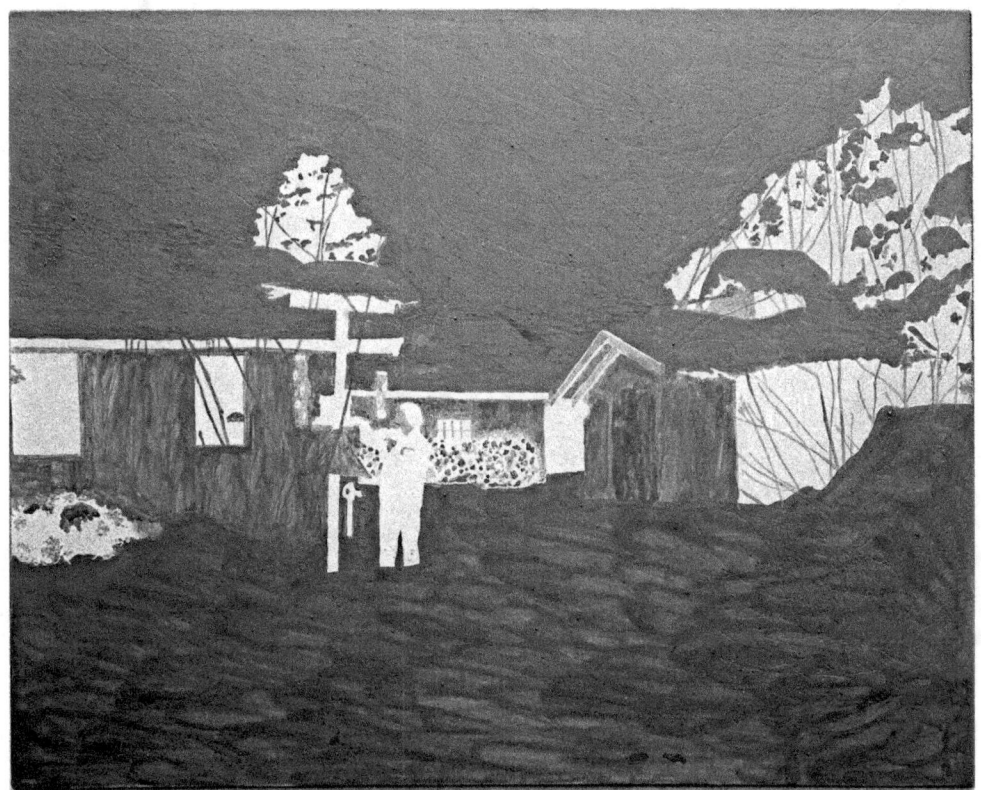

FIGURE 6.69

Here the 40% tones have been stopped out, and it's ready to go to 50%, which is an additional 1 minute and 14 seconds in the acid.

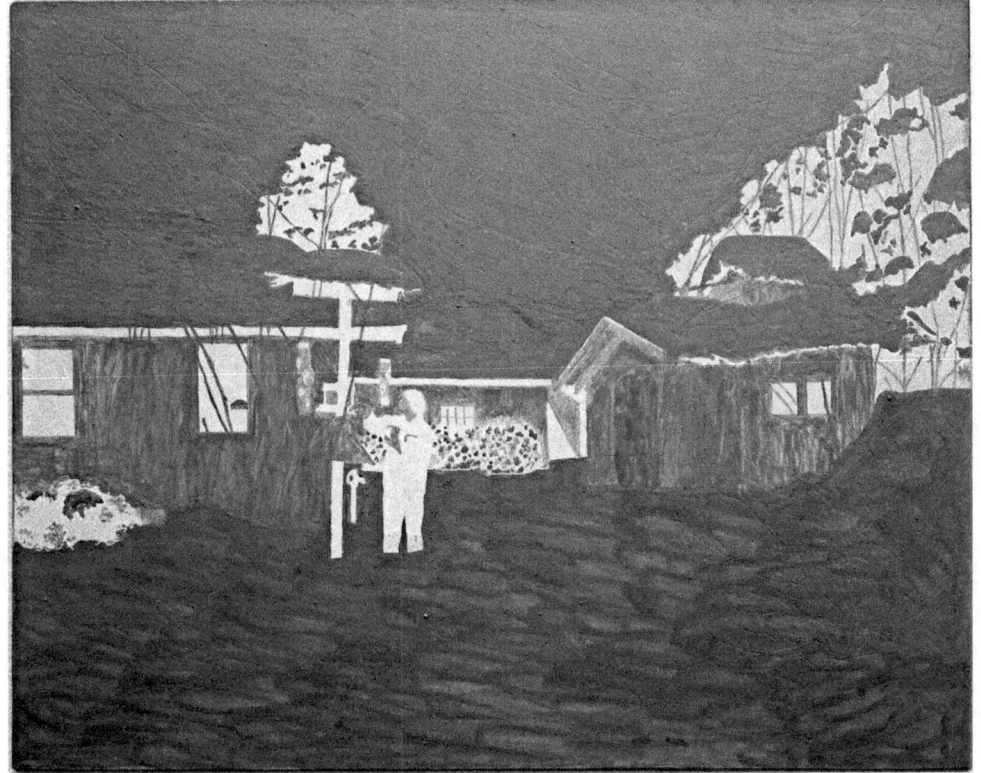

FIGURE 6.70

50% has been stopped out, and it's ready for 60%: an additional 1 minute and 49 seconds in the acid.

Here the 60% items have been stopped out, and it's ready for 80%: an additional 5 minutes and 53 seconds etch time.

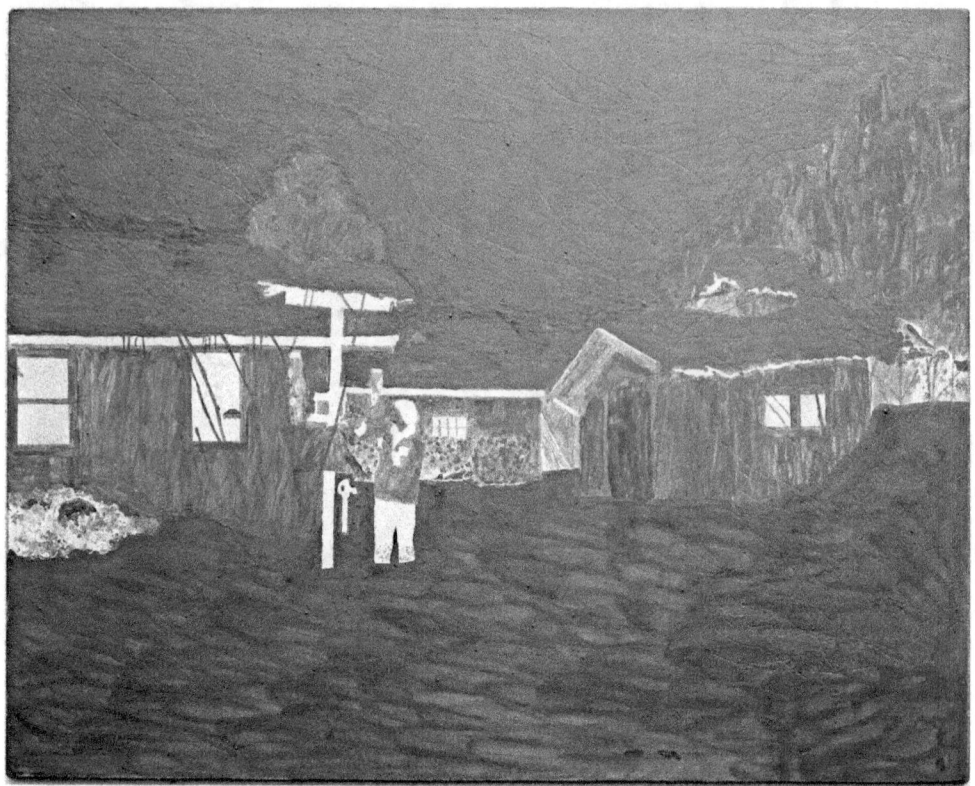

FIGURE 6.71

The 80% tones have been stopped out, and all that's left is the 90% tones, which will require an additional 4 minutes and 12 seconds in the acid.

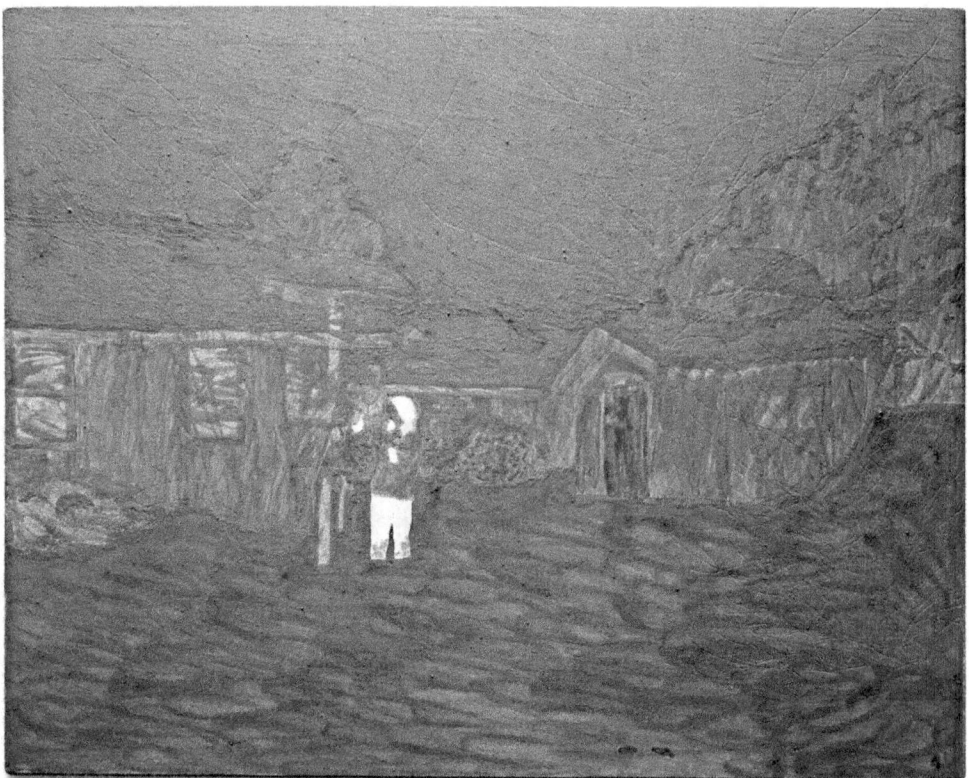

FIGURE 6.72

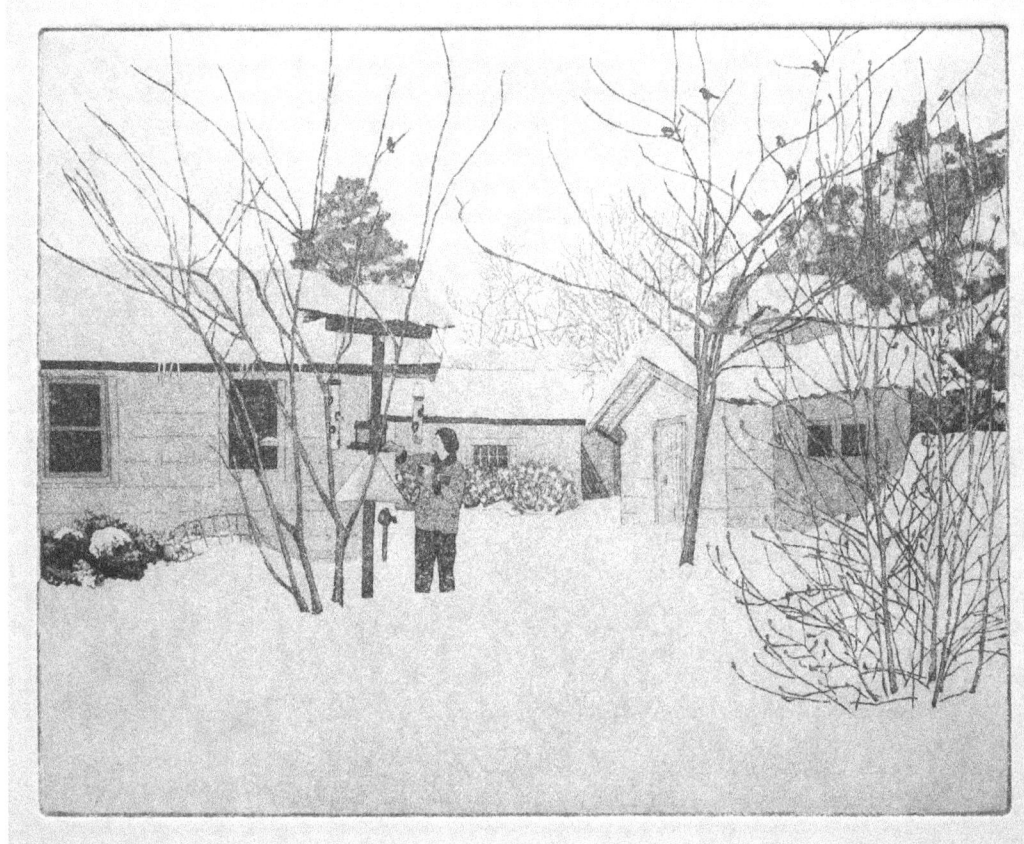

FIGURE 6.73

Figure 6.73 is a proof print of the plate after etching the tones as described above.

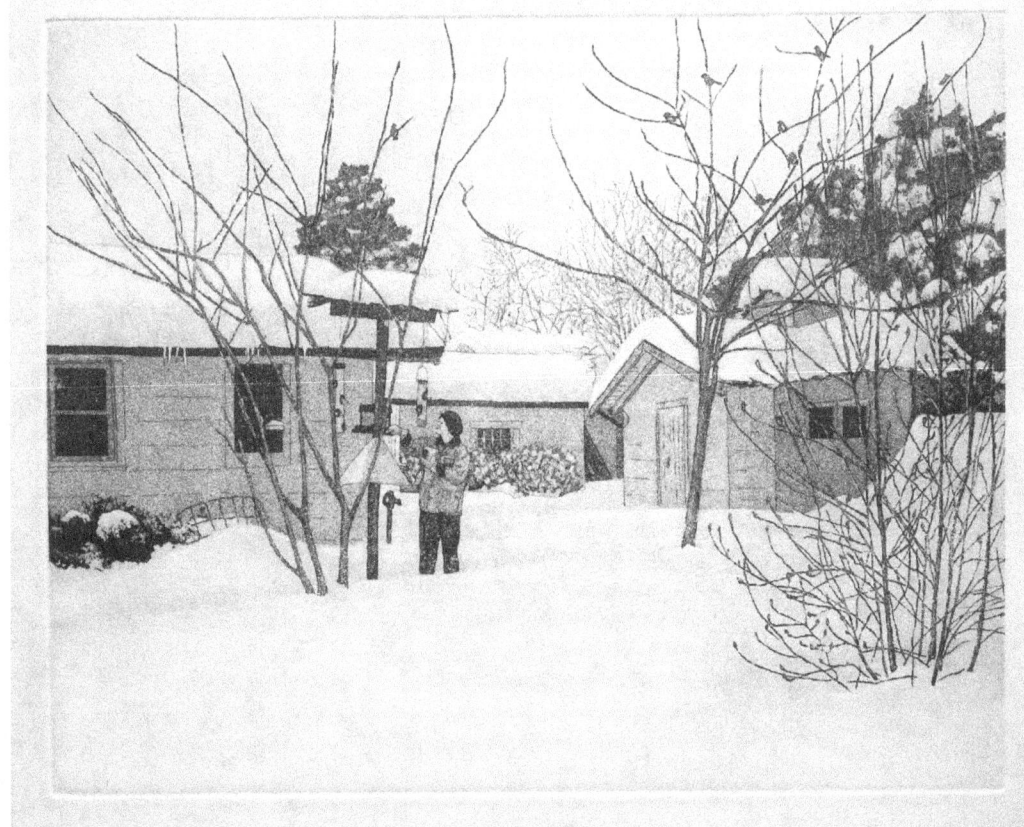

FIGURE 6.74

Figure 6.74 is a print from the completed plate, after some burnishing, sanding, steel wool, and drypointing.

Even though the aquatint itself was made with a permeable ground (PG-11), I wanted to have maximum control in a complex situation, so I created the tones in this image by timed step bites and stopping out with a nonpermeable stopout (SO-11), which creates flat tones. I chose to rely on sanding, burnishing, and steel wool for gradations and modeling in the tones because tonal precision and control are more easily achieved with these techniques than by relying on the permeability of a ground or stopout.

Recipes

(All measuring spoon references are level, not heaping.)

PG-11

INGREDIENTS:

4 teaspoons unsalted butter

1 cup Titanium White (Titanium dioxide) dry pigment

1 teaspoon Zinc White dry pigment

5⅓ Tablespoons Ivory Soap granules softened with 6 Tablespoons water. (Grate a bar of Ivory soap, place 5⅓ Tbsp. granules in closed container overnight with 6 Tbsp. water)

Mix ingredients. Screening and mulling is good for smooth consistency. See Chapter 1 for detailed production instructions.

To be used with copper and ferric chloride or with Edinburgh Etch. (Can also be used with zinc and nitric acid.)

Thins with water.

Makes about 5 oz.

■   ■   ■

Medium and Soft Variants of PG-11

For **PG-11 Medium**, combine 1 part glycerin with 4 parts PG-11.

For **PG-11 Soft**, combine 1 part glycerin with 3 parts PG-11.

You can add a small amount of dry pigment to the mixture to be able to easily distinguish one from another. I add lampblack dry pigment to them to make Medium a pale gray and more to Soft to make it a darker shade of gray.

See Appendix 5 for a detailed discussion of controlling permeability with the three variants of PG-11: Regular, Medium, and Soft.

■   ■   ■

SO-11

INGREDIENTS:

1 Tablespoon of Petroleum Jelly

1 Tablespoon of Titanium White
 (Titanium dioxide) dry pigment

½ teaspoon Zinc White dry pigment

4 Tablespoons of Senefelder's Asphaltum

2 Tablespoons of fine Powdered Rosin

6 Tablespoons softened Ivory Soap granules. (Grate a bar of Ivory
 soap, and soften by adding 4 Tbsp. of water to 6 Tbsp. of granules
 and let sit overnight in a closed container.)

Mix ingredients. Screening and mulling is good for smooth consistency. See Chapter 1 for detailed production instructions. To be used with copper and ferric chloride or with Edinburgh Etch. (Can also be used with zinc and nitric acid.)

When applied to the plate with a brush, it makes a good alternative to asphaltum when you want feathered, scumbled, or slightly softer edge effects. Can be used with or without an aquatint for tonal or textural effects or as a soft ground. Good as a general purpose stopout (doesn't lift asphaltum or bleed in aquatints) or for reinforcing or blocking thin spots in asphaltum or a block out for permeable grounds to prevent further etching.

Thins with water.

Makes about 8 oz.

■ ■ ■

Hydrogen Peroxide Copper Oxidizer

A copper oxidizing agent can be useful for fixing visible reference imagery on a plate so you can see where to etch tones, lines, etc., but not have the reference imagery show up in the print. Typically this is used when doing an image with multiple plates and the imagery from the key plate needs to be transferred to the subsequent plate/plates in a way that is visible, accurate, and detailed, but will not show up in the imagery printed from the subsequent plates. You do this by counterproofing the wet inked image from the key plate to a subsequent plate, then putting the subsequent plate into the oxidizer.

The counterproofed ink acts as a resist, keeping the inked parts of the plate shiny while the non-inked areas of the plate get oxidized, resulting in shiny lines where the ink was that contrast with the oxidized background. It is also useful as a visual indicator of where and how readily etching will occur on a plate where there may be trace substances on the plate that are not visible but may block etching. You simply put a small quantity of oxidizer on the plate for a few seconds or a minute and see if oxidation occurs. If it does, etching will occur and if not, it won't. Oxidizing chemicals are commonly available from jewelry supply places or chemists, but if you want to mix your own this is one way to do it.

INGREDIENTS:

1 cup Hydrogen Peroxide (the 3% stuff, commonly available at
    drug and grocery stores)
3 drops Ferric Chloride (the 40° Baumé strength)

Mix the ingredients together and watch for small bubbles. It only works when it's bubbling. Ferric chloride acts as a catalyst when added to hydrogen peroxide, causing it to release its extra oxygen as bubbles, so when you mix the two it looks like a bottle of ginger ale, with fine bubbles streaming upward. A small amount of heat is released. Theoretically, when the bubbles stop (after usually an hour or several hours, depending on the quantity and freshness), you are left with a bottle of water with a small amount of ferric chloride in it.

Don't throw it out after the bubbles stop. Store it in a plastic container and when needed, reactivate it by pouring a small quantity of hydrogen peroxide into the spent solution. Mix, give it a couple minutes, and it will be good to use for an hour or so. You get a better patina with old solution.

The copper has to be clean or the bubbling solution won't oxidize it evenly. Brasso it, then scrub it lightly with scouring powder and rinse until it holds a film of water. Place it in the oxidizing solution while it is still wet with the film of water. Rinse thoroughly and dry it with a clean cotton towel. Always use only as much oxidation as is necessary. Very heavy oxidation on copper can begin to act as a resist to the etchant and cause unwanted imagery to become visible in the print.

When no longer needed, the oxidation can be removed from the plate with Brasso or other metal polish.

■　■　■

The Cassara recipe for White Ground

The Cassara recipe calls for four ingredients:

1 volume of linseed oil

2 volumes of Titanium white, dry pigment

4 volumes of Ivory Snow (mild soap granules)

2 volumes of water

Mix the ingredients, adding as much of the water as necessary to get a creamy consistency. At first it will be quite runny, but will thicken after sitting for a day or two. If substituting grated Ivory Soap bars for Ivory Snow, use only 2 volumes of grated bars because they will weigh about the same as 4 volumes of Ivory Snow.

This recipe was originally published in the article "A Unique One-bite White Etching Ground" by Frank Cassara, *Artist's Proof*, Issue No. 5/Spring-Summer 1963/Vol III, No. 1, pp. 36–38. To view the full article online, go to http://etchings.org/grounds/Cassara Index.html.

Timing Charts

The rationale behind these timing charts is to enable an etcher to plan more realistically, should he or she wish to. It's still all an educated guess, but with a chart the scope of the guesswork is significantly reduced. The question is "How dark will my aquatint be if I leave it in the acid for X amount of time?"

The answer is based on another question that these charts don't help answer and that is: "How long should I leave my plate in the acid before the aquatint etches to a 100% black and starts to break down?"

The etcher has to guess the answer to that, and the answer can only be based on his or her knowledge and experience. It is based on how large the dots of resist are in the aquatint, how far apart they are, how strong the acid is, how warm the acid is, and how much permeable ground the acid has to get through to do anything to the plate. This is a function of conditions that tend to fluctuate and are determined by an individual etcher's habits and preferences.

It is assumed, for the purposes of this book, that the etcher is familiar enough with etching aquatints to be able to judge with reasonable accuracy the amount of time the plate can stay in the acid before the aquatint starts to break down. He or she should be able to tell by looking at the plate, when that is starting to happen.

The etcher also needs to be able to tell by looking at the plate with a magnifying glass whether the aquatint is lightly etched, moderately etched, or is approaching the breakdown stage (see page 15, paragraph 5, and page 79, paragraph 1). If an aquatint looks like it isn't etching fast enough for the chart in use, move to a chart with more "maximum time" on it. This will give you longer etch-time intervals. If the aquatint looks like it is going to break down before reaching the end of the chart, move to a chart with a shorter maximum time on it and if necessary, spatter the failing aquatint with a can of spray paint (or similar) to reinforce the resist so you can keep on etching darks.

You can "push" an etch toward a darker or lighter result by using a "longer" or "shorter" chart. In my opinion, this is one time when it's better to err toward the dark side since you can extend the etch time by adding spatters to a failing aquatint, and you can scrape and burnish if the result is too dark, but if it's too light all you can do is start over.

While the accuracy of the target "100% black" depends on the knowledge and skill of the etcher, the generation of the shades of tone ranging from white to black depends on physics and chemistry, which makes a predictive tool like these charts possible. This enables an etcher to more realistically plan tonal ranges and relationships or the distribution of target tones throughout an image.

Seven charts are provided with maximum etch times ranging from 10 to 60 minutes. Charts are designed to be copied and displayed near an acid tray for reference.

TIMING CHART

10 Minutes Maximum Etch Time

% OF TONE DESIRED	TOTAL TIME *minutes : seconds*	ADDED (INCREMENTAL TIME) *minutes : seconds*
5%	0 : 04	
		+ 0 : 05
10%	0 : 09	
		+ 0 : 08
20%	0 : 17	
		+ 0 : 15
30%	0 : 32	
		+ 0 : 24
40%	0 : 56	
		+ 0 : 37
50%	1 : 33	
		+ 0 : 55
60%	2 : 28	
		+ 1 : 16
70%	3 : 44	
		+ 1 : 40
80%	5 : 24	
		+ 2 : 06
90%	7 : 30	
		+ 2 : 30
100%	10 : 00	

TIMING CHART

15 Minutes Maximum Etch Time

% OF TONE DESIRED	TOTAL TIME *minutes : seconds*	ADDED (INCREMENTAL TIME) *minutes : seconds*
5%	0 : 06	
		+ 0 : 07
10%	0 : 13	
		+ 0 : 13
20%	0 : 26	
		+ 0 : 22
30%	0 : 48	
		+ 0 : 36
40%	1 : 24	
		+ 0 : 55
50%	2 : 19	
		+ 1 : 22
60%	3 : 41	
		+ 1 : 54
70%	5 : 35	
		+ 2 : 31
80%	8 : 06	
		+ 3 : 09
90%	11 : 15	
		+ 3 : 45
100%	15 : 00	

Estimate the number of minutes needed to etch the aquatint to a 100% black, and use the chart that has that number of minutes shown as the "Maximum Etch Time." The "% of tone desired" column indicates the grayscale percentage of tone desired in the aquatint. The "Total Time" column shows the TOTAL time the plate should be in the acid to achieve each percentage of tone, shown in minutes and seconds. The "Added (incremental) Time" column shows the amount of time in minutes and seconds needed to get from one "Total" time to the next. To skip "Total" time increments, add the intervening incremental times together to time the etch. For example, to darken a tone that is at 30% to 60%, add the incremental times between 30% and 40%, between 40% and 50%, and between 50% and 60% together, and leave it in the acid for that amount of time.

TIMING CHART

20 Minutes Maximum Etch Time

% OF TONE DESIRED	TOTAL TIME minutes : seconds	ADDED (INCREMENTAL TIME) minutes : seconds
5%	0 : 08	
		+ 0 : 10
10%	0 : 18	
		+ 0 : 16
20%	0 : 34	
		+ 0 : 30
30%	1 : 04	
		+ 0 : 48
40%	1 : 52	
		+ 1 : 14
50%	3 : 06	
		+ 1 : 49
60%	4 : 55	
		+ 2 : 32
70%	7 : 27	
		+ 3 : 21
80%	10 : 48	
		+ 4 : 12
90%	15 : 00	
		+ 5 : 00
100%	20 : 00	

TIMING CHART

30 Minutes Maximum Etch Time

% OF TONE DESIRED	TOTAL TIME minutes : seconds	ADDED (INCREMENTAL TIME) minutes : seconds
5%	0 : 13	
		+ 0 : 13
10%	0 : 26	
		+ 0 : 26
20%	0 : 52	
		+ 0 : 43
30%	1 : 35	
		+ 1 : 12
40%	2 : 47	
		+ 1 : 52
50%	4 : 39	
		+ 2 : 44
60%	7 : 23	
		+ 3 : 48
70%	11 : 11	
		+ 5 : 01
80%	16 : 12	
		+ 6 : 18
90%	22 : 30	
		+ 7 : 30
100%	30 : 00	

Estimate the number of minutes needed to etch the aquatint to a 100% black, and use the chart that has that number of minutes shown as the "Maximum Etch Time." The "% of tone desired" column indicates the grayscale percentage of tone desired in the aquatint. The "Total Time" column shows the TOTAL time the plate should be in the acid to achieve each percentage of tone, shown in minutes and seconds. The "Added (incremental) Time" column shows the amount of time in minutes and seconds needed to get from one "Total" time to the next. To skip "Total" time increments, add the intervening incremental times together to time the etch. For example, to darken a tone that is at 30% to 60%, add the incremental times between 30% and 40%, between 40% and 50%, and between 50% and 60% together, and leave it in the acid for that amount of time.

TIMING CHART

40 Minutes Maximum Etch Time

% OF TONE DESIRED	TOTAL TIME minutes : seconds	ADDED (INCREMENTAL TIME) minutes : seconds
5%	0 : 17	
		+ 0 : 18
10%	0 : 35	
		+ 0 : 34
20%	1 : 09	
		+ 0 : 58
30%	2 : 07	
		+ 1 : 36
40%	3 : 43	
		+ 2 : 29
50%	6 : 12	
		+ 3 : 38
60%	9 : 50	
		+ 5 : 04
70%	14 : 54	
		+ 6 : 42
80%	21 : 36	
		+ 8 : 24
90%	30 : 00	
		+ 10 : 00
100%	40 : 00	

TIMING CHART

50 Minutes Maximum Etch Time

% OF TONE DESIRED	TOTAL TIME minutes : seconds	ADDED (INCREMENTAL TIME) minutes : seconds
5%	0 : 21	
		+ 0 : 23
10%	0 : 44	
		+ 0 : 42
20%	1 : 26	
		+ 1 : 13
30%	2 : 39	
		+ 2 : 00
40%	4 : 39	
		+ 3 : 06
50%	7 : 45	
		+ 4 : 33
60%	12 : 18	
		+ 6 : 20
70%	18 : 38	
		+ 8 : 22
80%	27 : 00	
		+ 10 : 30
90%	37 : 30	
		+ 12 : 30
100%	50 : 00	

Estimate the number of minutes needed to etch the aquatint to a 100% black, and use the chart that has that number of minutes shown as the "Maximum Etch Time." The "% of tone desired" column indicates the grayscale percentage of tone desired in the aquatint. The "Total Time" column shows the TOTAL time the plate should be in the acid to achieve each percentage of tone, shown in minutes and seconds. The "Added (incremental) Time" column shows the amount of time in minutes and seconds needed to get from one "Total" time to the next. To skip "Total" time increments, add the intervening incremental times together to time the etch. For example, to darken a tone that is at 30% to 60%, add the incremental times between 30% and 40%, between 40% and 50%, and between 50% and 60% together, and leave it in the acid for that amount of time.

TIMING CHART

60 Minutes Maximum Etch Time

% OF TONE DESIRED	TOTAL TIME minutes : seconds	ADDED (INCREMENTAL TIME) minutes : seconds
5%	0 : 25	
		+ 0 : 28
10%	0 : 53	
		+ 0 : 50
20%	1 : 43	
		+ 1 : 28
30%	3 : 11	
		+ 2 : 24
40%	5 : 35	
		+ 3 : 43
50%	9 : 18	
		+ 5 : 27
60%	14 : 45	
		+ 7 : 36
70%	22 : 21	
		+ 10 : 03
80%	32 : 24	
		+ 12 : 36
90%	45 : 00	
		+ 15 : 00
100%	60 : 00	

Estimate the number of minutes needed to etch the aquatint to a 100% black, and use the chart that has that number of minutes shown as the "Maximum Etch Time." The "% of tone desired" column indicates the grayscale percentage of tone desired in the aquatint. The "Total Time" column shows the TOTAL time the plate should be in the acid to achieve each percentage of tone, shown in minutes and seconds. The "Added (incremental) Time" column shows the amount of time in minutes and seconds needed to get from one "Total" time to the next. To skip "Total" time increments, add the intervening incremental times together to time the etch. For example, to darken a tone that is at 30% to 60%, add the incremental times between 30% and 40%, between 40% and 50%, and between 50% and 60% together, and leave it in the acid for that amount of time.

APPENDIX 3

An Examination of PG-11, White Ground, Heat, and Rosin Aquatint

Grounds can react in very unpredictable ways to things like being subjected to heat, or to being applied to a plate in combination with other materials. Since permeable grounds are commonly used with aquatints, I wanted to take a close look at how these two permeable grounds (PG-11 and Cassara recipe White Ground) react to these conditions (being applied with a heated rosin aquatint) and how they compare with each other. This experiment was conducted to answer several questions:

1. How are PG-11 and White Ground affected by the heat applied to a plate while melting a rosin aquatint?

2. How does putting the aquatint on top of PG-11 or White Ground compare with putting it under the ground with regard to permeability and the overall visual effect obtained?

3. How does applying unheated PG-11 or White Ground on top of an aquatint compare with the unheated ground being applied to the plate with no aquatint, with regard to the visual effect obtained?

Admittedly, this is a minimal experiment to yield so many answers, but I was only looking for very general information and I think the results did yield some valid indications. Actually, I was very surprised by the results concerning PG-11. I fully expected it to melt into a greasy blur at the first sign of heat, but it didn't.

I designed the experiment as follows. There were two plates, each one 3.5 inches by 5 inches and each one divided into four quarters. For reference purposes, I will refer to the four quarters of each plate as seen in a vertical format as A and B across the top and C and D across the bottom. One plate would be for PG-11 and the other for White Ground.

Step 1 (Figures A3.1 and A3.2) was to apply PG-11 and White Ground to quarters A and B of the respective plates. I tried to apply a simple graded application within each quarter, starting at the top with thick enough ground to block out 100% of the etch and grading it downward so that at the bottom it was feathered down to nothing. (Minor textures or patterns were condoned.) This was allowed to dry overnight.

Step 2 was to place the two plates in an aquatint box and simultaneously dust them with rosin dust, with quarters A and C of each plate covered with a piece of mat board so that only quarters B and D of each plate would get aquatint. (As can be seen in Figures A3.3 and A3.4, the mat board moved so the edge of the aquatint actually came a little way into quarters A and C.) At this stage, quarters A (PG-11 and White Ground) had only ground, quarters B had ground with rosin dust on top of it, quarters C had nothing, and quarters D had only rosin dust. Both plates were simultaneously heated over a gas flame to melt the rosin and allowed to cool.

Step 3 was to apply similarly graded applications of ground to quarters C and D, so that now quarters C had unheated ground with no aquatint, and quarters D had unheated ground on top of an aquatint. This was allowed to dry overnight.

To sum up, in Figures A3.3 and A3.4 on both plates quarters A had ground only, heated, with no aquatint. Quarters B had a rosin aquatint on top of the heated ground, quarters C had only unheated ground with no aquatint, and quarters D had a rosin aquatint underneath the unheated ground.

Step 4 was to simultaneously place the two plates in a 1:1 ferric chloride bath which, as this was happening in January, was quite cold at 59°F, and let them etch with occasional agitation for 20 minutes.

Step 5 was to clean the plates and print them.

Following are images of the results.

Pictures of the Plates

STEP 1: This shows the bare copper plates (actual size) with PG-11 and White Ground applied to quarters A and B.

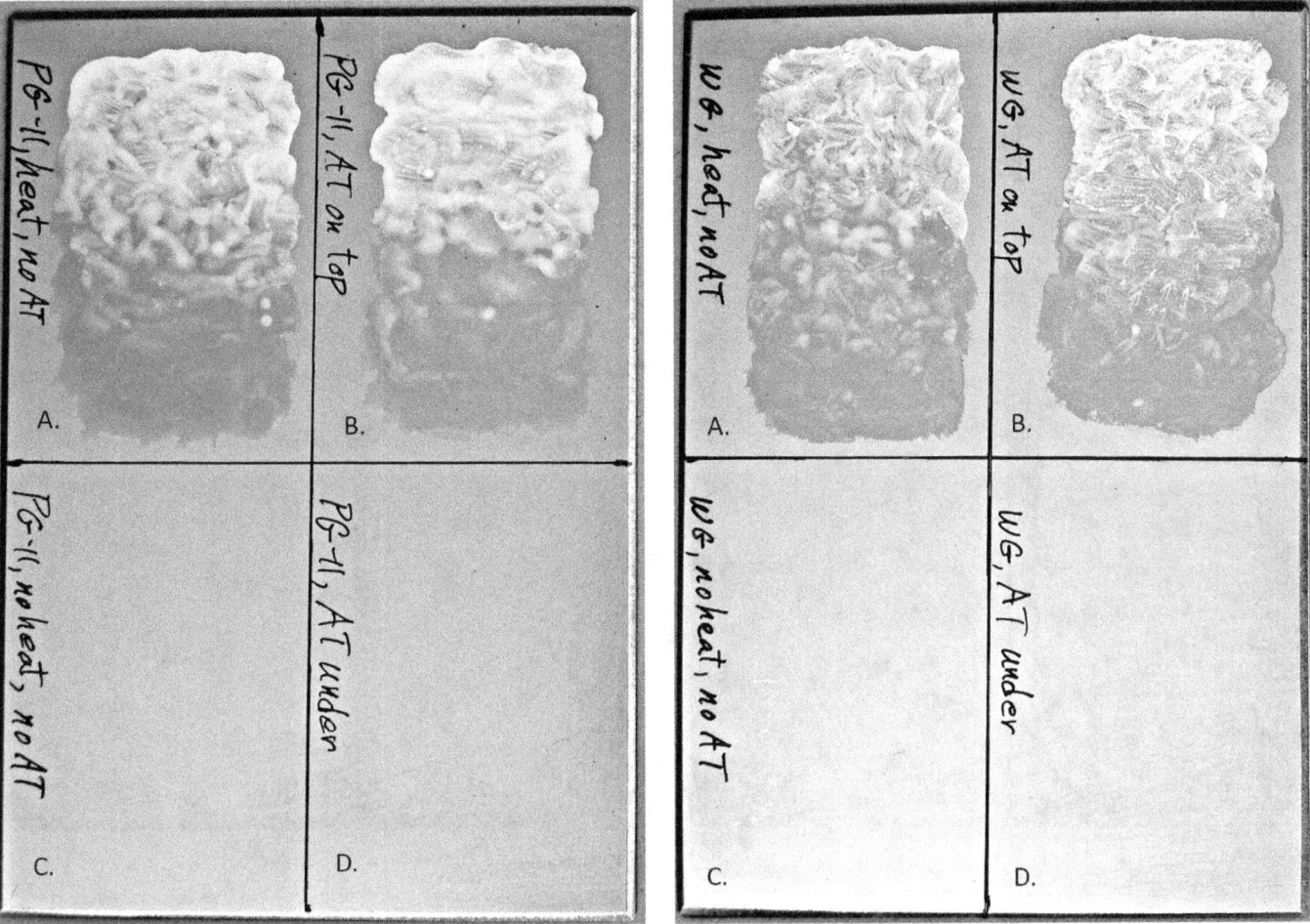

FIGURE A3.1   FIGURE A3.2

STEPS 2 AND 3: These are the plates after aquatint has been applied to quarters B and D, the aquatint has been cooked, and fresh, unheated ground has been applied to quarters C and D.

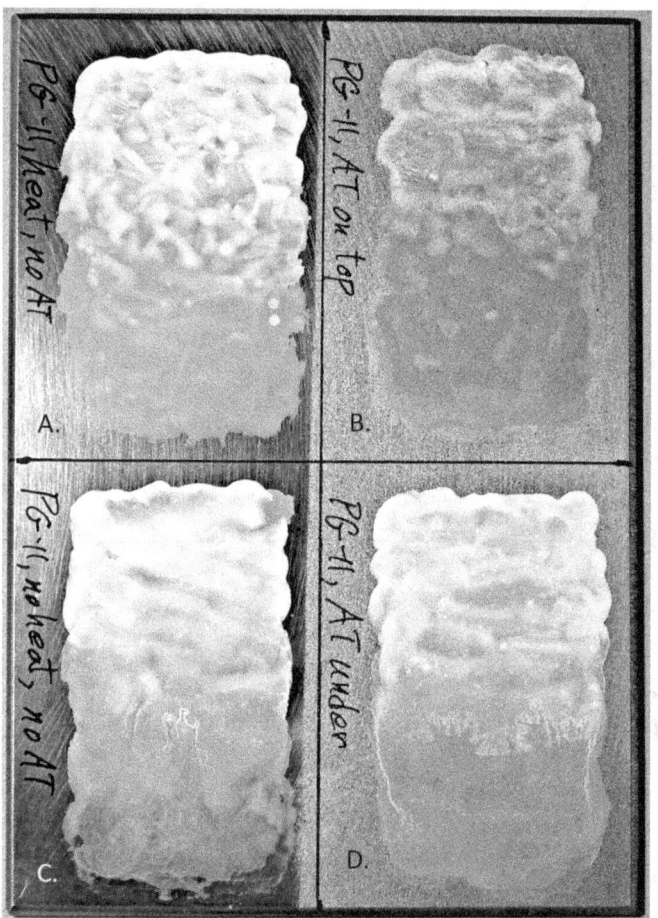

FIGURE A3.3

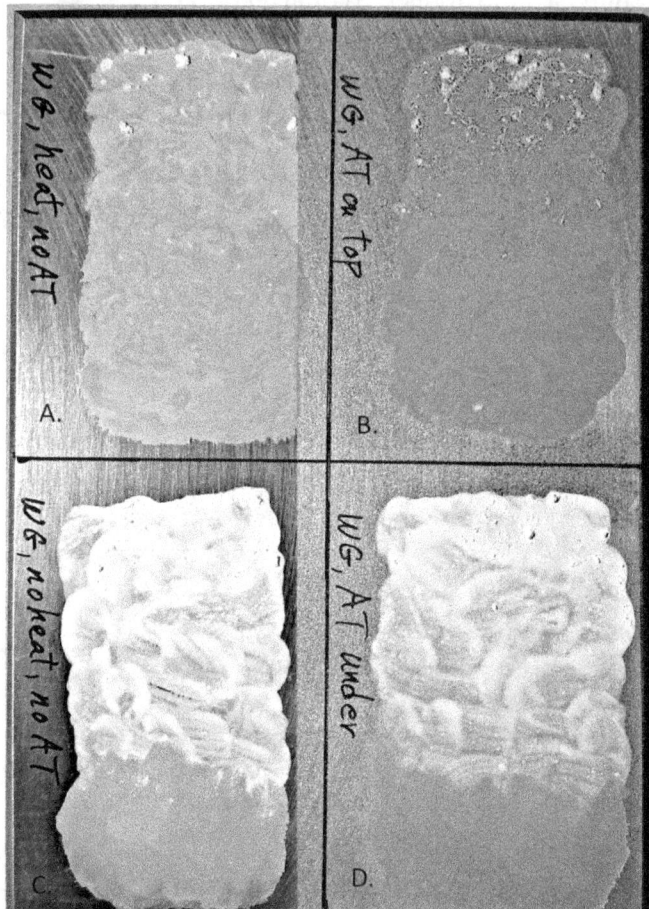

FIGURE A3.4

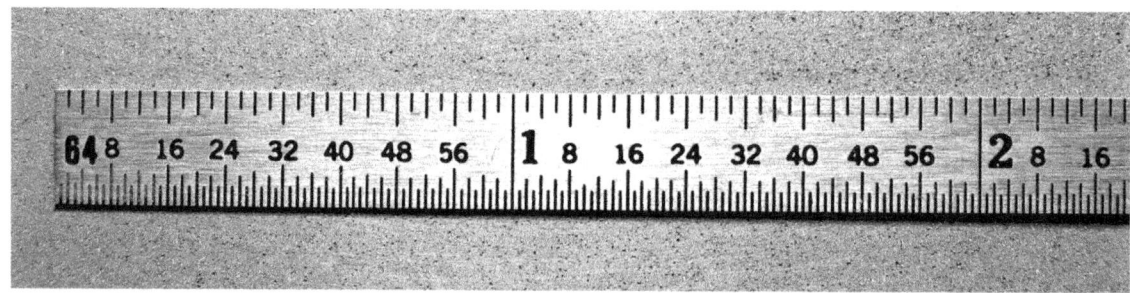

FIGURE A3.5: the aquatint with a ⅟₆₄-inch ruler showing particle size and density

Figure A3.5 shows a finer and a more open (less dense) aquatint than I would normally use, but with slow (cold) acid and no concerns about its durability (through editioning), I felt it was a good one for this test.

I don't know of anything in etching that is more sensitive to trace contamination on the surface of a copper plate than a rosin aquatint while it is being heated and is melting. The sensitivity shows up as unwanted patterns in a tone that is supposed to be flat. The patterns are created because a particle of rosin dust sitting on a copper surface looks about like the other particles of rosin dust around it, but as it is heated and melts it will spread out more (or less) if it is sitting on a trace of rosin varnish, asphaltum, oil from a fingerprint, residue from water, etc., than if it is sitting on clean copper. If it spreads out more, it stops out more copper and creates a lighter tone than the particles near it that don't spread as much (and vice versa), and patterns that mysteriously appear in an aquatint as it cooks tend to show up at least as clearly in the print.

I was surprised therefore to find that rosin cooked on top of PG-11, as far as I can tell (see Figure A3.12), behaved identically to the rosin cooked on the bare copper. This made for a very slight increase in the permeability of the PG-11 compared to the permeability of the corresponding White Ground sample, but both stopped out pretty much everything. I would say that the rosin on top of the PG-11 significantly reduced its permeability.

It was also interesting to see that the rosin particles cooked on top of White Ground (Figure A3.15) where it was thick (compared to those on the bare copper), dramatically fused together and spread out into relatively coarse patterns but, paradoxically, where it was thin they tended to remain in little balls and spread out less that those on the adjacent bare copper. (In the end, none of it mattered. Since this was White Ground on copper, not zinc, where it probably would have enhanced contrast, the ground pretty much stopped out everything so none of the interesting stuff going on on top of it had any effect on the copper plate underneath, which remained largely blank.)

The following pages show pictures of the individual quarters, for comparison. Each page has an enlarged, detail view which has been split to show the plate before etching on the left and after etching on the right. There are also two other small (approximately actual size) images, one showing the un-etched plate with the ground applied, and below that an image of the print (flipped) taken from the plate.

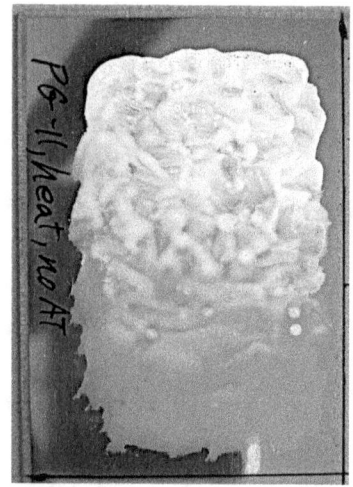

FIGURE A3.7: Plate with ground applied

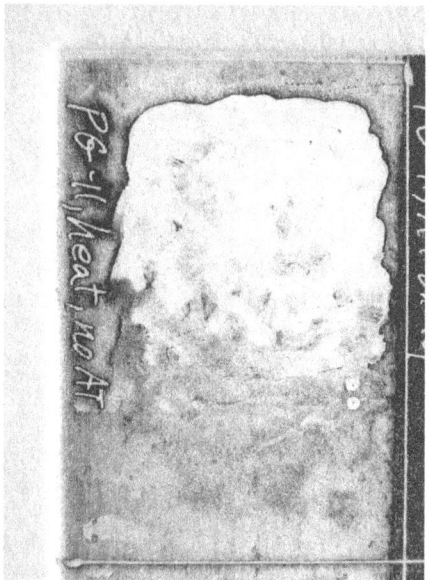

FIGURE A3.8: Print taken from the plate

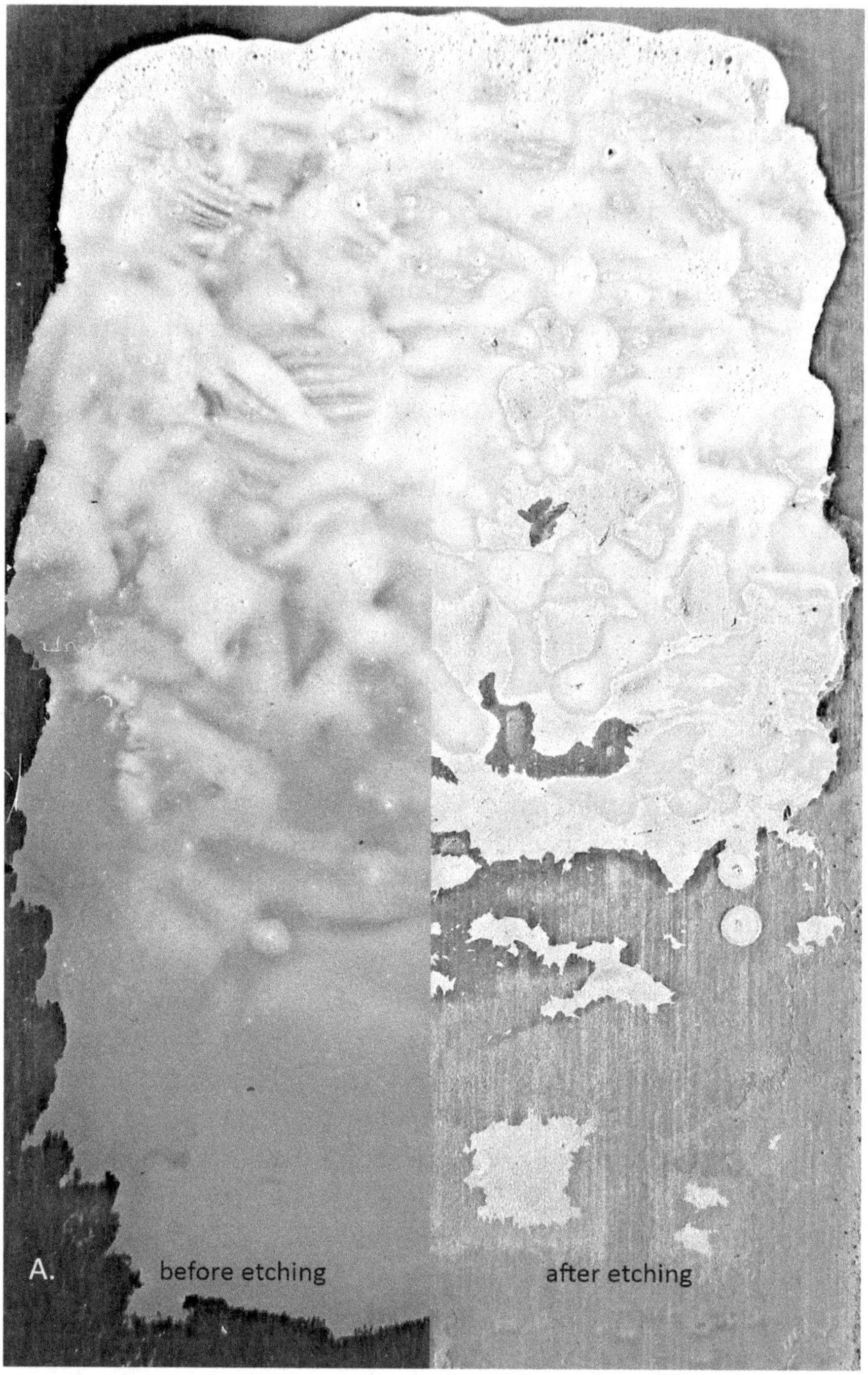

A. before etching   after etching

FIGURE A3.6: PG-11, heated, no aquatint

White Ground With Heat and No Aquatint
(Quarter A)

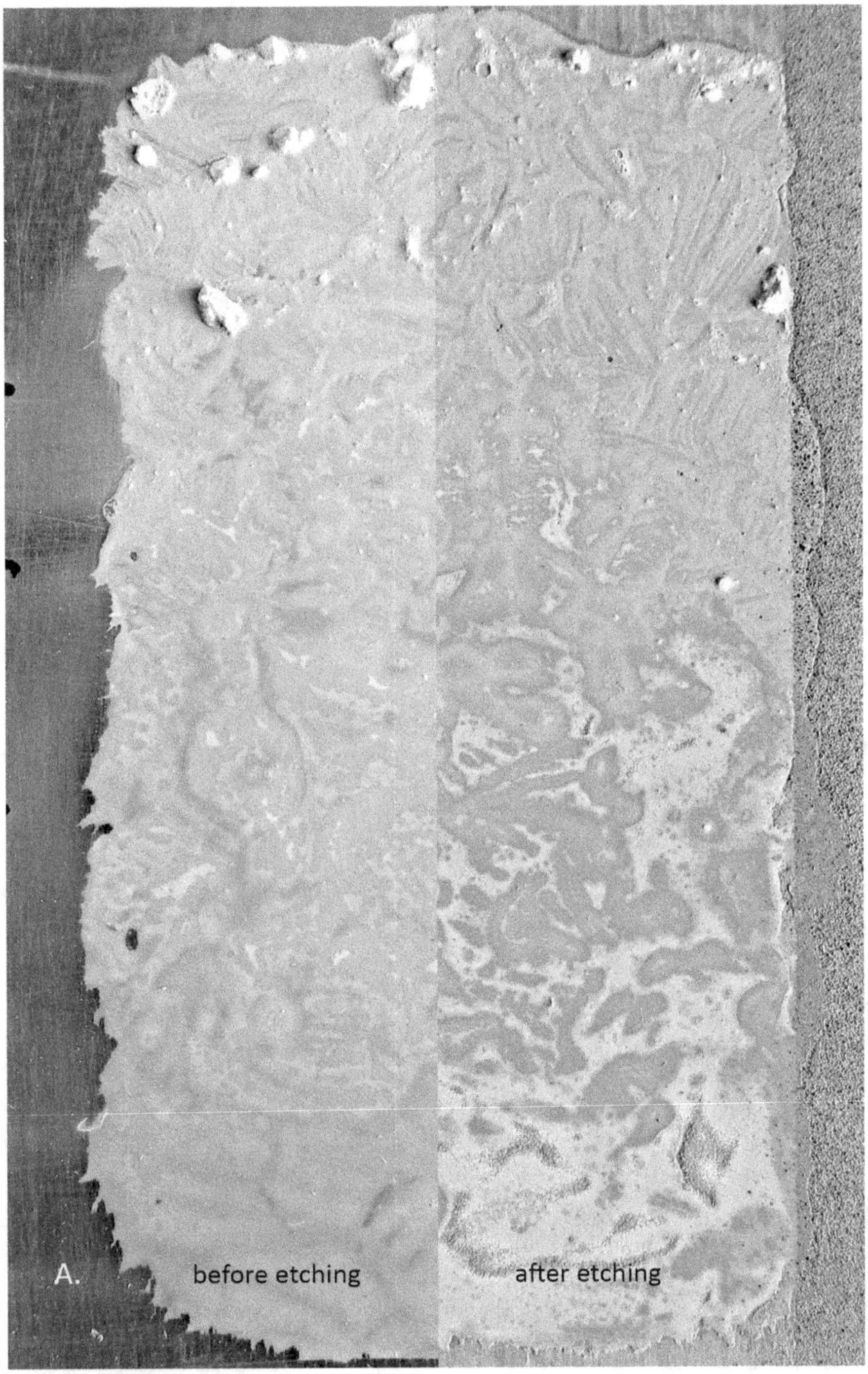

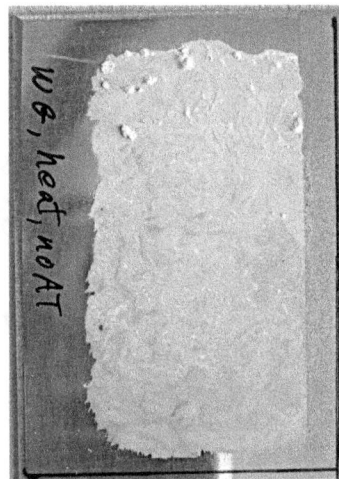

FIGURE A3.10: Plate with ground applied

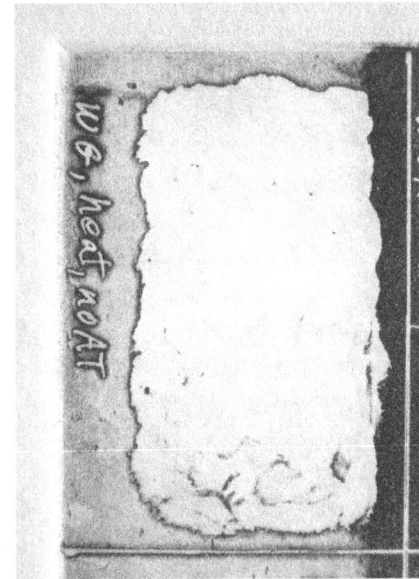

FIGURE A3.11: Print taken from the plate

A.   before etching   after etching

FIGURE A3.9: White Ground, heated, no aquatint

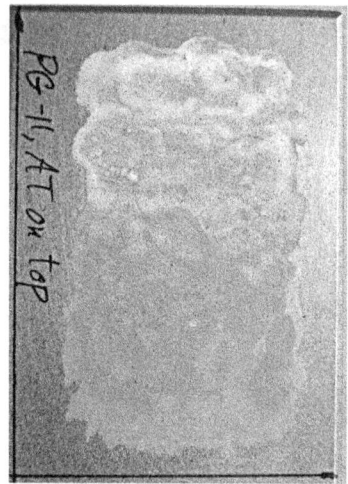

FIGURE A3.13: Plate with ground applied

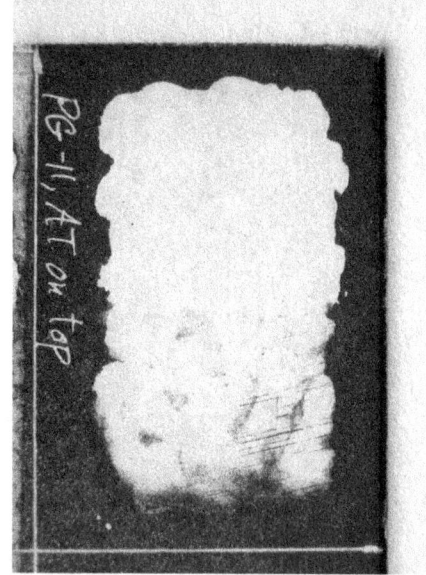

FIGURE A3.14: Print taken from the plate

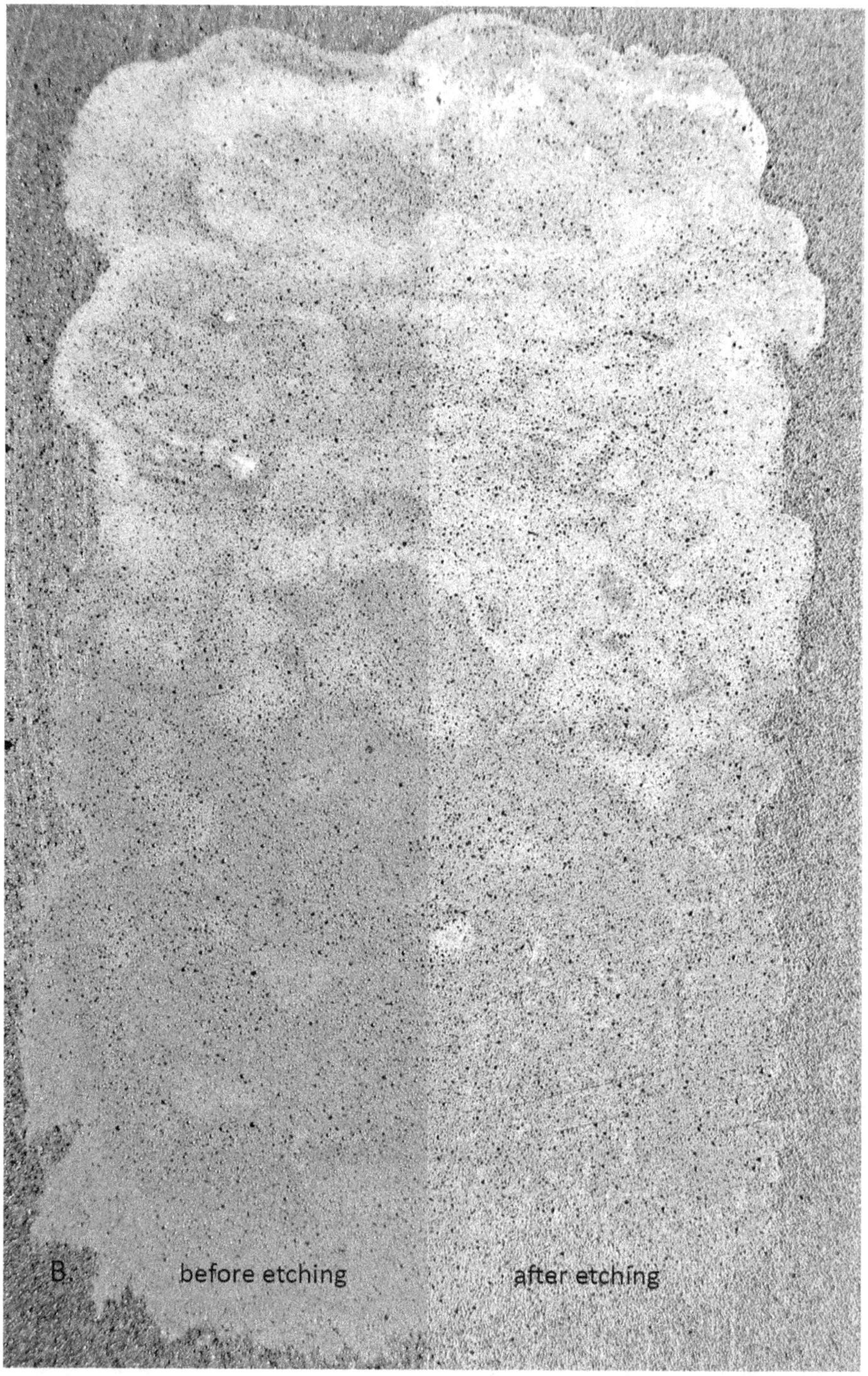

B. before etching   after etching

FIGURE A3.12: PG-11, rosin on top

White Ground With Rosin Aquatint on Top
(Quarter B)

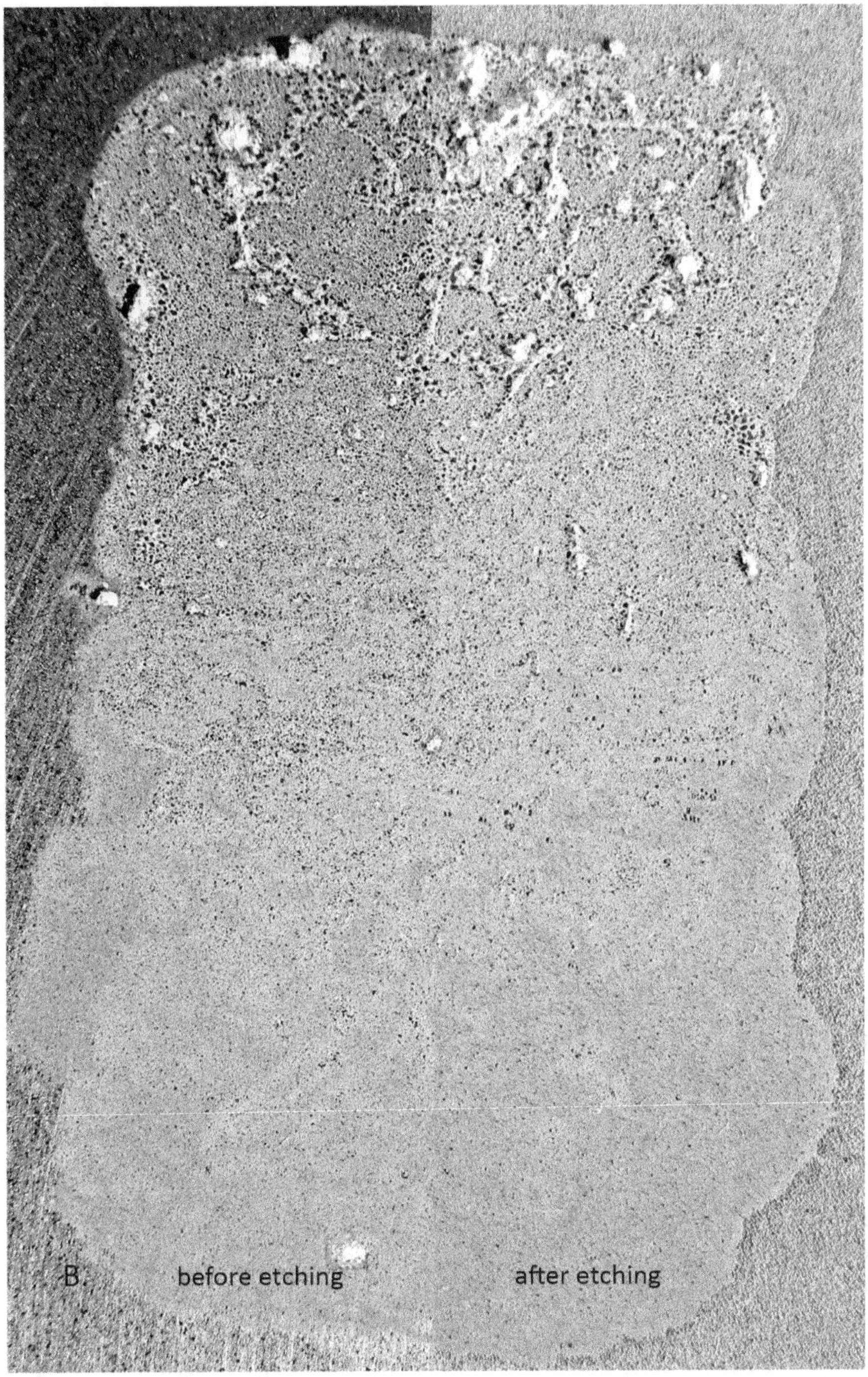

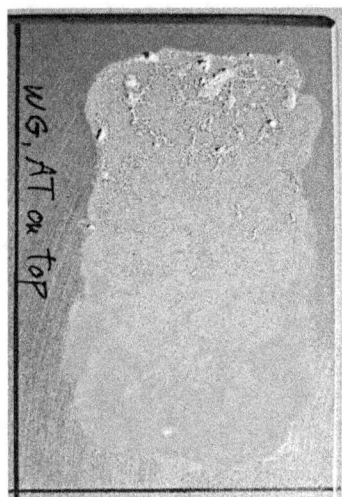

FIGURE A3.16: Plate with ground applied

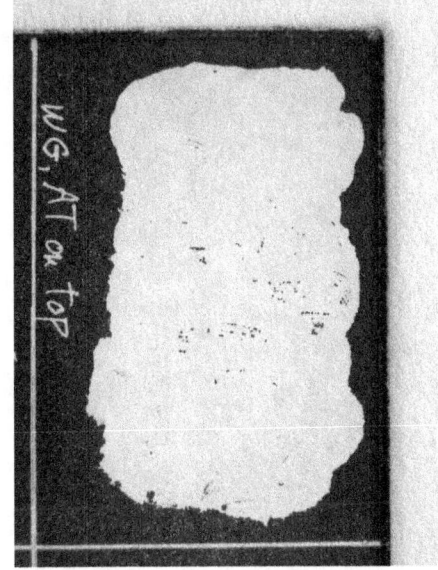

FIGURE A3.17: Print taken from the plate

B.   before etching   after etching

FIGURE A3.15: White Ground, rosin on top

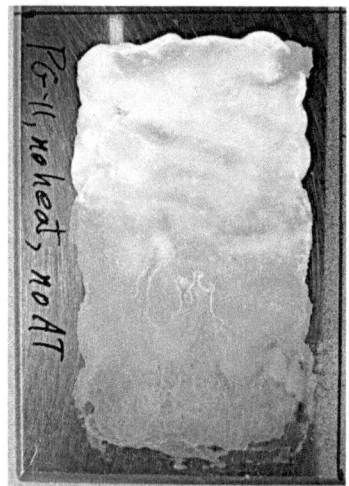

FIGURE A3.19: Plate with ground applied

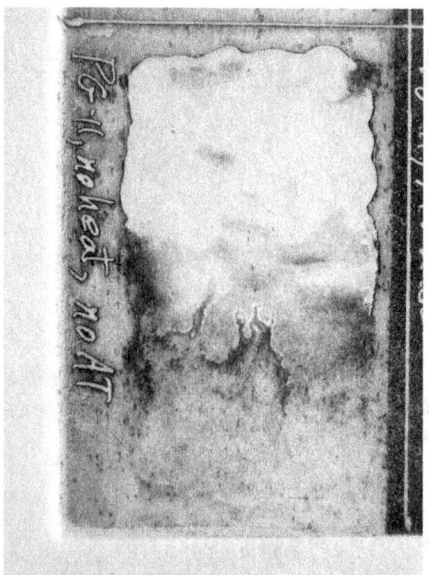

FIGURE A3.20: Print taken from the plate

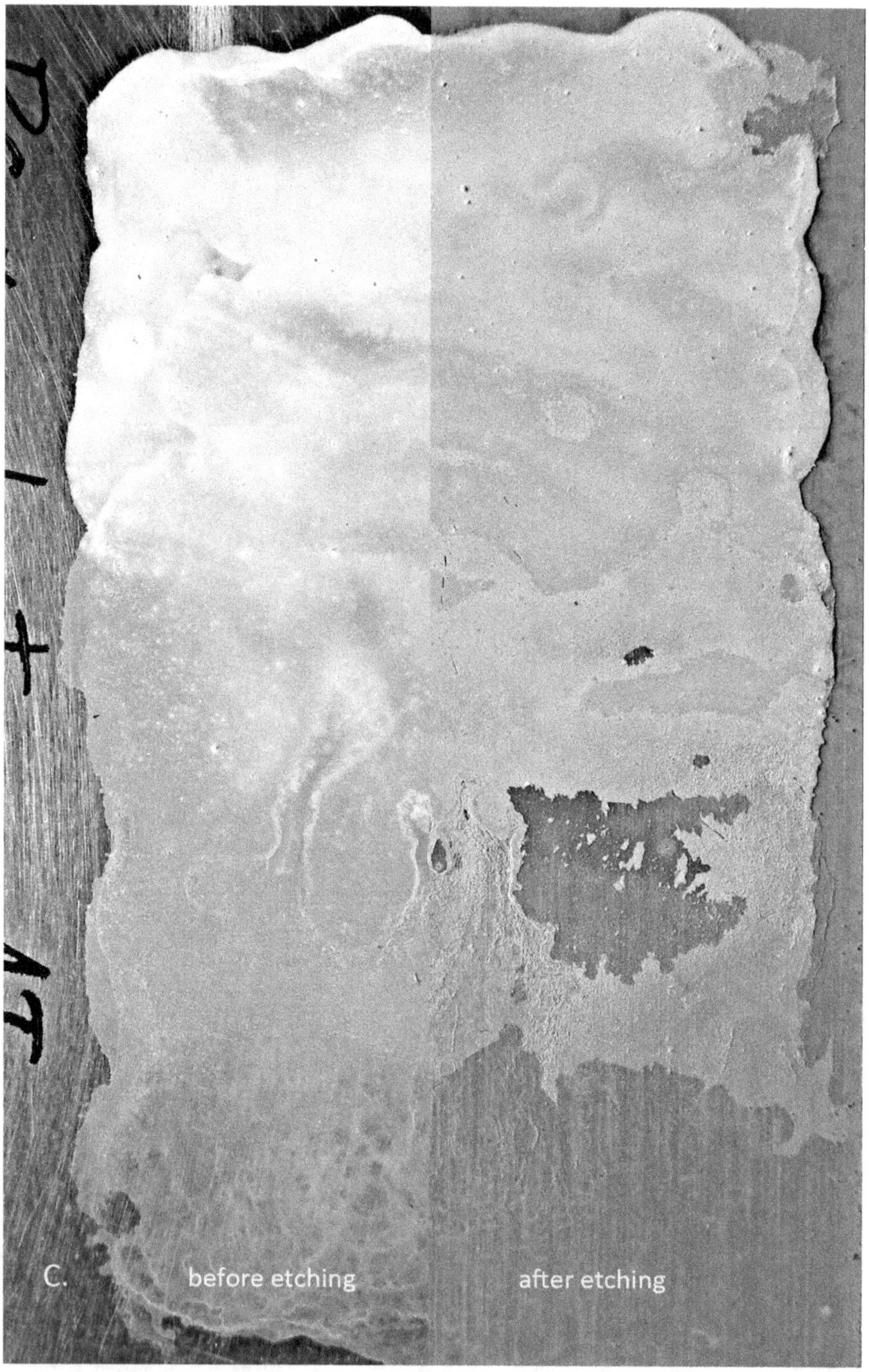

C. before etching after etching

FIGURE A3.18: PG-11, no heat and no aquatint

White Ground with No Heat and No Aquatint
(Quarter C)

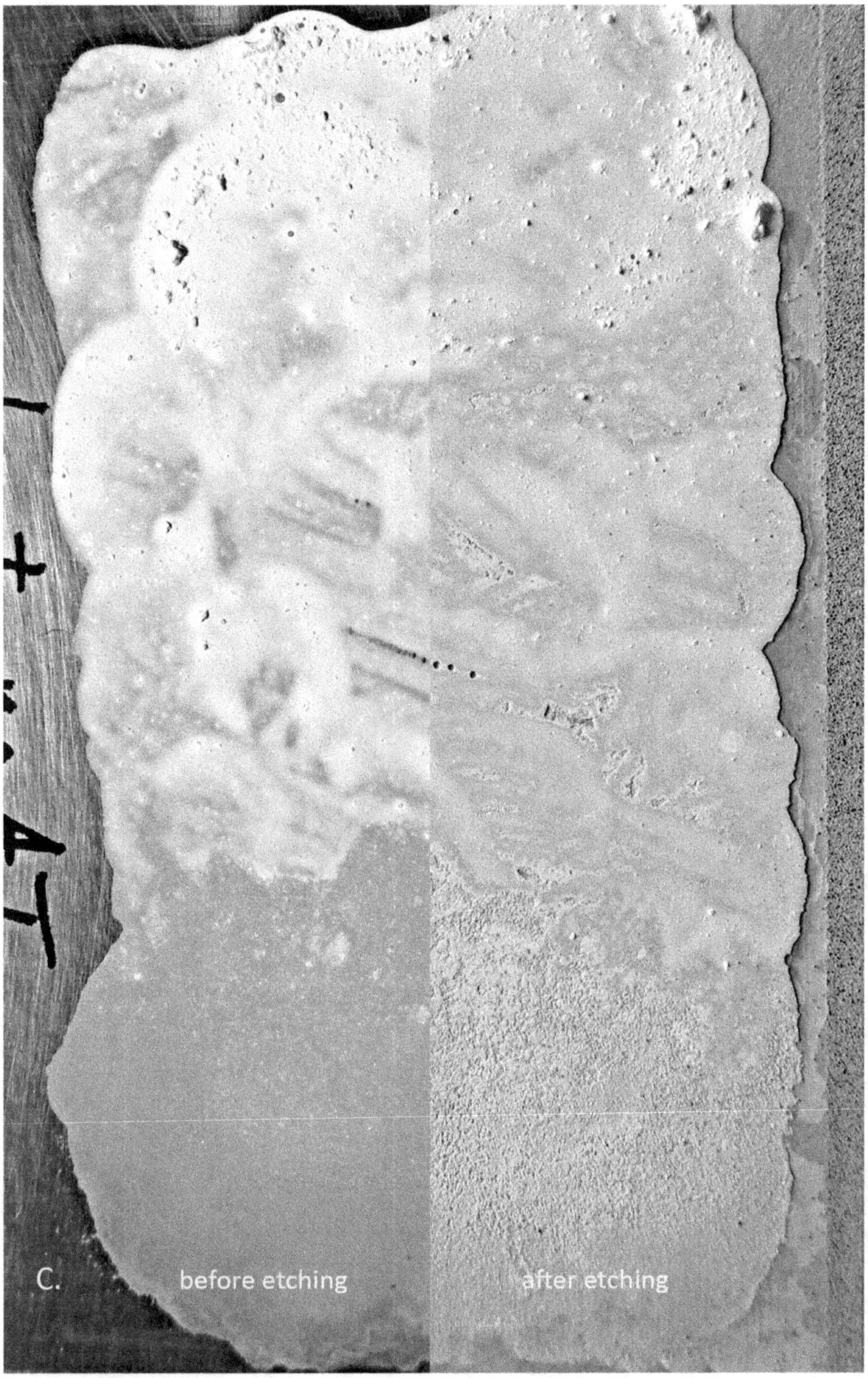

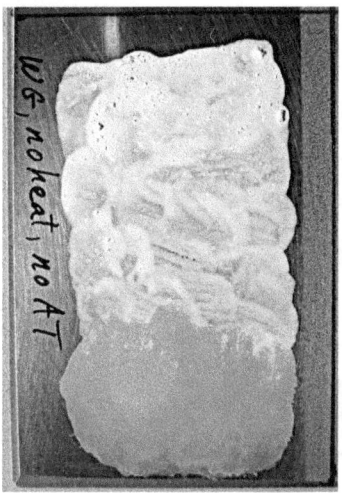

FIGURE A3.22: Plate with ground applied

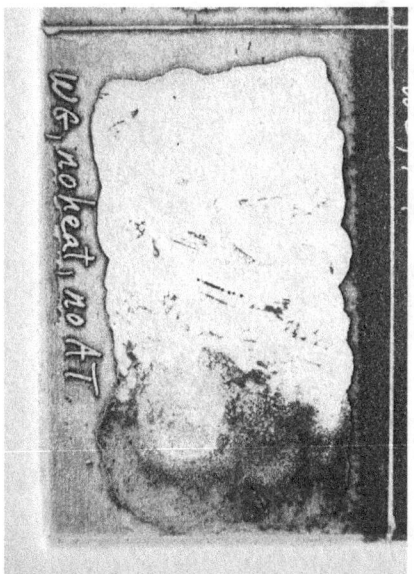

FIGURE A3.23: Print, taken from the plate

C. before etching   after etching

FIGURE A3.21: White Ground, no heat and no aquatint

PG-11 on Top of Rosin Aquatint (Quarter D)

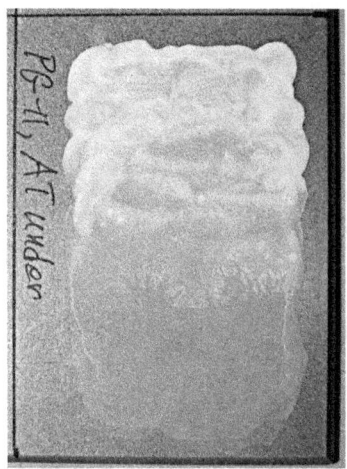

FIGURE A3.25: Plate with ground applied

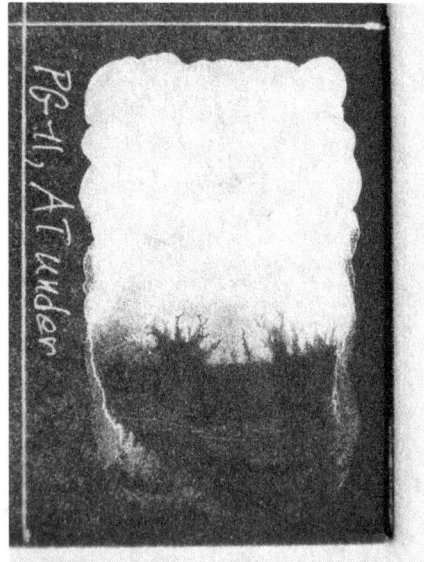

FIGURE A3.26: Print, taken from the plate

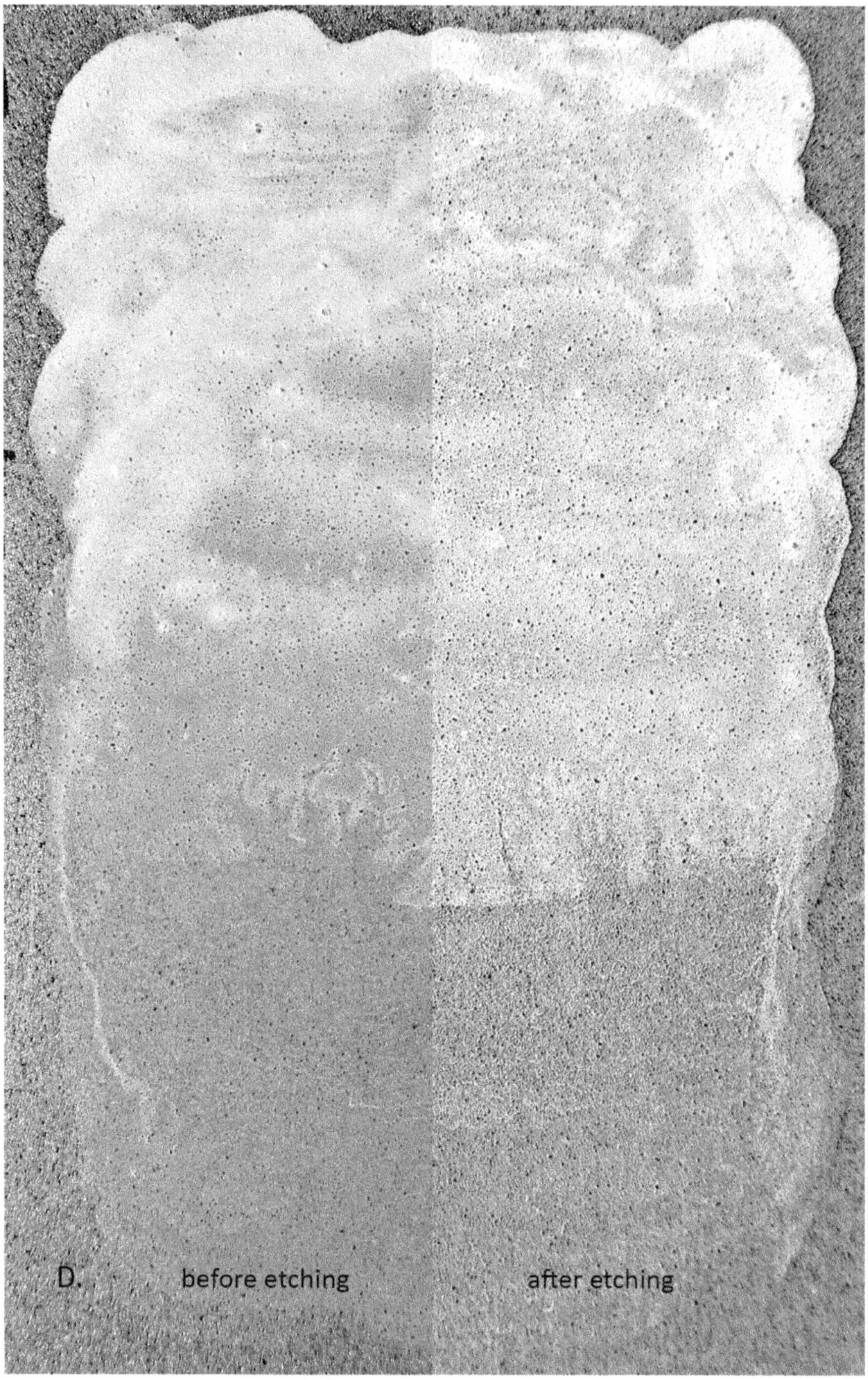

D.   before etching   after etching

FIGURE A3.24: PG-11 on top of rosin aquatint

White Ground on Top of Rosin Aquatint (Quarter D)

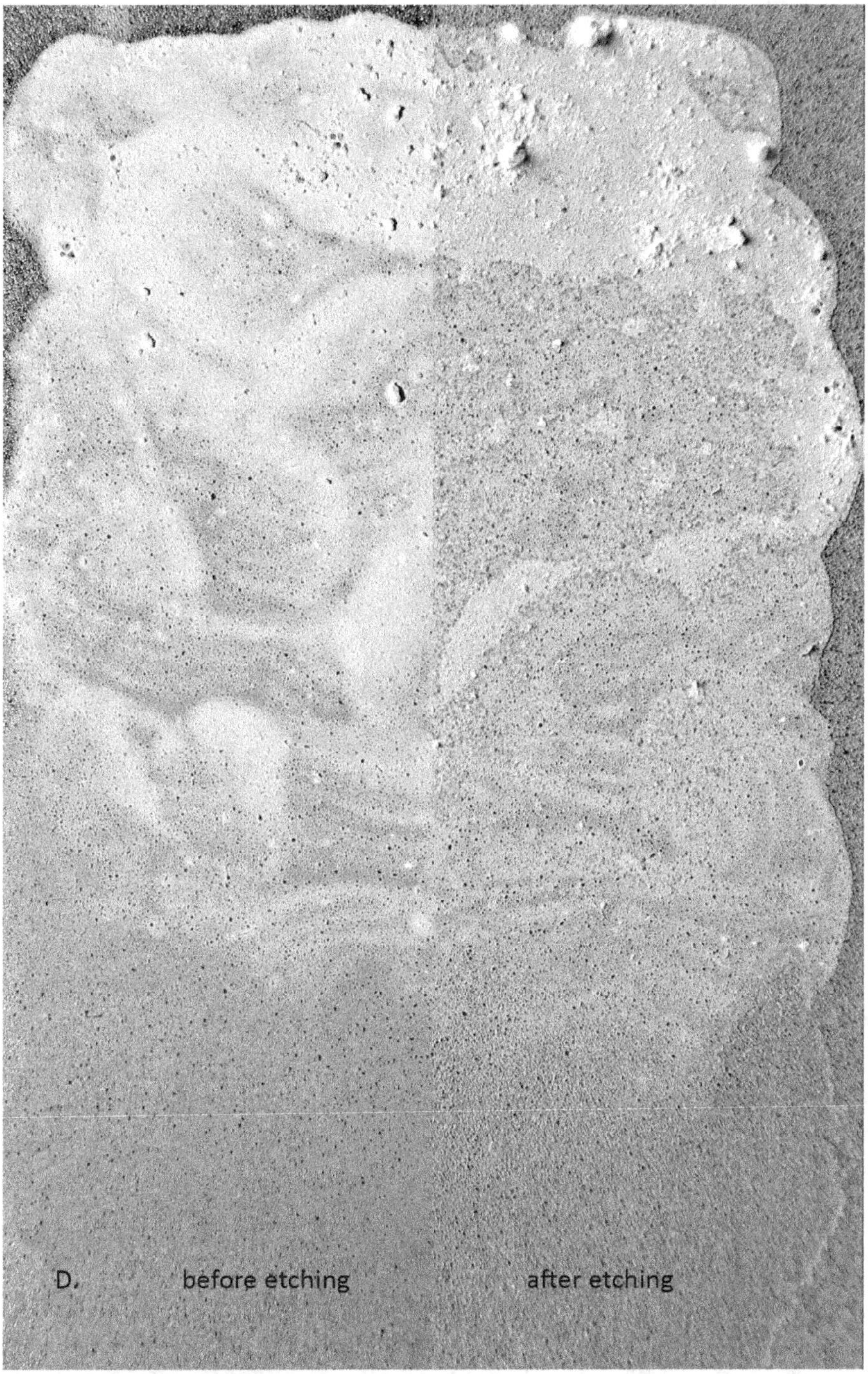

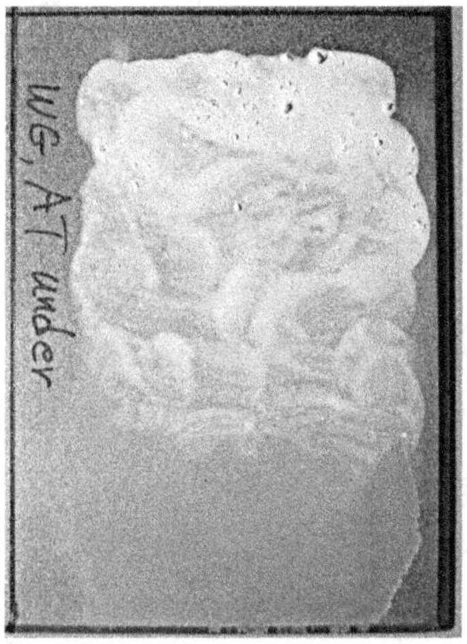

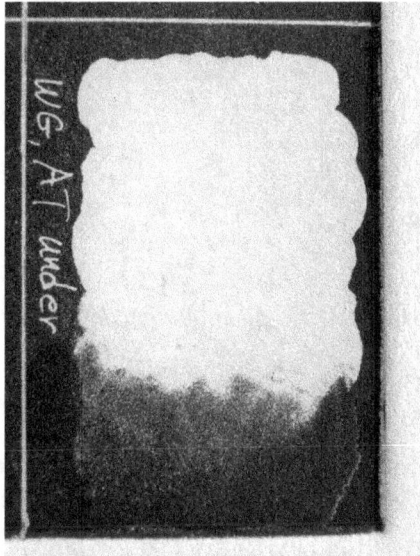

FIGURE A3.28: Plate with ground applied

FIGURE A3.29: Print taken from the plate

D.   before etching   after etching

FIGURE A3.27: White Ground on top of rosin aquatint

Discussion of the Results

So did the questions get answered?

QUESTION 1: How are PG-11 and White Ground affected by the heat applied to a plate while melting a rosin aquatint?

This question involves only heat and ground, not rosin, so the quarters to look at for a comparison would be A, which had only heated ground, and C, which had only unheated ground.

Looking at the prints for PG-11, quarters A (Figure A3.8) and C (Figure A3.20) showed the best breakdown (i.e. permeability) characteristics of all the samples. Where it was thinnest, there are little or no indications of stopping out. Where it was thickest, it stopped out completely and there is a fairly well distributed range of acid permeation between the two. I was unable to see any clear evidence that heat had any effect on the permeability of the ground.

For White Ground, as is typical of White Ground on copper, there was inadequate permeability in both quarters, but the one with no heat, C (Figure A3.23), appears to be more permeable than A (Figure A3.11), which was heated. (This probably would have looked quite different if done on zinc or if it had been etched with full strength Edinburgh Etch.) The acid only broke through in places where the ground was very thin. I would say from this that heating White Ground significantly, but not radically, reduces its permeability.

QUESTION 2: How does putting the aquatint on top of PG-11 or White Ground compare with putting it under the ground with regard to permeability and the overall visual effect obtained?

The best evidence for answering this would come from comparing quarters B (aquatint on top of heated ground) and D (aquatint under unheated ground).

For PG-11, quarter B (Figure A3.14) shows very little permeation and quarter D (Figure A3.26) shows a fair amount of permeation. For White Ground, quarter B (Figure A3.17) shows almost no permeation and quarter D (Figure A3.29) shows only slightly more. It looks to me like both PG-11 and White Ground are most permeable with no aquatint and that putting an aquatint under them significantly reduces permeability and putting a rosin aquatint on top of them drastically reduces permeability. This is the kind of thing an artist needs to keep in mind when applying the ground.

The main overall visual effect in these test results is an obvious lack of tonalities when the aquatint is under the ground and an even greater lack of tonalities when it is on top of the ground: too much white. One can't blame this entirely, if at all, on the materials. An artist needs to correct for or even take advantage of it by better coordinating the thickness of the ground (i.e. putting it on very thinly) in view of the fact that it is going to be reinforced by having an aquatint under it or applied on top of it, or alternatively the artist could use a more aggressive etchant. A ground with reduced permeability is what makes possible techniques with exaggerated contrast similar to the dramatic *maniere noire* effects seen in many monotypes. (See Chapter 2, Example 2.)

QUESTION 3: How does applying unheated PG-11 or White Ground on top of an aquatint compare with the unheated ground being applied to the plate with no aquatint, with regard to the visual effect obtained?

For this, compare quarters C and D. The effects are the same for both PG-11 (Figures A3.20 and A3.26) and White Ground (Figures A3.23 and A3.29). There is a radically different overall visual effect when comparing having the ground on top of an aquatint with having only the ground and no aquatint. With the permeable ground on top of an aquatint (Figures A3.26 and A3.29) you get the rich darks and deep spatial effects that aquatints offer. Without the aquatint (Figures A3.20 and A3.23) you get excellent textures and imagery with as much detail but with more of a feeling of "surface" to it and mostly grays with few darks, like collage, bas-relief, or something bonded to a piece of leather, rather than something involving dark spatial volumes like *maniere noire* or *chiaroscuro*.

APPENDIX 4

A Comparison of Ferric Chloride and Edinburgh Etch

Prior to writing this book, I was familiar with ferric chloride but had not used Edinburgh Etch, so I wanted to become more acquainted with Edinburgh Etch, especially in relation to PG-11 and SO-11. This appendix contains the results of an experiment I did to become more familiar with the characteristics of ferric chloride and Edinburgh Etch (an etchant introduced by Friedhard Kiekeben in 1997) when used with PG-11 on copper. Edinburgh Etch is ferric chloride with citric acid added, so the two etchants are closely related but also distinctly different.

Questions I had about them were:

1. How fast do they etch copper?

2. Do they affect the permeability of PG-11?

3. Are they both compatible with PG-11?

To do the experiment I cut three copper plates all to the same size, 2.5 inches by 4 inches. I then divided each plate in half lengthwise and put a rosin aquatint on half of each plate and left the other half bare copper (Figure A4.2). I wanted to have as smooth and even a gradation of PG-11 as possible covering both halves of the plate, applied very thinly at one end of the plate and ranging to a fairly heavy coating at the other, so I placed the plates together and simultaneously applied PG-11 to them with an airbrush (Figure A4.3). I did not dip the plates in vinegar, as I sometimes do to stabilize the ground.

Once the PG-11 had dried overnight I divided the un-aquatinted half of each plate into three strips and made various markings in each of the strips with the corner of a plastic spreader, a common No. 2 pencil, and a mechanical pencil with a 0.5 mm 3H lead in it for wide, medium, and fine lines (Figures A4.4, A4.5, and A4.6).

Nothing more was done to the aquatint with the graduated coating of PG-11 on it. The idea with the aquatint was to see how far along the length of the plate tone would be created by the acid penetrating the PG-11. With the un-aquatinted side the idea was to see how quickly the varied thickness of PG-11 would break down in the acid and what kind of linear and textural elements would be created.

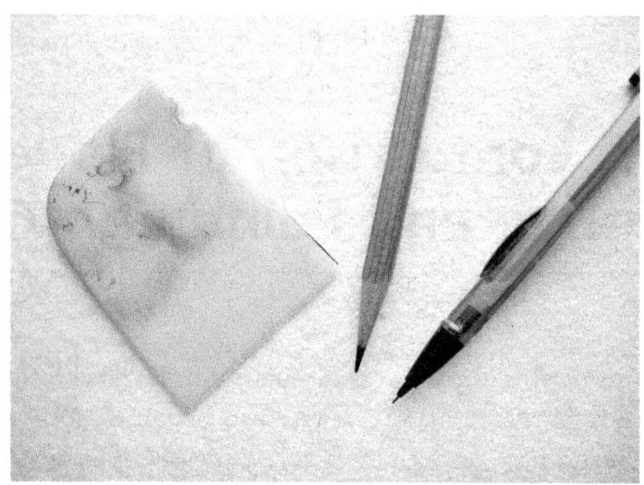

FIGURE A4.1: Implements used for making marks on the plates

I used three different etchants. One was ferric chloride consisting of one volume of approximately a 40° Baumé solution diluted with an equal volume of municipal chlorinated tap water, which I refer to as "1:1 ferric chloride."

The second was a full strength Edinburgh Etch, which I made by combining 2 quarts (8 cups) of 40° Baumé ferric chloride with 1.5 cups of tap water that had .5 cup (4 oz.) of citric acid crystals dissolved in it. I believe this conforms to the standard Edinburgh Etch recipe given by Kiekeben for etching copper.

The third etchant consisted of one volume of the above full strength Edinburgh Etch diluted with an equal volume of tap water, for a half-strength solution of Edinburgh Etch, which I refer to as "1:1 Edinburgh Etch."

Prior to etching the plates, I tested the "speed" of the three etchants by measuring the amount of time they took to etch through a thin copper wire. The test was repeated three times for each etchant, and the etchants were all at 63° F.

Timings were as follows:

1:1 ferric chloride:	8:19; 9:00; 8:01.
Full strength Edinburgh Etch:	13:19; 12:56; 14:19
1:1 Edinburgh Etch:	8:40; 8:31; 8:45

Faster etching at a 1:1 dilution is generally consistent with ferric chloride and copper.

The three plates were all etched for 20 minutes uninterrupted in the three etchants at 70° F, with occasional agitation, then rinsed with water and dried.

The Prepared Plates

FIGURE A4.2: Plates with aquatint.

FIGURE A4.3: Plates with airbrushed PG-11 (no vinegar).

Plates Before Etching

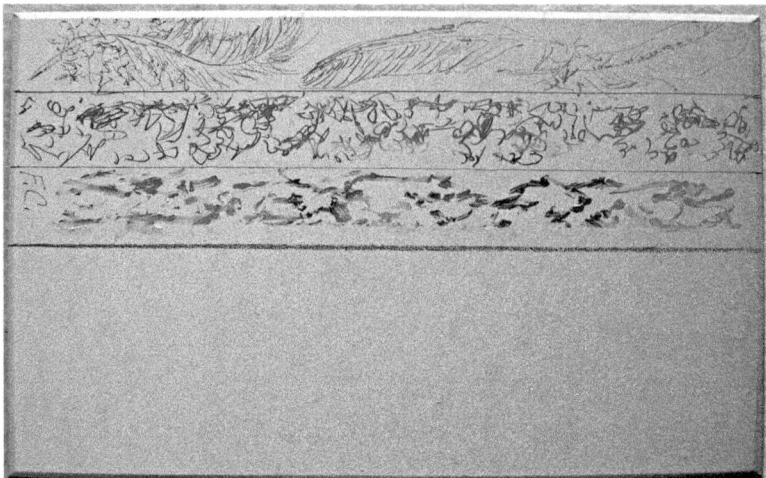

FIGURE A4.4: Plate prepared for etching in diluted ferric chloride.

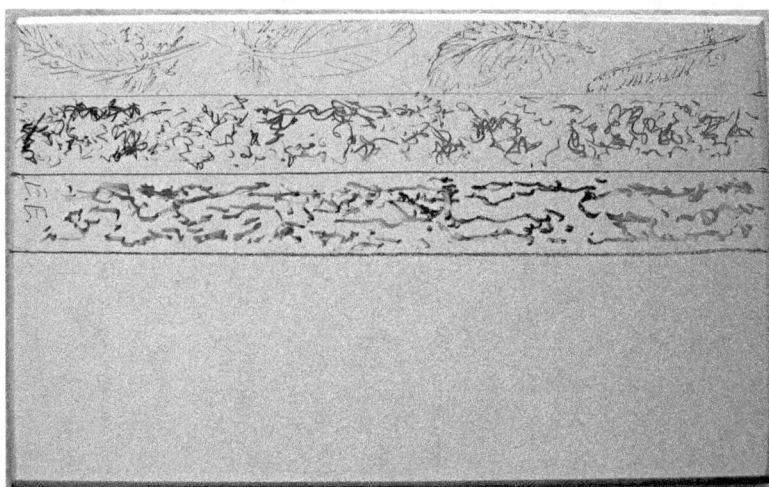

FIGURE A4.5: Plate prepared for etching in full-strength Edinburgh Etch.

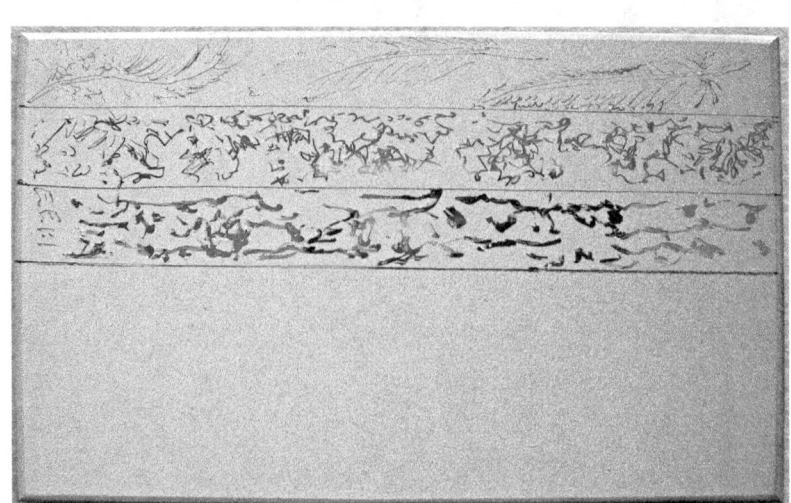

FIGURE A4.6: Plate prepared for etching in half-strength Edinburgh Etch.

Plates After Etching

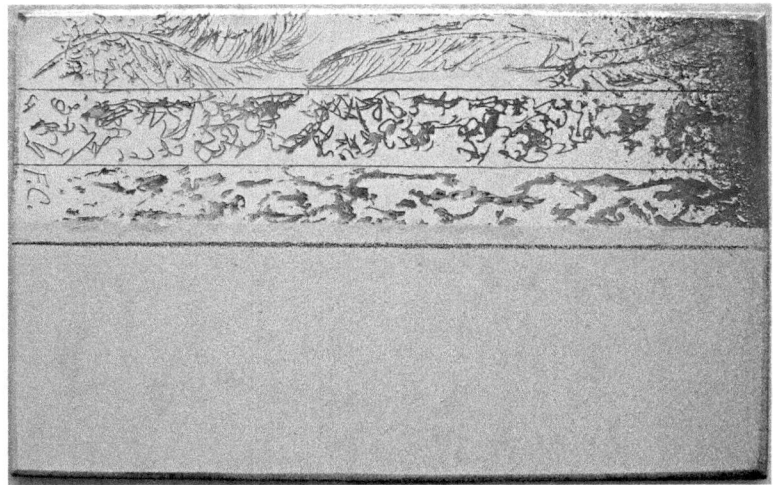

FIGURE A4.7: Plate after etching 20 minutes with diluted ferric chloride.

FIGURE A4.8: Plate after etching 20 minutes with full-strength Edinburgh Etch.

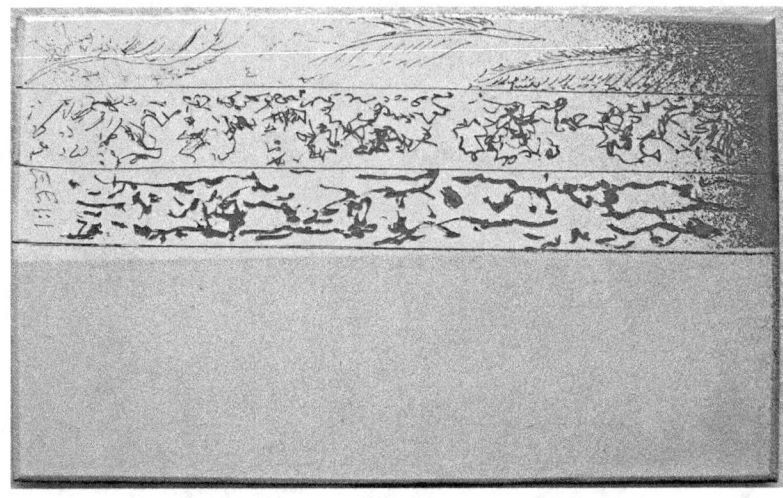

FIGURE A4.9: Plate after etching 20 minutes with half-strength Edinburgh Etch.

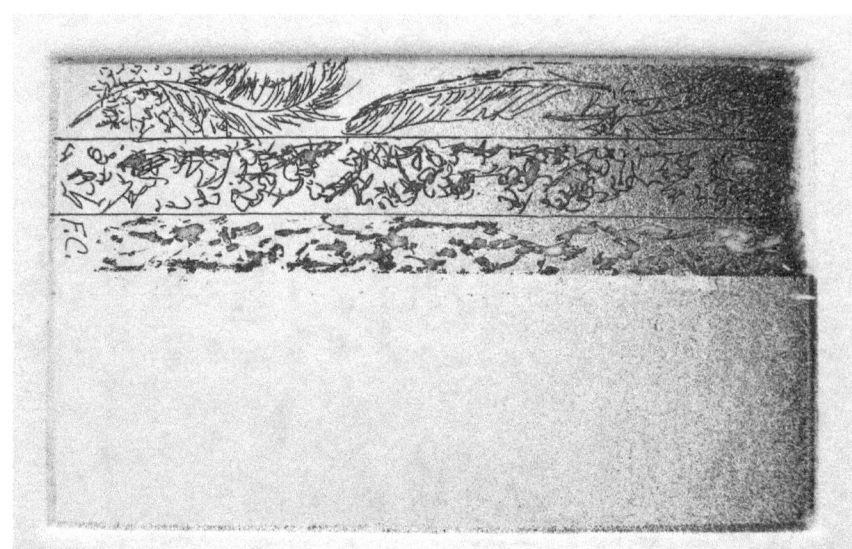

FIGURE A4.10: Print, from the plate etched in diluted ferric chloride.

FIGURE A4.11: Print taken from the plate etched in full-strength Edinburgh Etch.

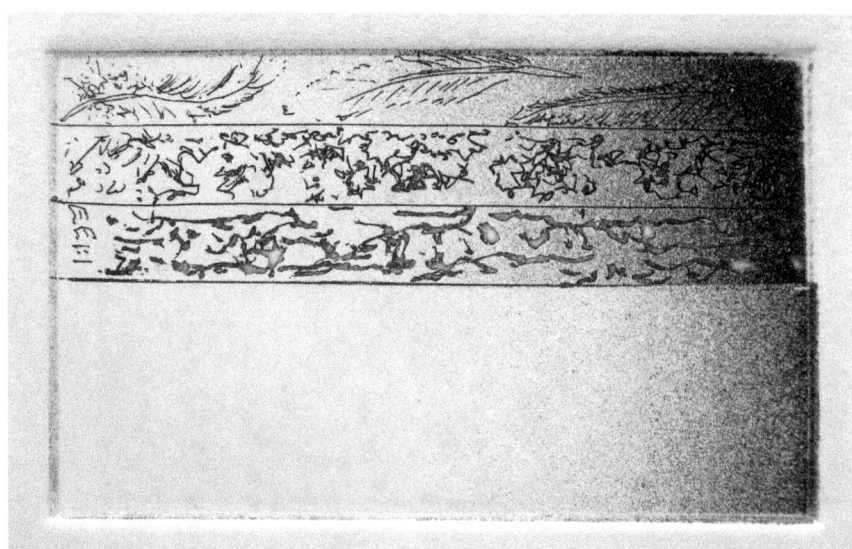

FIGURE A4.12: Print from the plate etched in half-strength Edinburgh Etch.

Close-ups of the Plates, End of Plate Where PG-11 Was Applied Heavily

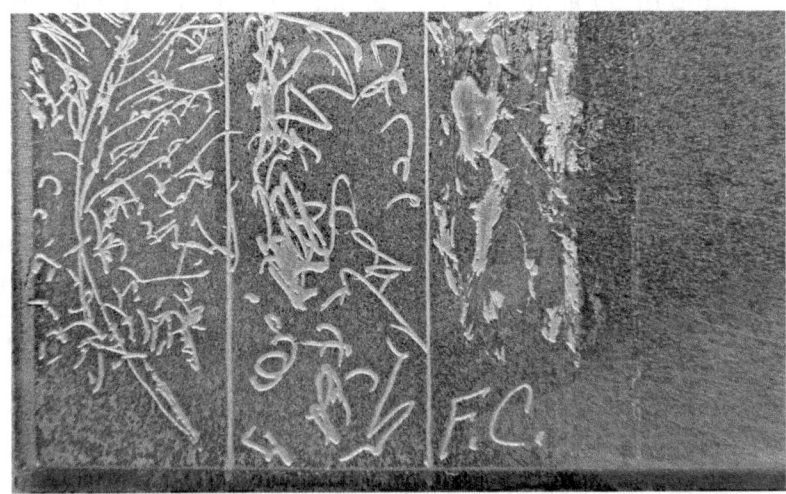

FIGURE A4.13: Ferric chloride (1:1), showing etched lines and background acid permeation.

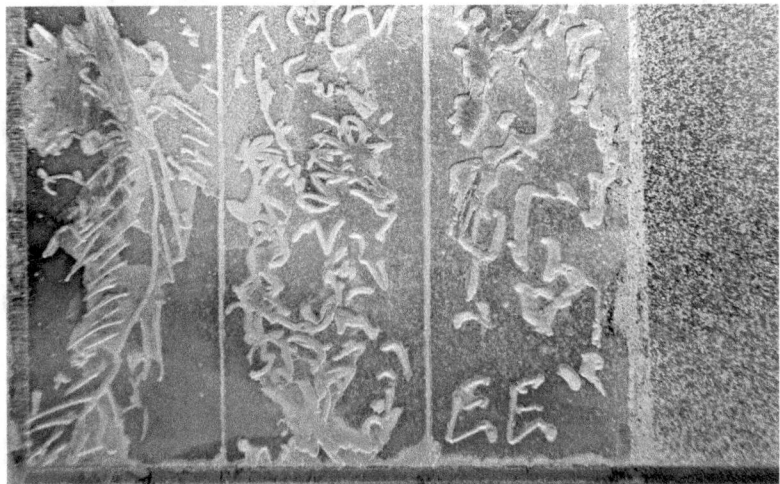

FIGURE A4.14: Full strength Edinburgh Etch, showing foul bite and heavy acid permeation.

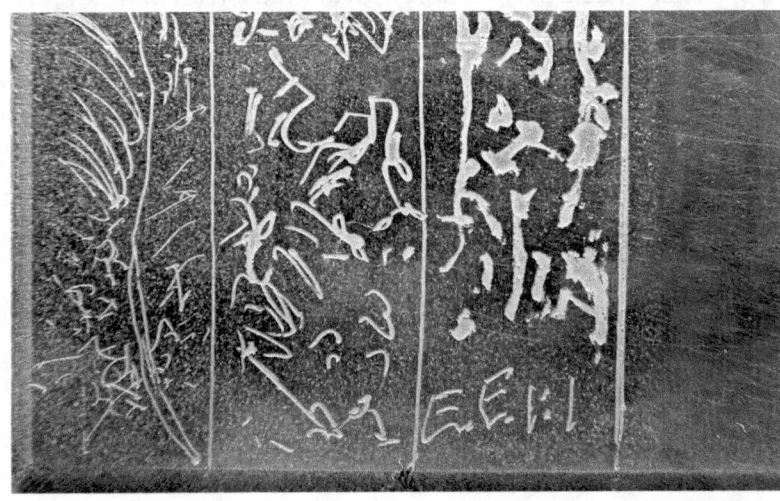

FIGURE A4.15: Half strength (1:1) Edinburgh Etch, showing clean etch and scant acid permeation.

Discussion of the results

The most obvious piece of information gained from this experiment is that it's not a good idea to etch PG-11 with full strength Edinburgh Etch. On top of an aquatint, maybe, but not on bare copper unless you want a very foul-bitten-looking result (Figure A4.8). PG-11 breaks down quickly when exposed to full strength Edinburgh Etch. More visible on the plate than in the print is evidence of acid permeation all across the aquatinted area. As can be seen in the print (Figure A4.11) in the un-aquatinted (line) area, the PG-11 persisted in the full strength Edinburgh Etch long enough to create some imagery but after a short time white flecks and fragments of ground could be seen floating around in the acid and heavy foul biting occurred.

There was also information to be gained from examining the results of the other two etchants. The diluted ferric chloride worked well, in that it etched the copper effectively and permeated the ground at a reasonable rate. The 1:1 Edinburgh Etch etched the copper at about the same rate as the 1:1 ferric chloride, but broke down the ground less and therefore gave a cleaner etch.

To describe the findings in more detail, the diluted ferric chloride obviously permeated the ground more than the half strength Edinburgh Etch did. This is more obvious when looking at the plate than at the print, but it's also visible in the print.

With the 1:1 ferric chloride (see Figure A4.13, right edge of image where the aquatint was) there is evidence over the entire surface of the plate of acid permeation, though some of it is more "pre-etch oxidation" rather than actual etching of the copper.

With the half strength Edinburgh Etch (Figure A4.15, right quarter of image), part of the plate remained completely protected, which was not true with either of the other two etchants. The part of the plate (Figure A4.13, right edge of image) that had aquatint and thick PG-11 shows evidence of acid permeation with diluted ferric chloride and even more (Figure A4.14, right edge of image) with full strength Edinburgh Etch, but with the half strength Edinburgh Etch (Figure A4.15, right edge of image) there is none. In the left three quarters of the image, the area where lines were scribed into thick PG-11, the diluted ferric chloride plate (Figure A4.13) shows background pitting (obvious evidence of acid permeation), but the half strength Edinburgh Etch plate (Figure A4.15) although showing some, shows significantly less.

The etched features also show a difference. The diluted (1:1) ferric chloride lines (Figure A4.10) are heavier than the half strength (1:1) Edinburgh Etch lines (Figure A4.12) in the print, but in the area where the PG-11 was thin (the right side of the image), the diluted ferric chloride lines are less distinct than the corresponding half strength Edinburgh Etch lines. I would attribute that to the half strength Edinburgh Etch's slower breaking down of the ground.

You can even feel the difference in the three etchants by dragging the edge of a fingernail across the etched lines on the plate. With the full strength Edinburgh Etch the lines are so foul bitten you can hardly feel them. With the diluted ferric chloride the lines are moderately "catchy," but with the half strength Edinburgh Etch the lines have a palpably sharper, crisper, "catchy" feel to them.

So, for etching copper with PG-11, I would recommend the diluted ferric chloride if you want a softer, warmer character to the print, or the half strength Edinburgh Etch for a cleaner, crisper look. Save the full strength Edinburgh Etch for etching White Ground on copper.

APPENDIX 5

Controlling Permeability of PG-11

As mentioned in the Introduction, being able to control the permeability of PG-11 is integral to its successful use. This will be more of an issue for some etchers than for others and in some situations more than in others. Most people (at least initially) will probably settle on a recipe that has a permeability that works for them and will use that for most of what they do. If you find that PG-11 generally stops out more than you want it to, thin it or add some glycerin. However, for etchers who are interested in trying to closely control what happens in a wider variety of situations, there will be times when alternative degrees of permeability are called for.

Permeability generally needs to be boosted (a "softer" stopout) when etching in light (10% to 50%) tonal ranges with the PG-11 on top of an aquatint, since the aquatint tends to significantly reduce permeability. Less permeability (a "harder" stopout) works better with dark tones (longer etches, more contrast) and when etching with no aquatint, or aquatint that is on top of the ground.

I usually deal with this by having a couple of small containers available, one with a Medium PG-11 and one with Soft (highest permeability). Regular PG-11 provides the "hardest" stopout. All of these variations of PG-11 will be slightly more permeable when etched with 1:1 ferric chloride than when etched with 1:1 Edinburgh Etch.

More specifically, the Regular, Medium, and Soft variations of PG-11 should be approximately coordinated with the following target tonal ranges. (All these refer to PG-11 applied on top of an aquatint.) If you're etching tones in the 0% (white) to 40% range, stop out with Soft PG-11. For tones in the 40% to 70% tonal range stop out with Medium, and for tones in the 70% to 100% (black) range stop out with Regular PG-11. (See Appendix 2 for timing the etching/step biting of target aquatint tones.)

During step biting of a plate, the more permeable grounds will have to be stopped out or reinforced with "harder" ground or SO-11 (depending on how complete a stopout you want) once the target tone has been etched, before proceeding to etch the darker tones.

So, if you're etching an aquatinted plate with target tones of 10%, 40%, 50%, 80%, and 100%, you would stop out the 10% areas with

Soft PG-11; etch that, reinforce it, and stop out the 40% areas with Soft PG-11; etch that and then cover those areas with either Medium PG-11 or SO-11 to block further etching there, being careful to blend or feather edges so as not to create unwanted hard edges when further etching occurs. Then you would apply Medium PG-11 to the 50% areas, etch that and stop it out with Regular PG-11 or SO-11. Then you would apply Regular PG-11 to the 80% areas, etch that, block it, stop out the 100% areas with Regular PG-11, and etch that. The more steps you break it down into, the more control you have over the results.

Figure A5.1 is a print from a test plate etched with Regular, Medium, and Soft PG-11 as described above.

The top three rows were etched with 1:1 ferric chloride and the bottom three rows with 1:1 Edinburgh Etch. Since I expected the Edinburgh Etch to etch faster than ferric chloride, I etched the ferric chloride half of the plate with a 20-minute chart and the Edinburgh Etch half with a 15-minute chart. However, in doing so, I overcompensated so the ferric chloride percentages came out darker than their respective Edinburgh Etch counterparts.

I etched the ferric chloride half of the plate first with the Edinburgh Etch half stopped out, then stopped that out and etched the Edinburgh Etch half of the plate.

For each half I applied Soft PG-11 to the 40% stripe, very thin at one end and thick at the other, and etched all three stripes to a target 40% tone. If the permeability of the Soft PG-11 was in an acceptable range, I should get slight stopping out where it was thin and progres-

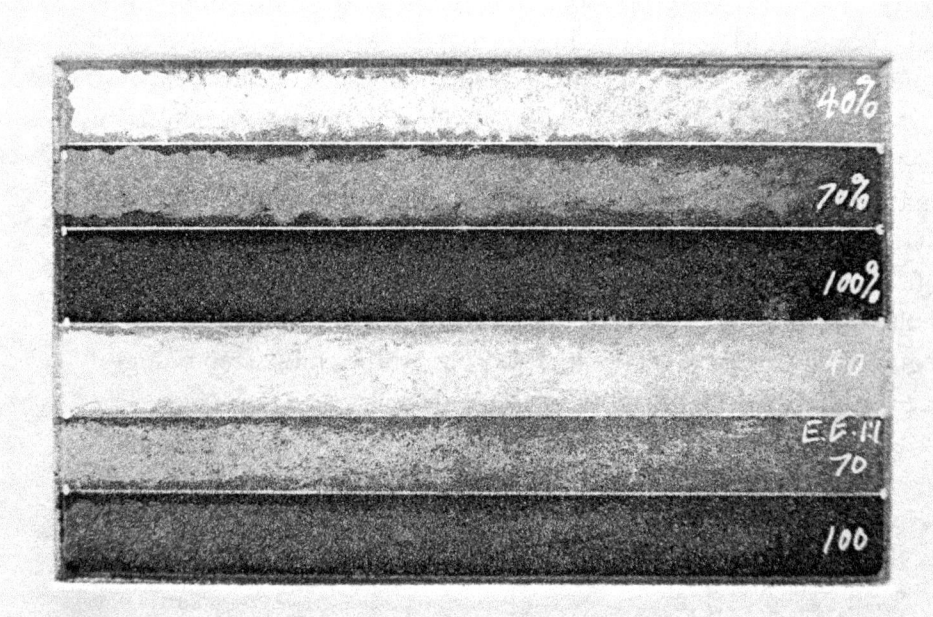

FIGURE A5.1

sively more stopping out moving toward the end where it was thick against a background tone of 40%, which is what happened. (If the permeability had been too high I would have gotten tone where the stopout was thick and if too low I would have gotten white at the end where it was thin.)

I then stopped out the 40% stripe and applied Medium PG-11 to the target 70% stripe (which at this point had 40% background tone etched in it) similarly, thick grading to thin, and etched that and the remaining 100% stripe to a target 70% tone.

Again, I got complete stopping out at the thick end—it stayed at 40%—ranging to slight stopping out at the thin end, where it feathered into the 70% background tone.

I then stopped out the 70% stripe and applied a graded application of Regular PG-11 to the 100% stripe and etched that to 100% background tone. The ferric one came fairly dark (the 70% background ended up more like a 90%), but a graded progression of tone is visible from a "70%" at the thick end to a fade into 100% at the thin end.

SO-11 and PG-11 Used As an Aquatint Resist

(etchant: 1:1 ferric chloride; 20-minute timing chart)

Dots of pretty much anything stuck on a piece of copper and put in acid will make an aquatint of some kind, but I wanted to get a clearer understanding of how serviceable SO-11 and PG-11 are for aquatints. Neither one is a prime candidate for creating aquatints.

The most useful materials for aquatints tend to be things that are physically durable (which these are not), compatible with only one solvent (I have yet to find a solvent these won't dissolve in), and are highly acid-resistant (i.e. not a permeable ground). Yet I found myself using these to create aquatints, just because I had some in the airbrush, and cleaning the plate is simpler if everything comes off at the same time.

For this experiment I divided a test plate in half, sprayed PG-11 on one half and SO-11 on the other. Then I etched five target tones of 20%, 40%, 60%, 80%, and 100% across both grounds at the same time.

Since the initial (20% tone) step bite was short (34 seconds), I put the plate with the spatters in a tray of salt and vinegar to fix the ground before I started etching. Immersion in vinegar or a salt and vinegar solution is always a good idea to prepare these grounds for being placed in the etchant.

Figure A6.1 is the plate, spattered with PG-11 on the left and SO-11 on the right, using an airbrush. The plate has been in the acid for 34

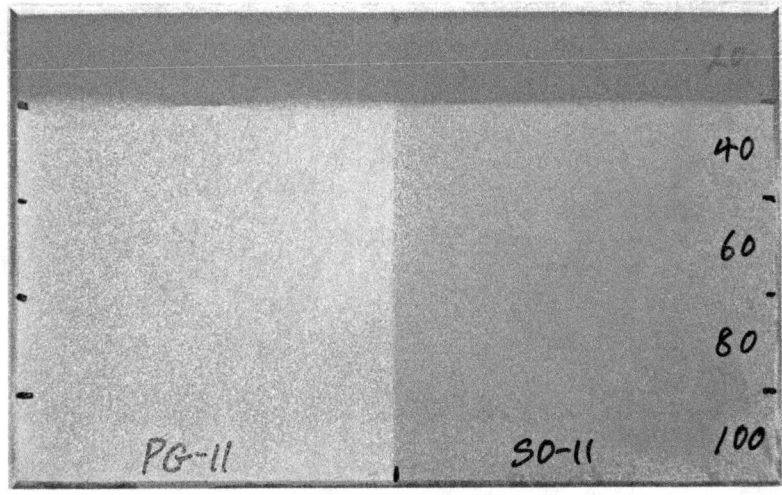

FIGURE A6.1

seconds to etch it to a target tone of 20%, and the 20% band has been stopped out with SO-11 from the airbrush.

I should caution that (as mentioned in Chapter 1) these grounds make extremely fragile resists. I would recommend rinsing plates in a tray of water or when possible letting a flow of water hit a stopped out area of the plate and flowing from there across the aquatinted areas. Rinse quickly, shake excess water off, and dry immediately with compressed air.

As can be seen, the rinse water left watermarks in the SO-11 side and I was curious to see if they would show up in the print. As it turned out, they were not visible (Figure A6.2).

I found that I had a tendency to spray on too much ground with both of them. Coverage and dot-pattern are pretty much what-you-see-is-what-you-get when viewing them under a magnifying glass, though especially with the brown SO-11 there is a tendency to underestimate the amount of coverage. (For more discussion of this see page 20.) I sprayed with the plates laying flat, face-up, with the airbrush about a foot from the plate.

Timings for the other target tones were: 40%—additional 1:18; 60%—3:03; 80%—5:53; and 100%—9:12, based on the 20-minute chart.

Figure A6.2 is a print of the tones created by the steps described above.

The SO-11 aquatint (impermeable) gives a resist that etches very similarly to a rosin aquatint. The PG-11 resist gives a softer, richer tone due to the partial breakdown of the resist. I didn't test PG-11 Medium

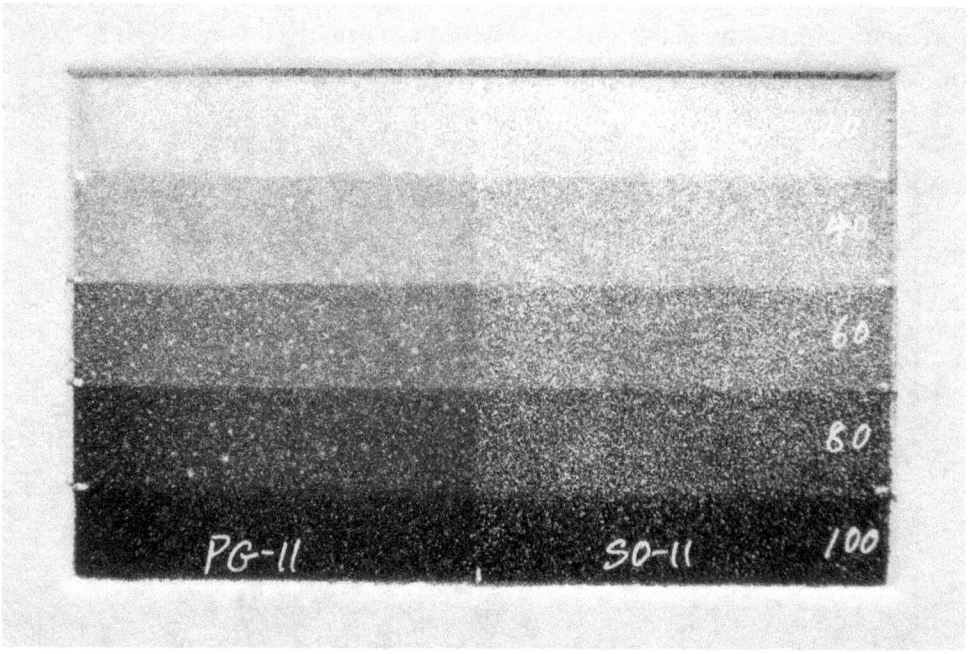

FIGURE A6.2

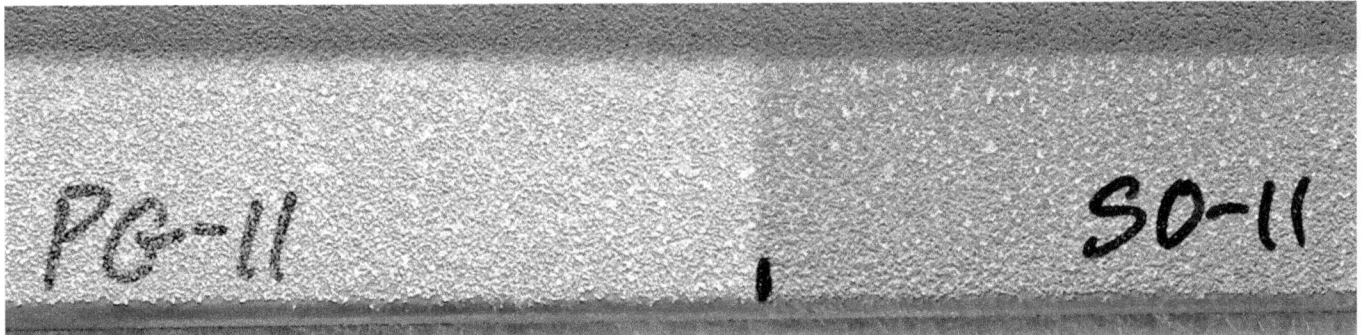

FIGURE A6.3

and Soft, but I expect they would give soft shades of gray and not last long enough in the acid to create a black.

Figure A6.3 shows the 100% band of tone on the plate after being in the acid for 20 minutes and before the surviving spatters of ground were cleaned off of the plate prior to proofing.

A Comparison of Nonpermeable and Permeable Grounds

(etchant: 1:1 ferric chloride)

As with the term "stopout" (the noun) the definition of a permeable or a nonpermeable ground derives more from usage than from strict fact. Any ground if it is thin enough will break down in the acid if left in long enough. Practically speaking, however, any ground that would be primarily useful for completely blocking something out for as long as a plate is likely to be in the acid would be a "nonpermeable" ground, and any ground that would be primarily useful because it is likely to break down in the acid and thereby do something interesting to the plate would be a "permeable" ground.

The following pictures are intended to illustrate what I'm talking about. Three grounds are used: one nonpermeable and two permeable. I wanted the grounds to look as similar as possible on the plate since this is a comparison of "what you see on the plate" with "what you get in the print." For the nonpermeable ground I mixed dry titanium white pigment with acrylic matte medium. For the two permeable grounds I used White Ground (Cassara recipe) and PG-11. The PG-11 was not dipped in vinegar. I used a large round bristle brush to apply a single brushstroke to each plate.

The first three plates (Examples A–C) show the grounds applied to a bare copper plate after which an aquatint was applied on top of the ground by spattering with PG-11 from an airbrush at 30 psi and a can of enamel spray paint. They were each etched in 1:1 ferric chloride for a total of 35 minutes. Plates are shown before the aquatint was applied. All of the plates in both sets were oxidized to darken the surface and make the grounds more visible, and are shown actual size.

The second three plates (Examples D–F) show the same grounds applied on top of a rosin box aquatint and the differences in permeability show up more dramatically in the resulting prints. These three plates were each etched in 1:1 ferric chloride for a total of 55 minutes. The surface effect of a ground being painted on to an aquatint is more like that of paint being applied to canvas than a ground that is being painted on to the surface of a bare metal plate, which tends to have more of the look and feel of a monotype.

Example A: Nonpermeable Acrylic Ground, Aquatint on Top of Ground

With the nonpermeable acrylic (Figure A7.1), places where the ground was very thin etched slightly, but overall there was very little etching where there was any ground, so the resulting image is mostly white with light grays.

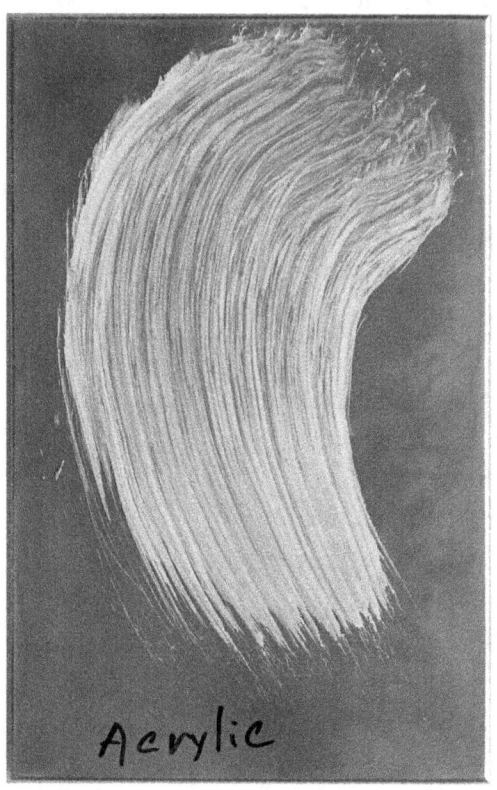

FIGURE A7.1: The plate with ground applied.

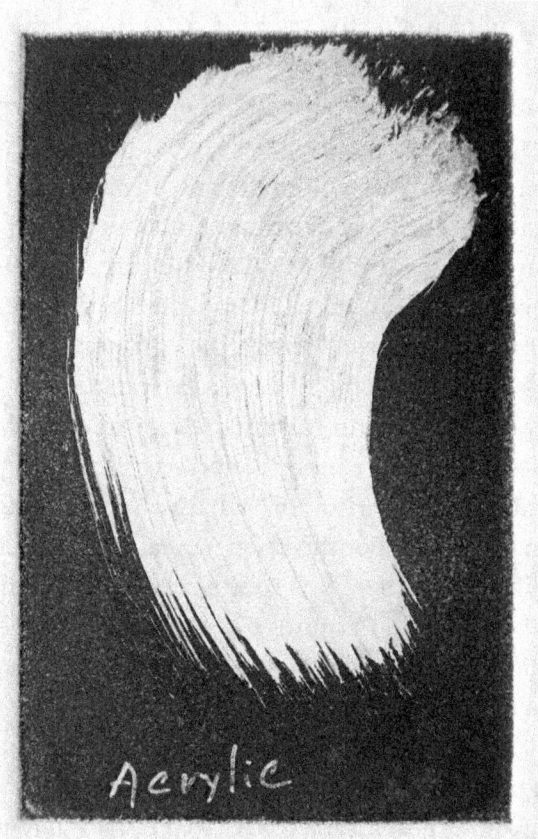

FIGURE A7.2: Resulting print.

Example B: Permeable White Ground
(Cassara Recipe), Aquatint on Top of Ground

With the permeable White Ground (Figure A7.3), places where the ground was thin broke down, allowing the acid to etch and create tones.

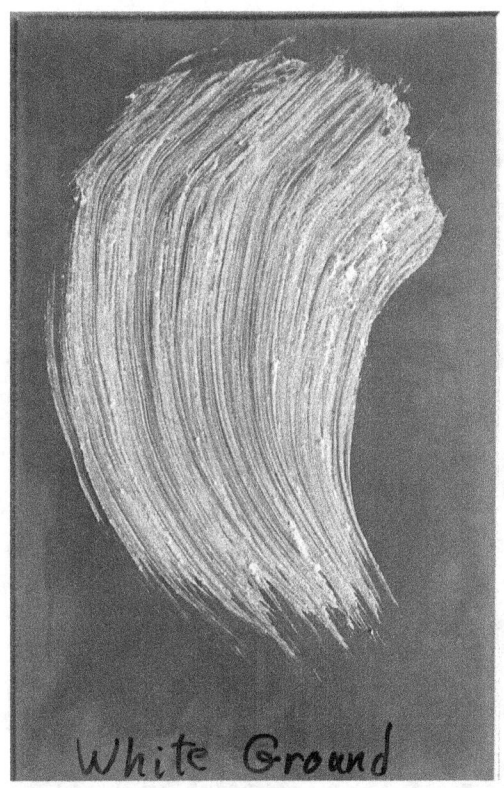

FIGURE A7.3

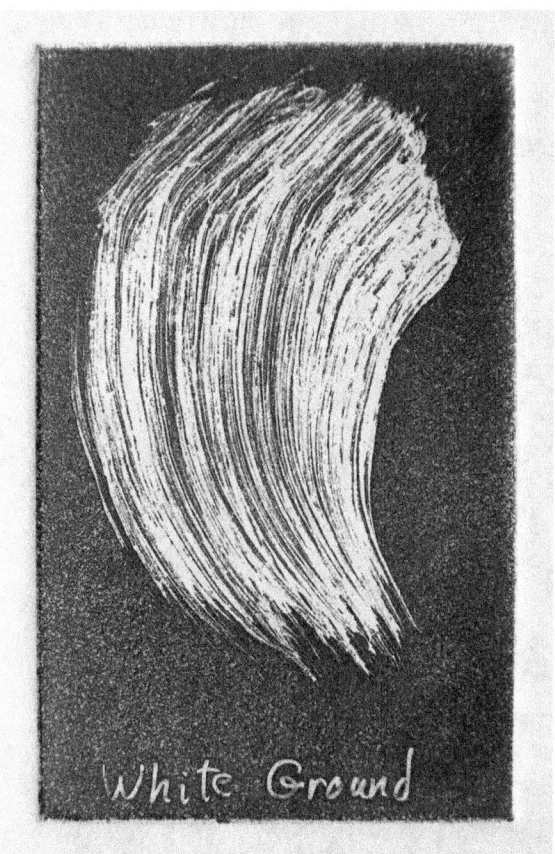

FIGURE A7.4

Example C: Permeable Ground PG-11, Aquatint on Top of Ground

With the permeable ground PG-11 (Figure A7.5) there is more break-down than with the preceding White Ground, although the difference is fairly subtle. Notice that, unlike with the White Ground (Figures A7.3 and A7.4), in Figure A7.5 the ground comes all the way down to the barely visible writing at the bottom of the plate, while in the print (Figure A7.6) the white brushstroke has receded upward above the writing due to the breaking down of the ground in the acid.

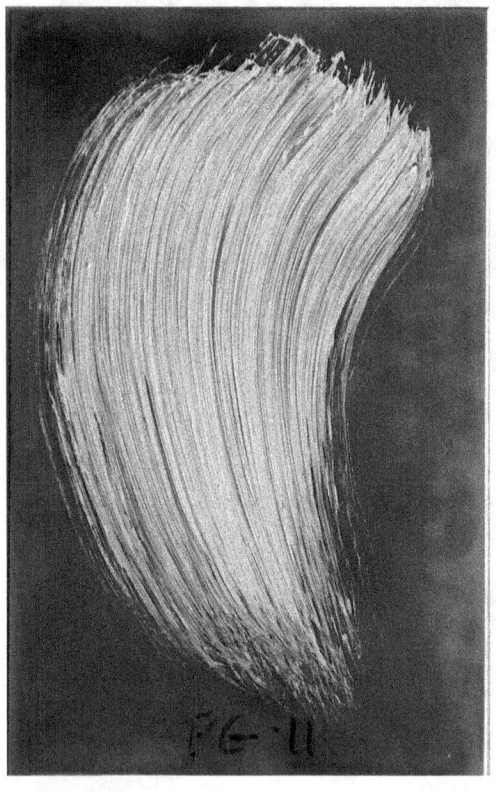

FIGURE A7.5

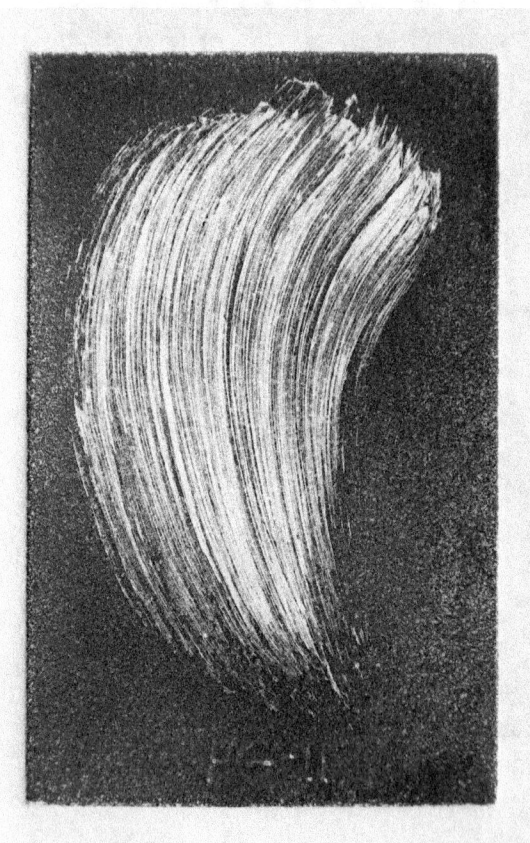

FIGURE A7.6

Example D: Nonpermeable Acrylic Ground on Top of a Rosin Aquatint

With a nonpermeable acrylic ground on a rosin aquatint (Figure A7.7), there is only a minute amount of breakdown, resulting in an almost completely stopped out brushstroke (Figure A7–8).

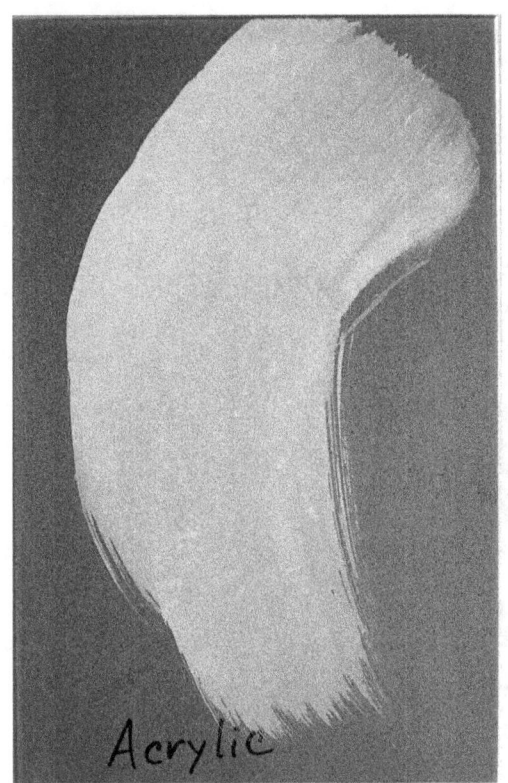

FIGURE A7.7

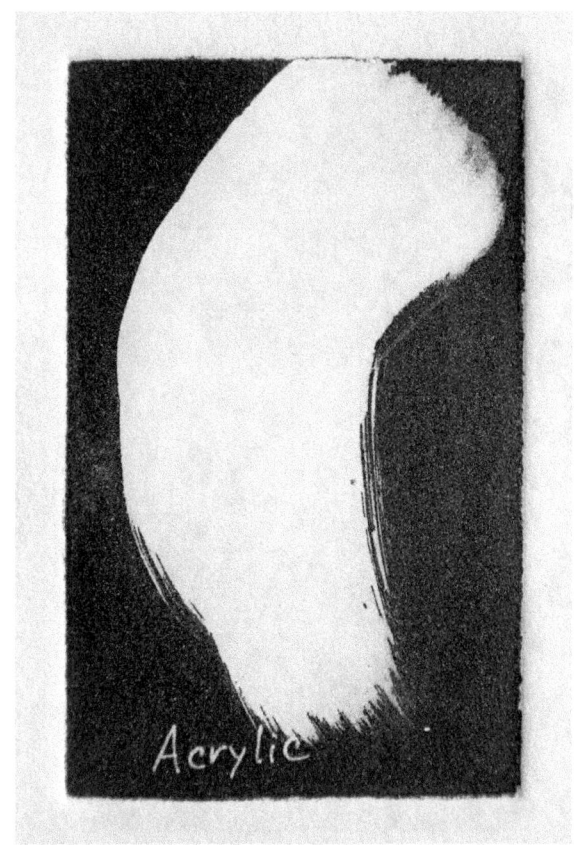

FIGURE A7.8

Example E: Permeable White Ground (Cassara Recipe) on Top of a Rosin Aquatint

Here the White Ground broke down where thin, and stopped out where thick. If the White Ground had been slightly more permeable, the range of values in the print would have more closely matched those seen on the plate. As it is, there is good permeability but the print has exaggerated contrast relative to the image seen on the plate.

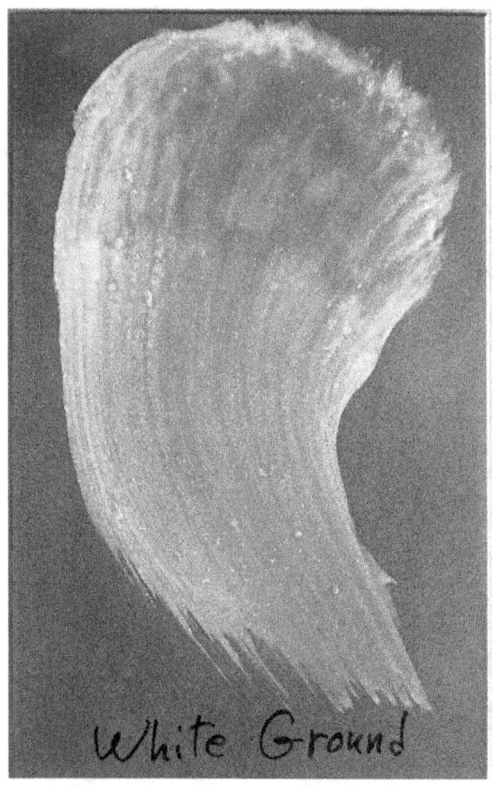

FIGURE A7.9

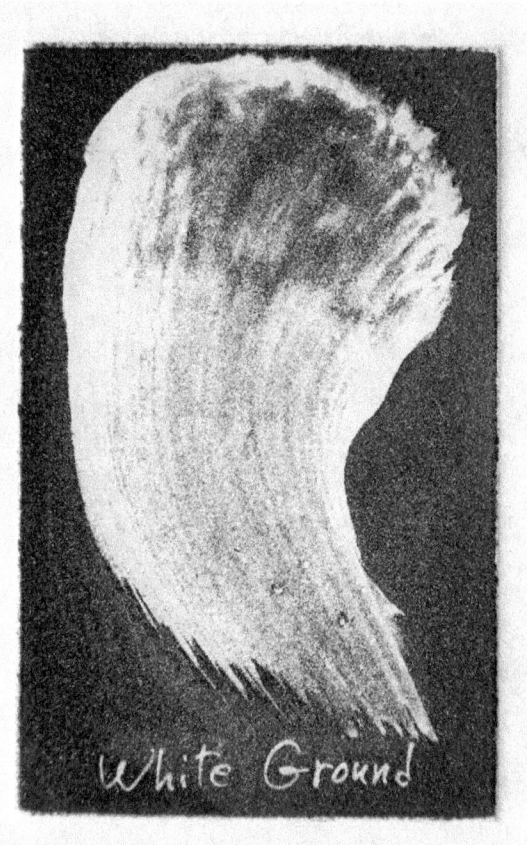

FIGURE A7.10

Example F: Permeable Ground PG-11 on Top of a Rosin Aquatint

After 55 minutes in the acid, the brushstroke made with PG-11 has all but disappeared due to its relatively high degree of permeability.

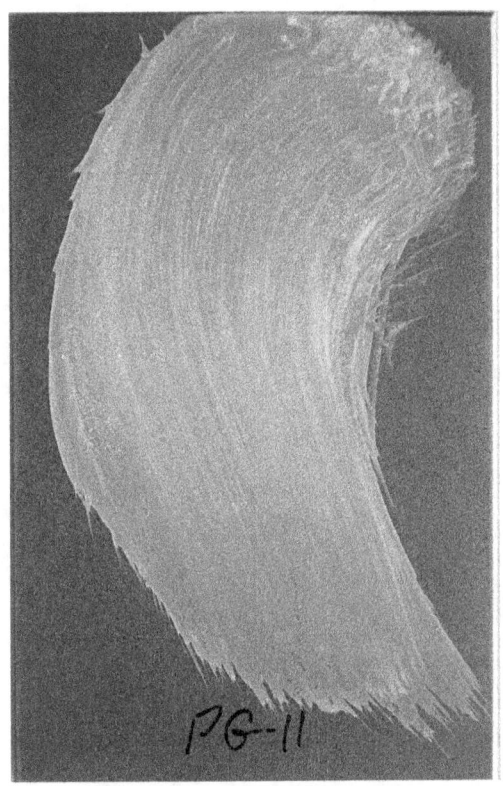

FIGURE A7.11

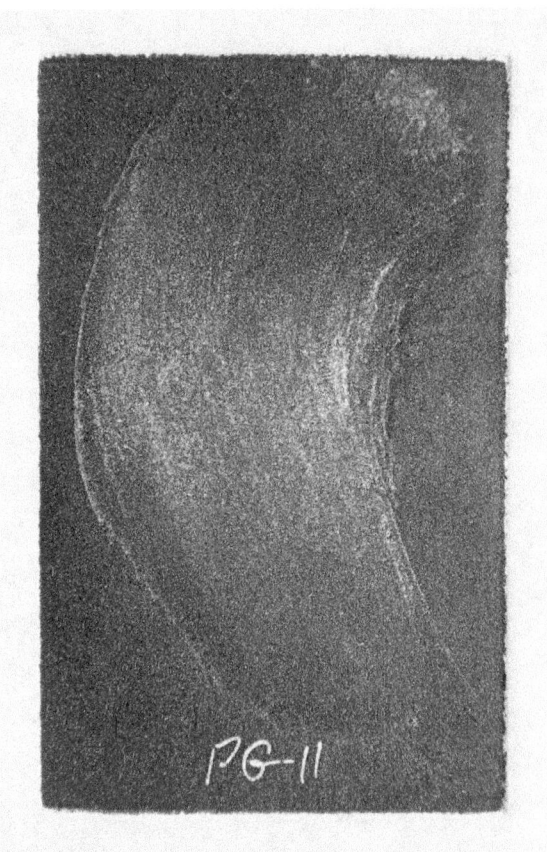

FIGURE A7.12

INDEX